Colloquies on European Civil Procedure

Colloquies on European Civil Procedure

Exploring the ELI-UNIDROIT Model European Rules of Civil Procedure

Edited by

Marco de Benito

BRILL | NIJHOFF

LEIDEN | BOSTON

This book is the result of the research and dissemination activities of the Jean Monnet Chair in European Civil Procedure Law at IE University, directed by Marco de Benito, with the support of the Erasmus + programme of the European Union.

Co-funded by the European Union

ie UNIVERSITY LAW SCHOOL

JEAN MONNET CHAIR IN EUROPEAN CIVIL PROCEDURE

Library of Congress Cataloging-in-Publication Data

Names: de Benito, Marco, editor.
Title: Colloquies on European Civil Procedure: Exploring the ELI-UNIDROIT Model European Rules of Civil Procedure / edited by Marco de Benito.
Description: Leiden; Boston: Brill Publisher, 2025. | Includes bibliographical references and index.
Identifiers: LCCN 2025014911 (print) | LCCN 2025014912 (ebook) | ISBN 9789004533240 (hardback) | ISBN 9789004533257 (pdf)
Subjects: LCSH: Civil procedure--Europe.
Classification: LCC KJC3815 .C65 2025 (print) | LCC KJC3815 (ebook) | DDC 347.4/05--dc23/eng/20250411
LC record available at https://lccn.loc.gov/2025014911
LC ebook record available at https://lccn.loc.gov/2025014912

Typeface for the Latin, Greek, and Cyrillic scripts: “Brill”. See and download: brill.com/brill-typeface.

ISBN 978-90-04-53324-0 (hardback)
ISBN 978-90-04-53325-7 (e-book)
DOI 10.1163/9789004533257

This book is printed on acid-free paper and produced in a sustainable manner.

Contents

Preface VII
Acknowledgments IX
Notes on Contributors X

1 Goals and Methodology 1
Marco de Benito, Fernando Gascón, Xandra Kramer, and Paul Oberhammer

2 Case Management 17
Marco de Benito, Anna Nylund, John Sorabji, and Rolf Stürner

3 Party Autonomy 36
Remo Caponi and Marco de Benito

4 Obligations of Parties, Lawyers, and Judges 58
Marco de Benito, Marco Gradi, (C. H.) Remco van Rhee, and Alan Uzelac

5 Service of Process 77
Astrid Stadler, Eva Storskrubb, Alan Uzelac, Enrique Vallines, and María Luisa Villamarín

6 Evidence 98
Marco de Benito, Fernando Gascón, Michele Angelo Lupoi, and Michael Stürner

7 Provisional and Protective Measures 113
Marco de Benito, Javier Gilsanz, Fernando de la Mata, and Jaime Vegas

8 Collective Proceedings 135
Marco Gradi, Elisabetta Silvestri, Ianika Tzankova, and Stefaan Voet

9 Costs and Funding 156
Albert Henke, Paul Oberhammer, and Eva Storskrubb

10 Judgments, *Lis Pendens*, *Res Judicata* 178
Christoph Kern, Enrique Vallines, Tanja Domej, and Jesús Loma

11 Appeals 208
Marco de Benito, Frédérique Ferrand, and Christoph Kern

12 Translation 226
Marco de Benito and Emmanuel Jeuland

13 Where from Here? 250
Paolo Biavati, Marco de Benito, Frédérique Ferrand, and Burkhard Hess

Appendix: ELI-UNIDROIT Model European Rules of Civil Procedure 265
Index 329

Preface

This book presents a series of colloquies between lawyers.[1]

Dialogue represents the primary communicative vehicle for thought. As social animals,[2] reflection on any topic inherently entails dialogue with others.[3] We humans *talk* with each other about things. An *ego-alter-object* triad is arguably our most profound epistemological structure.[4]

Since Antiquity, the increasing complexity of human knowledge has made writing the preferred format for communicating ideas. Nevertheless, the publication of any new work in any given field represents a further contribution to the ongoing dialogue. It is also evident that oral dialogue has never been superseded, even in the most formalised and esoteric disciplines.

Like philosophy, ethics, or politics, we *talk* and we *write* about law. Oral dialogue has historically constituted the principal vehicle for the expression and reflection on legal studies. In our classrooms and conference halls, we still emulate the model of Irnerius, who gathered a small group of students to explore together the recently rediscovered Digest.[5] Similarly, jurists have used a variety of literary forms: consultations, glosses, commentaries, summaries, questions and answers, dissertations, monographs, treatises, handbooks, encyclopaedias, lexicons, journal articles, blogs.[6]

The aim of this book is to contribute to the ongoing debate on European civil procedure in the form of a written dialogue. One of the most ancient and enduring forms of literary expression, written dialogue is particularly suited to capturing and reflecting the inherently dialogical structure of the

---

1 The word 'colloquy' (derived from the plural 'colloquies') comes from Latin *colloquium*, also *conloquium* ('conversation'), from *com-* ('together, with') + *loquor* ('speak').

2 ἐπειδὴ φύσει πολιτικὸν ὁ ἄνθρωπος ('since man is by nature a political thing': ARISTOTLE, *Nicomachean Ethics*, 1097b), a 'political animal': ὁ ἄνθρωπος φύσει πολιτικὸν ζῷον ('man is by nature a political animal', ARISTOTLE, *Politics I*, 2, 1253a2).

3 The word 'dialogue' comes from Latin *dialogus*, from Greek διάλογος ('conversation, dialogue'), from δια- ('across, between') + λέγω ('to speak'). The misconception that it can only mean 'conversation between two persons' is due to the confusion of δια- and δι- ('two').

4 See MOSCOVICI, S., *La psychanalyse, son image et son public*, Paris: Presses Universitaires de France, 1976.

5 See WAUTERS, B., DE BENITO, M., *The History of Law in Europe*, Cheltenham: Edward Elgar, 2017, pp. 50–57.

6 See WAUTERS, B., DE BENITO, M., *The History of Law in Europe*, Cheltenham: Edward Elgar, 2017, pp. 52–57, 94.

intellect. Since the time of Plato and his Socratic dialogues, this genre has demonstrated its capacity to express, structure, and convey complex ideas in an effective manner.

This book is inspired by a series of discussions that took place between 2020 and 2024. It should be noted, though, that this is far from a transcript. Those discussions provided only the initial material with which to create something completely new. For example, some of the chapters contain conversations that never took place, and some of the participants in one chapter actually discussed several topics with authors of another chapter. In sum, this book contains the freest literary exercise, completely detached from what may have been said in any oral conversation. *We wrote as if we were talking* because we enjoy discussing legal matters and thought it would be interesting to share our ideas with others in a conversational style. This is what the written dialogue genre is all about. This format allows us to convey the feeling of a real conversation, a polyphony[7] in two, three, four, or five voices that flows naturally and perhaps even rhythmically.

It would have been inconsistent with the fundamental premise of the book to present comprehensive, systematic accounts of each topic. The discourse is deliberately fragmented, moving fluidly from one idea to the next to reflect an authentic intersubjective exchange (and maybe even a postmodern scepticism of systematicity)[8]. Nevertheless, we have tried to arrange the sequence of topics in a rational way, with each section having a kind of invisible theme that the attentive reader will easily notice.

A text of this nature can only serve to complement more conventional and scientific methodologies (of which all of us are *guilty* in one way or another). It is our intention, therefore, to present the reader with a modest but possibly fruitful instrument for navigating the largely uncharted waters of European civil procedure.

---

7 See BAKHTIN, M. M., Проблемы поэтики Достоевского, Moscow: Khudozhestvennaya, 1963; in English, *Problems of Dostoevsky's Poetics* (edited and translated by EMERSON, C.), Minneapolis: University of Minnesota Press, 1984; BAKHTIN, M. M., Вопросы литературы и эстетики, Moscow: Khudozhestvennaya, 1975; in English, *The Dialogic Imagination. Four Essays* (edited by HOLQUIST, M., translated by EMERSON, C., HOLQUIST, M.), Austin: University of Texas Press, 1981.

8 See, e.g., BLANCHOT, M., *L'Entretien infini*, Paris: Gallimard, 1969; in English, *The Infinite Conversation* (translated by HANSON, S.), Minneapolis: University of Minnesota Press, 1993.

Acknowledgments

I take full responsibility for the idea, direction, and coordination of this book. I am also responsible for the first draft and final editing of all chapters, and therefore for any errors. However, this is by its very nature a truly collaborative work. It is a great privilege for me to have had the opportunity to work with scholars and practitioners of such calibre in the production of each chapter.

I would like to express my profound gratitude to all those who participated in the discussions that informed the development of this book. I would like to acknowledge Elina Asimakopoulou, Sergi Corominas, Ignacio Díez-Picazo, Miguel García Casas, Luis Gómez-Iglesias, Jorge González Carvajal, Andrzej Olaś, Laura Pérez, Pascal Pichonnaz, Elena Pineros, Inés de San Martín, Cindy Seinen, Alessandro Spinillo, Carlota Ucín, Anna Veneziano, and Diana Wallis for their active engagement and insightful contributions.

I would also like to acknowledge the contributions of Eliza Rose McNamara, Tomasz Dudek, and Valentina Viganò, from IE, ELI, and UNIDROIT respectively, in facilitating some of the discussions that helped shape this book.

I am also indebted to my former students, Adriana Martínez, Macarena Villa, and especially Yury Zakaznov, with whom I have since had the privilege of working on numerous occasions in my academic and professional endeavours. Their assistance with legal research and editing was invaluable to the completion of this book.

I would also like to thank Nikole Hyndman and Mary Kresge, then at VeraContent, for their help with style corrections; and to Elena Ortolà and Juan Torres, of Ortogràfic, for their exquisite renderings of contemporary chair designs that evoke the joy of convivial conversation.

I am also grateful to the Brill team, especially Lauren Danahy, who believed in the value of the project from the outset, and Akiko Hakuno and Mervin Ebenezer, who demonstrated remarkable patience and commitment to excellence. I would also like to thank the anonymous reviewers for their constructive feedback.

My gratitude extends to Soledad Atienza, dean of IE Law School, and Lupicinio Rodríguez, my steadfast ally in all legal ventures, for their encouragement and friendship.

A final word of thanks goes to Zahira for her loving motivation.

Notes on Contributors

Paolo Biavati
is professor emeritus at the University of Bologna and a partner at Studio Biavati.

Remo Caponi
is a judge (for outstanding achievements) at the Italian Supreme Court. He is a former full professor at the University of Florence.

Marco de Benito
is an associate professor at IE University and a partner at de Benito Arbitration.

Fernando de la Mata†
was an adjunct professor at ESADE University and a partner at Pérez-Llorca.

Tanja Domej
is a full professor at the University of Zurich.

Frédérique Ferrand
is a full professor at the University of Lyon 3 and a *Honorarprofessorin* at the University of Augsburg.

Fernando Gascón
is a full professor at the Complutense University of Madrid.

Javier Gilsanz
is an adjunct professor at IE University and a partner at PwC.

Marco Gradi
is a full professor at the University of Messina.

Albert Henke
is an associate professor at the University of Milan.

Burkhard Hess
is a full professor at the University of Vienna.

Emmanuel Jeuland
is a full professor at Paris 1 Panthéon-Sorbonne University.

Christoph Kern
is a full professor at the University of Heidelberg.

Xandra Kramer
is a full professor at both Erasmus University Rotterdam and Utrecht University.

Jesús Loma
is an adjunct professor at IE University, as well as a partner at Dlvlb.

Michele Angelo Lupoi
is a full professor at the University of Bologna and a partner at Studio Lupoi-Falvo.

Anna Nylund
is a full professor of law at the University of Bergen.

Paul Oberhammer
is a full professor at the University of Vienna, as well as of counsel at WilmerHale.

Elisabetta Silvestri
was an associate professor at the University of Pavia.

John Sorabji
is an associate professor at University College London.

Astrid Stadler
is a full professor at the University of Konstanz.

Eva Storskrubb
is an associate professor at Uppsala University.

Michael Stürner
is a full professor at the University of Konstanz, as well as a judge at the Higher Regional Court in Karlsruhe.

Rolf Stürner
is professor emeritus at the University of Freiburg.[1]

(C. H.) Remco van Rhee
is a full professor at Maastricht University.

Ianika Tzankova
is a full professor at Tilburg University.

Alan Uzelac
is a full professor at the Faculty of Law of the University of Zagreb.

Enrique Vallines
is an associate professor at the Complutense University of Madrid.

Jaime Vegas
is a full professor at the Juan Carlos I University of Madrid.

María Luisa Villamarín
is a full professor at the Complutense University of Madrid.

Stefaan Voet
is a full professor at KU Leuven and counsel at DLPA. He is also a substitute justice of the peace.

1 Professor Stürner does not assert authorship of the work, but rather acknowledges the excellent editorial reformulation and restructuring of several of his contributions to various academic forums and the inclusion of references in this volume.

CHAPTER 1

Goals and Methodology

Marco de Benito, Fernando Gascón, Xandra Kramer, and Paul Oberhammer

The objective of the Rules is not to establish a uniform civil procedure code. Instead, they present a set of best practices that can inspire legal reform, provide useful tools to litigants, lawyers, and judges, and serve as a valuable point of reference for comparative legal studies.

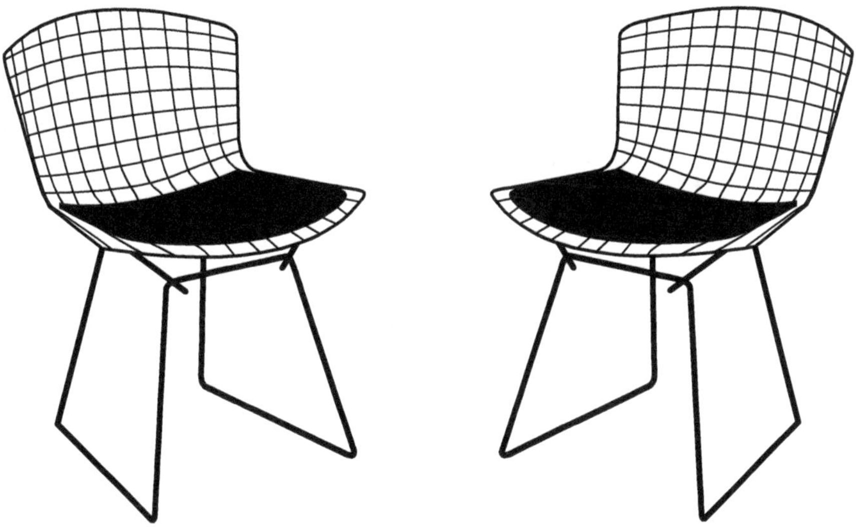

DE BENITO: The EU has developed an ambitious programme of action in civil procedure. Judicial cooperation has been strengthened. Exequatur has been abolished. Credit has been solidly protected. Sectorial action regularly includes procedural rules. Despite this considerable *acquis*, the core of procedural systems has remained anchored in national traditions. By 'national traditions', I am referring to the centuries-old codes, case law, and legal doctrine of countries such as France, Germany, England, Italy, or Spain. This core of civil procedure is being harmonised for the first time. As such, it is a turning point. From now on, talking about civil procedure in Europe will

 | DOI:10.1163/9789004533257_002

require us all to make at least some reference to these new harmonised rules and concepts.

OBERHAMMER: That's very true. But that's probably also the reason why it will encounter resistance.

People involved in the law-making process in Europe are used to being part of a process in which EU law is constantly being expanded. And we tend to think of this deeper integration as a positive development in the project of peace and prosperity that is the EU. However, this approach is not universally shared. Hence, additional arguments for the approximation or unification of procedural law in Europe may be useful. After all, civil procedure is practical and technical; some more down-to-earth arguments might be useful in advocating such unification.

Before returning to Austria, I taught in Switzerland. There I had the opportunity to witness the process of drafting and enacting the Swiss uniform code of civil procedure[1] and how it was received by the legal community. I remember the debate on whether there should be a uniform judicial structure, with a uniform name for the appellate courts throughout Switzerland. The idea was not generally well received. In the debate, 'legal culture' was used as an argument against the idea. In fact, culture will be used as an argument against any serious attempt at harmonisation. I suggest asking: whose culture: the culture of a society or a nation, or rather the culture of certain groups? I'm thinking here of the legal profession: judges often, lawyers here and there. Precisely those people who, because they work with civil procedure daily, are in a better position to question the harmonisation project.

As I have already said, typical arguments against harmonisation refer to the fact that a particular procedural code or judicial practice is said to be the expression of the legal culture of a particular jurisdiction. Bringing up the legal culture argument appears as a scholarly contribution, as adding a humanistic touch to the discussion. Sometimes, however, it simply functions as a camouflage of one's own personal or national idiosyncrasies.

DE BENITO: Perhaps academics are in a better position to encourage specialists to adopt a more flexible approach. After all, they have been advocating procedural approximation for quite some time.

1 Enacted on 19 December 2008, in force since 1 January 2011.

OBERHAMMER: I have my doubts. In our discussions within the working groups of the Rules project, someone – usually an academic – would suggest a certain solution. When confronted with the fact that it was their own jurisdiction's solution, the response would usually be that it was just a coincidence. Some would eventually change their minds; others, in turn, would defend their own treasure trove of national rules, which they know by heart and recite in their lectures just as previous generations did.

DE BENITO: Good legal harmonisation isn't about serving the convenience or interests of groups, whether they are judges, lawyers, or academics. It's always about serving the interests of citizens.

KRAMER: Exactly. The overall aim of any legislator, whether *hard* or *soft*, is to improve the effectiveness, efficiency, and reliability of civil procedure in the service of citizens.

OBERHAMMER: I would like to think that most citizens have an interest in the rule of law, as it is their main safeguard for their freedom and property. And, as Hayek – the only Viennese jurist to have been awarded a Nobel Prize – said, a crucial element of the idea of the rule of law is legal certainty and, more generally, foreseeability or predictability.[2] Some might argue that traditional notions of civil procedure provide for such predictability, as there is established judicial practice or perhaps even case law. This is only partly true. If we look at arbitration, we might think that the low degree of regulation of the process might lead to a continuing lack of predictability. However, the opposite is true. Businesses tend to prefer arbitration partly because they want to avoid the unpleasant surprises that they know first-hand from national court systems.[3]

Let me give you an example from my jurisdiction. In Austrian judicial practice, there are very complicated and detailed court traditions and practices on how to argue grounds of appeal; even Austrian lawyers find it difficult to get it right in many cases, let alone foreign lawyers. They may be

2 VON HAYEK, F. A., *The Road to Serfdom* London: Routledge, 1944, pp. 75 ff. See also VON HAYEK, F. A., *The Political Ideal of the Rule of Law*, Cairo: National Bank of Egypt, 1955.

3 See any of the empirical studies conducted by the School of International Arbitration of Queen Mary University of London, available at https://www.qmul.ac.uk/arbitration/research/; particularly, on the risk of 'judicialisation' of arbitration, 'Corporate Choices in International Arbitration: Industry Perspectives', 2013, p. 22.

able to say exactly what they think is wrong with the first instance judgment, both factually and legally; but they will not manage to say it *the Austrian way*. The problem is that clients will simply lose chances of success if their lawyers don't follow established practice.

Every foreign procedure is full of surprises, often unpleasant. What seems natural for professionals in one jurisdiction is considered parochial and arbitrary in another. Hence our need to work towards a uniform civil procedure, a uniform civil procedure that makes sense across the border. To do that, we need to discuss solutions that make sense to people in different jurisdictions. That is what we did in the ELI-UNIDROIT project.

DE BENITO: But to get back to the start of our chat, the project is going to meet with some resistance…

OBERHAMMER: Precisely for this reason, I prefer not to be too optimistic. The Swiss code of civil procedure is now more than ten years old; even so, it makes a big difference whether your case is heard in Geneva or Zurich. I have also mentioned the intricacies of Austrian appellate court practice: it has virtually no legal basis and couldn't be changed simply by changing the law. Some procedural idiosyncrasies may never go away. But we can work to provide future generations with a more rational and predictable civil procedure in the service of citizens.

GASCÓN: However, we must not lose sight of the fact that harmonisation is not the same as standardisation, nor does it imply standardisation. Harmonisation aims primarily at making systems comprehensible, understandable to others. It is of interest insofar as it helps systems in dialogue to understand each other better. For example, it will facilitate greater recognition and enforcement of judgments in all countries because we will all understand more easily what that document or judgment *means* in each country. This does not mean that every system must be identical.

DE BENITO: Moreover, to quote Hayek again, decentralisation, and with it difference and diversity, has the virtue of fostering competition, healthy emulation, and systemic improvement through individual action.[4]

4 VON HAYEK, F. A., *Law, Legislation and Liberty. A New Statement of the Liberal Principles of Justice and Political Economy*, London: Routledge and Kegan Paul, 1973–1979, especially vol. 1, *Rules and Order*, 1976.

GASCÓN: It also turns out that perfect uniformity is politically unattainable; and, as Ortega y Gasset said, futile effort leads to melancholy.[5] A well-directed effort simply leads us into the future. Once we have left one stage behind, another journey begins that will require time, talent, and enthusiasm.

Besides, just as having a plethora of different languages is an essential part of Europe's rich heritage, having different legal and procedural approaches – and (if Paul will allow me) cultures – is also a richness that I do not see why we should relegate to the dustbin of history.

KRAMER: Interestingly, many of us try to detach ourselves from our own systems. Of course, you can say: 'I see that in my system too'. But at some point, you must let go and take a step back: understand how it works in other countries; looking at what works and what doesn't work. In the structure group we had a lot of people from England, France, Germany, and the Netherlands. We had to be honest and look not only at our respective systems, but also at Italy or Norway, even outside our own countries, with which we are more familiar.

OBERHAMMER: The Rules are not a comparative handbook on European civil procedure, but the result of a long and intensive dialogue between people from jurisdictions all over Europe, who have contributed their experiences and concepts.

KRAMER: The starting point was the ALI-UNIDROIT Principles. Next, the entire *acquis* of binding EU law was considered. Although it was unwise to depart from binding EU law, the best practice approach allowed us to consider other perspectives. Common traditions of European countries, the work of the Storme Commission (as published in 1994),[6] and other pertinent European sources, such as soft law, were all considered. As the working groups consisted of at least four, but usually six or seven members from different countries, national approaches were also widely discussed. It was important to balance these sources and approaches to make sure that certain national systems did not dominate the Rules.

5 '*¿Adónde puede llevar el esfuerzo puro? A ninguna parte; mejor dicho, sólo a una: a la melancolía*': ORTEGA, J., 'Meditación del Escorial', *Obras completas*, vol. II (1916), Barcelona: Taurus, 2004, pp. 658–664, at 664.

6 STORME, M., *Study on the Approximation of the Laws and Rules of the Member States Concerning Certain Aspects of the Procedure for Civil Litigation* (final report), Dordrecht, 1994.

Another important source was the system of fundamental rights, in particular the right to a fair trial as set out in the Charter of Fundamental Rights of the EU, the European Convention on Human Rights, and the case law from the European Court of Human Rights. What's interesting is that the technical discussion is intertwined with the discussion on how to incorporate fundamental rights. Think of what we call principles of civil procedure. Most of them incorporate fundamental rights and, from a more technical or pragmatic point of view, also make civil procedure work. This intersection is evident not only in the general part, which we approach very carefully from this dual perspective, but throughout the Rules. Ideas such as settlement, cooperation, proportionality, and case management, or concentration of the procedure in different phases, are omnipresent and aim both to improve the efficiency of the procedure and to safeguard the fundamental rights of the parties.

The structure group, set up in 2016, had the difficult task of overseeing the drafts and merging them into a coherent set of standards, both in content and language. In the end, this was a more demanding task than we could have anticipated – we didn't know what we were getting into!

I remember a discussion about the project at the ELI annual conference in 2016. The structure group had barely started its work and we had more questions than answers. I raised the question of the precise scope of the project; whether it would cover both domestic and cross-border cases; its relationship with the ALI-UNIDROIT Principles, EU civil procedure, and national rules. In addition, I wondered how we could ensure coherence between the emerging drafts from the different working groups, and whether we would also have to fill in the gaps by adding a general part. In initial meetings with my fellow co-reporter, Loïc Cadiet, we agreed to include a general part to create more coherence.[7] One of the first steps we agreed on for the same purpose was to design a format for each working group that would consist, in turn, of a general part and then special parts. The idea was to *pre-harmonise* what each group would elaborate in their unique working dynamics. Some of the standards drafted by the working groups could then be incorporated individually into the general part, as was the case for the working group on obligations; others were drafted directly by the structure group.

---

7 See generally, on the function and technique of general parts in civil law legislation, MERRYMAN, J. H., PÉREZ-PERDOMO, R., *The Civil Law Tradition. An Introduction to the Legal Systems of Europe and Latin America*, Redwood City: Stanford University Press, 2018, pp. 68–79.

We also discussed the status of the commentary and how detailed it should be, as the approach varied greatly from one group to another. Finally, we agreed that we should have about one page per provision explaining what the rule is about and how it came about.

DE BENITO: I know that the Rules aren't a *code* as such. However, with their 245 articles covering general principles, parties, case management, service, access to information and evidence, judgment, *res judicata* and *lis pendens*, means of review, provisional measures, collective proceedings, costs, and more, we have never had such a comprehensive account of civil procedure in Europe.

KRAMER: Yes, but the idea was not to create an all-encompassing normative text like a national code, but simply to cover the essential elements of civil procedure, such as those you mentioned. We made it explicit in the preamble: the Model Rules are not intended to be exhaustive, but to reasonably cover the essential elements of civil procedure.[8]

In terms of the number of provisions, each working group had a slightly different approach, and in general the trend was towards an increasing number of articles. We strived to keep the size manageable, and the structure group merged certain standards. However, the general part involved adding quite a few rules.

In any case, they are called 'Model Rules' mainly because they do not cover everything. We cannot call it a code, as many parts would be missing, such as the small claims procedure. The Dutch code includes more than a thousand provisions.

DE BENITO: The figure is revealing, but codes – and 'model codes' even more so – can exist without including small claims procedures or other relatively minor aspects, which would remain outside of the code, *quasi vagantes extra corpus juris*, like the constitutions of the popes after the decrees of Gratian.[9] Consider the *Código Procesal Civil Modelo para Iberoamérica*, which consists of 393 articles and is nevertheless called a code. The terms 'model laws' or 'model codes' have a long tradition. Perhaps the extensive scope of this project and the inevitable fragmentation of its contents may explain the modest, unassuming title of 'Rules'?

---

8 Preamble, Section IV.

9 See, *inter alia multa*, WAUTERS, B., DE BENITO, M., *The History of Law in Europe*, Cheltenham: Edward Elgar, 2017, pp. 57–61.

KRAMER: There's something to it, yes.

DE BENITO: The final text reflects the sequence of the procedural model proposed by the Rules. The arrangement of the chapters and articles itself reflects a policy choice. Was this structure clear to the *structure group* from the outset?

KRAMER: When we submitted our first simple outline of the whole work, including the full drafts of the first three working groups, to UNIDROIT in 2018, we were told that the work lacked structure, and we were advised to try to follow the sequence of the procedure more closely. This is of course a challenge, and national codes differ on this point. Provisional measures are a good example. Often, provisional measures can be requested before the proceeding on the merits is commenced, but they can also be requested during the proceeding, or even later, at the enforcement stage. This raised questions as to which is the best option, and how best to follow the structure. Indeed, it was a choice we made after careful deliberation.

DE BENITO: Tell us more about your choices in terms of structure.

KRAMER: The Rules are divided into twelve parts, the first of which consists of 26 general provisions. Much thought has been given to how to structure the Rules so that they provide an internal logic. The 20-page preamble explains the main ideas and recognises that the Rules are neither exhaustive nor complete. For example, some rules are more detailed than others.

We also explain that digital procedures and the use of artificial intelligence are not treated as separate issues, but that the use of electronic means is outlined where it is most relevant.

Our mission was to try to make the Rules more compatible with technology, or at least technologically neutral. We were aware that digitalisation and artificial intelligence are growing at an ever-faster pace.[10] Consequently, you will see references to communications that can also be digital without going into more detail.

10 See generally THEMELI, E., 'The Frontiers of Digital Justice in Europe', in KRAMER, X., HOEVENAARS, J., KAS, B., THEMELI, E. (eds.), *Frontiers in Civil Justice. Privatisation, Monetisation and Digitisation*, Cheltenham: Edward Elgar, 2022, pp. 102–120. See also STÜRNER, R., 'The ELI / UNIDROIT Model European Rules of Civil Procedure. An Introduction to Their Basic Conceptions', *RabelsZ*, 86, 2022, pp. 421–472, at 469–471.

DE BENITO: In terms of methodology, the preamble is clear: the aim was not to draft a restatement, nor to identify a *tronc commun*, nor to follow a majority approach, nor to reach a compromise, but to identify best practice in each case:

> The methodological approach taken to devising the Rules themselves was determined by the Steering Committee from the outset. The aim was not to devise a set of rules articulating common practices, i.e. a 'restatement' of European civil procedure, nor was it to devise a set of rules based on the predominance of approaches across European jurisdictions, or based on compromise. The project's aim was to devise a set of best practice rules for the future development of European civil procedure.[11]

The challenge lies in identifying the most effective practices, which requires a complex process: first, there is the task of collecting practices, and then a delicate value judgement. How did this play out in practice?

GASCÓN: I would like to share my experience on this crucial point. I participated in three of the working groups: access to information and evidence, *res judicata* and *lis pendens*, and appeals. These working groups corresponded, moreover, to the three phases of the project's development. We were always faced with the same challenge: how to create model rules that would not only be accepted by the working group but could reach a level of general acceptance. In the working groups, we were in a good position to test the potential for wider acceptance. Essentially, if a group of colleagues representing different legal traditions could agree on a particular rule, then the rule was likely to be more generally accepted.

In finding the best solution in converging and diverging legal traditions, I found that three factors were important: the objective of the project, the role of comparative research, and awareness of disruptive effects.

Firstly, we had to keep in mind the objective of the project: to draft model rules. This means not only being aware that there are different solutions to the same procedural problem, but also selecting the preferred option both from an internal point of view and from the point of view of the potential for future European harmonisation.

---

11 Preamble, Section III, para. 9.

Secondly, we had to carry out comparative research. We needed context and to know how different procedural rules are performing in different European jurisdictions. In other words, what works and what does not. It was important for us to consider whether good performance is linked to the procedural solution itself or is simply a function of other features of a given judicial system. Sometimes a good rule will not work well simply because it exists within a weak or underperforming system. In any case, we understand that the best solutions come from the comparative study of both normative solutions and practical performance.

Finally, we needed to examine how the Model Rules impact on different systems, especially those where the Rules diverge significantly from standard practice. Whenever we define a set of *best* rules, there will be individuals or even communities that feel excluded.

OBERHAMMER: That comes with the best practice approach. There will always be people who feel neglected, either because of decisions made or because they were not consulted about the construction of the new system.

DE BENITO: Along these lines, there is also the question of how the Rules function in the context of different justice systems, constitutional traditions, or (once again) legal cultures.

GASCÓN: This was one of the most serious and permanent obstacles to reaching consensus in the working groups. Two examples come to mind, both in the field of evidence.

The first concerns addressing the scope of the court's powers to take evidence on its own motion, without prior request by the parties. Some countries find it unacceptable for the judge to assume the role of a party proposing evidence; in others, it is not at all extraordinary, especially regarding expert evidence. Both options are acceptable. This time we decided that a compromise *is* the best practice. We stated that proposing evidence is primarily the responsibility of the parties, but the court may exceptionally suggest that new evidence be added:

> Rule 25. *Evidence*
>
> (1) Each party is required to prove all the relevant facts supporting its case. Parties must offer evidence supporting their factual contentions. Substantive law determines the burden of proof.

> (2) In so far as appropriate the court may invite the parties to supplement their offers of evidence. Exceptionally, it may take evidence on its own motion.

This is adaptable to the circumstances, but it also makes clear our choice in favour of the parties retaining the primary responsibility to offer evidence.

The second example is illegally obtained evidence. We found a profound clash between systems for which illegally obtained evidence is a completely unacceptable violation of fundamental rights, and others which consider it unavoidable in cases where no other evidence is available. Once again, we reached a compromise:

> Rule 90. *Illegally obtained evidence*
>
> (1) Except where Rule 90(2) applies, illegally obtained evidence must be excluded from the proceedings.
>
> (2) Exceptionally, the court may admit illegally obtained evidence if it is the only way to establish the facts. In exercising its discretion to admit such evidence the court must take into account the behaviour of the other party or of non-parties and the gravity of the infringement.

In other words, illegally obtained evidence should not be accepted as a rule, but the court may grant evidentiary effect to illegally obtained evidence in exceptional situations due to the circumstances of the case and with careful use of proportionality.

DE BENITO: As you said, you also took part in the working groups on *res judicata* and *lis pendens*, as well as on appeals. Did you face similar difficulties in those areas?

GASCÓN: The block of rules on *res judicata* was more technical, but it also has a clear impact on the way strategic decisions are taken in litigation. In the different legal traditions, we see different approaches regarding, for instance, the scope of *res judicata*.

For example, in the German legal tradition, the scope of *res judicata* is rather limited, as it only covers the explicit decisions made by the court in the judgment. In the English tradition, by contrast, under the *Henderson v*

Henderson rule, a party cannot raise in subsequent litigation any claim that he should have raised in an earlier action, with a consequent broad preclusive effect.[12] In France we see something similar following the *arrêt Césareo*.[13] The same in Spain with the Civil Procedure Code of 2000.[14] In the ELI-UNIDROIT project, we decided to follow the German rule instead,[15] and offer a narrow scope for *res judicata*:

> Rule 149. *Material scope of* res judicata
>
> (1) The material scope of *res judicata* is determined by reference to the claims for relief in the parties' pleadings, including amendments, as decided by the court's judgment.
>
> (2) *Res judicata* also covers necessary and incidental legal issues that are explicitly decided in a judgment where parties to subsequent proceedings are the same as those in the proceedings determined by the prior judgment and where the court that gave that judgment could decide those legal issues.

We think that a broader scope of *res judicata* may not be considered acceptable in jurisdictions accustomed to understanding the effects of the judgment as strictly limited to what has been expressly discussed in the case.

DE BENITO: What about the third set of rules you took part in: appeals?

GASCÓN: There was a major clash over how different legal traditions and procedural cultures approach the right to appeal and the differences between the first and second appeal. Here, especially with the first appeal, there is a clash between common law and civil law. Within the working group, some of the main questions were: should the first appeal be limited? Should we require leave to appeal, as is customary in English law, or should we grant more general access to the first appeal?

---

12 Judgment of 20 July 2843, available at http://www.worldlii.org/int/cases/EngR/1843/917.pdf.

13 Judgment of 7 July 2006, available at https://www.legifrance.gouv.fr/juri/id/JURITEXT000007054984/.

14 LEC, Art. 400(2): 'For the purposes of *lis pendens* and *res judicata*, the facts and legal grounds put forward in a proceeding shall be deemed to be the same as those alleged in a previous proceeding, if such allegation was possible.'

15 ZPO, § 322(1): 'Judgments are capable of binding effect only to the extent that a claim raised by the complaint or the counterclaim has been decided.' See MURRAY, P. L., STÜRNER, R., *German Civil Justice*, Durham: Carolina Academic Press, 2004, pp. 355–366.

Again, we found the best-rule approach through a compromise. We decided to include a common rule that would grant leave to appeal for cases that have reached a certain monetary threshold (which should not be too high) and cases below this threshold, where the court has the possibility to grant leave to appeal.

Regarding the second appeal, we encountered the so-called 'Italian red line': the fact that Italian citizens have a constitutional right to access the *Corte suprema di cassazione* and have the opportunity for a last appeal.[16] How can we create Model Rules that limit access to first appeal and grant more access to second appeal simultaneously? By ignoring the 'Italian red line' and accepting the possibility that some Italian readers may find this section unacceptable.

KRAMER: Another example is the very idea to draft a general part with principles, which came from the French *Code de procédure civile* with its *principes directeurs*.[17] Or the idea of a pre-commencement duty to try to settle disputes, which was first fully realised in England with Woolf's pre-action protocols.[18]

OBERHAMMER: All these examples show how difficult it was to follow this best-rule approach. It may seem that we are close in terms of legal traditions, but when it comes to the details – and procedural law has a lot to do with the details –, cultures and traditions can differ enormously.

DE BENITO: Then there is the human factor. Apart from the systemic and cultural factors, which are crucial, it is the human factor that makes the difference between a regulation that works and one that is theoretically perfect but unworkable.

KRAMER: Of course, the human factor is key. This is the case for any harmonisation project or binding rules, which must be operational within EU Member States, for instance. Even in the context of binding European rules we see that they aren't always applied identically.

---

16 Italian Constitution, Art. 111: 'Jurisdiction is implemented through due process regulated by law. Every trial is conducted in an adversarial manner between the parties, on equal terms, before a third and impartial judge. The law ensures its reasonable duration. (…)'

17 CPC, Arts. 1–24.

18 Available at https://www.justice.gov.uk/courts/procedure-rules/civil/protocol.

In any case, this is a work in progress. The training of judges and lawyers will have to incorporate the Rules in one way or another. In general, more interaction between lawyers is already a strong trend. We can all spread our knowledge and learn from each other.

DE BENITO: How did you see the future of the Rules at that time – what could they mean for the legal development of European countries, how could they be useful for national legislators, for EU institutions, and even for other regions?

KRAMER: For national legislators in Europe, we knew that only certain elements would be immediately relevant and that the Rules cannot be fully incorporated one by one. But we were convinced that, if we all did a good job, the Rules could serve as a useful reference point when a country wished to revise, in part or in full, its own civil procedures.

For the various European and international institutions – particularly those that have been close observers of the project –, the Rules feed into future and current initiatives. Within the European legislator, we can already see that the Rules have played an important role in, among other smaller initiatives,[19] the revision of the Evidence Regulation[20] and the Service Regulation.[21]

For other legislatures around the world, the Rules offer important takeaways. In regions where UNIDROIT collaborates, such as Latin America,

19 See https://www.europarl.europa.eu/legislative-train/theme-area-of-justice-and-fundamental-rights/file-common-standards-in-the-field-of-civil-procedure. See also MAŃKO, R., *Europeanisation of Civil Procedure. Towards Common Minimum Standards?*, Brussels, Strasbourg: European Parliament, 2015, available at https://www.europarl.europa.eu/thinktank/en/document/EPRS_IDA(2015)559499.

20 Council Regulation (EC) 1206/2001 of 28 May 2001 on cooperation between the courts of the Member States in the taking of evidence in civil or commercial matters, now replaced by Regulation (EU) 2020/1783 of the European Parliament and of the Council of 25 November 2020 on cooperation between the courts of the Member States in the taking of evidence in civil or commercial matters (taking of evidence) (recast).

21 Council Regulation (EC) 1393/2007 of 13 November 2007 on the service in the Member States of judicial and extrajudicial documents in civil or commercial matters, now replaced by Regulation (EU) 2020/1784 of the European Parliament and of the Council of 25 November 2020 on the service in the Member States of judicial and extrajudicial documents in civil or commercial matters (service of documents) (recast). See generally ANTHIMOS, A., REQUEJO, M. (eds.), *The European Service Regulation. A Commentary*, Cheltenham: Edward Elgar, 2023.

there is great interest in the way we have developed the ALI-UNIDROIT Principles into the more detailed Rules within the European context.

GASCÓN: We were also aware that national codes of civil procedure cannot simply be replaced by the Rules in the relevant language. They were designed to serve as model rules. Some provisions could perhaps be imported from time to time, but we knew that this would not always be possible, nor was it our aim.

KRAMER: Exactly. It can only be done in bits and pieces.

GASCÓN: In bits and pieces, yes; but always keeping in mind the Model Rules as an integral whole. One of the revolutionary aspects of this project is that it proposes a complete model for declaratory proceedings.

Bibliography

ANTHIMOS, A., REQUEJO, M. (eds.), *The European Service Regulation. A Commentary*, Cheltenham: Edward Elgar, 2023.

MAŃKO, R., *Europeanisation of Civil Procedure. Towards Common Minimum Standards?*, Brussels, Strasbourg: European Parliament, 2015, available at https://www.europarl.europa.eu/thinktank/en/document/EPRS_IDA(2015)559499.

MERRYMAN, J. H., PÉREZ-PERDOMO, R., *The Civil Law Tradition. An Introduction to the Legal Systems of Europe and Latin America*, Redwood City: Stanford University Press, 2018.

MURRAY, P. L., STÜRNER, R., *German Civil Justice*, Durham: Carolina Academic Press, 2004.

STORME, M., *Study on the Approximation of the Laws and Rules of the Member States Concerning Certain Aspects of the Procedure for Civil Litigation* (final report), Dordrecht, 1994.

STÜRNER, R., 'The ELI / UNIDROIT Model European Rules of Civil Procedure. An Introduction to Their Basic Conceptions', *RabelsZ*, 86, 2022, pp. 421–472.

THEMELI, E., 'The Frontiers of Digital Justice in Europe', in KRAMER, X., HOEVENAARS, J., KAS, B., THEMELI, E. (eds.), *Frontiers in Civil Justice. Privatisation, Monetisation and Digitisation*, Cheltenham: Edward Elgar, 2022, pp. 102–120.

VON HAYEK, F. A., *Law, Legislation and Liberty. A New Statement of the Liberal Principles of Justice and Political Economy*, London: Routledge and Kegan Paul, 1973–1979.

von Hayek, F. A., *The Political Ideal of the Rule of Law*, Cairo: National Bank of Egypt, 1955.

von Hayek, F. A., *The Road to Serfdom* London: Routledge, 1944.

Wauters, B., de Benito, M., *The History of Law in Europe*, Cheltenham: Edward Elgar, 2017.

CHAPTER 2

Case Management

Marco de Benito, Anna Nylund, John Sorabji, and Rolf Stürner

The historical tendency towards a more proactive role on the part of the judge has given rise, in the 21st century, to the so-called case management model of civil procedure. Consequently, the Rules establish the overarching obligation of the court to facilitate the efficient management of cases. This is regarded as an essential component of the broader principle of cooperation between the court and the parties.

The comprehensive list of case management tools at the disposal of the judge is indicative of this encouragement of a more assertive, creative, and collaborative involvement of the court. Nevertheless, the case management model is not limited to its expression in this or that provision; rather, it is reflected in numerous provisions throughout the Rules.

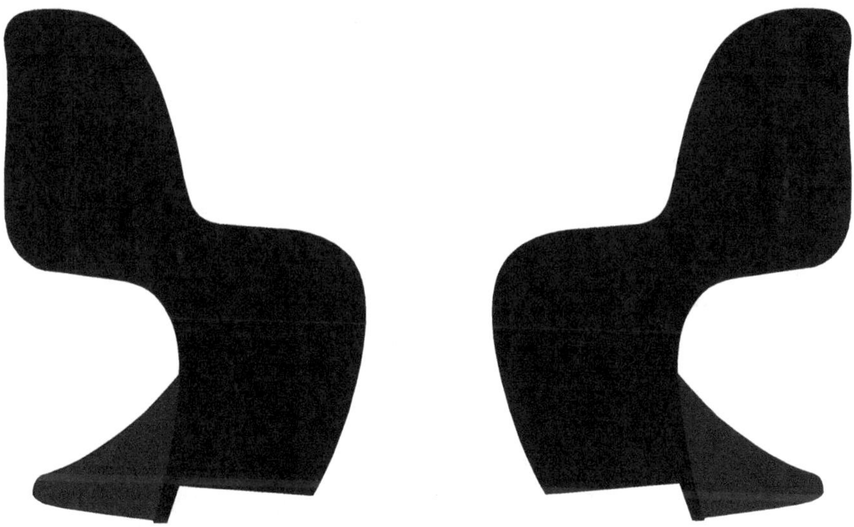

 | DOI:10.1163/9789004533257_003

Sorabji: The Rules eschew the distinction whether case management should focus on procedure only – as in England and Wales – or both substance and procedure – as in Austria. Take Rule 4, for instance, which sets out the general case management obligation:

> Rule 4. *Role of the court – the general case management duty*
>
> The court is responsible for active and effective case management. The court must ensure that parties enjoy equal treatment. Throughout proceedings it shall monitor whether parties and their lawyers comply with their responsibilities under these Rules.

This provision accepts that the two, procedure and substance, are functionally interdependent. And the better approach is one which looks to the court's role in assisting the parties and the parties' role in assisting the court to reach substantively correct decisions.

de Benito: What has been described as a partnership, a cooperative model of case management that is focused on the duty of loyal cooperation.[1]

Sorabji: This still seems strange for me to say, as it's not entirely an expression that would be used in English procedure or in English generally. Nevertheless, that duty of loyal cooperation between the court and the parties took centre stage in terms of case management. The idea was particularly championed by Remco van Rhee and Alan Uzelac.

The duty would exist even before proceedings through the adoption of pre-commencement duties, which would of course continue after commencement. These duties require parties to cooperate with each other to seek to settle their disputes consensually. And the role of the court here is to help and to some extent facilitate such endeavours once proceedings have commenced.

1 See generally van Rhee, C. H. (ed.), *Judicial Case Management and Efficiency in Civil Litigation*, Antwerp, Oxford: Intersentia, 2007; Cabral, A., 'New Trends and Perspectives on Case Management', *International Journal of Comparative Law*, 2018, 8, pp. 10–36; García Odgers, R., *El* case management *en perspectiva comparada. Teoría, evolución histórica, modelos comparados y un caso en desarrollo*, Valencia: Tirant lo Blanch, 2019; Nylund, A., 'Case Management in a Comparative Perspective: Regulation, Principles and Practice', *Revista do processo – RePro*, 2019, 292, pp. 377–398; Chan, C. H., van Rhee, C. H. (eds.), *Civil Case Management in the Twenty-First Century: Court Structures Still Matter*, Cham: Springer, 2021.

NYLUND: In part, these developments are not novel. They can be traced to Franz Klein,[2] and they can be found in Norwegian civil procedure as well as other – although not all – procedural codes and rules across Europe.

DE BENITO: To some, they may be controversial. Procedural rules applying to pre-commencement party activity?

STÜRNER: I have contributed to a lot of discussions on comparative civil procedure during my time as a professor and judge; nevertheless, while working on this project, I gained a lot of new knowledge on the variety of conflict resolution mechanisms implemented by different legal and procedural cultures, and at times I was forced to change my mind, open it up, and adapt it to other concepts and ideas.

SORABJI: Reforming procedural culture was, thankfully, outside the scope of the project! However, the working group that devised case management rules in the project was alive to the controversial aspects of this issue. And the conclusion they drew was that best practice would require formalizing the cooperative approach in the Rules. This is because it properly cohered with the idea of a partnership between the court and the parties to promote a proportionate litigation process – one of the aims identified in the general principles identified at the beginning of the Rules, namely Rules 2 to 10.

Now, such points can be made throughout the Rules. It is hoped that the approach taken – for example, in respect of case management – will raise questions, debates, and discussions, and will challenge our traditions. This will hopefully lead to the development of new cultures and traditions. This may in turn inspire future reform across Europe and hopefully, over time, the greater coherence and convergence the project seeks to achieve. If it does so, this project will have gone a long way in achieving its aim to improve European civil procedure law.

DE BENITO: Why do we need a cooperative civil procedure instead of simply party autonomy in some areas and a commanding judge in others?

NYLUND: Leaving even bits of the procedure solely in the parties' hands is often far from ideal. It can even reduce the quality of justice and cause

2 KLEIN, F., *Pro futuro. Betrachtungen über Probleme der Civilproceßreform in Oesterreich*, Leipzig, Vienna: Deuticke, 1891.

delay. The parties need assistance to effectively exercise their party autonomy. They need someone to pinpoint common ground and identify inconsistencies and unclear assertions. In short: they need an active judge.[3]

DE BENITO: An actively listening judge, might we say?

NYLUND: Perhaps! That cooperation between the court and the parties, which shifts procedural relations from *dyadic* to *triadic*,[4] is what enhances and secures that the parties can make informed decisions and be autonomous.[5] It's interesting to see how Rules 2, 3, and 4 manifest the principle of party cooperation and case management in an integrated, amalgamated, interdependent manner:

> A. *Co-operation*
>
> Rule 2. *General*
>
> Parties, their lawyers and the court must co-operate to promote the fair, efficient and speedy resolution of the dispute.
>
> Rule 3. *Role of the parties and their lawyers*
>
> Parties and their lawyers must:
>
> (a) take reasonable and appropriate steps to settle disputes amicably;
>
> (b) contribute to the proper management of the proceedings;
>
> (c) present facts and evidence;
>
> (d) assist the court in the determination of the facts and the applicable law;
>
> (e) act in good faith and avoid procedural abuse when dealing with the court and other parties.

---

3 NYLUND, A., 'Oral Proceedings During the Preparatory Stage', *International Journal of Procedural Law*, 2022, 12, pp. 57–74, at 68–69.

4 BRAUN, J., *Lehrbuch des Zivilprozessrechts*, Tübingen: Mohr Siebeck, 2014, pp. 66–69.

5 *Cfr*. GALIČ, A., '(In)compatibility of Procedural Preclusions with the Goals of Civil Justice: An Ongoing Debate in Slovenia', in UZELAC, A. (ed.), *Goals of Civil Justice and Civil Procedure in the Contemporary Judicial Systems*, Cham: Springer, 2014, pp. 221–243.

Rule 4. *Role of the court – the general case management duty*

The court is responsible for active and effective case management. The court must ensure that parties enjoy equal treatment. Throughout proceedings it shall monitor whether parties and their lawyers comply with their responsibilities under these Rules.

STÜRNER: The commentary to those Rules tries to clarify that the idea of a well-working community between parties and court, and especially between two parties, might be a bit idealistic. Each party in civil procedure wants to be the winner. Consequently, there is a competition between parties to convince the court of the factual basis of their cases and the correctness of the legal theory underlying them. The principle of cooperation is concretised in the Rules by the parties' special duties, mainly the duty to facilitate settlement, to disclose evidence in favour of the opponent, and to act fairly.[6] This concretisation by the Rules is to be read as an expression of realistic expectations. The Rules are not naïve, and thus do not suggest any kind of romantic idealisation of a community working together, especially regarding the relationship between parties.

NYLUND: From this point of view, and picking up on John's argument at the beginning, it's interesting to see how the Rules link cooperation, party autonomy, and the management of procedure, substance, and evidence. Procedural case management refers to the court setting the schedule, assigning the case to different procedural tracks, appointing experts, ruling on access to evidence. Substantive aspects refer to the court assisting the parties in identifying core factual and legal points by separating disputed from undisputed issues, or discerning core issues from peripheral, irrelevant issues. By management of evidence, I mean limiting evidence-taking to whatever is relevant and proportional to prove the disputed facts and sometimes making the parties aware that they might need to add evidence.[7]

6 STÜRNER, R., 'The ELI / UNIDROIT Model European Rules of Civil Procedure. An Introduction to Their Basic Conceptions', *RabelsZ*, 86, 2022, pp. 421–472, at 451–453.

7 See, e.g., CHAN, C. H., VAN RHEE, C. H. (eds.), *Civil Case Management in the Twenty-First Century: Court Structures Still Matter*, Cham: Springer, 2021, p. 140; ANDREWS, N., *Andrews on Civil Processes: Court Proceedings, Arbitration & Mediation*, Cambridge: Intersentia, 2019, pp. 175–195; NYLUND, A., 'Case Management in a Comparative Perspective: Regulation, Principles and Practice', *Revista do processo – RePro*, 2019, 292, pp. 377–398; CABRAL, A., 'New Trends and Perspectives on Case Management', *International Journal of Comparative Law*, 2018, 8, pp. 10–36; PÉREZ-RAGONE, Á., 'An Approach to Case

SORABJI: These three aspects of case management are very much interconnected.

NYLUND: But they appear in each proceeding with different intensity. If it turns out that the main disputed issue is legal, then the proceeding should focus on the law: evidence would be secondary, and the proceeding should be shaped to better address those legal issues. If a party becomes aware that if they want to prove some core disputed facts that would require costly evidence, such as an expert report, then the party might be more inclined to agree to mediation or may consider modifying the claim to forego the evidence. In this way, the court exercising substantive case management promotes party choices – supports the parties in making informed decisions regarding procedure, substance, and evidence.[8]

In an ideal world, the parties would have identified core disputed issues before commencing court proceedings; but this does not always happen, and we must regulate civil procedure for the world as it is and not as we would wish it to be.

DE BENITO: Even if they do, they're not alone. As you said before, Anna, any proceeding is an *actus trium personarum*: there are the parties, but there is also the judge. And it is essential that the judge is fully engaged with the dispute, as this will ensure a successful outcome.[9] Effective case management is the most effective way to achieve this. We may describe this

---

Management from the Horizontal and Vertical Structure of Court Systems', *Zeitschrift für Zivilprozess International*, 2018, 23, pp. 353–354; GASCÓN, F., 'Between Reform and Dejudicialisation: Current Trends in Spanish Civil Litigation', in UZELAC, A., VAN RHEE, C. H. (eds.), *Transformation of Civil Justice. Unity and Diversity*, Cham: Springer: 2018, pp. 119–143, at p. 125; GALIČ, A., 'The Preparatory Stage of Civil Proceedings in Slovenia, the Czech Republic and Slovakia: Halfway There Yet?', in ERVO, L., NYLUND, A. (eds.), *Current Trends in Preparatory Proceedings*, Cham: Springer, 2016, pp. 111–140; NYLUND, A., 'Norway: Efficiency by Flexible Preparatory Proceedings and Case Management', in ERVO, L., NYLUND, A. (eds.), *Current Trends in Pre-Trial Proceedings*, Cham: Springer, 2016, pp. 57–79; JEULAND, E., 'Case Management in France', in VAN RHEE, C. H., FU, Y. (eds.), *Civil Litigation in China and Europe: Essays on the Role of the Judge and the Parties*, Dordrecht: Springer, 2014, pp. 349–358; GENSLER, S. S., 'Judicial Case Management: Caught in the Crossfire', *Duke Law Journal*, 2010, 60, pp. 669–744, at 692.

8 NYLUND, A., 'Oral Proceedings During the Preparatory Stage', *International Journal of Procedural Law*, 2022, 12, pp. 57–74, at 68–69.

9 DE LA OLIVA, A., *El papel del juez en el proceso civil. Frente a ideología*, prudentia iuris, Cizur Menor: Civitas, 2012, p. 46.

as 'procedural immediacy'.[10] The concept of immediacy is often associated with the judge's direct contact with evidence. However, in a broader sense, it encompasses the relationship between procedure and decision.

All authentic judgement, whether moral or intellectual, is formed through a procedure. This includes the weighing of the various arguments and proofs presented. One might argue that God alone does not require a procedure to judge.[11] To judge is to proceed and to proceed is to judge; they are two sides of the same coin. The procedure may itself become a more important factor of legitimacy than the substantive rule.[12] Hence, a judgement that has renounced its own formative process is necessarily unfair.[13]

Precisely because it is formed through a procedure, the dispute is apprehended through a kind of osmosis. The judge becomes familiar with the lawsuit in a gradual, natural way, and the solution is arrived at in a similar manner. The just decision 'filters into the mind of the judge' through the procedure.[14]

In my view, case management is thus closely linked to this notion of procedural immediacy.

NYLUND: That consideration brings me to another: what matters is not so much regulation but rather bring about a change in mindset. Put differently, more effective case management has a lot to do with changing procedural and cultural aspects of civil procedure, rather than its technical aspects. And these rest on tacit assumptions of the proper role of the judge and in what ways a judge can intervene without becoming impartial and encroaching on party autonomy. Rule 49 has a very comprehensive list of procedural matters that need to be addressed:

---

10 DE BENITO, M., *Justicia o burocracia* (foreword by TARUFFO, M.), Cizur Menor: Civitas, 2017, pp. 127–134.

11 FENECH, M., *Derecho procesal penal*, Barcelona: Labor, 1960, p. 37.

12 LUHMANN, N., *Legitimation durch Verfahren*, Frankfurt: Suhrkamp, 1969.

13 See GRADI, M., 'Cornelis Saftleven e l'allegoria del processo', in FARALLI, C., GIGLIOTTI, V., HERITIER, P., MITTICA, M. P. (eds.), *Il diritto tra testo e immagine. Rappresentazione ed evoluzione delle fonti*, Milan: Mimesis, 2015, pp. 151–165, esp. at 160 ff.

14 CALAMANDREI, P., 'La genesi logica della sentenza civile', in *Opere giuridiche*, vol. I, *Problemi generali del diritto e del processo*, Rome: Roma TrE-Press, 2019, pp. 11–54, at 12 and *passim*; 'Il proceso come giuoco', in *Opere giuridiche*, vol. I, *cit.*, pp. 537–562, at 539. See also MERRYMAN, J. H., PÉREZ-PERDOMO, R., *The Civil Law Tradition*, Redwood City: Stanford University Press, 2007, p. 115.

Rule 49. *Means of case management*

Where necessary for the proper management of proceedings, the court shall, in particular:

(1) encourage parties to take active steps to settle their dispute or parts of their dispute and, where appropriate, to use alternative dispute resolution methods;

(2) schedule case management conferences;

(3) determine the type and the form of the procedure;

(4) set a timetable or procedural calendar with deadlines for procedural steps to be taken by parties and/or their lawyers;

(5) limit the number and length of future submissions;

(6) determine the order in which issues should be tried and whether proceedings should be consolidated or separated;

(7) determine the separation of questions concerning jurisdiction, provisional measures and statutes of limitation for early decision upon special hearings;

(8) consider necessary amendments regarding the parties' proper representation, the consequences of changes related to the parties to litigation and the participation of third parties, intervenors, or other persons;

(9) consider amendments to the pleadings or offers of evidence in the light of the parties' contentions;

(10) require a party's appearance in person or require a party's representative, who should be fully informed of all matters relevant to the proceedings, to be present at a court hearing;

(11) address the availability, admissibility, form, disclosure and exchange of evidence and, if adequate to the state of proceedings,

(a) determine the admissibility of evidence;

(b) order the taking of evidence.

The rule, comprehensive as it is, could have perhaps more forcefully clarified that we need a case management hearing, held either in person or remotely, for the court to efficiently exercise procedural case management.

Sorabji: What about substantive case management?

NYLUND: The Rules demonstrate how difficult it is to regulate that. Rule 61 (4) attempts to do that by allowing the court to provide parties with advice relevant to their preparation for the final hearing:

> Rule 61. *Case management hearings to prepare for the final hearing and determination*
>
> (4) Whenever appropriate, the court may provide parties with advice relevant to their preparation for the final hearing and judgment. Such advice should, in so far as possible, be given in the early case management hearing. Case management orders should be made in or immediately after the early case management hearing.

This wording is vague, and many European lawyers will raise their eyebrows on the term 'advice' on substance. I understand that *advising* is different from *assisting* the parties in pinpointing core issues and in identifying the core of the case to have concentrated and proportional proceedings. The commentary to Rule 61 says nothing more on this topic.

There is also Rule 63, which refers to the court having the opportunity to clarify issues:

> Rule 63. *The closing of preparatory proceedings*
>
> (1) As soon as the court is satisfied that both parties have had a reasonable opportunity to present their case during the preparatory proceedings and that it has had an opportunity to clarify issues …

Yet, again, it doesn't define what clarification means. I miss a provision that would require the court to address unclear, incomplete, inconsistent information; this would also help the parties exercise their autonomy and would concentrate the proceedings.

Also, judges need good tools to perform good case management. Perhaps case summaries might help in this regard by identifying the core issues of the case and background. This would be done in writing, either by the parties or by the court prior to the case management hearing, and then the summary would be updated after that case management hearing and prior to the final hearing. Written summaries have been a successful tool in Swedish civil procedure.[15] Electronic case management systems could enable the court and the parties to work on a single document rather than using

15 NYLUND, A., 'Case Management in a Comparative Perspective: Regulation, Principles and Practice', *Revista do processo – RePro*, 2019, 292, pp. 377–398.

separate documents. This could change the way courts and the parties cooperate and really empower cooperation for better party autonomy – and for better justice.

DE BENITO: We see this often in international arbitration, especially in the initial phases of the procedure. The arbitral tribunal can facilitate a joint effort with the parties to ascertain the specific claims and facts in contention and delineate the fundamental structure of the procedure. The national and linguistic diversity among lawyers can result in the formulation of claims that adhere to disparate conceptual and terminological frameworks, or even simply usages. In such cases, the tribunal's (circumspect) request for clarification can be invaluable for a true and effective comprehension of the dispute. By reducing the terminology employed by the parties to a common language, the tribunal can facilitate communication and understanding between the parties. The tribunal and the parties may even find that multiple litigious issues may be manifestations of a single underlying debate.[16]

Moreover, any proceeding involves intellectual communication between individuals. It can be reasonably deduced that the quality of communication is directly proportional to the degree of mutual understanding between the sender and receiver. It is therefore essential to eliminate any impediments to effective communication.[17]

For this reason, the court's or tribunal's primary contribution to a fair and efficient procedure is not quantitative, but qualitative. Should the parties accept the challenge of working together in good faith, the tribunal's leadership can facilitate significant savings in time and money. This alone may entail a reduction in the number of rounds of pleadings, the establishment of transparent criteria for the admission or rejection of evidence, greater clarity in the resolution of requests for documentary evidence, and an enhancement in the organisation of hearings.[18]

STÜRNER: What is the core element of these Rules? In my eyes, it's the duty of the court to give hints and feedback, *Hinweise* in German,[19] to enable parties to develop and present their cases efficiently, giving due regard to the

16 DE BENITO, M., 'Eficiencia y fe en el derecho', *Spain Arbitration Review*, 36 (2019), pp. 83–87, at 86.

17 DE BENITO, M., 'Eficiencia y fe en el derecho', *Spain Arbitration Review*, 36 (2019), pp. 83–87, at 86.

18 DE BENITO, M., 'Eficiencia y fe en el derecho', *Spain Arbitration Review*, 36 (2019), pp. 83–87, at 86.

19 MURRAY, P. L., STÜRNER, R., *German Civil Justice*, Durham: Carolina Academic Press, 2004, pp. 164–177.

court's preliminary assessment of the decisive factual, evidentiary, and legal issues and any lacking factual assertions or evidence necessary for success in the eyes of the court. Ultimately, the fundamental idea underlying these Rules is dialogue: a dialogical civil procedure, a dialogical interaction between the parties and the court.

If the court does not fulfil its duty to monitor missing facts and evidence, the court is not permitted to draw negative conclusions. This is first and foremost to protect parties from judicial arbitrariness practising capricious and unfair preclusion. Consequently, the court cannot simply forbid or disregard late factual or evidential contentions without any warning in the first or even second instance. This results in a well-working balance of the distribution of duties between judge and parties.

DE BENITO: Anna, you have been mentioning party autonomy when talking about the court's case management duty. Let me try to look at case management from the parties' perspective.

First, the party disposition principle is reaffirmed in the Rules. Parties alone institute proceedings (Rule 21); they determine the scope of the dispute (Rule 23); they can even waive remedies such as provisional measures or appeals (Rule 154).

What's more, the parties frame the facts (Rule 24); and they can even 'agree on the legal basis of the claim or on specific issues in the claim', which 'binds the court' (Rule 26).[20]

Also, it's for the parties to offer evidence. The court can invite the parties to supplement their offers and can suggest evidence, but only exceptionally can it take evidence on its own motion (Rules 25 and 92). The parties can seek access to evidence orders at any time, even before commencement (Rule 25). And this applies not only to the production of documents, but 'all forms of relevant and non-privileged evidence' (Rule 100), including witness or party depositions or investigations leading to an expert report.

It's only the actual taking of evidence and the external aspects of evidence that begin to fall primarily in the court's hands. The parties retain control over the innermost aspects of the proceedings. Only in the outermost layer does the court's role become prevalent.

SORABJI: Even then, case management is not designed in the Rules as a top-down activity. As Rolf said, it's a dialogue in which the parties, counsel, and the court can all put forward ideas and initiatives.

---

20 See STÜRNER, R., 'The ELI / UNIDROIT Model European Rules of Civil Procedure. An Introduction to Their Basic Conceptions', *RabelsZ*, 86, 2022, pp. 421–472, at 465–466.

NYLUND: I fully agree that the Rules emphasise party autonomy, and that the bottom-up, cooperative, dialogic approach to case management of the Rules enhances party autonomy. By enhancing the parties' understanding of the costs and risks involved, it puts them in a position to make informed decisions regarding procedural and substantive aspects of the case.

DE BENITO: Even by mutual agreement: the parties can 'agree on a case management measure', i.e., make procedural arrangements (*Prozessverträge*), and the court cannot depart from them 'without good reason' (Rule 50).

This cooperative approach is underlined from the very outset of the Rules. The first actual provision is Rule 2: 'Parties, their lawyers and the court' – in that order – 'must cooperate'. Then Rule 3 directs parties and lawyers to 'contribute to the proper management of the proceedings'. Hence, it's not that the courts' powers are increased or decreased at the expense of those of the parties. What increases is the overall flexibility of the system. What sets the tone of the Rules are sentences such as this one: '*whenever necessary and appropriate*, the court must order the taking of relevant evidence offered by a party' (Rule 92).

And this is not a trivial matter. The need for procedural certainty and a certain some degree of procedural rigidity, such as a fixed pattern of phases and deadlines defined by the legislature in a detailed and comprehensive manner, is deeply ingrained in some legal cultures.[21] For instance, the ALI-UNIDROIT Principles draw a very clear outline: 'the pleading phase, the interim phase, and the final phase' (Principle 9). Each phase has a concrete and precise content. There is a connection between a *what* and a *when*: what to do and when to do it.

STÜRNER: Indeed, the interim phase is perhaps the most important phase of the structure proposed. In this stage of procedure, parties can supplement their means of evidence and improve their factual assertions.[22] This stage is especially flexible, as it does not presuppose a clear and strict differentiation between disclosure and the taking of evidence. The example of

21 See CAPPELLETTI, M., GARTH, B.G., 'Introduction. Policies, Trends and Ideas in Civil Procedure,' 1988, pp. 5–13, in CAPPELLETTI, M. (ed.), vol. XVI: *Civil Procedure*, in ZWEIGERT, K., DROBNIG, K. (eds.), *International Encyclopedia of Comparative Law*, Tübingen, Dordrecht, Boston, Lancaster: Mohr Siebeck / Martinus Nijhoff. See also MERRYMAN, J. H., PÉREZ-PERDOMO, R., *The Civil Law Tradition*, Redwood City: Stanford University Press, 2007, p. 112–113.

22 See, for Germany, MURRAY, P. L., STÜRNER, R., *German Civil Justice*, Durham: Carolina Academic Press, 2004, pp. 12–14, 225–245.

witness statements presented in the interim phase – traditional US-style witness depositions are not typically taken in this stage in the Model Rules – may illustrate this flexibility of the interim stage for disclosure or evidence taking.

Witness statements may only disclose the contents of a possible testimony in the main hearing to the satisfaction of both parties, making further evidence-taking unnecessary. Alternatively, they may in part replace the main examination when taking evidence in the main hearing by cross-examination. In this case, the traditional strict differentiation between disclosure and evidence-taking no longer exists. The results of the interim phase are not only designed to inform the parties to prepare for the main hearing but also to inform the court, permitting a concentration of the main hearing on still seriously disputed issues worthy to be tried intensively in the main hearing.

A strict differentiation between disclosure and evidence-taking has been also abandoned in the legal or procedural culture where this differentiation originally comes from, because England had already changed the purpose of the pre-trial stage before the Woolf reforms, which affirmed and extended the results of this development. After all, it's no longer possible, even in English civil procedure, to make a strict and clear differentiation in this regard.

DE BENITO: I agree, Rolf, that the choice for the main hearing model is clear in the Rules, with a preparatory phase and a final hearing (Rules 61 and 64).[23] However, when I read Rule 49, which Anna mentioned earlier, I see that those case management powers are not delineated within any given timeframe. Case management powers exist in an overarching or *delocalised* manner, so to speak. The Rules avoid defining too much the *what* and *when* of proceedings. The interim phase is thus rendered more abstract: it becomes less of a tangible phase and more of a path leading from pleading to trial.

STÜRNER: We did prefer flexible rules that do not provide rigid dates and time limits for party activities or allow the court to give strict orders to parties. But bear in mind that the desirable dialogue between court and parties

---

23 See KRAMER, X. E., 'The Structure of Civil Proceedings and Why It Matters: Exploratory Observations on Future ELI-UNIDROIT European Rules of Civil Procedure', *Uniform Law Review*, 19:2 (2014), pp. 218–238; NYLUND, A., 'The Structure of Civil Proceedings. Convergence Through the Main Hearing Model?', *Civil Procedure Review*, 9:2 (2018), pp. 13–39.

also includes an attempt to establish a well-working procedural calendar that details all necessary steps to be taken.

NYLUND: In that regard, I think judges need skills to understand at what stage of the proceedings it's appropriate to do what, and to exercise case management in different kinds of cases: cases where mandatory rules come into play, cases where parties are self-represented or not adequately represented, cases with a power imbalance between the parties, and to raise these issues in an effective yet neutral manner.

STÜRNER: Always bearing in mind that judges shouldn't be authoritarian, but cooperative. In my experience as a judge in the German courts of appeals of Stuttgart and Karlsruhe for nearly three decades, it's very rare that lawyers refuse cooperation when it is amicably offered by the judge. Therefore, I have continuously put emphasis on the described dialogical character of civil procedure, which is the source of a sound balance between party and court competences.

DE BENITO: That remark, Rolf, makes me think that case management in the Rules isn't more authoritarian or liberal, but simply looser, more focused on trust rather than compliance with a predetermined series of specific mandates. Trust in a sense of initiative and *prudence* in the exercise of discretion, which is primarily, but not exclusively, with judges.[24] Trust in a sense of loyalty and responsibility, which rests primarily, but again not exclusively, with the parties.

'Prudence' may seem an odd choice of words in this context, but I can think of no more expressive term. φρόνησις, *prudentia*, 'prudence:' the classical Aristotelian virtue that Aquinas elegantly defined as *recta ratio agibilium*, 'right reason in action.'[25]

Consequently, if there is a shift in power, it's not between the court and the parties, as previously stated, like in some zero-sum game, but rather from the legislative to the judiciary, from central codification committees to each individual judge, lawyer, and party. From this structuralist perspective, there is indeed a shift of procedural authority.

---

24 See generally STORME, M., HESS, B. (eds.), *Discretionary Power of the Judge. Limits and Control / Discretionaire bevoegdheid van de rechter: grenzen en controle*, Mechelen: Kluwer, 2003.

25 ARISTOTLE, *Nicomachean Ethics*, VI:7–8, available at https://oll.libertyfund.org/title/peters-the-nicomachean-ethics.

STÜRNER: Which in turn affects the idea of what judges are and do, and all our underlying cultural and political assumptions, or pre-conceptions. The idea of a judge of not the same in the US, the UK, Germany, or Spain.

DE BENITO: This, Rolf, might be one of the most interesting points of the whole project: how the Rules interact with the different notions of judicial office: the professional model and the bureaucratic model.[26] Because the Rules are the rough equivalent to a small *Zivilprozessordnung*, a civil procedural code; not a *Richtergesetz*, not a judiciary law, and certainly not a *Gerichtsverfassungsgesetz*, a court organisation code, either.

The issue is that the notion of judicial office and the organisation of the courts has far-reaching implications. These extend not only to the role of judges, their responsibilities, their background, their appointment, their career progression, their relations with counsel and staff, but also to the way civil procedure *works*. Judicial office and civil procedure are inextricably linked. If the Rules lean towards a professional model to some extent, would not having them applied mainly by judges of the bureaucratic persuasion cause a certain degree of cognitive dissonance?

STÜRNER: Indeed, the idea of a certain judicial office model underlying the Rules and their procedural model is very demanding. Judges should not be authoritarian and bureaucratic. They should be real partners of the parties, at least as long as the parties don't obstruct the judges' decision and play a fair game. The faces of justice are conceived as authoritarian, hierarchical, and bureaucratic in civil law countries, while in common law countries they might be perceived as more liberal and personalised, as the judicial positions are filled by former lawyers within well-working democracies. However, this notion may not always be aligned with the realities of the present time, because the political history of the last fifty years changed the physiognomy of many societies in civil law countries. Model Rules are always drafted with the expectation and hope that their spirit might influence national judicial attitudes.

It is true that this model of civil procedure is a relatively new phenomenon. In my eyes, it is the result of a shift towards democracy in more than one European country. Traditionally, this occurred in England, though we could add France thanks to its role in the continental democratic revolution

26 DAMAŠKA, M. R., *The Faces of Justice and State Authority. A Comparative Approach to the Legal Process*, New Haven: Yale University Press, 1986.

and its democratic performance over the past century. These Model Rules closely reflect elements of proceedings which are adequate to democracies, treating parties as real subjects of proceedings invested with personal dignity, and not as mere objects of a technical procedure.

In the future, a significant question may arise as to whether court hearings with judges, parties, and lawyers will be in person or virtual only, as is the case with today's roundtable. Indeed, we can hear each other speak and see each other, but there is no real, personal presence like in the *analogue* world. Personally, I don't believe that future generations will not prefer in-person, *analogue* interactions. In my eyes, the corona crisis – with its video conferences for professional collaboration, private discussions, and university or even high school lectures – has shown us that video conferences may replace some traditional meetings.[27] However, all of us – even the youngest generations – feel unhappy with permanent video conferencing, longing for the return of the *analogue* world. The Rules try to strike the right balance when it comes to video technology.

Another future danger addressed in the official commentary is that oral proceedings and in-person civil procedure could increasingly be replaced by computerised and automated proceedings, eventually disappearing altogether. This is especially likely in small claims proceedings, where decisions could be taken by artificial intelligence. The question will be whether justice can be carried out without a human's participation in the final decision – whether (or not) justice will retain a human face.[28]

Modern techniques could take us back to older times, in a way. During the period of the 'learned procedure' in the *jus commune*, parties didn't make the acquaintance of the judges and the court, hence the blind *justitia* with her eyes blindfolded.[29] For most participants in the project, radical

27 See Krans, B., Nylund, A., *Civil Courts Coping with Covid-19*, The Hague: Eleven, 2021.

28 Stürner, R., 'The ELI / UNIDROIT Model European Rules of Civil Procedure. An Introduction to Their Basic Conceptions', *RabelsZ*, 86, 2022, pp. 421–472, at 469–471.

29 See generally van Caenegem, R. C., 'History of European Civil Procedure', 1973, pp. 16 ff., and Cappelletti, M., Garth, B. G., 'Introduction – Policies, Trends and Ideas in Civil Procedure', 1988, pp. 5 ff., in Cappelletti, M. (ed.), vol. XVI: *Civil Procedure*, in Zweigert, K., Drobnig, K. (eds.), *International Encyclopedia of Comparative Law*, Tübingen, Dordrecht, Boston, Lancaster: Mohr Siebeck / Martinus Nijhoff. See also, more summarily, Wauters, B., de Benito, M., *The History of Law in Europe*, Cheltenham: Edward Elgar, 2017, pp. 70–74.

solutions that further the 'dehumanisation of justice' would be regrettable. Nevertheless, the future depends on social development as a whole, and future generations may have a different point of view on the topic, even to the point of feeling more content, at least in part, with artificial intelligence decisions than with individual human decisions. It's hard to give a prognosis about details of the distant future.

Bibliography

ANDREWS, N., *Andrews on Civil Processes: Court Proceedings, Arbitration & Mediation*, Cambridge: Intersentia, 2019.

ARISTOTLE, *Nicomachean Ethics*, VI:7–8, available at https://oll.libertyfund.org/title/peters-the-nicomachean-ethics.

BRAUN, J., *Lehrbuch des Zivilprozessrechts*, Tübingen: Mohr Siebeck, 2014.

CABRAL, A., 'New Trends and Perspectives on Case Management', *International Journal of Comparative Law*, 2018, 8, pp. 10–36.

CALAMANDREI, P., 'La genesi logica della sentenza civile', in *Opere giuridiche*, vol. I, *Problemi generali del diritto e del processo*, Rome: Roma TrE-Press, 2019, pp. 11–54.

CALAMANDREI, P., 'Il proceso come giuoco', in *Opere giuridiche*, vol. I, *Problemi generali del diritto e del processo*, Rome: Roma TrE-Press, 2019, pp. 537–562.

CAPPELLETTI, M., GARTH, B. G., 'Introduction – Policies, Trends and Ideas in Civil Procedure', 1988, in CAPPELLETTI, M. (ed.), vol. XVI: *Civil Procedure*, in ZWEIGERT, K., DROBNIG, K. (eds.), *International Encyclopedia of Comparative Law*, Tübingen, Dordrecht, Boston, Lancaster: Mohr Siebeck / Martinus Nijhoff.

CHAN, C. H., VAN RHEE, C. H. (eds.), *Civil Case Management in the Twenty-First Century: Court Structures Still Matter*, Cham: Springer, 2021.

DAMAŠKA, M. R., *The Faces of Justice and State Authority. A Comparative Approach to the Legal Process*, New Haven: Yale University Press, 1986.

DE BENITO, M., *Justicia o burocracia* (foreword by TARUFFO, M.), Cizur Menor: Civitas, 2017.

DE LA OLIVA, A., *El papel del juez en el proceso civil. Frente a ideología*, prudentia iuris, Cizur Menor: Civitas, 2012.

FENECH, M., *Derecho procesal penal*, Barcelona: Labor, 1960.

GALIČ, A., '(In)compatibility of Procedural Preclusions with the Goals of Civil Justice: An Ongoing Debate in Slovenia', in UZELAC, A. (ed.), *Goals of Civil Justice and Civil Procedure in the Contemporary Judicial Systems*, Cham: Springer, 2014, pp. 221–243.

Galič, A., 'The Preparatory Stage of Civil Proceedings in Slovenia, the Czech Republic and Slovakia: Halfway There Yet?', in Ervo, L., Nylund, A. (eds.), *Current Trends in Preparatory Proceedings*, Cham: Springer, 2016, pp. 111–140.

García Odgers, R., *El* case management *en perspectiva comparada. Teoría, evolución histórica, modelos comparados y un caso en desarrollo*, Valencia: Tirant lo Blanch, 2019.

Gascón, F., 'Between Reform and Dejudicialisation: Current Trends in Spanish Civil Litigation', in Uzelac, A., van Rhee, C. H. (eds.), *Transformation of Civil Justice. Unity and Diversity*, Cham: Springer: 2018, pp. 119–143.

Gensler, S. S., 'Judicial Case Management: Caught in the Crossfire', *Duke Law Journal*, 2010, 60, pp. 669–744.

Gradi, M., 'Cornelis Saftleven e l'allegoria del processo', in Faralli, C., Gigliotti, V., Heritier, P., Mittica, M. P. (eds.), *Il diritto tra testo e immagine. Rappresentazione ed evoluzione delle fonti*, Milan: Mimesis, 2015, pp. 151–165.

Jeuland, E., 'Case Management in France', in van Rhee, C. H., Fu, Y. (eds.), *Civil Litigation in China and Europe: Essays on the Role of the Judge and the Parties*, Dordrecht: Springer, 2014, pp. 349–358.

Klein, F., *Pro futuro. Betrachtungen über Probleme der Civilproceßreform in Oesterreich*, Leipzig, Vienna: Deuticke, 1891.

Kramer, X. E., 'The Structure of Civil Proceedings and Why It Matters: Exploratory Observations on Future ELI-UNIDROIT European Rules of Civil Procedure', *Uniform Law Review*, 19:2 (2014), pp. 218–238.

Krans, B., Nylund, A., *Civil Courts Coping with Covid-19*, The Hague: Eleven, 2021.

Luhmann, N., *Legitimation durch Verfahren*, Frankfurt: Suhrkamp, 1969.

Merryman, J. H., Pérez-Perdomo, R., *The Civil Law Tradition*, Redwood City: Stanford University Press, 2007.

Murray, P. L., Stürner, R., *German Civil Justice*, Durham: Carolina Academic Press, 2004.

Nylund, A., 'Case Management in a Comparative Perspective: Regulation, Principles and Practice', *Revista do processo – RePro*, 2019, 292, pp. 377–398.

Nylund, A., 'Oral Proceedings During the Preparatory Stage', *International Journal of Procedural Law*, 2022, 12, pp. 57–74.

Nylund, A., 'Norway: Efficiency by Flexible Preparatory Proceedings and Case Management', in Ervo, L., Nylund, A. (eds.), *Current Trends in Pre-Trial Proceedings*, Cham: Springer, 2016, pp. 57–79.

Nylund, A., 'The Structure of Civil Proceedings. Convergence Through the Main Hearing Model?', *Civil Procedure Review*, 9:2 (2018), pp. 13–39.

Pérez-Ragone, Á., 'An Approach to Case Management from the Horizontal and Vertical Structure of Court Systems', *Zeitschrift für Zivilprozess International*, 2018, 23, pp. 353–354.

Storme, M., Hess, B. (eds.), *Discretionary Power of the Judge. Limits and Control / Discretionaire bevoegdheid van de rechter: grenzen en controle*, Mechelen: Kluwer, 2003.

Stürner, R., 'The ELI / UNIDROIT Model European Rules of Civil Procedure. An Introduction to Their Basic Conceptions', *RabelsZ*, 86, 2022, pp. 421–472.

van Caenegem, R. C., 'History of European Civil Procedure', 1973, in Cappelletti, M. (ed.), vol. XVI: *Civil Procedure*, in Zweigert, K., Drobnig, K. (eds.), *International Encyclopedia of Comparative Law*, Tübingen, Dordrecht, Boston, Lancaster: Mohr Siebeck / Martinus Nijhoff.

van Rhee, C. H. (ed.), *Judicial Case Management and Efficiency in Civil Litigation*, Antwerp, Oxford: Intersentia, 2007.

Wauters, B., de Benito, M., *The History of Law in Europe*, Cheltenham: Edward Elgar, 2017.

CHAPTER 3

Party Autonomy

Remo Caponi and Marco de Benito

The procedural model proposed by the Rules is characterised by a commitment to respecting the parties' autonomous decisions. The parties define the scope of the dispute and make all the major decisions regarding the claim, including settlement, withdrawal, or appeal.

Furthermore, by adopting a flexible and cooperative model of civil procedure, the Rules presuppose and rely on the active involvement of the parties in the shaping of procedural matters.

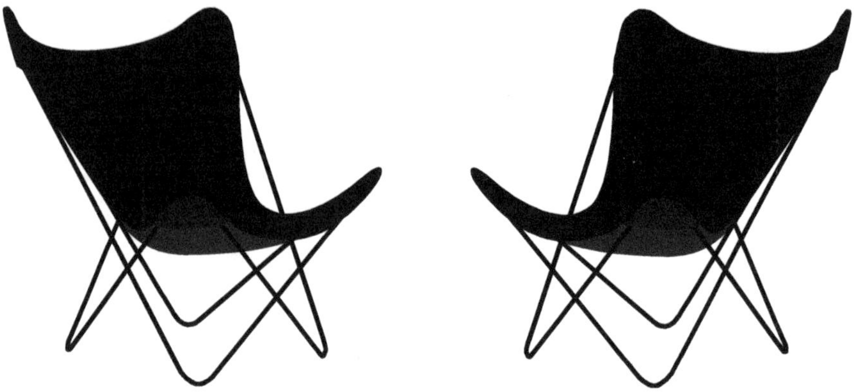

CAPONI: I'd like to begin by citing Hegel. (It's hard for me to imagine doing procedural discourse outside the framework of Hegel's thought; but that's just me.) Hegel asserts that, 'in speculative thinking, the negative belongs to the content itself'.[1] In line with this premise, I'll initially examine what isn't implied by party autonomy in civil procedure.

Let's start with the question of who is responsible for introducing facts into the proceedings. This question revolves around arguments of efficiency,

1 *'Gehört im begreifenden Denken das Negative dem Inhalte selbst an'*: HEGEL, G. W. F., *Phänomenologie des Geistes*, Bamberg, Würzburg: Verlag Joseph Anton Goebhardt, 1807; in English, *Phenomenology of Spirit* (translated by MILLER, A. V.), Oxford: Oxford University Press, 1977, Preface, § 59, p. 36.

 | DOI:10.1163/9789004533257_004

not autonomy. It's a matter of organising resources that happens to be consistent with private autonomy but doesn't necessarily follow from it.

DE BENITO: The official commentary reflects this view:[2]

> For a court to be required to conduct its own factual inquiries, it would need to be provided with sufficient inquisitorial procedures, powers and administrative staff. Such an apparatus, in order to be efficient, would necessarily be a very expensive form of dispute resolution process.

CAPONI: Let's now look at the power of the court to introduce facts. The general rule, as set out in Rule 24(2), is that 'the court must not consider facts not introduced by the parties'. But Rule 24(3) does allow the court to consider facts that are 'necessarily implied' by the parties' factual contentions or simply 'contained within the case file'. Therefore, the court's power isn't entirely excluded by party disposition.[3]

Let's move to the presentation of evidence. Each party is 'required to prove all the relevant facts supporting its case' and 'must offer evidence supporting their factual contentions' (Rule 25). Once again, this isn't necessarily a result of party autonomy, but a way of sharing risks and distributing tasks based on efficiency. After all, parties are closer to the evidence than the court.

DE BENITO: The commentary also reflects this view:[4]

> The burden of proof in sentence 1 of Rule 25 (1) distributes the risk that evidential support for the existence of facts favourable to a party's case fails because their non-existence becomes clear or their existence remains unclear (on the standard of proof, see Rule 87). Such a distribution of risk between claimants and defendants is common to all developed legal systems (see Rule 24, comment 2).

2 Rule 24, comment 1.

3 CAPONI, R., 'Le regole modello europee ELI-UNIDROIT del processo civile sullo sfondo della riforma italiana', *Rivista trimestrale di diritto e procedura civile*, 3-2022, pp. 717–753, at 736–737.

4 Rule 25, comment 2.

CAPONI: Now that we've got the lowdown on what party autonomy isn't, let's try to figure out what it is.

The notion of party autonomy encompasses the free decision to exercise or not procedural powers (*Befugnisdisposition*). The term 'disposition' suggests the capacity to make a decision and enforce that decision upon others. This can be either *in actu* or *in potentia*: 'disposition' suggests both the act of deciding and the possibility of deciding.

This begins with the decision whether to take legal action and against whom (Chiovenda defined the right of action as 'the *power* to implement the law in one's favour through the courts').[5] It therefore includes the authority to start or discontinue proceedings (Rule 21).

Party autonomy also includes the power to define the scope of the dispute (Rules 23, 167).

Nothing more, but nothing less.

DE BENITO: However, perhaps we can find other instances of decision-making power throughout civil procedure. Let me explain.

The Rules point to four layers or instances of decision-making authority: over rights; facts and law; evidence; and case management. We can order these layers from the *innermost* to the *outermost*, or vice versa, in terms of how deeply they impact or guide civil procedure.

The innermost layer, disposition over rights, is naturally within the parties' domain (in accordance with the *Dispositionsprinzip*). It's the parties who institute or terminate proceedings (Rule 21) and determine the scope of the dispute (Rule 23). They can even waive remedies such as provisional measures or appeals (Rule 154).

The second layer also pertains to the parties, who are responsible for framing the facts (Rule 24) and may even 'agree on the legal basis of the claim or on specific issues in the claim' (Rule 26). In this less profound layer of the procedure, which remains infused by party autonomy (as a corollary of the *Dispositionsprinzip*),[6] considerations of efficiency begin to emerge, as you previously highlighted.

5 'L'autonomo potere giuridico di realizzare per mezzo degli organi giurisdizionali l'attuazione della legge in proprio favore': CHIOVENDA, G., *Principi di diritto processuale civile (Le azioni. Il processo di cognizione)*, Naples: Jovene, 1923, p. IX.

6 DE LA OLIVA, A., *El papel del juez en el proceso civil. Frente a ideología*, prudentia iuris, Cizur Menor: Civitas, 2012, pp. 32–43.

As we ascend to the third layer, which is focused on fact- and law-finding, practical (or prudential) considerations become more important than either axiological (or ideological) ones.[7]

CAPONI: As I said before, this stage is about ensuring that tasks are efficiently assigned and that relevant materials are easily accessible.

DE BENITO: Also, this stage is crucial to make sure that the grounds for the case decision are well formed (since '*fact-finding* is the business of the judge', not the parties).[8]

CAPONI: Hence, it's for the parties to offer evidence, but the court can invite the parties to supplement their offers and can suggest evidence, and even exceptionally it can take evidence on its own initiative (Rules 25, 92).

DE BENITO: It's only at the outermost layer, which deals with the external shaping of the proceeding, that authority is primarily vested in the court. The court has extensive decision-making authority at this upper, crustal level.

CAPONI: Even in this regard, the key idea in the Rules isn't 'disposition', but cooperation towards a fair and efficient management of the dispute.

DE BENITO: Indeed. After an initial delineation of their scope of application (Rule 1), the Rules commence with a call to cooperation, which is directed first to the parties, then to their counsel, and finally to the court: 'parties, their lawyers and the court must cooperate' (Rule 2). Then they continue requiring parties and counsel to 'contribute to the proper management of the proceedings' (Rule 3), thereby underscoring their active role in the case's management.

CAPONI: The court is in charge, oversees the joint effort, and makes the right decisions 'where appropriate' (Rule 49), as someone has to be ultimately responsible for case management (Rule 4).

7 DE LA OLIVA, A., *El papel del juez en el proceso civil. Frente a ideología,* prudentia iuris, Cizur Menor: Civitas, 2012, pp. 32–43.

8 See generally JOLOWICZ, J. A., 'Fact-Finding', in JOLOWICZ, J. A., *On Civil Procedure*, Cambridge: Cambridge University Press, 2000, pp. 205–221, at 211–212.

DE BENITO: In conclusion, the parties maintain control over the core aspects of the proceedings. Only at the most superficial level does the court's role become prominent; and, even then, the parties are jointly responsible.

CAPONI: The model proposed by the Rules is founded upon the principles of cooperation and flexibility,[9] which, in turn, facilitate and require dialogue.[10] It thus follows that the parties are involved in the shaping of procedural matters and that their individual preferences are duly considered.

This is not only from a theoretical perspective, but also from a practical one. During the corona crisis, flexibility in proceedings – the possibility of holding oral acts in writing, or agreeing to waive some types of evidence, etc. – was the key factor in continuing to bring cases forward. Countries with a less flexible approach in this regard generally coped worse with the situation.[11]

DE BENITO: We can't forget, in this regard, Rule 50(2):

> Rule 50. *Case management orders*
>
> (2) If the parties agree on a case management measure the court shall not determine differently without good reason.

CAPONI: That's the provision of the Rules about *Prozessverträge*, procedural contracts.[12]

---

9 See generally CAPONI, R., 'Rigidità e flessibilità del processo civile', *Rivista di diritto processuale*, 6, 2016, pp. 1442–1458. See also NYLUND, A., CABRAL, A., 'General Report: Contractualisation of Civil Litigation', in NYLUND, A., CABRAL, A. (eds.), *Contractualisation of Civil Litigation / Contractualisation de la procédure civile*, Cambridge: Intersentia, 2024, pp. 1–38, at 19–21.

10 UZELAC, A., 'Flexible Proceedings and Procedural Contracts', in NYLUND, A., CABRAL, A. (eds.), *Shaping Civil Litigation Using Procedural Agreements*, The Hague: Eleven, 2024, pp. 131–147, at 146.

11 See generally KRANS, B., NYLUND, A., *Civil Courts Coping with Covid-19*, The Hague: Eleven, 2021.

12 See generally WAGNER, G., *Prozeßverträge. Privatautonomie im Verfahrensrecht*, Tübingen: Mohr Siebeck, 1998; CADIET, L., 'Les conventions relatives au procès en droit français. Sur la contractualisation du règlement des litiges', en VV.AA., *Accordi di parte e processo*, Milan: Giuffrè, 2008, pp. 8–35; CAPONI, R., 'Autonomia privata e processo civile: gli accordi processuali', in VV.AA., *Accordi di parte e processo*, Milan: Giuffrè, 2008, pp. 99–119; CABRAL, A. P., 'Designing Procedure by Contract: Litigation Agreements in Contemporary Civil Procedure', in *International Journal of Procedural Law*, 9, 2-2019, pp. 363–380; TRENKER, M., *Einvernehmliche Parteidisposition im Zivilprozess*.

DE BENITO: Which is ambivalent in nature. On the one hand, it welcomes the procedural arrangements proposed by the parties. On the other hand, it makes it clear that the parties cannot dispose of procedural issues. They can and must cooperate, but the court is the ultimate decision maker.

From this angle, it's difficult to view procedural contracts under Rule 50(2) (the ones that affect the outermost layer of proceedings, case management) as genuine contracts. Indeed, since they take effect when the parties are already engaged in a triadic, dynamic environment – the effort to win over the judge's *conviction intime* –,[13] discussing private autonomy and the power of disposition seems misplaced.

Hence the final paragraph of Rule 50(2) of the Rules: if the parties agree on a case management measure, 'the court shall not determine differently *without good reason*'. The whole group of problems raised by these agreements is summed up in this phrase, 'without good reason'.

CAPONI: Rule 50(2) gives the court the final say in this instance. But what exactly is meant by 'good reason' in this context? Should the court only look at the formal aspects, like whether the agreement breaks a mandatory rule? Or could the court consider broader principles of due process, such as equality or fairness? Could the court even consider factors like efficiency or proportionality if they think it's appropriate?

Ultimately, the court is responsible for managing the case, so it's logical to conclude that the assessment of whether an agreed-upon measure is with or 'without reason' covers all elements inherent to the court's authority. The court can decline a valid procedural agreement if there's a more efficient way to arrange the procedure and it makes sense to do so.

DE BENITO: I agree. The parties own their civil or arbitral proceeding just as shipowners own their ship. The owners can suggest where to dock, and the captain will usually follow their lead – unless it's not safe for nautical reasons. The parties can even end the journey (and in arbitration, they can

Parteiautonomie im streitigen Erkenntnisverfahren, Vienna: Manz, 2020; SCHUMANN, G., *Derecho a la tutela judicial efectiva y autonomía de la voluntad: los contratos procesales*, Madrid: Marcial Pons, 2022; NYLUND, A., CABRAL, A. (eds.), *Contractualisation of Civil Litigation / Contractualisation de la procédure civile*, Cambridge: Intersentia, 2024; NYLUND, A., CABRAL, A. (eds.), *Shaping Civil Litigation Using Procedural Agreements*, The Hague: Eleven, 2024.

13 See GOLDSCHMIDT, J., *Der Prozess als Rechtslage. Eine Kritik des prozessualen Denkens*, Berlin: Springer, 1925 (reprinted in Aalen: Scientia, 1968).

even dismiss the captain in the next port), but until then, the captain is in charge on board.[14]

In any case, there are expressions of party autonomy that don't refer to the external shaping of the procedure but rather to the substantive right, to jurisdiction, and so forth.

CAPONI: The extent of court control varies considerably in each of these instances, ranging from no influence at all to the ultimate decision-making authority.

DE BENITO: This heterogeneity calls into question the utility of the *Prozessvertrag* as a unified concept. Although the concept has some intuitive contours, a closer analysis reveals a reality that is excessively variegated to sustain a coherent system.

I'd rather propose a three-fold classification that, without assuming a unified 'procedural contract' category, differentiates between manifestations of private autonomy *propter actionem* (in relation to the substantive right and the right of action), *propter jurisdictionem* (in matters of jurisdiction), and *propter processum* (on the procedure itself and the judgment). A court settlement would be an example of party disposition *propter actionem*; an arbitration or prorogation agreement would be an act of disposition *propter jurisdictionem*; a pact over the shifting of the burden of proof would be an instance of *propter processum* party disposition.

If we apply this framework, we can see that both the French experience with the *contrats de procédure*[15] and the Brazilian experience with the *convençoes processuais*[16] both revolve around agreements *propter processum*.

The ship analogy is a good way to show how these three areas of party autonomy and disposition work together and why they can't really be

---

14 See BLACKABY, N., PARTASIDES, C., REDFERN, A., *Redfern and Hunter on International Arbitration*, Oxford: Oxford University Press, 2022, c. 6: Conduct of the Proceedings, 6.03. The analogy is originally Veeder's and can be found in VEEDER, V. V., 'Whose Arbitration Is It Anyway – The Parties' or the Arbitration Tribunal's?', in WORDSWORTH, S., VEEDER, M. (eds.), *Selected Writings and Contributions to the Development of Law*, Oxford: Oxford University Press, 2023, pp. 345–359.

15 See French CPC, Art. 781. See, *inter alia*, CANELLA, M. G., 'Gli accordi processuali francesi volti alla "regolamentazione collettiva" del processo civile', *Rivista trimestrale di diritto e procedura civile*, 64, 2–2010, pp. 549–580.

16 See Brazilian CPC, Art. 190. See, *inter alia multa*, CABRAL, A., NOGUEIRA, P. H., 'Brazil', in NYLUND, A., CABRAL, A. (eds.), *Contractualisation of Civil Litigation / Contractualisation de la procédure civile*, Cambridge: Intersentia, 2024, pp. 79–90.

reduced to common principles and rules. Each of these types of procedural autonomy brings its own set of challenges (*Problemkreise*).[17]

Caponi: Which are not trivial: for, as Satta said, the subject of procedural contracts 'transcends its singular manifestation to reach the innermost roots of the whole of procedural law'.[18]

de Benito: I agree with the Sardinian jurist and writer. The subject matter addresses the intertwined legal, cultural, and societal foundations of civil procedure[19] in a manner that few other topics do.

Caponi: The tripartite classification proposed provides an elegant framework for analysis. However, it's important to note that party autonomy is a single, indivisible concept. Parties are involved in decision-making at every stage of the procedure.

de Benito: Indeed, party autonomy and party disposition are pervasive and multifaceted. First and foremost, the claimant is obliged to select and define the desired outcome from the court – the remedy, the *actio*. Facts and law are only relevant to the extent that they support the relief being sought.

Caponi: In accordance with Rules 23 and 24, 'the scope of the dispute is determined by the claims and defences', and 'the court must decide on, and only on, the relief claimed'.

de Benito: The thing is, the 'relief claimed' is made up of a petition (*petitum*) and a cause of action (*causa petendi*). And neither of the two elements naturally results from a set of given facts. Life doesn't know about *facts*. Life, to us, is only undifferentiated, formless matter. Only God knows, in his omniscience, life or reality as such in its infinitude. But, for us human creatures, we must work with *facts* due to the limitations of our intelligence. We need

17 de Benito, M., 'La autonomía privada en el proceso civil: apuntes taxonómicos', in Banacloche, J., Gascón, F. (eds.), *Logros y retos de la justicia civil en España*, Valencia: Tirant lo Blanch, 2022, pp. 251–262.

18 Satta, S., *Contributo alla dottrina dell'arbitrato*, Milan: Giuffrè, 1931, p. 50.

19 Nylund, A., Cabral, A., 'General Report: Contractualisation of Civil Litigation', in Nylund, A., Cabral, A. (eds.), *Contractualisation of Civil Litigation / Contractualisation de la procédure civile*, Cambridge: Intersentia, 2024, pp. 1–38, at 10.

to grasp this reality through an ultimately arbitrary selection that is accessible to our senses and intellect.

CAPONI: To re-present, to 'bring again' reality. Francesco Carnelutti liked to stress this etymology.

DE BENITO: And what facts? The set of facts that best fit a rule. Lawyers don't select the facts *as such*; they select only those that fit well with the article or precedent that leads them to the result their clients are looking for. That result isn't just a legal abstraction; it's an actual change in social life.[20]

CAPONI: Which will be enforced by physical coercion, if necessary. The original meaning of 'disposition' is about deciding what to do with something that has been pledged or with the debtor's body.

DE BENITO: As in Cubism, objects can be depicted from multiple angles simultaneously. Think of a business transaction that didn't go as planned. One party wants to void the contract because of fraud and, on a subsidiary basis, terminate it because of breach of the representations and warranties. While the *petitum* may be identical, the particular facts selected are contingent upon the *causæ petendi* (which, in this example, are inherently incompatible with one another). The *causæ petendi* in question are, in turn, contingent on the wording of a specific article, legal principle, or precedent. Which, once again, will differ depending on the law that governs the contract. In a nutshell, we choose the facts that are relevant and useful for us.

CAPONI: Law is *ars inveniendi*, an art of discovery; more a *quæsitum* than a *datum*.[21]

DE BENITO: I think it was Calamandrei who explained this with a brilliant analogy: a painter in front of a landscape. Landscapes don't actually exist. They are just our subjective representations of reality. We can admire the painting and think that this mountain here on the canvas is astonishingly similar to that mountain on the horizon. But it's just an illusion. The artist freely chose to paint that mountain because it was more inspiring than the

20 See, e.g., CALAMANDREI, P., 'La genesi logica della sentenza civile', in *Opere giuridiche*, vol. I, *Problemi generali del diritto e del processo*, Rome: Roma TrE-Press, 2019, pp. 11–54.

21 See DÍEZ-PICAZO, L., *Experiencias jurídicas y teoría del derecho*, Barcelona: Ariel, 1999, pp. 220–234.

less poetic view of the smoky factory to our left or the ugly concrete apartment buildings in front of us.

That's what we do when we select the *actio* and frame the facts and legal basis of the dispute – the *legal qualification of facts*. From this perspective, the main facts of the claim are an integral part of the *causa petendi*.

CAPONI: Hence the qualification of facts might be reviewed as a *quæstio juris* in a court of *cassation* or *Revision*.[22]

DE BENITO: In a way, Rule 24 is a natural specification of Rule 23:

> Rule 23. *Scope*
>
> (1) The scope of the dispute is determined by the claims and defences of the parties in the pleadings, including amendments.
>
> ...
>
> Rule 24. *Facts*
>
> (1) The parties must put forward such facts as support their claim or defence. ...

From this perspective, one should recognise that the legal basis for the claim is an indispensable element of the *causa petendi*.[23] This challenges the traditional view expressed in the phrase *da mihi factum, dabo tibi jus*.

Perhaps this is why the ALI-UNIDROIT Principles of Transnational Civil Procedure set out the presentation of legal arguments as a duty:

> 11. *Obligations of the parties and lawyers*
>
> (3) In the pleading phase, the parties must present in reasonable detail the relevant facts, their contentions of law, and the relief requested ...

Nevertheless, the Rules establish the presentation of legal arguments as a mere possibility:

---

22 JOLOWICZ, J. A., 'Introduction: Recourse against Civil Judgments in the European Union: A Comparative Survey', in JOLOWICZ, J. A., VAN RHEE, C. M., *Recourse against Civil Judgments in the European Union*, The Hague: Kluwer, pp. 1–11.

23 See DALLA BONTÀ, S., *L'introduzione della causa tra sostanziazione e individuazione. Premesse teorico-ricostruttive*, Naples: Edizioni Scientifiche Italiane, 2018.

> Rule 26. *Applicable law*
>
> (1) … [T]he parties may present legal arguments supporting their claim or defence.
>
> (2) The court must determine the correct legal basis for its decision. …
>
> (3) Where parties are free to dispose of their rights, they may agree on the legal basis of the claim or on specific issues in the claim. … The agreement binds the court.

Maybe this less demanding approach reflects an overly schematic notion of *causa petendi*, which leaves key elements unresolved. For instance, a claimant could submit a claim by asking for a change in social life – like ending a contract or getting paid money – and then just stating the facts. However, the desired end of a contract can take place, e.g., by either avoidance or termination. And the requested payment of a sum of money can be, e.g., by way of restitution or compensation.

If we don't make this legal qualification part of what the parties are expected to do, the defendant may then rightly say that it's difficult to prepare a defence strategy that covers all the possible legal bases. This raises issues related not only to the constitutional right to be heard, but also to the principle of equality of arms and even simply to a fair and efficient resolution of the dispute – which is ultimately the court's responsibility (Rule 4).[24]

CAPONI: Such a strategy could potentially lead to the manipulation of the *jura novit curia* rule. A modification of *jura novit curia* is permissible only – if the rights are under the control of the parties – through mutual agreement, not through unilateral actions.

DE BENITO: Furthermore, it's likely that this would encourage the court to conduct its own factual investigations, which could potentially lead to the misuse or misapplication of Rule 24(3).

> Rule 24. *Facts*
>
> (3) The court may consider such facts not specifically addressed by a party but that are necessarily implied by matters of fact put forward by the parties or which are contained within the case file. It may only

24 See, e.g., Shandong Chenming Paper Holdings Limited v. Arjowiggins HKK 2 Ltd., Decision of the High Court of Hong Kong, HKCFI 128, 12 January 2022, para. 45.

> do so if they are relevant to a party's claim or defence and the parties have been given a reasonable opportunity to respond.

CAPONI: However, the court should avoid applying legal rules or re-characterising claims if this involves facts that the parties never mentioned. This new configuration in the negative is important in the *corrélation de forces* between the court and the parties.

DE BENITO: In conclusion, the legal characterisation of facts supporting the relief sought is vital for all the participants of the civil procedure to *breathe life* into the raw material of facts. As I said earlier, 'facts' alone are meaningless (*sinnlos*) as life is essentially matter void of form.

CAPONI: In any case, the courts have the tools to deal with any potential abuses. The Rules clearly set out the concentration principle, which is a duty to bring all the facts and the legal elements, along with the sanction: inadmissibility of the second procedure based on the same cause of action (Rule 22). If a party brings the same lawsuit under a different legal basis, it'll be considered estopped. Omitting legal elements is risky. The Rules *strongly recommend* that parties actively assist the court in determining the applicable law by speaking openly about their legal views on the dispute.[25]

The same applies, of course, to the relief. It's essential to determine or clarify the actual relief being sought as a priority, as this forms the reference point for assessing the relevance of facts and law. The court should maintain neutrality on this crucial matter while encouraging parties to discuss the legal nature of the relief sought.

DE BENITO: This, which has been termed 'substantive case management', represents a crucial component of a collaborative procedural model. When viewed through this lens, the differences with the ALI-UNIDROIT Principle appear less significant.

CAPONI: The parties also have a procedural tool to eliminate *l'aléa de la requalification par le juge*, the risk that the court may attempt a legal re-characterisation of the facts. I'm referring to the joint application for

---

25 CADIET, L., AMRANI-MEKKI, S., 'General Principles: Party Disposition and Principle of Party Autonomy', in STADLER, A., SMITH, V., GASCÓN, F. (eds.), *European Rules of Civil Procedure. A Commentary on the ELI/UNIDROIT Model Rules*, Cheltenham: Edward Elgar, 2023, pp. 42–43.

proceedings, also known as *'requête conjointe'* in French law, which binds the court in that regard.[26] The Rules have incorporated this mechanism in Rule 57:

> Rule 57. *Contents of the joint application*
>
> (1) A joint application is a statement of claim in which parties jointly may submit to the court their agreement according to Rule 26, their respective claims and defences, the issues on which they disagree and which are to be determined by the court, and their respective arguments on those disputed issues.

This is an innovative provision for an Italian.

DE BENITO: It's also for a Spaniard.

CAPONI: It's based on Rule 26(3): the parties may agree not only on 'the legal basis of the claim', but also 'on specific issues in the claim'. And the latter expression doesn't make a distinction between *quæstiones facti* and *quæstiones juris*.

DE BENITO: The pervasive nature of party autonomy, which intertwines all aspects of civil procedure, extends beyond the definition of the relief, the selection of the facts and the law. The very prorogation of jurisdiction entails an act of disposition.

CAPONI: Depending on the context, the term 'disposition' may encompass a departure from the established procedural norms that would otherwise apply (*Normdisposition*).[27] It should be noted, however, that this is only possible under certain conditions, such as minimum contacts with the chosen forum, absence of *forum non conveniens* restrictions, and so on.

DE BENITO: In those same borders, it'd also be an act of disposition when, in a contract case, the claimant chooses to bring the lawsuit in the courts of the defendant's domicile or in the place of performance of the obligation, or in any other applicable *forum* that the law leaves for the claimant's choice.

---

26 DONNIER LE GALLOU, A., 'Le juge et le droit: présentation de l'article 12 NCPC', *Revue Juridique de l'Ouest*, 4, 1995, pp. 477–499, p. 499.

27 CAPONI, R., 'Autonomia privata e processo civile: gli accordi processuali', in VV.AA., *Accordi di parte e processo*, Milan: Giuffrè, 2008, pp. 99–119, at 103.

Also in this context, parties enjoy a wide sphere of autonomy, and therefore power of disposition.

Pulling on the thread of the discourse, by disposing of jurisdiction, a claimant can affect the relief it seeks. For example, if there is some connection with the US, a claimant can perhaps take the case there and seek punitive damages, which he could not otherwise do.[28] A mere act of disposition over jurisdiction has the potential to result in a significant alteration to the content of the remedy.[29]

In sum, the scope of party autonomy is much wider than is normally considered.

CAPONI: Why do we tend to oversee this when we discuss these topics?

DE BENITO: Maybe it's because we see ourselves more as legislators than parties. But litigation, especially international litigation, doesn't work that way. There's forum shopping, parallel proceedings, contradictory decisions, races just to see who's first to attach assets.

CAPONI: Perhaps with time. In the EU, efforts at rationalisation date back half a century to the Brussels I Convention,[30] today Brussels I Regulation,[31] a key piece of legislation to avoid parallel litigation. In the international arena, the Hague Conference on Private International Law has made a tremendous effort to produce, among others, the Choice of Court Convention[32] and the Judgments Convention:[33] two treaties that, if successfully ratified, will increase legal certainty in cross-border disputes.

DE BENITO: We've been discussing the concepts of party autonomy and party disposition for some time. I've used both terms interchangeably in

28 Spanish Supreme Court, 12 January 2009. See DE BENITO, M., *El convenio arbitral: su eficacia obligatoria*, Madrid: Civitas, 2010, pp. 89–95.

29 On the relationship between the right of action and the arbitration agreement, see DE BENITO, M., 'El arbitraje y la acción', *Arbitraje: Revista de Arbitraje Comercial y de Inversiones*, 7, 2014-2, pp. 409–420.

30 Convention on Jurisdiction and the Enforcement of Judgments in Civil and Commercial Matters, signed in Brussels on September 27, 1968.

31 Regulation (EU) 1215/2012 of the European Parliament and of the Council of 12 December 2012 on Jurisdiction and the Recognition and Enforcement of Judgments in Civil and Commercial Matters (recast).

32 Convention on Choice of Court Agreements, concluded in The Hague on June 30, 2005.

33 Convention on the Recognition and Enforcement of Foreign Judgments in Civil or Commercial Matters, concluded in The Hague on July 2, 2019.

various contexts. Could I have been more precise in distinguishing between the two?

CAPONI: I believe I made a brief mention of this earlier. The original meaning of 'disposition' refers to a decision about what to do with a pledged thing (*in rem*) or even the debtor's body (*in personam*), as seen in the two executive *legis actiones*: the *pignoris capio* and the *manus injectio*. (Some national legal systems still have personal imprisonment for debt, which is a form of disposition over the debtor's body.)

As the legal process became increasingly abstract and complex, the term 'disposition' was expanded to encompass the decision-making process regarding the various rights held by creditors, whether *in rem* or *in personam*, including options such as waiver, debt recognition, settlement, etc.

A further extension of the semantic field of the word 'disposition' occurred with the autonomous development of civil procedure as a distinct legal domain, separate from civil law. An illustrative example is what I refer to as a 'negative disposition' over civil proceedings (adopting the Hegelian negative stance). A unilateral act of withdrawal or a court settlement, for instance, entail a negative disposition of the proceedings. By virtue of an act of withdrawal, the proceeding ceases to exist. Through a court settlement, both the proceedings and the dispute cease to exist.

In both instances, the decision was reached outside the proceedings but came into effect through the proceedings. The concept of autonomy is characterised by an inward-looking orientation, whereas the disposition is defined by an outward-looking perspective. A decision is reached through a process of deliberation (we 'make up our minds'), whereby a decision is made and then acted upon in the external world.

DE BENITO: It's a powerful idea. Human action is purposeful behaviour.[34]

CAPONI: It seems that the Indo-European root of the Greek word νόμος means to assign, to allot, to take. In this light we can understand autonomy as taking oneself (*seriously*), assigning rules to oneself. However, since man is by nature a social being,[35] we cannot be autonomous by ourselves. We

34 VON MISES, L., *Human Action. A Treatise on Economics*, Auburn: The Ludwig von Mises Institute, 1998, p. 11.

35 ἐπειδὴ φύσει πολιτικὸν ὁ ἄνθρωπος ('since man is by nature a political thing', *Nicomachean Ethics*, 1097b), a 'political animal': ὁ ἄνθρωπος φύσει πολιτικὸν ζῷον ('man is by nature a political animal', *Politics I*, 2, 1253a2).

are, by nature, in need of recognition by others. Hegel echoed this idea.[36] For autonomy to truly exist, we need power of disposition over rights and things in the outside world. This is thus the sequence: private autonomy, recognition by others, disposition over things. The extent to which external parties (such as the legislature or the court) recognise your decisions (your acts of disposition) determines the actual scope of your autonomy.

DE BENITO: I believe that it's within this Aristotelian framework that we can gain insight into the nature of procedural law as an area of public rather than private law.

In seeking public approval for an individual claim, a claimant resorts to an adjudicatory authority. The adjudicatory body represents or substitutes the community, defined as the national community, the transnational community of merchants, the community of sportsmen in the context of sports arbitration, etc. The representative role may be performed by a person or a fraction of the community, including a popular assembly, a jury, a professional committee, a court, an arbitral tribunal. (In contrast, in an enforcement action, the authority in charge will typically be a state official, as the state holds a monopoly on legitimate violence. In this instance, the official does not represent or substitute the public; rather, they represent or substitute the claimant, preventing him from taking the law into his own hands.)

Consequently, the inclusion of procedural law within the sphere of public law isn't contingent on the state's frequent involvement in the adjudication of disputes, which is an incidental and far from universal phenomenon.[37] Rather, procedural law belongs to public law because the conflict that arises from someone asserting a right that's denied by another necessarily requires a value judgment by the community. This is so precisely because man is by nature a social being.

CAPONI: Just a note of caution: the whole dichotomy of public and private law can sometimes be a bit confusing. Have a look at how legal history reflects Hegelian thesis-antithesis-synthesis dialectics. It started with a highly formalised, public, sacred system of social regulation governing transactions and procedure. This was followed by a reaction which created a strict

---

36 HEGEL, G. W. F., *Phänomenologie des Geistes*, Bamberg, Würzburg: Verlag Joseph Anton Goebhardt, 1807; in English, *Phenomenology of Spirit* (translated by MILLER, A. V.), Oxford: Oxford University Press, 1977, §§ 178–185, pp. 111–113, *passim*.

37 See generally DE JOUVENEL, B., *De la Souveraineté*, Paris: Génin, 1955.

dichotomy between private and public law. Over time, the border between these fundamental systems has become blurred.[38]

In practice, public and private lawyers tend to espouse disparate views on the purposes of the legal system. When applied to the topic under discussion, this different perspective will likely prompt the following question: should civil justice be fundamentally a tool for implementing values in society ('to bring a recalcitrant reality closer to our chosen ideals'[39]), or should it be mainly a tool for an expedient and cost-effective resolution of disputes among private parties?[40]

DE BENITO: The acknowledgement of autonomous realms within the domain of civil procedure – and, indeed, the broader field of dispute resolution, encompassing its most purely consensual forms –[41] calls into question an excessively statist, hierarchical notion of the purpose of civil justice and, ultimately, the legal system itself.[42]

CAPONI: The individual is the cornerstone of modernity. In the Western legal tradition, the liberty of the individual is regarded as unlimited in

38 On the need for a historical perspective on any procedural research, see CAPONI, R., 'Frammenti di teoria del processo civile. Una premessa introduttiva', *Il Processo*, 2019, pp. 1–11, at 7–8. For a succinct history of forms of pleading in both civil and common law, see CLARK, C. E., 'History, Systems and Functions of Pleading', *Virginia Law Review*, 11-1925, pp. 517–552.

39 A court's 'job is not to maximize the ends of private parties, nor simply to secure the peace, but to explicate and give force to the values embodied in authoritative texts such as the Constitution and statutes': FISS, O. M., 'Against Settlement', *Yale Law Journal*, 93, 1984, pp. 1073–1090, at 1089, 1085.

40 CAPONI, R., 'Harmonizing Civil Procedure: Initial Remarks' in HESS, B., KRAMER, X. E. (eds.), *From Common Rules to Best Practices in European Civil Procedure*, Oxford: Hart, 2017, pp. 43–62, p. 62. See generally CALAMANDREI, P., 'La relatività del concetto di azione', in *Opere giuridiche*, vol. I, *Problemi generali del diritto e del processo*, Rome: Roma TrE-Press, 2019, pp. 427–449. See also JOLOWICZ, J. A., 'On the Nature and Purposes of Civil Procedural Law', in JOLOWICZ, J. A., *On Civil Procedure*, Cambridge: Cambridge University Press, 2000, pp. 59–80.

41 See SORABJI, S., CAO, H., 'Principles of Civil Procedure'; and DE BENITO, M., 'Untimely Concordance: The Discreet Convergence of Civil and Arbitral Proceedings', both in WOO, M., VAN RHEE, C. M. (eds.), *Comparative Civil Procedure*, Cheltenham: Edward Elgar, 2025, pp. 63–90 and 470–500. See also MOFFITT, M. L., 'Three Things to Be Against ('Settlement' Not Included)', *Fordham Law Review*, 78, 2009, pp. 1203–1245.

42 See generally DAMAŠKA, M. R., *The Faces of Justice and State Authority. A Comparative Approach to the Legal Process*, New Haven: Yale University Press, 1986.

principle, whereas the powers of the polity (e.g. the state) are viewed as limited in principle.[43]

DE BENITO: Has anything changed since the corona crisis, or even since 9/11? It seems like governments are getting more and more inclined to sacrifice fundamental rights for some kind of *common good* or *collective threat*. A negative perception of individual rights may be driving a shift away from the humanistic paradigm that has defined modernity.

CAPONI: It's interesting to see that as the liberal, individualistic paradigm declines, a public-private collaborative model is taking over. This makes room for consensual forms along with the traditional legal mandates.[44] In today's legal landscape, characterised by heightened polycentricity[45] and permeability, private parties are assuming a more active role as co-producers and intermediaries of meaning for procedural norms.[46]

DE BENITO: Any legal system is inextricably linked to the social fabric of a given society. And social life is, by nature, irreducible to a collective, uniform, ultimately coactive implementation of an ideal. The trend you mention may indicate an acknowledgment of the failure of the 20th century state's grand promises.

What is clear, in any event, is that party autonomy isn't opposed to civil procedure; it's an integral part of it.

CAPONI: Chiovenda initially acknowledged that procedural law is a subset of public law. However, he then proceeded to develop a rationale that positioned procedural law as an autonomous domain, citing the intertwining of the general and individual interests in civil procedure as a key factor.[47] He advanced the position that an intermediate or *intermediary* position of civil procedure should be established as a *tertium genus* within

43 See SCHMITT, C., *Verfassungslehre*, Berlin: Duncker & Humboldt, 2003, p. 158.

44 CAPONI, R., 'Autonomia privata e processo civile: gli accordi processuali', in VV.AA., *Accordi di parte e processo*, Milan: Giuffrè, 2008, pp. 99–119, at 100–101.

45 PICARDI, N., *Manuale del processo civile*, Milan: Giuffrè, 2006, p. 208.

46 CAPONI, R., 'Autonomia privata e processo civile: gli accordi processuali', in VV.AA., *Accordi di parte e processo*, Milan: Giuffrè, 2008, pp. 99–119, at 118–119.

47 CHIOVENDA, G., *Istituzioni di diritto processuale civile*, Naples: Jovene, 1935, I, p. 102.

the public-private law dichotomy. This could be described as an 'interstitial' or even 'hermaphrodite' area of law.[48]

DE BENITO: I think that procedural law would be well-served by the protection of Janus, the Roman god associated with beginnings, transitions, time, duality, doorways, passages, frames, and endings. Janus is typically depicted with two faces. One of these faces regards the parties and their individual struggles, while the other considers the community's value judgement of each party's actions as legitimate or illegitimate, to give everyone their due (*suum cuique tribuere*).[49]

CAPONI: I find Janus an appropriate and mighty protector indeed!

Bibliography

BLACKABY, N., PARTASIDES, C., REDFERN, A., *Redfern and Hunter on International Arbitration*, Oxford: Oxford University Press, 2022.

CABRAL, A. P., 'Designing Procedure by Contract: Litigation Agreements in Contemporary Civil Procedure', in *International Journal of Procedural Law*, 9, 2-2019, pp. 363–380.

CABRAL, A., NOGUEIRA, P. H., 'Brazil', in NYLUND, A., CABRAL, A. (eds.), *Contractualisation of Civil Litigation / Contractualisation de la procédure civile*, Cambridge: Intersentia, 2024, pp. 79–90.

CADIET, L., 'Les conventions relatives au procès en droit français. Sur la contractualisation du règlement des litiges', en VV.AA., *Accordi di parte e processo*, Milan: Giuffrè, 2008, pp. 8–35.

CADIET, L., AMRANI-MEKKI, S., 'General Principles: Party Disposition and Principle of Party Autonomy', in STADLER, A., SMITH, V., GASCÓN, F. (eds.), *European Rules of Civil Procedure. A Commentary on the ELI/UNIDROIT Model Rules*, Cheltenham: Edward Elgar, 2023, pp. 42–43.

48 'Diritto intermedio': CAPONI, R., Autonomia privata e proceso civile: gli accordi processuali', in VV.AA., *Accordi di parte e processo*, Milan: Giuffrè, 2008, pp. 99–119, at 116; 'ermafrodita ed interstiziale': CAPONI, R., 'Autonomia del processo costituzionale: note preliminari', *Forum di Quaderni Costituzionali*, 2010, available at https://www.forumcostituzionale.it/wordpress/images/stories/pdf/documenti_forum/paper/0171_caponi.pdf.

49 ULPIAN, Digest 1,1,10,1.

Calamandrei, P., 'La genesi logica della sentenza civile', in *Opere giuridiche*, vol. I, *Problemi generali del diritto e del processo*, Rome: Roma TrE-Press, 2019, pp. 11–54.

Calamandrei, P., 'La relatività del concetto di azione', in *Opere giuridiche*, vol. I, *Problemi generali del diritto e del processo*, Rome: Roma TrE-Press, 2019, pp. 427–449.

Canella, M. G., 'Gli accordi processuali francesi volti alla "regolamentazione collettiva" del processo civile', *Rivista trimestrale di diritto e procedura civile*, 64, 2-2010, pp. 549–580.

Caponi, R., 'Autonomia del processo costituzionale: note preliminari', *Forum di Quaderni Costituzionali*, 2010, available at https://www.forumcostituzionale.it/wordpress/images/stories/pdf/documenti_forum/paper/0171_caponi.pdf.

Caponi, R., 'Autonomia privata e processo civile: gli accordi processuali', in vv.aa., *Accordi di parte e processo*, Milan: Giuffrè, 2008, pp. 99–119.

Caponi, R., 'Frammenti di teoria del processo civile. Una premessa introduttiva', *Il Processo*, 2019, pp. 1–11.

Caponi, R., 'Rigidità e flessibilità del processo civile', *Rivista di diritto processuale*, 6, 2016, pp. 1442–1458.

Caponi, R., 'Harmonizing Civil Procedure: Initial Remarks', in Hess, B., Kramer, X. E. (eds.), *From Common Rules to Best Practices in European Civil Procedure*, Oxford: Hart, 2017, pp. 43–62.

Caponi, R., 'Le regole modello europee eli-unidroit del processo civile sullo sfondo della riforma italiana', *Rivista trimestrale di diritto e procedura civile*, 3-2022, pp. 717–753.

Chiovenda, G., *Istituzioni di diritto processuale civile*, Naples: Jovene, 1935.

Chiovenda, G., *Principi di diritto processuale civile* (*Le azioni. Il processo di cognizione*), Naples: Jovene, 1923.

Clark, C. E., 'History, Systems and Functions of Pleading', *Virginia Law Review*, 11-1925, pp. 517–552.

Dalla Bontà, S., *L'introduzione della causa tra sostanziazione e individuazione. Premesse teorico-ricostruttive*, Naples: Edizioni Scientifiche Italiane, 2018.

Damaška, M. R., *The Faces of Justice and State Authority. A Comparative Approach to the Legal Process*, New Haven: Yale University Press, 1986.

de Benito, M., 'El arbitraje y la acción', *Arbitraje: Revista de Arbitraje Comercial y de Inversiones*, 7, 2014-2, pp. 409–420.

de Benito, M., *El convenio arbitral: su eficacia obligatoria*, Madrid: Civitas, 2010.

de Benito, M., 'La autonomía privada en el proceso civil: apuntes taxonómicos', in Banacloche, J., Gascón, F. (eds.), *Logros y retos de la justicia civil en España*, Valencia: Tirant lo Blanch, 2022, pp. 251–262.

DE BENITO, M., 'Untimely Concordance: The Discreet Convergence of Civil and Arbitral Proceedings', in WOO, M., VAN RHEE, C. M. (eds.), *Comparative Civil Procedure*, Cheltenham: Edward Elgar, 2025, pp. 470–500.

DE LA OLIVA, A., *El papel del juez en el proceso civil. Frente a ideología*, prudentia iuris, Cizur Menor: Civitas, 2012.

DÍEZ-PICAZO, L., *Experiencias jurídicas y teoría del derecho*, Barcelona: Ariel, 1999.

DONNIER LE GALLOU, A., 'Le juge et le droit: présentation de l'article 12 NCPC', *Revue Juridique de l'Ouest*, 4, 1995, pp. 477–499.

FISS, O. M., 'Against Settlement', *Yale Law Journal*, 93, 1984, pp. 1073–1090.

GOLDSCHMIDT, J., *Der Prozess als Rechtslage. Eine Kritik des prozessualen Denkens*, Berlin: Springer, 1925 (reprinted in Aalen: Scientia, 1968).

HEGEL, G. W. F., *Phänomenologie des Geistes*, Bamberg, Würzburg: Verlag Joseph Anton Goebhardt, 1807; in English, *Phenomenology of Spirit* (translated by MILLER, A. V.), Oxford: Oxford University Press, 1977.

JOLOWICZ, J. A., 'Fact-Finding', in JOLOWICZ, J. A., *On Civil Procedure*, Cambridge: Cambridge University Press, 2000, pp. 205–221.

JOLOWICZ, J. A., 'Introduction: Recourse against Civil Judgments in the European Union: A Comparative Survey', in JOLOWICZ, J. A., VAN RHEE, C. M., *Recourse against Civil Judgments in the European Union*, The Hague: Kluwer, pp. 1–11.

JOLOWICZ, J. A., 'On the Nature and Purposes of Civil Procedural Law', in JOLOWICZ, J. A., *On Civil Procedure*, Cambridge: Cambridge University Press, 2000, pp. 59–80.

KRANS, B., NYLUND, A., *Civil Courts Coping with Covid-19*, The Hague: Eleven, 2021.

MOFFITT, M. L., 'Three Things to Be Against ('Settlement' Not Included)', *Fordham Law Review*, 78, 2009, pp. 1203–1245.

NYLUND, A., CABRAL, A. (eds.), *Contractualisation of Civil Litigation / Contractualisation de la procédure civile*, Cambridge: Intersentia, 2024.

NYLUND, A., CABRAL, A., 'General Report: Contractualisation of Civil Litigation', in NYLUND, A., CABRAL, A. (eds.), *Contractualisation of Civil Litigation / Contractualisation de la procédure civile*, Cambridge: Intersentia, 2024, pp. 1–38.

NYLUND, A., CABRAL, A. (eds.), *Shaping Civil Litigation Using Procedural Agreements*, The Hague: Eleven, 2024.

PICARDI, N., *Manuale del processo civile*, Milan: Giuffrè, 2006, p. 208.

SATTA, S., *Contributo alla dottrina dell'arbitrato*, Milan: Giuffrè, 1931.

SCHMITT, C., *Verfassungslehre*, Berlin: Duncker & Humboldt, 2003.

SCHUMANN, G., *Derecho a la tutela judicial efectiva y autonomía de la voluntad: los contratos procesales*, Madrid: Marcial Pons, 2022.

SORABJI, S., CAO, H., 'Principles of Civil Procedure', in WOO, M., VAN RHEE, C. M. (eds.), *Comparative Civil Procedure*, Cheltenham: Edward Elgar, 2025, pp. 63–90.

TRENKER, M., *Einvernehmliche Parteidisposition im Zivilprozess. Parteiautonomie im streitigen Erkenntnisverfahren*, Vienna: Manz, 2020.

UZELAC, A., 'Flexible Proceedings and Procedural Contracts', in NYLUND, A., CABRAL, A. (eds.), *Shaping Civil Litigation Using Procedural Agreements*, The Hague: Eleven, 2024, pp. 131–147.

VEEDER, V. V., 'Whose Arbitration Is It Anyway – The Parties' or the Arbitration Tribunal's?', in WORDSWORTH, S., VEEDER, M. (eds.), *Selected Writings and Contributions to the Development of Law*, Oxford: Oxford University Press, 2023, pp. 345–359.

VON MISES, L., *Human Action. A Treatise on Economics*, Auburn: The Ludwig von Mises Institute, 1998.

WAGNER, G., *Prozeßverträge. Privatautonomie im Verfahrensrecht*, Tübingen: Mohr Siebeck, 1998.

CHAPTER 4

Obligations of Parties, Lawyers, and Judges

Marco de Benito, Marco Gradi, (C. H.) Remco van Rhee, and Alan Uzelac

Classical doctrine posits that parties are the bearers of burdens, not obligations. The notion that parties are obliged to each other in a relevant manner has not been a dominant one in legal discourse. This reflects a fundamental understanding of civil procedure as an inherently conflictual process, in which the resolution of private interests is the primary objective. This perspective remained in place even as the public interest gained increasing recognition.

In the present day, the prevailing paradigm regards civil procedure as a collaborative endeavour. The Rules reflect this paradigm by requiring a higher standard of conduct from parties and counsel: they must cooperate loyally with each other and the court to achieve a fair and efficient resolution of the dispute. Parties will continue to assert their rights and interests; counsel will continue to devise procedural strategies for favourable outcomes. Nevertheless, instances of abusive behaviour will result in sanctions being imposed. The new paradigm also attributes duties to the court, encouraging a permanent dialogue with the parties and more attentive consideration of their demands.

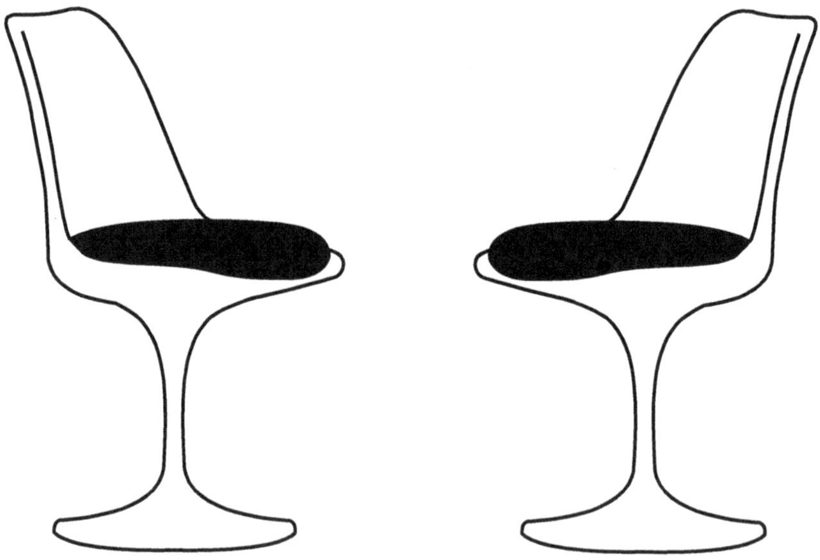

 | DOI:10.1163/9789004533257_005

DE BENITO: Most of the working groups dealt with a specific topic, which then became a specific chapter of the Rules. However, there is no chapter in the Rules devoted to the duties of parties and lawyers. This information must be found elsewhere: scattered or in provisions dealing with other issues. This is probably because the issue of the obligations of parties and lawyers concerns the very model of litigation proposed by the Rules.

UZELAC: Usually, it is Remco who talks about history, but this time it is I who will talk about the history of this fundamental part of the project. The Rules could probably have been clearer and more precise, as our working group produced what we felt was a more coherent whole than the couple of provisions that made it into the final text.

Initially, the scope assigned to us was 'obligations of the parties and lawyers'. Only later did we add 'judges' alongside parties and lawyers; from the point of view we adopted, it was essential that courts have specific obligations in the proceedings.

As we know, the working groups were formed in waves. The creation of the individual working groups was something of a piecemeal process; there was a first wave of three initial groups and, six months later, two new intermediate groups were formed. Six months later, these groups were followed by another wave of three new groups, which were supposed to be the final ones. Eventually, another group on appeals and a supergroup on structure were formed.

As co-reporters of the 'obligations' group that was formed in the second wave, Remco and I were tasked with assembling a well-dimensioned and balanced working group: one that brought together experts from various parts of Europe; one that included not only the academic but also the practical perspective; and whose members were fluent in both English and French, as the Rules would be written in these two languages. In the end, the group consisted of Emmanuel Jeuland, Bartosz Karolcyzk, Walter Rechberger, Elisabetta Silvestri, John Sorabji – who was our native English speaker and a member of the steering committee –, and Magne Strandberg.

The group was created in late 2014 and its mission[1] was to further develop Principle 11 of the ALI-UNIDROIT Principles,[2] which reads:

---

1 For a more extensive presentation of the mandate and the approach of the working group on obligations of parties, lawyers, and judges, see UZELAC, A., 'Towards European Rules of Civil Procedure: Rethinking Procedural Obligations', *Acta Iuridica Hungarica / Hungarian Journal of Legal Studies*, 58-1, 2017, pp. 3–18, at 3–7.

2 THE AMERICAN LAW INSTITUTE, UNIDROIT, *ALI/UNIDROIT Principles of Transnational Civil Procedure*, New York: Cambridge University Press, 2006.

Principle 11. *Obligations of the parties and lawyers*

11.1 The parties and their lawyers must conduct themselves in good faith in dealing with the court and other parties.

11.2 The parties share with the court the responsibility to promote a fair, efficient, and reasonably speedy resolution of the proceeding. The parties must refrain from procedural abuse, such as interference with witnesses or destruction of evidence.

11.3 In the pleading phase, the parties must present in reasonable detail the relevant facts, their contentions of law, and the relief requested, and describe with sufficient specification the available evidence to be offered in support of their allegations. When a party shows good cause for inability to provide reasonable details of relevant facts or sufficient specification of evidence, the court should give due regard to the possibility that necessary facts and evidence will develop later in the course of the proceeding.

11.4 A party's unjustified failure to make a timely response to an opposing party's contention may be taken by the court, after warning the party, as a sufficient basis for considering that contention to be admitted or accepted.

11.5 Lawyers for parties have a professional obligation to assist the parties in observing their procedural obligations.

We were faithful to the spirit of the ALI-UNIDROIT Principles, but we also wanted to deepen these principles in various areas of importance.

We started by dividing the work into different areas and topics, each of which was initially covered by two members of our team. The general part was the task of Remco and Walter; case management was assigned to John and Magne; factual and legal determination were assigned to Bartosz and Emmanuel. Together with Elisabetta, I initially prepared the part of the text that dealt with consensual dispute resolution.[3] Over time, we discussed our draft together, so that our text is, in all its parts, truly the result of collective work.

3 See, for further information about the draft rules produced by the working group, UZELAC, A., 'Towards European Rules of Civil Procedure: Rethinking Procedural Obligations', *Acta Iuridica Hungarica / Hungarian Journal of Legal Studies*, 58–1, 2017, pp. 3–18, at 8–12.

We had nine meetings. In three years, we met in Maastricht, Dubrovnik, Leuven, Pavia, Paris, Bergen, Vienna, and Rome: quite a pan-European project! This shows that the members of our group were all proactive hosts and collaborators.

I do not recall any major disagreements on any aspect of our work or the draft rules themselves. The final product was fully supported by every single member of our group. However, unlike the text produced by most of the other working groups, which was incorporated into the final text of the Rules with virtually no changes, ours was partly modified.

We tried to achieve a new understanding of civil procedure that could overcome the old adversarial-inquisitorial dichotomy. Never in history have these two opposing models existed in pure form. However, to illustrate the extreme positions, the Romano-canonical procedure was certainly adversarial in many respects, whereas the socialist civil procedure could rightly be called inquisitorial. We wanted to find a virtuous middle way in which both the parties and the court contributed equally to a common task. We found this in the principle of loyal cooperation, which eventually found its deserved place in Rule 2:

> Rule 2. *General*
>
> Parties, their lawyers and the court must co-operate to promote the fair, efficient and speedy resolution of the dispute.

The common procedural interest of the parties should transcend their mutual differences as to the merits. That common interest lies at the core of our approach to procedural obligations. The final purpose – the 'overriding objective' in English legal terminology[4] – is to contribute to fair and efficient proceedings. The cooperation principle requires from everyone that partakes in the adjudication process behaviour that is just, effective, and adequate in costs. It also requires all participants to refrain from any actions that would abuse the process and be contrary to the overriding objective.

We were convinced that civil procedure should be based on cooperation. Of course, civil procedure should incorporate other goals and aims,[5] which

---

4 Sorabji, J., *English Civil Justice after the Woolf and Jackson Reforms. A Critical Analysis*, Cambridge: Cambridge University Press, 2014, pp. 135–254.

5 Uzelac, A., 'Goals of Civil Justice and Civil Procedure in the Contemporary World', in Uzelac, A. (ed.), *Goals of Civil Justice and Civil Procedure in Contemporary Judicial Systems*, Cham: Springer, 2014, pp. 3–31.

are sometimes also called 'principles'; but most of them revolve around the central idea of cooperation. This is the case with proportionality, the need to attempt an amicable settlement of disputes, etc. Even the fundamental right to be heard can be considered an expression of cooperative behaviour.

VAN RHEE: All participants in civil litigation share one responsibility: to bring an end to the dispute in a fair, efficient, and speedy manner. This cooperative approach[6] goes back some time in history. In Austria, we already find the *Kooperationsprinzip* formulated by Franz Klein,[7] although its contents differ slightly from the way we use it in our draft. The *principe de coopération* is currently present in French procedural law. We thought of it as a best practice and thus as a starting point for our work.

When does cooperation start? In our framework, it starts before the case is brought before the court, in what we may call the pre-commencement or pre-action stage. In that stage, the parties should cooperate to avoid unnecessary disputes and costs and to facilitate the early consensual resolution of the dispute. Where such early resolution or settlement is not possible, the parties should cooperate to encourage proportionate management of the proceedings. In this endeavour for proportionality, the court is at the centre, but it should also have the cooperation of the parties. With their help, the court should consider the nature, importance, and complexity of the individual case to deal with it fairly.

DE BENITO: With all these *shoulds*, I wonder if this is really how things play out in the courts or if it is just a case of wishful thinking.

VAN RHEE: In our framework, we want the parties and the lawyers to get together and, in a certain way, already be prepared before the action is brought in court. This is aligned with the idea of the pre-action protocols, which were introduced in England and Wales by Lord Woolf.

---

6 VAN RHEE, C. H., 'Principe de coopération / Cooperation Principle', in JEULAND, E., LALANI, S. (eds.), *Recherche lexicographique en procédure civile / Lexicographical research in civil procedure*, Paris: IRJS, 2017, pp. 207–214; VAN RHEE, C. H., 'Judicial Case-Management and Loyal Cooperation. Towards Harmonized European Rules of Civil Procedure', in AARLI, R., SANDERS, A. (eds.), *Courts in Evolving Societies. A Sino-European Dialogue between Judges and Academics*, Leiden: Brill, 2020, pp. 168–202.

7 KLEIN, F., Pro futuro. *Betrachtungen über Probleme der Civilproceßreform in Österreich*, Leipzig, Vienna: Deuticke, 1891, pp. 10–50.

DE BENITO: But going to the extreme of making settlement talks mandatory?

VAN RHEE: Reaching an amicable settlement is a central task for the parties and their lawyers.[8] According to the Rules (in their current wording), the court must facilitate settlement at any stage of the proceedings. Both the court and the lawyers should inform the parties of the different settlement methods that can be used, and even suggest some of them to the parties. Often the parties are not aware of the different alternatives, so it is necessary to inform them. We thought it would be a good idea for the judge to do this in addition to the lawyers. This is more efficient and could reduce the workload of state courts, often overloaded. From this point of view, settlement discussions result in fewer cases coming to court or in better prepared cases where lawyers and parties have established contact and exchanged information.

DE BENITO: What happens to cooperation after settlement attempts have failed and the parties enter the courtroom? How does the case develop according to the Rules?

VAN RHEE: In court, parties and lawyers are expected to show a cooperative attitude.[9] As we said before, they must contribute to the proper management of the proceedings; this is a shared responsibility. They must of course present their claims and defences, including facts and offers of proof. They must also assist the court in determining the relevant facts and applicable law. All this must be done as promptly and completely as possible and as appropriate to the careful conduct of the case to ensure expediency.

Effective case management is primarily the responsibility of the court, albeit with the assistance of the parties.[10] The court must ensure that the way

8 VAN RHEE, C. H., 'Mandatory Mediation before Litigation in Civil and Commercial Matters: A European Perspective', *Access to Justice in Eastern Europe*, 4-2021, 12, pp. 7–24.

9 VAN RHEE, C. H., 'Obligations of the Parties and their Lawyers in Civil Litigation: The ALI/UNIDROIT Principles of Transnational Civil Procedure', in ADOLPHSEN, J., GOEBEL, J., HAAS, U., HESS, B., KOLMANN, S. (eds.), *Festschrift für Peter Gottwald zum 70. Geburtstag*, Munich: Beck, 2014, pp. 669–679.

10 VAN RHEE, C. H., 'Case Management in Europe: A Modern Approach to Civil Litigation', *International Journal of Procedural Law*, 8-2018, 1, pp. 65–84; VAN RHEE, C. H., 'Gerenciamento de casos e cooperação na Europa: uma abordagem moderna sobre a litigância cível', in *Civil Procedure Review*, 13-2022, 2, pp. 157–170; VAN RHEE, C. H.,

the case is dealt with is in accordance with the nature of the dispute. To this end, case management conferences are crucial.

DE BENITO: Etymologically, to confer, *con-ferre,* means to 'bring together'. However, we must acknowledge that most of the time the parties will just *agree to disagree…*

VAN RHEE: The essence of cooperation is to bring the parties together! But let us now turn to Rule 11:

> Rule 11. *Fair opportunity to present claim and defence*
>
> The court must manage proceedings to ensure that parties have a fair opportunity to present their case and evidence, to respond to their respective claims and defences and to any court orders or matters raised by the court.

An honest and orderly exchange of claims and defences is necessary for the proceedings to proceed fairly and efficiently.

The same approach is needed with the determination of the applicable facts and legal rules. Bartosz Karolcyzk and Emmanuel Jeuland led this part of our project. It is the traditional task of the parties to present the relevant facts: *da mihi factum, dabo tibi jus.* We added that the court may invite the parties to clarify or supplement these facts. The court does not merely passively receive the facts. The court will initiate a dialogue with the parties to ascertain whether further clarification or the provision of additional facts is required.

The court may only consider facts that have not been presented by the parties if there is good reason to do so. Thus, to a certain extent the parties are still the masters of the facts of the case, but the court may take facts that have not been pleaded by the parties into consideration if they are relevant and implied by the facts pleaded or appear from the case file:

'Case Management and Co-Operation in the Model European Rules of Civil Procedure', *Journal of International and Comparative Law,* 9-2022, 2, pp. 1–16.

Rule 24. *Facts*

(1) The parties must put forward such facts as support their claim or defence. The court may invite the parties to clarify or supplement these facts.

(2) The court must not consider facts not introduced by the parties.

(3) The court may consider such facts not specifically addressed by a party but that are necessarily implied by matters of fact put forward by the parties or which are contained within the case file. It may only do so if they are relevant to a party's claim or defence and the parties have been given a reasonable opportunity to respond.

Obviously, this is a rather different approach from what we are used to in some more traditional jurisdictions.

Proof of the relevant facts is, again, the task of the parties. In effect, this means that the parties should, as a rule, offer evidence in support of the facts they introduce:

Rule 25. *Evidence*

(1) Each party is required to prove all the relevant facts supporting its case. Parties must offer evidence supporting their factual contentions. ...

(2) Each party has, in principle, a right to access all forms of relevant, non-privileged and reasonably identified evidence. In so far as appropriate, parties and non-parties must contribute to disclosure and production of evidence. It is not a basis of objection to such disclosure by a party that disclosure may favour the opponent or other parties.

The traditional rule is that no one is obliged to disclose facts, especially when these are damaging to one's case: *nemo contra se edere tenetur*. We felt that another approach, reminiscent of the common law approach to disclosure, is preferable. Also, the court may ask the parties to supplement their offers of evidence, or even suggest the introduction of additional evidence. This requires a certain degree of cooperation between the parties and the court.

DE BENITO: When it comes to legal grounds, however, a more traditional *jura novit curia* approach seems to appear in the Rules. The parties 'must' put forward the facts (Rule 24) and are 'required' to prove them (Rule 25); but they merely 'may' present legal arguments:

> Rule 26. *Applicable law*
>
> (1) While taking account of any applicable special provisions, the parties may present legal arguments supporting their claim or defence.

VAN RHEE: This is the final version of the Rules, and it differs from our draft. We set forth an obligation to also provide legal arguments. Fortunately, however, in practice it is difficult to find proceedings in which the parties merely present facts and not legal arguments, if only because the selection of these facts is guided by the *Tatbestand*, the general and abstract factual assumption from which certain consequences are derived: the ones sought. Therefore, even if there is no specific obligation in the Rules in their final version, this duty or rule – or burden – of providing a legal context will, in the end, be respected.

DE BENITO: Even if the parties provided only the facts, substantive case management, as opposed to purely procedural case management, would probably require the court to ask the parties to identify the relevant legal grounds at an early stage. And not only those necessary to simply identify the cause of action and thus the scope of the claim, but also the broader and more elaborate ones necessary to clarify the *thema decidendum* and with it the terms of the debate and the judgment. The second paragraph of Article 26 indirectly indicates this possibility:

> Rule 26. *Applicable law*
>
> (2) The court must determine the correct legal basis for its decision. … It may only do so having provided the parties a reasonable opportunity to present their arguments on the applicable law.

The consequence is certainly a relativisation of that initially surprising contrast between the 'shall' we read about facts and the 'may' we find about the law.

UZELAC: According to older procedural theory, the parties are *domini litis*: they do everything themselves, without *proper* obligations in the strict sense. Everything the parties do is an expression of their freedom to take or not take a certain action. The only thing that can be said about a party's obligation is that there is a certain self-interest in the party's actions. The dichotomy between *Lasten* and *Pflichten*, that is, the dichotomy between *proper* and *mere* obligations, was fundamental in older procedural theory.[11] For various reasons, it does not seem a productive dichotomy today.[12]

GRADI: That is a bold statement! I think the distinction between duties and burdens is still useful, at least in the determination of facts. These are conventional distinctions and definitions that have been accepted almost universally. One speaks of a procedural burden when the activity requested by the party is in its own interest, to enable it to gain an advantage. Conversely, we speak of a procedural duty when the conduct required is aimed at protecting a different interest, particularly that of the other party.

With respect to the determination of facts, the procedural burdens are the burden of proof and the burden of allegation. Each party bears the burden of alleging and proving facts in support of its case. Proof of a fact, of course, requires its prior allegation, its prior introduction into the procedural debate. In my view, the burden of allegation is implicit in the burden of proof. The burden of proof and allegation allocate the risk of the absence of allegation and the absence of proof in the sense that, if at the end of the proceedings, the fact is not proved, the party with an interest in it loses the case.

It is also generally recognised that, after a limited time, it is no longer possible for the parties to introduce new facts or new evidence. As Remco said, there is a kind of collaboration: the judge can invite the party to modify or complete the facts; however, there comes a time when it is no longer possible to introduce new facts or evidence. In my opinion, this is acceptable because each party is responsible for protecting its interests promptly and adequately.

It is well known that James Goldschmidt taught that civil procedure should only consist of burdens.[13] Therein lies, of course, a major problem:

---

11 See UZELAC, A., 'Towards European Rules of Civil Procedure: Rethinking Procedural Obligations', *Acta Iuridica Hungarica / Hungarian Journal of Legal Studies*, 58–1, 2017, pp. 3–18, at 12–13. The classical work on the concept of burden is GOLDSCHMIDT, J., *Der Prozess als Rechtslage. Eine Kritik des prozessualen Denkens*, Berlin: Springer, 1925 (later in Aalen: Scientia, 1962), although the idea can be found earlier in KISCH, W., *Deutsches Zivilprozessrecht*, Berlin, Leipzig: De Gruyter, 1922, vol. 1, pp. 18 ff.

12 On contemporary trends and the change in the approach to civil litigation, see UZELAC, A., VAN RHEE, C. H., 'The Metamorphoses of Civil Justice and Civil Procedure: The Challenges of New Paradigms – Unity and Diversity', in UZELAC, A., VAN RHEE, C. H. (eds.), *Transformation of Civil Justice. Unity and Diversity*, Cham: Springer, 2018, pp. 3–21.

13 GOLDSCHMIDT, J., *Der Prozess als Rechtslage. Eine Kritik des prozessualen Denkens*, Berlin: Springer, 1925, pp. 335–362.

the problem of asymmetric information. With reference to fact-finding, burdens only work if both parties have equal access to information and evidence. If there is asymmetric information, we have what Rolf Stürner called 'Darwinian litigation',[14] which is not acceptable. We must introduce a duty of cooperation in fact-finding: a duty of clarification. The duty of clarification – *Aufklärungspflicht*, in German – is the duty to answer, to give information, to give evidence, to explain and disclose information and evidence[15]. It is usually a duty that works upon request.

Both principles – the burden of allegation and proof and the duty of clarification – have been incorporated into the Rules. For example, Rules 24 and 25 burden the parties with the introduction of facts and evidence. The sanction is given by Rule 27:

> Rule 27. *Sanctions for non-compliance with rules and court orders*
>
> (1) The court shall disregard factual allegations, modifications of claims and defences, and offers of evidence that are introduced later than permitted by these rules or by court orders, including those concerning amendment. Preclusion does not apply if the court could have taken notice of the party's failure or mistake and itself failed to raise with the parties whether they wished to seek an amendment or relief from sanction.
>
> (2) As a general rule, the court may continue the proceedings and decide on the merits based on the facts and evidence available to it.
>
> ...

This is the idea of a burden in the party's own interest.

On the other hand, we have the duty of cooperation in the determination of facts; in particular, Rule 25(2) on access to information and evidence. It is possible to request information and evidence, but the duty of clarification of the opponent party is a duty upon request, not an automatic duty – which is reasonable and proportionate. And then there's the judge, who

14 Stürner, R., 'Zur allgemeinen Aufklärungspflicht der nicht beweisbelasteten Partei im Zivilprozeß', *Zeitschrift für Zivilprozess*, 1991, 104, pp. 208–217.

15 von Hippel, F., *Wahrheitspflicht und Aufklärungspflicht der Parteien im Zivilprozess*, Frankfurt: Klostermann, 1939, pp. 282–381; Stürner, R., 'Die Aufklärungspflicht der Parteien des Zivilprozesses', *Tübinger rechtswissenschaftliche Abhandlungen*, 44, 1976, pp. 134–151; Gradi, M., *L'obbligo di verità delle parti*, Turin: Giappichelli, 2018, pp. 343–400.

controls the proportionality of the request. The Rules also provide sanctions for uncooperative behaviour. In this respect, the Rules provide every possible sanction that exists in comparative civil procedure:[16]

> Rule 27. *Sanctions for non-compliance with rules and court orders*
>
> (3) The court may draw negative factual inferences, order a party or their lawyer to bear the costs of non-compliance, or in serious cases of non-compliance render an *astreinte*, an order for payment of a fine, administrative sanction as provided by national law, or hold the non-compliant party in contempt.

The first sanction, adverse inferences, is probably the most important sanction in practice and my preferred solution; it is a simple and inexpensive sanction. Of course, it does not guarantee that truth in fact-finding will be established. But if one party has asymmetric information, and the other party who has evidence refuses to cooperate, the decision against the non-cooperating party is not unfair.

Another duty is the prohibition of lying and withholding essential information. In Germany, this type of duty is called *Wahrheitspflicht* and *Vollständigkeitspflicht*.[17] These issues are not directly addressed in the Rules, but some provisions lead to the conclusion that lies and concealment of information are not permitted. For example, Rule 47:

> Rule 47. *Careful conduct of litigation by the parties*
>
> Parties must present their claims, defences, factual allegations and offers of evidence as early and completely as possible and as appropriate to the careful conduct of litigation in order to secure procedural expedition.

---

16 Gradi, M., 'The Right of Access to Information and Evidence and the Duty of Truthful Disclosure of Parties in Comparative Perspective', in Cadiet, L., Hess, B., Requejo, M. (eds.), *Procedural Science at the Crossroads of Different Generations*, Baden-Baden: Nomos, 2015, pp. 93–122.

17 Olzen, D., 'Die Wahrheitspflicht der Parteien im Zivilprozeß', *Zeitschrift für Zivilprozess*, 1985, 98, pp. 403–426; Gomille, C., *Informationsproblem und Wahrheitspflicht. Ein Aufklärungsmodell für den Zivilprozess*, Tübingen: Mohr Siebeck, 2016, pp. 18–23; Carratta, A., 'Dovere di verità e completezza', *Rivista trimestrale di diritto e procedura civile*, 2014, pp. 47–76.

I do not think, however, that this is the most important rule concerning this matter, given the comment on Rule 24:

> These Rules do not establish as a procedural principle a general obligation upon parties to provide the court from the start of proceedings with a full account of the information about all the facts known by that party and which are possibly relevant to the case.[18]

Therefore, the Rules generally exclude the obligation not to withhold information. However, there are other Rules that seem to indicate otherwise. First, Rule 186:

> Rule 186. *Without-notice* (ex parte) *procedure*
>
> (3) An applicant must fully disclose to the court all facts and legal issues relevant to the court's decision whether to grant relief and, if so, on what terms.

In the case of *inaudita altera parte* proceedings, there is a duty to be as complete as possible in the provision of facts and legal grounds. But this is only a special rule. In general, we can refer to Rule 3(e), which imposes a duty on the parties to act in good faith. A party who makes a false statement is not acting in good faith.

However, a statement is false not only when it is untrue, but also when it is incomplete and lacks information essential to the case. In this situation, the party who does not act in good faith may be sanctioned when deciding on costs:

> Rule 241. *General rule*
>
> (1) When determining upon which party the obligation to reimburse costs shall be placed under Rule 239, the court shall take into account the circumstances of the specific proceedings, in particular whether and to what extent the parties' claims were successful.
>
> (2) The court may also take into account the parties' conduct, in particular, whether and to what extent they acted in good faith and contributed to the fair, efficient and speedy resolution of the dispute.

18 Rule 24, comment 5.

Another example is in cases of extraordinary review. Reopening the procedure is possible if new evidence is discovered that was unavailable to one party because of the other party's behaviour:

> Rule 182. *Grounds for an extraordinary motion for review*
>
> (1) An extraordinary motion for review may only be brought against a judgment on the following grounds
>
> (d) after a judgment is issued, evidence that would have been decisive to it is recovered or obtained, and such evidence was not available prior to judgment being given due either to force majeure or improper conduct by the party in whose favour the judgment was made;

Obviously, these provisions do not directly sanction lying or withholding essential information; but they can be useful in sanctioning such behaviour.

DE BENITO: This is an interesting debate: does the distinction between duty and burden still make sense? From a theoretical point of view, the answer is clearly yes. However, considering that the principle of cooperation plays such an important role in the Rules, the difference may be blurred. It may be the case that parties are expected to act in their own interest as well as in the best interest of fair adjudication. It is therefore unclear whether the distinction between burden and duty is still relevant in the Rules.

UZELAC: *Lasten* and *Pflichten*, burdens and duties. I intentionally use German here because the terms are very precise and nuanced. Nowadays, however, people speak less German and more English. Some fine nuances are sacrificed in English. The English semantic field of 'obligations', with its plethora of 'must' and 'shall', encompasses both *Lasten* and *Pflichten*. This linguistic difficulty cannot be overlooked. Of course, in English there is also 'burden' – e.g., the burden of proof –, but trying to assign a very precise meaning to it leads to perplexity and is probably futile.

For certain purposes, distinguishing what is a burden and what is an obligation – in the proper sense of the term – may be useful. But when our approach to civil procedure is a practical one, we must ask ourselves what our objective is. Our aim is to insist on cooperation. And for that purpose, the distinction between burden and obligation is simply not very useful.

In the end, we felt that insisting too much on burdens and obligations would lead to something we wouldn't like to adopt. Therefore, even when sanctions were mentioned in our draft, we did not distinguish sanctions in the proper legal sense of the word – i.e., legally coercing the parties or other participants in the proceeding – from other types of sanctions.

Moreover, in our approach, sanctions cover something that may not be a sanction in the strict legal sense, but only a consequence. For example, negative inferences are not sanctions in the strict sense; but they can be effective. A negative inference is a sanction only in the sense that it motivates the parties and leads them to work towards the common goal of fair adjudication.

VAN RHEE: The distinction between *Pflichten* and *Lasten*[19] is in my opinion pertinent when discerning whether something is relevant for the parties only, or for society at large. I'd say that establishing true facts is not only relevant for the parties. Society at large has an interest in decisions based on true facts. Society at large has an interest in a judgment based on the correct legal grounds. Society at large has an interest in litigants who use scarce resources in an efficient way, because otherwise not all litigants have access to justice. The corresponding obligations must be considered as genuine duties (*Pflichten*) and not just burdens (*Lasten*). This means that many of the obligations that we find in the Rules need to be sanctioned; and sometimes not only by drawing adverse inferences.

GRADI: I believe that *Pflichten* and *Lasten* converge into one indistinct obligation only if we adopt a primarily public perspective on civil procedure. The collective or public interest requires an appropriate sanction even when a party's conduct is contrary to its own interest in establishing the facts. However, from the litigants' point of view, the distinction remains. This brings us to the crux of the matter: the fusion of duties and burdens presupposes a markedly public conception of civil litigation.

As regards the consequences of non-cooperation, I agree that adverse inference may seem, at first sight, an ambiguous sanction. However, I think it is an appropriate sanction against uncooperative behaviour of a party, especially if we focus on the private interest of the other party.

DE BENITO: Adverse inferences can function as a sanction, but also as a method of establishing facts, as a way of inferring facts from a party's failure to cooperate – a logical inference, according to the adjudicator's *conviction*

19 VAN RHEE, C. H., 'Charge et obligation / Burden and Duty', in JEULAND, E., LALANI, S. (eds.), *Recherche lexicographique en procédure civile / Lexicographical research in civil procedure*, Paris: ICRJ, 2017, pp. 77–80.

intime, in the light of the available facts and evidence. This is very different from a sanction for breach of duty. We see all this regularly in international arbitration.[20]

VAN RHEE: It is difficult to compare arbitration with proceedings before a court established by law. I would say that adverse inferences might not be a good sanction in a state court, although I realise that we have them in the Rules. Adverse inferences may lead to a decision based on facts other than the actual facts.

We have an interest, as a society at large, in the state courts delivering a judgment based on the correct law and the true facts. An adverse inference is, as Marco said, a way of establishing the facts, but not necessarily the true facts. In a state court, fact-finding should not only be seen as a burden, but also as a duty that comes with sanctions. This is different in arbitration. Arbitration does not have the same social significance as court proceedings. In arbitration, adverse inferences may be a good method of establishing the facts of the case because society's interest in a decision based on true facts is either non-existent or at least not as pronounced in arbitration.

DE BENITO: Should the old idea of burdens therefore remain alive in arbitration?

UZELAC: It is not important whether the cat is black or white; the important thing is that it catches mice. In the context of sanctions and negative inferences, the distinction between this or that item is less important than its effectiveness in its respective context.

I do not regard arbitration as socially indifferent. Arbitration has long ceased to be an alternative method of dispute resolution and has become the standard in certain contexts. And it is effective precisely because of its lack of formal and mandatory sanctions – sanctions in the sense of fines. However, cost sanctions exist in arbitration – even more so than in litigation – and can be quite effective.

---

20 See, e.g., AMARAL, G. R., 'Burden of Proof and Adverse Inferences in International Arbitration: Proposal for an Inference Chart', *Journal of International Arbitration*, 35, 2018, pp. 1–30.

DE BENITO: Indeed, arbitration has evolved to become a 'system of justice';[21] as such, it's hardly less socially relevant than court litigation. Furthermore, arbitrators and courts regularly collaborate in many ways; the relevant legal framework is designed and is constantly being refined to make this collaboration as smooth as possible.

VAN RHEE: I meant that litigation before a court of law, precisely because it is public, can convey messages. The proceedings are public, the judgements are public. Arbitration, on the other hand, is mostly a black box. It is therefore unable to convey the messages that court litigation conveys to the public.

Bibliography

AMARAL, G. R., 'Burden of Proof and Adverse Inferences in International Arbitration: Proposal for an Inference Chart', *Journal of International Arbitration*, 35, 2018, pp. 1–30.

CARRATTA, A., 'Dovere di verità e completezza', *Rivista trimestrale di diritto e procedura civile*, 2014, pp. 47–76.

GOLDSCHMIDT, J., *Der Prozess als Rechtslage. Eine Kritik des prozessualen Denkens*, Berlin: Springer, 1925.

GOMILLE, C., *Informationsproblem und Wahrheitspflicht. Ein Aufklärungsmodell für den Zivilprozess*, Tübingen: Mohr Siebeck, 2016.

GRADI, M., *L'obbligo di verità delle parti*, Turin: Giappichelli, 2018, pp. 343–400.

GRADI, M., 'The Right of Access to Information and Evidence and the Duty of Truthful Disclosure of Parties in Comparative Perspective', in CADIET, L., HESS, B., REQUEJO, M. (eds.), *Procedural Science at the Crossroads of Different Generations*, Baden-Baden: Nomos, 2015, pp. 93–122.

KISCH, W., *Deutsches Zivilprozessrecht*, Berlin, Leipzig: De Gruyter, 1922, vol. I.

KLEIN, F., Pro futuro. *Betrachtungen über Probleme der Civilproceßreform in Österreich*, Leipzig, Vienna: Deuticke, 1891.

MOURRE, A., 'Soft Law as a Condition for the Development of Trust in International Arbitration', *Revista Brasileira de Arbitragem*, 13-2016, 51, pp. 82–98.

21 MOURRE, A., 'Soft Law as a Condition for the Development of Trust in International Arbitration', *Revista Brasileira de Arbitragem*, 13-2016, 51, pp. 82–98.

OLZEN, D., 'Die Wahrheitspflicht der Parteien im Zivilprozeß', *Zeitschrift für Zivilprozess*, 1985, 98, pp. 403–426.

SORABJI, J., *English Civil Justice after the Woolf and Jackson Reforms. A Critical Analysis*, Cambridge: Cambridge University Press, 2014.

STÜRNER, R., 'Die Aufklärungspflicht der Parteien des Zivilprozesses', *Tübinger rechtswissenschaftliche Abhandlungen*, 44, 1976, pp. 134–151.

STÜRNER, R., 'Zur allgemeinen Aufklärungspflicht der nicht beweisbelasteten Partei im Zivilprozeß', *Zeitschrift für Zivilprozess*, 1991, 104, pp. 208–217.

THE AMERICAN LAW INSTITUTE, UNIDROIT, *ALI/UNIDROIT Principles of Transnational Civil Procedure*, New York: Cambridge University Press, 2006.

UZELAC, A., 'Goals of Civil Justice and Civil Procedure in the Contemporary World', in UZELAC, A. (ed.), *Goals of Civil Justice and Civil Procedure in Contemporary Judicial Systems*, Cham: Springer, 2014, pp. 3–31.

UZELAC, A. 'Towards European Rules of Civil Procedure: Rethinking Procedural Obligations', *Acta Iuridica Hungarica / Hungarian Journal of Legal Studies*, 58-1, 2017, pp. 3–18.

UZELAC, A., VAN RHEE, C. H., 'The Metamorphoses of Civil Justice and Civil Procedure: The Challenges of New Paradigms – Unity and Diversity', in UZELAC, A., VAN RHEE, C. H. (eds.), *Transformation of Civil Justice. Unity and Diversity*, Cham: Springer, 2018, pp. 3–21.

VAN RHEE, C. H., 'Judicial Case-Management and Loyal Cooperation. Towards Harmonized European Rules of Civil Procedure', in AARLI, R., SANDERS, A. (eds.), *Courts in Evolving Societies. A Sino-European Dialogue between Judges and Academics*, Leiden: Brill, 2020, pp. 168–202.

VAN RHEE, C. H., 'Case Management and Co-Operation in the Model European Rules of Civil Procedure', *Journal of International and Comparative Law*, 9-2022, 2, pp. 1–16.

VAN RHEE, C. H., 'Case Management in Europe: A Modern Approach to Civil Litigation', *International Journal of Procedural Law*, 8-2018, 1, pp. 65–84.

VAN RHEE, C. H., 'Charge et obligation / Burden and Duty', in JEULAND, E., LALANI, S. (eds.), *Recherche lexicographique en procédure civile / Lexicographical research in civil procedure*, Paris: ICRJ, 2017, pp. 77–80.

VAN RHEE, C. H., 'Gerenciamento de casos e cooperação na Europa: uma abordagem moderna sobre a litigância cível', in *Civil Procedure Review*, 13-2022, 2, pp. 157–170.

VAN RHEE, C. H., 'Mandatory Mediation before Litigation in Civil and Commercial Matters: A European Perspective', *Access to Justice in Eastern Europe*, 4-2021, 12, pp. 7–24.

VAN RHEE, C. H., 'Obligations of the Parties and their Lawyers in Civil Litigation: The ALI/UNIDROIT Principles of Transnational Civil Procedure', in ADOLPHSEN,

J., GOEBEL, J., HAAS, U., HESS, B., KOLMANN, S. (eds.), *Festschrift für Peter Gottwald zum 70. Geburtstag*, Munich: Beck, 2014, pp. 669–679.

VAN RHEE, C. H., 'Principe de coopération / Cooperation Principle', in JEULAND, E., LALANI, S. (eds.), *Recherche lexicographique en procédure civile / Lexicographical research in civil procedure*, Paris: IRJS, 2017, pp. 207–214.

VON HIPPEL, F., *Wahrheitspflicht und Aufklärungspflicht der Parteien im Zivilprozess*, Frankfurt: Klostermann, 1939.

CHAPTER 5

Service of Process

Astrid Stadler, Eva Storskrubb, Alan Uzelac, Enrique Vallines, and María Luisa Villamarín

The issue of service, which may appear to be a technical matter, is in fact linked to fundamental aspects of civil procedure, such as access to justice and the right to be heard.

The Rules offer a flexible regulatory framework that is designed to remain relevant and useful in the context of ongoing developments in globalisation and technological change, while safeguarding the fundamental procedural rights of citizens.

STADLER: Our working group consisted of six members. Eva and I, from Sweden and Germany respectively, acted as co-reporters. Members from the UK, France, Italy, and Greece completed the team. This diversity of legal backgrounds compensated for the relatively small size of the group.

We held five meetings between 2014 and 2017, plus the annual meetings with all the working groups and the steering committee, in which the co-reporters presented their respective drafts.

 | DOI:10.1163/9789004533257_006

VALLINES: What would you say were the main challenges you faced?

STADLER: Terminology was one of them for sure. It is always a sensitive issue in international projects like this. We worked in English, but we also tried to prepare a French translation in parallel to the English version. This turned out to be a productive idea: sometimes the first translations revealed shortcomings in the English version, so we would go back and try something like a simultaneous drafting in English and French.

The project's general policy was to avoid using terminology that might have different meanings in different jurisdictions. For instance, 'personal service', 'substituted service', or 'fictitious service' all have different meanings or connotations in different countries. We wanted to avoid that. We went for more neutral and explanatory terms, like 'service guaranteeing reception' or 'alternative service'. Sometimes we had to sacrifice conciseness or even elegance to get the clarity we needed and avoid any confusion.

VALLINES: I can imagine how challenging it must have been for the steering committee to define the most appropriate level of detail and to achieve a uniform degree of completeness of the regulation in the different chapters; to try to achieve a comprehensive regulation or rather to exercise self-restraint and leave room for national legislators. It is not easy to draw this line. In your working group, did you have a clear idea about this from the beginning?

STADLER: The dichotomy between minimum or maximum rules was always present. We used the ALI-UNIDROIT Principles as a starting point, as most of the working groups did. Regarding service, however, the ALI-UNIDROIT Principles are rather circumspect.

Furthermore, they are principles, not rules; and our mission was to draft a set of actual rules. Nevertheless, we soon realised that some issues cannot be solved in detail and are probably best left to national legislators. These would be open-ended rules rather than *principles*, anyway. Take Rule 71:

> Rule 71. *Responsibility for service*
>
> (1) Responsibility for service of documents lies with the court/parties.
>
> (2) If responsibility lies with the court, upon application the court may entrust a party with service of documents if appropriate.

(3) Where responsibility lies with the parties the court retains supervisory control which may include the power to set aside service.

Responsibility for service – who should be responsible for initiating and organising service – was obviously one of the key issues to tackle. The diversity of answers across Europe is remarkable. In some countries, responsibility lies with the court (Germany, England, Italy, etc.), in the others this falls upon the parties (Greece). However, in France, and countries which have adopted the French system (Belgium, Luxembourg), there is a well-established bailiff system, in which claimants first go to the bailiff, the bailiff takes care of service, and only after that is the statement of claim filed with the court.[1] We thought it would be better to leave it for legislators to choose: 'responsibility for service of documents lies with the court/parties'. We emphasised in the commentary that this is a deliberate option.

VALLINES: But you did set a hierarchy of preferred methods of service:

Rule 73. *Priority of methods guaranteeing receipt*

Documents shall be served using a method that guarantees receipt (Rules 74–76). If such service is not possible, alternative service methods apply, as specified in Rule 78. Where the address for service is unknown or other methods of service have failed, methods of last resort, specified in Rule 80, may be used to effect service.

STADLER: We discussed whether it was appropriate to list several options and leave it to the 'judge/parties' to choose between them or whether to adopt a hierarchy of service models. As you pointed out, we opted for a hierarchy, partly because most European countries favour a certain method – e.g., personal service or service with acknowledgement of receipt – over others.

Another reason in favour of a hierarchy of methods of service is that methods that guarantee reception offer greater protection of the defendant's right to be heard, particularly regarding service of the statement of

1 For a comparative overview, see SIMONI, A., PAILLI, G., *Study on the Service of Documents. Comparative Legal Analysis of the Relevant Laws and Practices of the Member States. Final Report*, JUST/2014/JCOO/PR/CIVI/0049, European Commission, 2016; see also TSIKRIKAS, D., KENNETT, W., 'Service and Notice of Proceedings', in STADLER, A., SMITH, V., GASCÓN, F. (eds.), *European Rules of Civil Procedure. A Commentary on the ELI/UNIDROIT Model Rules*, Cheltenham: Edward Elgar, 2023, pp. 219–251.

claim, but also it is crucial for other issues of substantial and procedural law, especially *lis pendens* and the interruption of prescription. Only when this is not possible, the 'judge/parties' may resort to alternative service rules.[2]

At the same time, when proceedings are already pending, Rule 79(1) allows service from lawyer to lawyer, which is the most widespread and surely the most efficient method:

> Rule 79. *Service of documents during proceedings*
>
> (1) During proceedings, if a party is represented by lawyer, service of documents may normally be effected on the lawyer or from lawyer-to-lawyer without Court intervention. Lawyers must provide an electronic address that can be used for service of documents.

VALLINES: What about the EU Service Regulation[3] and generally the EU acquis? Was it an important point of reference in your work?

STADLER: That was one of the first things we had to figure out: what to do with the Service Regulation. The question was, in turn, closely connected to whether we wanted to draft rules solely for domestic or also for cross-border disputes.

Regarding the first question, we all knew that the Service Regulation 2007 was not working very well in practice. Plus, when we started work, there was a reform underway. So, we decided not to take the Service Regulation or the EU acquis in this area as set in stone.

Regarding the second question, we opted to draft model rules including both domestic and cross-border cases because often the issues are the same in both settings. Only in limited situations is there a need for specific rules for cross-border cases, such as issues of language and translation

---

2 TSIKRIKAS, D., KENNETT, W., 'Service and Notice of Proceedings', in STADLER, A., SMITH, V., GASCÓN, F. (eds.), *European Rules of Civil Procedure. A Commentary on the ELI/UNIDROIT Model Rules*, Cheltenham: Edward Elgar, 2023, pp. 219–251, at 227.

3 Council Regulation (EC) 1393/2007 of 13 November 2007 on the service in the Member States of judicial and extrajudicial documents in civil or commercial matters, now replaced by Regulation (EU) 2020/1784 of the European Parliament and of the Council of 25 November 2020 on the service in the Member States of judicial and extrajudicial documents in civil or commercial matters (service of documents) (recast). See generally ANTHIMOS, A., REQUEJO, M. (eds.), *The European Service Regulation. A Commentary*, Cheltenham: Edward Elgar, 2023.

or slightly more generous deadlines (Rules 82 to 85). Rule 86 clarifies the relationship of the Rules with the Hague Service Convention, which applies 'where there is occasion to transmit a judicial or extra-judicial document for service outside the European Union'. It's also worth mentioning Rule 82, which sets a different standard for language requirements than the Service Regulation.

VALLINES: We therefore have a set of rules – not mere principles – that establish a hierarchy of notification methods, applicable to both domestic and cross-border cases. Now, how do the different methods work in practice?

STADLER: Let's take the example of a company that's being sued. If it's a domestic case, we would start with Rule 74(1)(b).

> Rule 74. *Service guaranteeing receipt*
>
> (1) Service guaranteeing receipt includes
>
> (b) service via a designated electronic information system using appropriately high technical standards attested to by an acknowledgement of receipt that the system generates automatically where the addressee has a legal obligation to register with that system. Such an obligation shall be imposed on legal persons and on natural persons engaging in independent professional activities for disputes relating to their trade or profession;

This article about electronic service reflects one of the most important decisions we made: to suggest that companies and legal persons should be bound to register and to provide an email address that can be used by courts – already a mandatory rule in some countries, such as Italy.[4]

Therefore, the first option, which is also the quickest and most effective way to perform the service, is electronic service. This method should be effective in most cases. Only if a company does not have a registered email address, or if it is not operational, will we need another means of service – physical delivery to a company representative at the company's premises, as set out in Rules 74(1)(a) and 75.

4 Art. 149 bis CPC, Art. 3 bis Legge № 53/1994, Decreto-Legge № 179/2012.

VALLINES: Indeed, physical delivery is a widely accepted method throughout Europe.[5] Even the European Commission has recognised, based on several studies, that 'service by post is a preferred method of service for the majority of stakeholders'.[6] And both electronic and physical delivery seem to be the most preferred options when it comes to direct methods of service, whereas the use of transmitting and receiving entities remains exceptional.

STADLER: That's right. The Rules reflect and emphasise that reality.[7]

If the representative or employee refuses to accept the documents, Rule 77 applies. This is a general rule on refusal of acceptance and states that refusal is, under certain conditions, equivalent to service.

> Rule 77. *Refusal to accept service*
>
> Service according to Rule 74(1)(a) also includes service attested to by a document signed by the competent person who effected the service and stating that the addressee refused to receive the document. The document must be deposited at a specified place for a certain period of time for the purpose of collection by the addressee who has been informed where and when to collect the document.

If no representative of the defendant company is met, physical delivery can also be done to an employee, if there is one, and will also often lead to successful service. Rule 78 provides a couple of methods of so-called alternative service methods. According to Rule 78(1)(c), the documents can also be deposited at the post office or at any other public authority. In this case it is necessary to notify the addressee that the documents are ready for collection and to tell him when and where to collect them. If the addressee

5 See, e.g., TSIKRIKAS, D., KENNETT, W., 'Service and Notice of Proceedings' in STADLER, A., SMITH, V., GASCÓN, F. (eds.), *European Rules of Civil Procedure. A Commentary on the ELI/UNIDROIT Model Rules*, Cheltenham: Edward Elgar, 2023, pp. 219–251, at p. 231.

6 Commission Staff Working Document Impact Assessment Accompanying the document Proposal for a Regulation of the European Parliament and of the Council amending Regulation (EC) 1393/2007 of the European Parliament and of the Council on the service in the Member States of judicial and extrajudicial documents in civil or commercial matters (service of documents), p. 16.

7 As encouraged by SIMONI, A., PAILLI, G., *Study on the Service of Documents. Comparative Legal Analysis of the Relevant Laws and Practices of the Member States. Final Report*, JUST/2014/JCOO/PR/CIVI/0049, European Commission, 2016, pp. 94 ff.

picks them up within that period, we will also have been successful in this case.

If none of the alternative methods leads to a successful notification – in particular, if the documents are not collected –, the method of last resort is service by publication, as provided for in Rule 80.

> Rule 80. *Service methods of last resort*
>
> (1) If service by methods that guarantee receipt (Rules 74–77) or alternative service (Rule 78) is not possible because the addressee's address is unknown or service has otherwise failed, service of documents may be effected as follows:
>
> (a) by publication of a notice to the addressee in a form provided for by law of the forum state, including publication in electronic registers accessible to the public, and
>
> (b) by sending a notice to the addressee's last known address or e-mail address, if applicable.

There are several means to carry out service by publication, including electronic social networks, if provided for by the law of the forum. We drafted a very flexible rule in this respect; whatever provides a chance that the information gets to the addressee is welcome under Rule 80.

VALLINES: With regard to electronic service, it may be of interest to note that you were one of the first working groups to be formed in 2014, so you were present from the outset of the project. In 2020, the Covid-19 crisis was declared, and many things changed.[8] In this regard, has the world moved beyond the Rules? Do they stand in the post-pandemic context? If you were to undertake this project now, would you propose any amendments to the text of the Rules?

STORSKRUBB: This is an excellent question, which could be applied to all sections of the Rules. As far as our side is concerned, I think we answered it quite well. The digitisation of civil justice was there before the pandemic, and we were aware of it. So, I'd like to think that the recent developments, although far-reaching in many respects, would not have significantly changed our approach to service.

8 See generally KRANS, B., NYLUND, A., *Civil Courts Coping with Covid-19*, The Hague: Eleven, 2021.

As Astrid said, the Rules impose an obligation on legal entities to be available for electronic service. When we proposed it, this felt quite avant-garde. Electronic service would be very efficient both nationally and cross-border compared to sending letters by post, which might work not-so-well in all countries. We still wanted acknowledgement of receipt. This was also included in the rules on electronic service for legal persons, which generate a formal acknowledgement of receipt in the system. But we also included an electronic means of service for natural persons:

> Rule 74. *Service guaranteeing receipt*
>
> (1) Service guaranteeing receipt includes
>
> (c) service by other electronic means if the addressee has previously and explicitly agreed to use this service method or is under a legal obligation to register an email address for the purpose of service. Such service must be attested to by the addressee's acknowledgement of receipt, which must include the date of receipt, and which is returned by the addressee;

We wouldn't go as far as to impose an obligation on natural persons to accept service by electronic means, hence the need for explicit consent. However, if there is consent to be served – for example, by email or some sort of digital platform –,[9] then there must be an acknowledgement of receipt. We need to make sure that the natural person has received the documents electronically.

Electronic means are present also in last resort service, as Astrid pointed out, in Rule 80: 'by publication of a notice to the addressee in a form provided for by law of the forum state, including publication in electronic registers accessible to the public', and 'by sending a notice to the addressee's last known address or e-mail address, if applicable'. This means that not only email, but also WhatsApp or any kind of electronic means, including Facebook Messenger or the like, can be used.[10] The idea is that the right of

9 For details on currently employed methods of electronic service and associated aspects of safety and authenticity, see TSIKRIKAS, D., KENNETT, W., 'Service and Notice of Proceedings', in STADLER, A., SMITH, V., GASCÓN, F. (eds.), *European Rules of Civil Procedure. A Commentary on the ELI/UNIDROIT Model Rules*, Cheltenham: Edward Elgar, 2023, pp. 219–251, at 232–233.

10 Rule 80, comment 3. See TSIKRIKAS, D., KENNETT, W., 'Service and Notice of Proceedings', in STADLER, A., SMITH, V., GASCÓN, F. (eds.), *European Rules of Civil*

defence can and must be protected in a digital context. This has not been and is not without controversy, both legally and culturally, in different parts of Europe.

UZELAC: Let's imagine that we have a young defendant, a German digital nomad that moves to a beautiful island in Croatia. His change of address has been stuck in the bureaucratic process. Meanwhile, an attempt is made to notify the German address of the trial, but the letter is misplaced and lost. Finally, we have the service of last resort according to Rule 80. The defendant has accounts on LinkedIn, Facebook, and Instagram. Furthermore, his friends and relatives should be able to find a way to contact him. Would Rule 80 be appropriate as a mechanism of last resort? Or would this be a case where the Rules would insist on surfing the web to find out what is happening to this person, especially knowing that he belongs to the younger generation?[11]

VALLINES: Your question seems to be, in essence, whether the court or the party responsible for service may be deemed to have made 'every reasonable effort to discover the addressee's present address' when they have failed to search for this address on the internet. This is an interesting question about the scope and meaning of Rule 80(2).

STORSKRUBB: This would be another example of the Rules not going into such detail. Rule 80(2) would allow such a search but would not make it mandatory. We have not imposed an obligation or offered any kind of explanation as to the specific scope of the court's duty to act. Moreover, where responsibility for service lies not with the court but with the parties, we have not specified how active or diligent the parties must be.

VALLINES: From this point of view, making 'every reasonable effort' to discover the defendant's address functions as an open standard of care, which only national law or jurisprudence can fully integrate.

Procedure. A Commentary on the ELI/UNIDROIT Model Rules, Cheltenham: Edward Elgar, 2023, pp. 219–251, at 243.

11 STORSKRUBB, E., 'E-Justice, Innovation and the EU', in HESS, B., KRAMER, X., *From Common Rules to Best Practices in European Civil Procedure*, Baden-Baden: Nomos, 2017, pp. 271–302, at 295.

STADLER: Exactly. What constitutes reasonable efforts can be decided on a case-by-case basis. Sometimes there is no way of knowing where the defendant is: there are always cases where the defendant escapes or simply disappears, especially in cross-border contexts.[12]

VALLINES: Indeed, the Service Regulation requires Member States to assist in locating the recipient's address.[13]

STADLER: This is precisely why we need Rule 80. Rule 80(2) imposes an obligation on the parties and the court to make reasonable efforts to discover the addressee's present address – efforts which must be documented in the files.[14] As a closing clause, Rule 80(3) sets forth that service shall be ultimately deemed to be made within two weeks of the last publication of the notice, subject to certain conditions. We must strike a balance between the defendant's right to be heard and the claimant's right to present his case. The *fictio juris* of a period of silence after publication is often the only way to achieve that balance.

VALLINES: Rule 80 is not the only rule regarding service methods of last resort; I see much room for flexibility in Rule 81, which allows parties to carry out service in whatever manner they think is best if there is acknowledgement of receipt by the defendant:

> Rule 81. *Cure for defective service*
>
> If service of documents does not meet the requirements of Rules 74–79, such non-compliance will be cured if the addressee's conduct proves that they received the document to be served personally and in sufficient time for them to arrange their defence or in any other way respond as required by the nature of the document.

---

12 See TSIKRIKAS, D., KENNETT, W., 'Service and Notice of Proceedings', in STADLER, A., SMITH, V., GASCÓN, F. (eds.), *European Rules of Civil Procedure. A Commentary on the ELI/UNIDROIT Model Rules*, Cheltenham: Edward Elgar, 2023, pp. 219–251, at 241.

13 Art. 7(1) of the Regulation (EU) 2020/1784 of the European Parliament and of the Council of 25 November 2020 on the service in the Member States of judicial and extrajudicial documents in civil or commercial matters (service of documents) (recast).

14 The Rules follow here the example of France, Art. 659 CPC; Italy, Art. 148 CPC; Luxembourg, Art. 157 NCP; and Spain, Arts. 156, 161(4), and 163 LEC.

I've witnessed this situation in Spain,[15] with courts circumventing the legal rules of service by sending emails or leaving individual letters in the defendant's briefcase. Later, the service was 'cured' by way of an acknowledgement of receipt. However, this is an illegal procedure. Also, it puts the defendant's right to defend themselves first, like Article 45(1)(b) Brussels I does. It doesn't say the document has to be served correctly, but it should be served in a way that lets the defendant arrange their right to defend themselves. It's a pretty general rule, but it gives more flexibility and less room for people to abuse the formality.[16]

STADLER: I am glad you mentioned Rule 81. It is an important article. We modelled it to follow the example of many European countries that already have a similar rule in place.[17] I think it is a reasonable standard, which is already in the European Enforcement Order Regulation.[18] What is the purpose of service? To make sure that the defendant knows what is going on: that a lawsuit has been filed and the relevant documents of the case. After all, the way a person has been served is often secondary to whether he has actually received the documents: *pas de nullité sans grief*.[19] This is what Rule 81 emphasises.

---

15 Under Art. 166 LEC, 'Service that has not been carried out in accordance with [the relevant provisions of the Code on service] and that may hamper the right of defence will be null and void. However, when the addressee has acted as if he had been served and has not invoked the nullity of the service in her first appearance before the court, service will then be fully effective, as if it had been conducted in accordance with the relevant legal provisions.'

16 GASCÓN, F., 'Service of Proceedings on the Defendant as a Safeguard of Fairness in Civil Proceedings: In Search of Minimum Standards from EU Legislation and European Case-Law', *Journal of Private International Law*, 13-3, 2017, pp. 475–518, at 499.

17 TSIKRIKAS, D., KENNETT, W., 'Service and Notice of Proceedings', in STADLER, A., SMITH, V., GASCÓN, F. (eds.), *European Rules of Civil Procedure. A Commentary on the ELI/UNIDROIT Model Rules*, Cheltenham: Edward Elgar, 2023, pp. 219–251, at 232–233, 242.

18 Rule 81 is based on Art. 18(1) of the Regulation (EC) 805/2004 of the European Parliament and of the Council of 21 April 2004 creating a European Enforcement Order for uncontested claims. See TSIKRIKAS, D., KENNETT, W., 'Service and Notice of Proceedings', in STADLER, A., SMITH, V., GASCÓN, F. (eds.), *European Rules of Civil Procedure. A Commentary on the ELI/UNIDROIT Model Rules*, Cheltenham: Edward Elgar, 2023, pp. 219–251, at 244.

19 TSIKRIKAS, D., KENNETT, W., 'Service and Notice of Proceedings', in STADLER, A., SMITH, V., GASCÓN, F. (eds.), *European Rules of Civil Procedure. A Commentary on the ELI/UNIDROIT Model Rules*, Cheltenham: Edward Elgar, 2023, pp. 219–251, at 244. Numerous Member States have similar provisions on the cure of defective service: e.g.,

VALLINES: Returning to electronic service: Eva, you said that the working group wouldn't go so far as to advocate a legal obligation for individuals to accept the service electronically. What factors did the group consider in reaching this conclusion?

STORSKRUBB: At the time, Denmark was the only country in Europe – perhaps things have changed since then – that obliged natural persons to be available for electronic service, even for the document instituting proceedings. Citizens in Denmark *must* have this kind of electronic mailbox for authorities of all kinds, even courts. Only people who are homeless, or who aren't accountable for themselves, can have an alternative system.

The same happens, after all, with a physical post-box. A natural person may be on holiday, but is assumed to be available 24/7, as in the digital sphere. This relates to the legal culture, but also to the general trend towards digitisation. Swedish media report that many companies now have a function to lock company email, so that an employee cannot be reached outside working hours. I think the model example can be France: taking into account the active use of digital means of communication, the French legislator nevertheless obliges companies to negotiate with employees about the right to disconnect (*droit à la déconnexion*) to 'assure the respect of rest, vacation along with personal and family life'.[20] I believe that this right should apply in a similar way to all types of notifications, otherwise the line between social life, availability, and privacy becomes blurred and even delusional.

If courts are allowed to serve people electronically, the question is when, or how quickly, will people access the service? How do we, as a society, perceive this kind of responsibility? With this sophistication of electronic communication and the implicit assumption that everyone is online, will the burden become insurmountable? This is a deep cultural issue that is constantly evolving.[21]

Art. 114(2) French CPC; judgment of the *Cour de cassation*, civil, dated 24 May 1984, Gaz. Pal. 1984, judgment of the *Cour de cassation*, civil, dated 18 January 1989, JCP 1989, III 21286; § 189 German ZPO; Art. 159(3) Greek CPC.

20 Art. L2242-17 *Code du travail*. See *Cour de cassation*, labour, 2 October 2001; *Cour de cassation*, labour, 17 February 2004.

21 STORSKRUBB, E., 'E-Justice, Innovation and the EU', in HESS, B., KRAMER, X., *From Common Rules to Best Practices in European Civil Procedure*, Baden-Baden: Nomos, 2017, pp. 271–302, at 296.

We see a similar reasoning behind the recast Service Regulation's rules on electronic service. Even in a cross-border setting, direct electronic service – not via the designated transmitting and receiving agencies – is in principle not possible without prior consent. If I understand correctly, if there is a platform of this kind, consent to join the platform does not suffice and there still needs to be specific consent. The same idea underlies the need for explicit acknowledgement of receipt of an email, even though the system *knows* when the addressee has received and read the message.

VILLAMARÍN: I see many of your ideas – cautiously opening to more electronic service to a greater extent, but without forcing everyone to be available for that purpose – incorporated in the recast Service Regulation.

Another issue in this regard is the interoperability of these platforms across Europe. In a cross-border context, digital platforms must be interoperable.

STORSKRUBB: They should. Currently, the reality is that only Danish courts or authorities can serve people on the Danish platform; a Finnish authority cannot.

VALLINES: This in turn poses a legal question: should the EU compel Member States to make their systems available to each other?

STORSKRUBB: In the first drafts of our accompanying commentary, we tried to encourage this, but it is easier to envision it than to put it into practice. In the EU context, the interoperability of platforms and digital tools in general is now being discussed more, but there is still a long way to go.

VALLINES: When electronic service or any other method of direct service to the addressee is unsuccessful, we must then turn, as Astrid explained, to the 'alternative methods' of service listed in Rule 78. What is the general approach of the Rules to these 'alternative methods'?

VILLAMARÍN: We can start by asking whether we need a standard for these cases. A first point of reference is the Henderson case at the European Court of Justice.[22] Mr. Henderson was sued by Novo Bank because of his repeated non-payments. After receiving an unanswered notice, he was

22 *Andrew Marcus Henderson v. Novo Banco S.A.*, Judgment of 2 March 2017, case 354/15, ECLI:EU:C:2017:157, paras. 97, 99.

condemned by the Portuguese courts. When he found out, he appealed the decision claiming that the notice was null and void, on the following grounds. First, because the 'acknowledgment of receipt of the registered letter was not included in the file, which constituted a breach of a formal requirement laid down by Portuguese legislation'. Second, because he did not personally accept service of the document instituting proceedings before the Court and ignored 'who had accepted the letter of service in question, so that he was not aware of the proceedings brought against him'. Third, Annex II to Regulation 1393/2007 was not transmitted to him and he was 'not informed of his right to refuse to receive service of a judicial document drawn up solely in the Portuguese language, whereas, in the present case, a translation into English or Irish would have been required'. Based on these questions, the Court of Justice analysed the minimum standards to be met in alternative methods. In this respect, two fundamental ideas can be highlighted: firstly, these alternative methods must 'offer sufficient guarantees that the addressee is properly informed within the required time limits'; secondly, the option of a third party validly accepting court documents on behalf of the addressee must be 'reserved for clearly defined situations' to guarantee the defendant's rights. Moreover, for this to be possible, the addressees must in any case be adult persons 'who are within the person's habitual residence and who are members of his family or employees in his service'.

VALLINES: Looking at Rule 78, how are these cases of alternative service defined?

VILLAMARÍN: Firstly, age or, more generally, capacity must be considered. National legislations vary considerably in this regard. For example, in France, recipients need to be older than twelve; older than fourteen in Spain, Italy, and Hungary; older than fifteen in Luxembourg and Finland; older than sixteen in Belgium.[23] The Recast Service Regulation is limited to adults. Rule 78 opted for a more open-ended, flexible rule, which avoids defining a threshold and which should include, for instance, minors close to legal age. The recipient should simply be 'able', which refers to a case-by-case assessment.[24]

---

23 TSIKRIKAS, D., KENNETT, W., 'Service and Notice of Proceedings', in STADLER, A., SMITH, V., GASCÓN, F. (eds.), *European Rules of Civil Procedure. A Commentary on the ELI/UNIDROIT Model Rules*, Cheltenham: Edward Elgar, 2023, pp. 219–251, at 238.

24 TSIKRIKAS, D., KENNETT, W., 'Service and Notice of Proceedings', in STADLER, A., SMITH, V., GASCÓN, F. (eds.), *European Rules of Civil Procedure. A Commentary on the ELI/UNIDROIT Model Rules*, Cheltenham: Edward Elgar, 2023, pp. 219–251, at 238.

Secondly, it is also necessary to define the relationship of these potential addressees to the defendants. Rule 78 limits the addressees to cohabitants and persons working for the defendant, in line with the recast service regulations. Furthermore, to avoid conflicts of interest, Rule 78(3) excludes those who are opposing parties to the defendant, as is the case in most European countries. Paragraphs (1) and (2) of Rule 78 require the will of the person served.

Thirdly, the place where alternative service is to be carried out must also be considered. Rule 78(1) limits the place to the defendant's residence or premises. Places *close* to the defendant's residence or premises are not acceptable.

Fourthly, the will of the person who receive the service is also required by Rule 78(1) and (2).

The use of open-ended criteria such as 'willing and able' is aimed not to confine ourselves in too concrete requirements. The purpose is to avoid excessive formality, but not to create some more. Therefore, the ascertaining of these characteristics is up to judges who must always bear in mind that the service must be effective and guaranteeing right of defence in reasonable terms.[25]

VALLINES: If alternative service also fails, we have no choice but to resort to the 'methods of last resort' provided for in Rule 80. Such cases are far from rare.

VILLAMARÍN: Of course, effective rules for such cases are essential. The dilemma is the conflicting rights and interests at stake. On the one hand, we have the claimant's right to legal protection, which could be totally impeded if the defendant could not be searched by all the legal available means, since this would leave this right devoid of content. In this sense, the Court of Justice of the EU states that a 'objective of general interest' in the EU is 'the aim of avoiding the situation of denial of justice in which the claimant would find himself if it were impossible to locate the defendant'.[26] On the other hand, there is the defendant's right of defence, which obliges us to be

25 AGUILERA, M., 'El Reglamento UE/2020/1784, sobre notificación y traslado transfronterizo de documentos: novedades e implicaciones internas', *Revista General de Derecho Europeo*, 53, 2022, pp. 1–31, at 16.

26 *G v. Cornelius de Visser*, Judgment of 15 March 2012, Case 292/10, ECLI:EU:C:2012:142, *Hypoteční banka a.s. v. Udo Mike Lindner*, Judgment of 17 November 2011, Case 327/10, ECLI:EU:C:2011:745.

especially cautious when serving judicial documents. For this reason, when it comes to the methods of last resort, a certain degree of diligence is required from both the court and the parties, particularly the claimant. Rule 80 doesn't refer to the standard of care required from the parties.[27]

The court's duty is clearly defined in Rule 80: it must make 'every reasonable effort', using similar terms as those of the recast Service Regulation,[28] which in turn mirrors case law from the European Court of Human Rights requiring that national authorities take the action that could legitimately and reasonably be expected from them.

For example, in the recent Karesvaara case,[29] a Spanish court had served the judicial document by means of public announcement, by attaching the summons to the court's physical bulletin board, without any other attempt to serve them personally. The ECHR determined that the national authorities had not taken all the measures that had been reasonably expected of them. This was particularly evident in the subsequent enforcement proceedings, where the claimants' property and alternative addresses were promptly located.[30]

In conclusion, it is not enough for the court to try to serve. The court must exhaust all means of service at its disposal. This means that, in some cases, it may be necessary to search for an alternative address or to carry out further investigations.

The claimant's burden in this regard is not expressly laid down in either Rule 80 or the Regulation, but we can find guidance in comparative case law. For example, in Spain, the applicant bears the procedural burden of verifying that such an act has been attempted in the number of places where there is a sufficient rational basis for estimating that the person lives, and must employ the ordinary diligence – not a heightened standard of care – to acquire the corresponding knowledge.[31] Therefore, it must provide the court with all information in its possession about the defendant, resulting in nullity of service if bad faith can be assumed, as usually happens when the claimant unlawfully conceals the defendant's address.

---

27 An example of this standard of care required to the defendant can be found in ECHR case *Inmoterra International Denia v. Spain*, 20 May 2020, where the unsuccessful service of document was attributed to the inaction and lack of diligence of the defendant (para. 30).

28 Art. 22(2)(c).

29 *Karesvaara and Njie v. Spain*, 15 December 2020 (Appl. 60750/15).

30 Para. 55.

31 Art. 155 LEC. See also Supreme Court Judgments 287/2017, of 12 May 2017; 2147/2016, of 18 May 2016; 2630/2016, of 9 June 2016.

VALLINES: In fact, an unscrupulous claimant might even think of playing with the rules of service to favour a method of last resort and thus curtail the defendant's right of defence.

VILLAMARÍN: Fictitious methods of last resort are indeed problematic and must be used carefully and exceptionally. Rule 80 addresses this problem with three proposals. First, it calls for the implementation of the most efficient channels for publication, recommending the generalisation of electronic registers or noticeboards (para. 1.b). Second, it calls to serve always to the last known address or email address, if applicable (para. c). Third, it establishes a further safeguard, because it also suggests accompanying the publication, where possible, with effective channels, such as warnings or alerts.

We can look at the fictitious service or last resort as a reversal of risks in the balance between the claimant's right of access to justice and the claimant's right of defence, when any diligent and good faith ways to locate a defendant have been exhausted. It is easier for the defendant to protect their rights afterwards with the *ex post* control of the lawfulness of the last resort service at the enforcement stage.[32]

Today, almost 85% of the world's population owns a smartphone. So why not use SMS, WhatsApp, social media, at least for alerts or to let people know there is a publication waiting to be read? Why not use these methods directly for publication? This is already happening in countries like the USA, the UK, Bulgaria, or Estonia. Rule 80 is open to this new option, as explained in the commentary.

UZELAC: In the wake of this technology note and the previous reflection on the changes brought about by the pandemic, perhaps some areas of the project are in danger of rapidly becoming obsolete. The chapter on process notification could be one of these areas.

Croatian law is usually rather conservative, yet I see that it exceeds some of the service standards of the Regulation, which should be cutting-edge and future oriented. In 2019, we started with a broad obligation – not only for legal persons but also for lawyers and other legal professionals such as experts – to open safe electronic mailboxes in the national system. We have been recently stretching this duty even further. This is to say that, if the

32 GASCÓN, F., 'Service of Proceedings on the Defendant as a Safeguard of Fairness in Civil Proceedings: In Search of Minimum Standards from EU Legislation and European Case-Law', *Journal of Private International Law*, 13-3, 2017, pp. 475–518, at 508.

rules are to be resistant to time, they must be drafted with electronic communication at the forefront. However, if I look at the current service rules, I find that most of them concern old-fashioned paper communication, while very few focus on electronic communication. This situation should probably be reversed, which leads me to believe that, after the pandemic, these rules could and probably should be revised.

The same happens with the 'reasonable effort' standard. According to Rule 80(2), 'reasonable effort' needs to be made only 'to discover the addressee's present address'. Nowadays, the best proof of communication is communication itself. As María Luisa said, people use their mobile phones for all kinds of communication. Therefore, it is not the case to strive to find an email address – which is already a slightly outdated method of communication. Instead, one should try to reach the recipient by the best means available. The decisions of the Court of Justice cited by María Luisa were also a bit broader.

Considering the pandemic and recent developments in civil procedure, we need to change our objectives, tools, and means. Yes, the Rules of Procedure could and should be revised, and better sooner than later.

Storskrubb: Not necessarily. Professionals are already mentioned in our rules for legal persons. As I said, we were quite avantgarde in 2014, where we said that legal persons and professionals are obliged to have a platform. We did not specify the type of electronic platform but said that they must be available for electronic service.

We distinguished between all legal persons, professionals, and individuals. Apart from Denmark, I know of no other European country that obliges every single citizen to set up an electronic mailbox to receive official communications from all authorities, including the courts.

What's more, I don't believe that all individuals in Europe can or should be required to use these electronic services. Some people can't, others simply don't want to. Can we really force everyone to be available? The question is broader. When and how should citizens be required to be available electronically? Will I be obliged to check my digital mailbox and even the spam that nobody checks daily? If I go on a meditation retreat for a week, will some procedural timetable collapse? Do we really want to relax on social media and suddenly find a court or tax notice on the screen?[33] This is a

33 Marchal, N., 'El nuevo marco europeo sobre notificación y obtención de pruebas en el extranjero: hacia un espacio judicial europeo digitalizado', *Revista Española de Derecho Internacional*, 74–1, 2022, pp. 155–179, at 174.

sensitive political or constitutional issue that affects the relationship between citizens and the state, and we cannot ignore it.

STADLER: I agree with Eva: Covid has not made these rules obsolete. We already have a strong emphasis on electronic service as the standard mode of service. We are not talking about e-mail, but about a designated electronic information system, as provided for in Rule 74. We have deliberately avoided going into technical detail, as this must remain open to technical developments.

For companies, this is the ordinary way of service. For individuals and consumers, it can become the normal mode if they give their explicit consent. I believe that the consent of natural persons is necessary. Otherwise, the courts will probably use email addresses that are no longer valid or are not regularly checked by the recipient. That would create a lot of uncertainty.[34]

According to Rule 78(1)(c), this may be 'at a post office or at the competent public authority', such as a town hall or police station; what is important is that the addressee knows where to collect them.[35]

In general, the Rules were designed to remain open to further development, a necessary feature of a good model regulation. After all, model rules are not immediately applicable laws. National legislators who wish to reform their service rules are free to make changes and adapt to new developments. Therefore, I do not believe that they are obsolete or outdated.

VILLAMARÍN: I'd make a distinction between the present and the future. Today, electronic service of documents can only be imposed on legal persons; natural persons must have given their consent beforehand – and with due safeguards. Tomorrow, electronic service will probably be made mandatory. But we must focus on the present. And today, whether we are using electronic, postal, or other personal services, flexibility is what matters most. We must avoid the temptation to impose an inflexible protocol that could end up being, *hic et nunc*, inefficient. Even if we will face

---

34 STORSKRUBB, E., 'E-Justice, Innovation and the EU', in HESS, B., KRAMER, X., *From Common Rules to Best Practices in European Civil Procedure*, Baden-Baden: Nomos, 2017, pp. 271–302.

35 For further details, see TSIKRIKAS, D., KENNETT, W., 'Service and Notice of Proceedings', in STADLER, A., SMITH, V., GASCÓN, F. (eds.), *European Rules of Civil Procedure. A Commentary on the ELI/UNIDROIT Model Rules*, Cheltenham: Edward Elgar, 2023, pp. 219–251, at 239.

compulsory electronic service, this system must be fast and secure and must guarantee access to justice and the right of defence.[36]

Vallines: Moreover, because this would freeze the law at some point, planting the seeds of legal obsolescence as soon as further technical developments appear, which we cannot foresee now.

Uzelac: I believe that the future is already here. As I said, in a country as antiquated as Croatia, an electronic signature chip with a simple reading device has been integrated into the judicial environment over the past five years. Whenever there is new documentation or a new movement in a case, I automatically receive a notification via my mobile phone. It also gets to my client's inbox a lot faster than it gets to my lawyer's (an interesting glitch of the system).

We no longer have only one channel of communication. Our world is based on communication redundancy. I wouldn't consider social media platforms like Facebook or Instagram as exclusive channels. Also, I don't think the obligation to notify the process is respected when sending something via Instagram. However, it might be the best way to inform the other party of the receipt of important court documents. This could trigger communication and is the only way to safeguard the right to be heard in the current times.

All this could perhaps have been emphasised more openly in the Rules. In any case, I think we must consider these issues and take them into account when interpreting the Rules; this is not a serious criticism of text itself.

Storskrubb: Whatever medium is used, be it postal or electronic platforms, it is necessary for people or companies to follow the Rules or go to the specified address for the system to work. However, when people are not registered, have multiple addresses, or run fictitious companies, these are the most difficult cases in terms of service. This makes it easier for them to hide as defendants. We need to have more layers. I agree that in the future the formal rules of electronic service may make it harder for people to hide.

36 Marchal, N., 'El nuevo marco europeo sobre notificación y obtención de pruebas en el extranjero: hacia un espacio judicial europeo digitalizado', *Revista Española de Derecho Internacional*, 74-1, 2022, pp. 155–179, p. 168.

Competing means of service will help us to facilitate access to justice.[37] It just needs to be coordinated, organised and formalised if everyone is to be available electronically.

Bibliography

AGUILERA, M., 'El Reglamento UE/2020/1784, sobre notificación y traslado transfronterizo de documentos: novedades e implicaciones internas', *Revista General de Derecho Europeo*, 53, 2022, pp. 1–31.

ANTHIMOS, A., REQUEJO, M. (eds.), *The European Service Regulation. A Commentary*, Cheltenham: Edward Elgar, 2023.

GASCÓN, F., 'Service of Proceedings on the Defendant as a Safeguard of Fairness in Civil Proceedings: In Search of Minimum Standards from EU Legislation and European Case-Law', *Journal of Private International Law*, 13-3, 2017, pp. 475–518.

KRANS, B., NYLUND, A., *Civil Courts Coping with Covid-19*, The Hague: Eleven, 2021.

MARCHAL, N., 'El nuevo marco europeo sobre notificación y obtención de pruebas en el extranjero: hacia un espacio judicial europeo digitalizado', *Revista Española de Derecho Internacional*, 74-1, 2022, pp. 155–179.

SIMONI, A., PAILLI, G., *Study on the Service of Documents. Comparative Legal Analysis of the Relevant Laws and Practices of the Member States. Final Report*, JUST/2014/JCOO/PR/CIVI/0049, European Commission, 2016.

STORSKRUBB, E., 'E-Justice, Innovation and the EU', in HESS, B., KRAMER, X., *From Common Rules to Best Practices in European Civil Procedure*, Baden-Baden: Nomos, 2017, pp. 271–302.

TSIKRIKAS, D., KENNETT, W., 'Service and Notice of Proceedings', in STADLER, A., SMITH, V., GASCÓN, F. (eds.), *European Rules of Civil Procedure. A Commentary on the ELI/UNIDROIT Model Rules*, Cheltenham: Edward Elgar, 2023, pp. 219–251.

---

37 GASCÓN, F., 'Service of Proceedings on the Defendant as a Safeguard of Fairness in Civil Proceedings: In Search of Minimum Standards from EU Legislation and European Case-Law', *Journal of Private International Law*, 13-3, 2017, pp. 475–518, at 517.

CHAPTER 6

Evidence

Marco de Benito, Fernando Gascón, Michele Angelo Lupoi, and Michael Stürner

Evidence occupies a central role in civil procedure as the primary means of establishing facts. A comparative overview reveals a fair degree of variation in terms of the evidentiary powers and responsibilities of judges and parties, the form of the taking of evidence, and the opportunity to obtain information in the control of opposing parties or non-parties.

The Rules propose a precise and consistent regulatory framework for these issues.

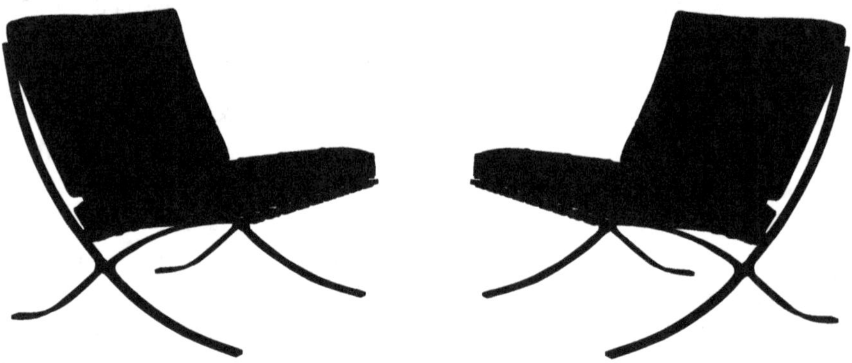

STÜRNER: The first three groups on service, provisional measures, and evidence started work in 2014 and completed their drafts by 2017. Other working groups joined later, as did the 'structure group'. The evidence group[1] was pleased to see its draft incorporated into the Rules.[2]

---

1 Co-reporters: Neil Andrews (England; until September 2016) and Fernando Gascón (Spain). Members: Laura Ervo (Sweden and Finland), Frédérique Ferrand (France), Viktória Harsági (Hungary), and Michael Stürner (Germany).

2 See GASCÓN, F., STÜRNER, M., 'Access to Information and Evidence in the ELI/UNIDROIT European Rules on Civil Procedure: Some Fundamental Aspects', *Uniform Law Review* (*Revue de droit uniforme*), 2019, pp. 14–41.

 | DOI:10.1163/9789004533257_007

GASCÓN: When we started working in 2014, the idea was to build a self-sufficient instrument, which could be used in different contexts if the rest didn't *fly*. Of course, there are some differences between what we presented in 2017 and what we find in the final text.

STÜRNER: Yes, some articles – for example on the burden of proof[3] – were deleted or moved from our draft to the general part. Of course, there is a logic behind this. The law of evidence is particularly complex to harmonise. The task of formulating a *better law* approach, and not just a *restatement*,[4] is difficult because there are so many different approaches to evidence.

GASCÓN: Ultimately, the formulation reflects what a particular group of people felt at a particular time was the *better* approach to address a particular issue.

STÜRNER: As we all know, the integral version of the Rules is composed of articles and commentary: first the article to formulate the norm or standard, and then the commentary to provide a brief background or rationale. Precisely because the project adopted this *better law* approach, rather than a *restatement*, we do not always find comparative remarks in the commentary.

GASCÓN: Fortunately, we had the ALI-UNIDROIT Principles, which we all agreed to take as a starting point.

STÜRNER: It is an excellent text.[5] The first thing we did was to check whether it was still up to date, and for the most part it was.[6] We also referred to instruments such as the IBA Rules on the taking of evidence in international arbitration, and sectoral European instruments such as the Directives on intellectual property rights,[7] competition damages claims,[8] and

3 Rule 25 (1).

4 On this goal, see the Preamble, at para. 8.

5 See STÜRNER, R., 'The Principles of Transnational Civil Procedure: An Introduction to Their Basic Conceptions', *RabelsZ*, 69:2, 2005, pp. 201–254.

6 TROCKER, N., 'From ALI-UNIDROIT Principles to Common European Rules on Access to Information and Evidence? A Preliminary Outlook and Some Suggestions', *Uniform Law Review* (*Revue de droit uniforme*), 19:2, 2014, pp. 239–291.

7 Directive 2004/48/EC of the European Parliament and of the Council of 29 April 2004 on the enforcement of intellectual property rights (IP Enforcement Directive).

8 Directive 2014/104/EU of the European Parliament and of the Council of 26 November 2014 on certain rules governing actions for damages under national law for infringements of

trade secrets.[9] We also consulted the EU small claims procedure,[10] and, finally, the case law of the Court of Justice of the EU and the European Court of Human Rights.

Gascón: With these materials on the table, we quickly put together a rough draft to get started. This draft was pretty comprehensive, with about fifty articles.

Stürner: A few provisions didn't make it into the final text – in the end the chapter comprises forty-two articles –; but the structure was maintained. We divided the chapter into four parts. The first is the general part, quite broad in scope, including provisions on standard of proof;[11] burden of proof; illegally obtained evidence; management of evidence; ways to establish facts such as admission by failure to challenge evidence; evaluation of evidence; sanctions concerning evidence. The second part – the most innovative section – regulates access to evidence orders.[12] The third part is rather classical in content and structure and offers an updated formulation of the discrete means of evidence: documents, witnesses, experts, party examination, judicial inspection. The fourth part deals with the cross-border taking of evidence in a very brief way: it refers to existing normative instruments, as we had a common feeling that we weren't going to reinvent the wheel in this area.

Lupoi: I became acquainted with the Storme Project[13] shortly after graduating, thanks to Federico Carpi. Upon reading the general part of the Rules, which focuses on the most modern procedural principles, such as flexibility,

---

the competition law provisions of the Member States and of the European Union (Competition Damages Directive).

9 Directive (EU) 2016/943 of the European Parliament and of the Council of 8 June 2016 on the protection of undisclosed know-how and business information (trade secrets) against their unlawful acquisition, use and disclosure (Trade Secrets Directive).

10 Regulation (EC) 861/2007 of the European Parliament and of the Council of 11 July 2007 establishing a European Small Claims Procedure, OJ L 199, 31.7.2007, p. 1.

11 See Stürner, M., 'Evaluation of Evidence and Standard of Proof in the ELI/UNIDROIT European Rules of Civil Procedure', in Tichý, L. (ed.), *Standard of Proof in Europe*, Tübingen: Mohr Siebeck, 2019, pp. 273–286.

12 See Gascón, F., Stürner, M., 'Access to Information and Evidence in the ELI/UNIDROIT European Rules on Civil Procedure: Some Fundamental Aspects', *Uniform Law Review (Revue de droit uniforme)*, 2019, pp. 14–41, at 29 ff.

13 Storme, M., *Study on the Approximation of the Laws and Rules of the Member States Concerning Certain Aspects of the Procedure for Civil Litigation* (final report), Dordrecht, 1994.

proportionality, and cooperation, I realised that this long march towards the harmonisation of civil procedure had continued.

In Italy, a new reform of the code of civil procedure entered into force as of 28 February 2023: the so-called Cartabia reform, from the name of the Minister of Justice who has promoted this reform.[14] As the drafts previously circulating led to believe, the reform has very little in common with any of these principles and rules. The procedural models it has introduced have very little flexibility and the new rules make no mention of proportionality or cooperation. It is regrettable that the Italian legislature has not drawn upon the Rules as a source of inspiration. This represents a missed opportunity.

DE BENITO: It's not easy to transfer the Rules, which is such a novel project, to national law, with its own inertias and priorities.

LUPOI: It certainly isn't easy. Take, for example, the court's wide-ranging evidentiary powers. The Rules empower the court to take evidence of its own initiative:

> Rule 25. *Evidence*
>
> (3) In so far as appropriate the court may invite the parties to supplement their offers of evidence. Exceptionally, it may take evidence on its own motion.

Italy has a different approach to this (apart from cases involving minors, where the principle has been codified in the new Article 473 bis.2 CPC). On the other hand, as the commentaries say, the more powers judges have in theory, the less they tend to use them in practice.[15] Therefore, Rule 25 is not really a problem, in my view.

It'd be harder to accept the principle of cooperation and the duty to facilitate access to information and evidence, especially when it could harm the interests of the party. But I'm convinced that the time has come to go beyond the principle that one has the right not to harm oneself, *nemo contra se edere tenetur*.

DE BENITO: Easier said than done. That maxim stems from the natural inclination of the parties or their lawyers to elicit only favourable information.[16]

---

14 *Decreto legislativo* Nº 149 of 10 October 2022.

15 Rule 25, comment 7.

16 DAMAŠKA, M. R., *Evidence Law Adrift*, New Haven: Yale University Press, 1997, p. 145.

LUPOI: Of course. I was recently involved in a project on a protocol for the Bologna Bar Association. We were trying to come up with a principle of clarity for drafting pleadings. I was chatting to a lawyer, and he told me that he has the *right* to draft unclear pleadings if he needs to. Given this stance, it seems that the principle of cooperation is not widely accepted in practice.

That said, the principle of cooperation is moving slowly but surely. Rule 93 provides that if one party does not contest a fact, the other is relieved of the burden of proving it:

> Rule 93. *Admission by a failure to challenge evidence*
>
> The court may take a party's unjustified failure to make a timely response to an opposing party's contention as a sufficient basis for considering that contention to be admitted or accepted. Before doing so the court must inform the party that it is considering drawing such a conclusion concerning the evidence and provide them with an opportunity to respond.

This is a manifestation of the duty of cooperation and is now enshrined also in the Italian code of civil procedure (Article 115 CPC).

DE BENITO: In any event, in the same Rule 93, the judge must inform the silent party that, unless he contests that fact, it will be deemed to be proven. This may appear somewhat paternalistic, but it is in line with Rule 24 on the framing of the disputed facts:

> Rule 24. *Facts*
>
> (1) The parties must put forward such facts as support their claim or defence. The court may invite the parties to clarify or supplement these facts.

LUPOI: The principle of cooperation and the court's duty to supervise the behaviour of the parties (Rule 4, on 'the general case management duty') inevitably has an element of paternalism.

DE BENITO: It also affects the burden of pleading and proof, where the boundaries between procedural and substantive law tend to become less obvious.[17]

---

17 See CALVINHO, G., *Carga de la prueba*, Buenos Aires: Astrea, 2016, pp. 8–10, 76–80, *passim*.

LUPOI: It is, of course, less obvious than in other areas and judicial mechanisms. There is a long-standing debate between jurisdictions as to whether certain elements are procedural or substantive. Do the Rules resolve this long-standing debate? Yes and no. On the one hand, according to Rule 25(1), '*substantive* law determines the burden of proof'. On the other, according to Rule 88(2), 'the existence of facts can be presumed on the basis of other proven facts': what in Italian law we would call a judicial and therefore *procedural* presumption. Although this is not necessarily problematic, one may ask: is this presumption mechanism always allowed, or are there limits? Under Italian law, for example, presumptions are left to the judge's *procedural* prudence unless expressly established by *substantive* law.[18]

GASCÓN: I wouldn't be too worried about these subtleties in the context of the Rules. As for presumptions, we included that reference in Article 88(2) just for the record, as a procedural tool that exists in many countries and contributes to a good and efficient procedural system.

LUPOI: Another example is the lack of definition of the notion of confidential information (Rule 103). This prompts the question of whether it will be governed by the *lex fori*, as a procedural matter, or by the substantive law governing the legal relationship.

GASCÓN: It really depends on how you understand the very notion of privilege. If you come from a common law culture where privilege represents someone's right not to do something, this is a more substantive perspective: it is the role of the legal relationship. By contrast, if you have a view of privilege as a means of making evidence inadmissible, then you have a procedural view. From that point of view, you would use the *lex fori* to deal with the nature of privilege. This is a very difficult thing to deal with and it would have been very difficult to find the common ground to propose a set of rules that would be universally acceptable.

LUPOI: Another area that I assume will end up being governed by substantive law is the 'admissibility' of witness testimony referred to by Rule 114. Should we assess that admissibility according to the law governing the merits? The Rules don't resolve this dilemma. The same is true of Rule 98, which stipulates that 'the court will freely evaluate evidence'. This principle of free assessment may be limited because certain means of evidence, such as public documents, are given full probative force – *plena probatio* – and

18 *Codice civile*, Art. 2729; Italian CPC, Art. 116.

the judge is bound by them. That said, the interesting question is whether Rule 98 eliminates the full probative force of certain means of evidence. I haven't seen an exception in other provisions of the Rules. Rule 112, which refers to 'authentic documents', seems to be more descriptive than prescriptive in terms of the assessment of evidence.

GASCÓN: In the working group we agreed that the free assessment of evidence shouldn't be an obstacle for a judge to give full probative value to a public document. The mere fact of having the free assessment rule shouldn't cause any problems with such evidence, which has traditionally been considered to have probative value in some countries. The idea was that the category of full probative value could be dangerous – we do not know what the future will bring in the field of evidence and fraud around documents – and we weren't entirely comfortable with including an express rule in that regard.

DE BENITO: Privilege, burden of proof, presumptions, admissibility, free assessment of evidence, legal force of public documents, inferences to be drawn from certain types of evidence (such as the examination of a party): all these complexities reveal different conceptions of what is substantive and what is procedural in each different culture or legal system. The Rules cannot yet function as a completely autonomous instrument; they are designed to operate in a particular context, and a common context doesn't yet exist.[19]

The same applies to the rules on access to evidence: what the Americans call, in the context of the production of documents, discovery.

STÜRNER: In the working group, we used to refer to discovery as 'that which must not be named', because it was quite clear that we could not use anything that even came close to discovery. We had to come up with our own European approach to this sensitive issue.

GASCÓN: We recognised that, in any modern evidentiary system, parties should be entitled to access relevant information that they do not have in their possession, but which may support their claims or affirmative defences, with the problem of information asymmetry that this situation entails.

---

19 See JOLOWICZ, J. A., *On Civil Procedure*, Cambridge: Cambridge University Press, 2000, pp. 205–221.

STÜRNER: Of course, in wanting to help a party gather information, there is also the risk – which has been described many times of so-called US-style discovery – of *fishing expeditions* in search of a lot of unnecessary information to prepare a lawsuit – or to force unfair negotiations and settlements.

GASCÓN: Our concern about that led us to what we call 'access to evidence orders' or 'orders to secure access to evidence', which are different names for the same reality, depending on the context and sometimes just to avoid being repetitive. In either format, you can read about it in Rules 100 to 110. Here we focus on conveying the idea that these measures are under strict judicial control, so it's not just a lawyer's plan, but something that is always supervised by a judge. And, of course, judges will decide based on strict proportionality. This concept is reinforced by the protection of confidentiality, and by a regime of severe sanctions in case of non-compliance with what the judge has established. Fundamentally, the idea was that US-style disclosure of evidence plays too much into the hands of lawyers. We want European disclosure to be much more in the hands of the judges. This I'd say is the main idea.

STÜRNER: We also wanted to convey another message. There is a tradition in many European cultures, as Michele pointed out in relation to Italy and the *nemo contra se edere tenetur* adagio, that a party is not expected to help his opponent by providing information and evidence, also in a civil and not only in a criminal context.[20]

GASCÓN: Of course. In Rule 25(2) we stated explicitly that 'it is not a basis of objection to such disclosure by a party that disclosure may favour the opponent or other parties'. We wished to make it clear that, under the regime proposed by the Rules, there is a duty, if the court so requests, to share information and sources of evidence with your opponent, present or even future.

DE BENITO: The very idea that you can force your opponent to help you find evidence in your favour is culturally sensitive; a cultural aspect that is, after all, another integral part of a legal system, along with substantive law or judicial organisation. I see that you have taken a firm stand on which is the *better law* on this point.

---

20 See Rule 25, comment 5.

GASCÓN: It necessarily derives, in my view, from the whole system of the Rules and the cooperative model that underpins them.

DE BENITO: These orders can be applied for even in relation to future opponents, to proceedings not yet commenced.

GASCÓN: Under the Rules, individuals and companies can ask a court to grant them access to evidence not only from someone who is or will clearly be a party, but also against non-parties or public authorities. You may find that many cases – especially collective cases involving legal areas under the strict regulatory power of public authorities – involve relevant documents and information held by those public regulators.

DE BENITO: Always with the burden of commencing the relevant proceedings 'within a specified, reasonable period of time', as provided for in Rule 106(2).

GASCÓN: Otherwise, as we can read in the same provision, the court may set aside the order, order the applicant to return the information thus obtained, and even impose a sanction on the non-complying party. However, each case is different: sometimes the result of one of these measures is that the potential claimant decides not to file a claim. In these cases, access to evidence orders can also have a deterrent effect.

DE BENITO: Tell us more about the procedure for applying for an access to evidence order. I have seen a lot of overlap with the provisional and precautionary measures regime.

GASCÓN: Both share many features. These orders are always at the request of the party. And they can generally only be granted after hearing the other party or a third party, although the door is open to granting the order *inaudita parte*, without hearing the other party, who will always be heard afterwards.

We also discussed whether these procedures should be done in writing or orally. In the end, we proposed that they should normally be in writing, except in specific cases. On this, the general rules on case management would have to be applied.

Our focus was to ensure that it was neither too difficult nor too easy to obtain an order. The party seeking an order will have to demonstrate a strong *prima facie* case, what in Spain and other countries we call *fumus boni juris* – as you point out, the same standard as for obtaining interim measures. What is particular to these orders is the need to be specific. We wanted to avoid *fishing expeditions*. The court cannot accede to any request that involves a great deal of speculation or an unjustifiably broad search for information, a concern that appears repeatedly in Rules 100 and 102.

DE BENITO: These, in turn, are indeterminate concepts. Can we say that virtue lies in the middle ground?

GASCÓN: An application may not be completely specific, but it certainly cannot be vague or speculative: yes, a middle ground. The court will have to address the issue with a necessity test, a subsidiarity test, and a proportionality test. The order will not be granted unless the judge finds that the evidence itself is necessary, or that you have no other means of accessing that information or source of evidence unless the court helps you. And, of course, they will not help you if the nature and quantity of the evidence that is the subject of the application is not reasonable and proportionate in a particular case.

Once the order has been issued, the party to whom it is addressed must comply with it, and the court is free to decide on the concrete means: it depends on the information to be provided and the type of source of evidence to be disclosed. Serious sanctions are provided for in case of noncompliance and in case of destruction or concealment of evidence. You must take it seriously.

DE BENITO: However, there may be situations where a party refuses to provide certain information because it considers it to be privileged, confidential, or sensitive for some other reason.

GASCÓN: The idea of proportionality is key in such cases. The court may decide that, in the interests of one party's access to justice, information should remain confidential. Or that the other party must provide information or sources of evidence that should normally remain confidential. Where this is the case, of course, specific measures will have to be put in place to protect confidentiality. There are some suggestions as to what could be done: closed hearings, or the use of access to information experts. In addition, there would be very severe sanctions for breaches of confidentiality.

DE BENITO: You mention experts. Indeed, the evidence that can be accessed is not limited to documents. Would it be possible to use this rule exceptionally regarding witnesses, for example?

GASCÓN: I don't think there is any problem in using these tools to find out who is a witness in a case. It is about 'information'. When information is collected, it is sometimes inseparable from the source of evidence.

DE BENITO: Imagine a US-trained lawyer living in Europe opening the Rules for guidance. Wouldn't he be inclined to see this section as an invitation to ask for a pre-trial deposition, an interview with potential witnesses – and then see if he wants to call them as witnesses or not? Isn't this possibility within the scope of the chapter?

GASCÓN: Possibly. But the court would have to give that order to the prospective or third party. And, of course, it would have to strike a balance between disturbing someone by subpoenaing them to testify and their duty to cooperate in the proper administration of justice. In most legal systems, witnesses – if that is what they really are – have a duty to cooperate. And this means, of course, giving evidence. I would not see too much of a problem with that.

STÜRNER: We could see these novel developments in the context of arbitration, which is more flexible and, above all, allows for a more thorough and comprehensive operation of the evidence.

DE BENITO: Indeed, I have begun to see the Rules as a guide for counsel and arbitrators; whenever I have raised them in arbitration, they have always been well received. Counsel and arbitral tribunals are constantly faced with the challenge of filling in the gaps in the applicable procedural rules, which are often cautious and overlapping. They are often forced to rely on general procedural rules.[21] Probably for this reason, arbitral communities are immersed in a kind of para-legislative apparatus from which they draw ideas, principles and rules: a contest of soft law of all kinds, conflicting and converging on a particular point.[22]

21 See PETROCHILOS, G., *Procedural Law in International Arbitration*, Oxford: Oxford University Press, 2004, pp. 174–176, 214–223.

22 See PARK, W. W., 'The Procedural Soft Law of International Arbitration', in MISTELIS, L. A., LEW, J. D. M. (eds.), *Pervasive Problems in International Arbitration*,

From this point of view, very few of these soft law instruments have the depth of knowledge that the Rules have. Some of the chapters – appeals or collective proceedings – will not, in principle, be widely used in arbitration. But others can effectively fill a gap or ratify a particular solution. I'm thinking, for example, of the parties. In arbitration, there is no *procedural* regulation of parties: capacity to be a party, litigation capacity, voluntary or necessary joinder, intervention. This would be an area where the Rules could fill a gap. Another example would be provisional and protective measures, where I see a particularly bright future for the Rules: aims, requirements, criteria, procedure… And especially the area we are dealing with today: means of evidence and access to information. The IBA Rules on the taking of evidence in international arbitration are well known, but are deliberately vague in certain respects.[23] The Prague Rules also fall short in this respect. Certainly, the Rules provide the most ambitious rules on access to information and evidence to be found as a guide in arbitration.

I agree with you, Michael: arbitration will be the first and perhaps the best place to test the Rules.

STÜRNER: The IBA Rules look like a kind of manual, a step-by-step guide to proceed. They are not very systematic, whereas our Rules are quite systematic and significantly more complex. However, this virtue can also be a drawback: precisely because of their complexity, lawyers and arbitrators may be reluctant to adopt these Rules: they are open waters.[24]

DE BENITO: I agree that it may be difficult to adopt the Rules for a particular proceeding where all parties have to agree. But I can well imagine a

Alphen aan den Rijn: Kluwer, 2006, pp. 141–154; KAUFMANN-KOHLER, G., 'Soft Law in International Arbitration: Codification and Normativity', *Journal of International Dispute Settlement*, 1:2, 2010, pp. 1–17; NEWMAN, L. W., RADINE, M. J. (eds.), *Soft Law in International Arbitration*, Huntington: Juris, 2014; FAVALLI, D. (ed.), *The Sense and Non-Sense of Guidelines, Rules and other Para-Regulatory Texts in International Arbitration*, Huntington: Juris, 2015; FERNÁNDEZ ARROYO, D. P., 'Soft Law and Arbitral Procedure: A Conditioned but Inescapable Couple', *European International Arbitration Review*, 7:2, 2018, pp. 71–86.

23 See ROJAS, J. A., 'La prueba en el arbitraje. Interpretación de las Reglas IBA en el arbitraje internacional', in IIDP-IAPL, *La prueba en el proceso / Evidence in the Process*, Barcelona: Atelier, 2018, pp. 583–594.

24 On the possible impact of the Rules, see STÜRNER, M., 'The ELI/UNIDROIT European Rules of Civil Procedure: Access to Information and Evidence', in GASCÓN, F., HESS, B. (eds.), *The Future of the European Law of Civil Procedure – Coordination or Harmonisation?*, Antwerp: Intersentia, 2020, pp. 205–222, at 217 ff.

party arguing that it needs access to documents or premises and raising the Rules as a point of reference in the process of persuasion. Without formally adopting the Rules, we can all use them as authoritative material in a persuasive effort to support a particular request. If an issue merits it, and the key to a procedural argument lies in the Rules, learned lawyers will raise them, and judges and arbitrators may well be receptive to them. This can be done at any time; and not just by young professionals, but by any conscientious professional who really wants to win an argument.

GASCÓN: Think of the Principles of European Contract Law (PECL) or the Draft Common Frame of Reference (DCFR): lawyers increasingly use them when the case requires and deserves it; and when lawyers use them, judges use them. Only this process takes time.

LUPOI: With the same flexibility, some jurisdictions are starting to use so-called procedural agreements, in which the parties agree in some way on how to conduct the proceedings. In Italy we do not have anything similar. But would it be feasible to envisage a future in which the parties could agree, for example, to regulate evidence in their proceedings in accordance with the Rules?

GASCÓN: If you address this question to our Brazilian colleagues, they will probably say: of course, why not? You can make a procedural contract by reference. However, the main question would be: would such a reference not clash with the rest of the Rules according to which the whole procedure must be conducted, and of which the evidence section is an integral and inseparable part?

DE BENITO: To begin with, consider the court's responsibility for case management, which is highlighted in Rule 4 and *passim*. For example, under Rule 50(2), 'if the parties agree on a case management measure the court shall not determine differently *without good reason*'. This means, *a contrario sensu*, that the court can and should determine otherwise if the circumstances warrant it. The court's responsibility is too deeply rooted in the litigation model articulated by the Rules.

LUPOI: In many jurisdictions, however, it is possible for the parties to agree to shift the burden of proof by limiting the use of certain evidence.

GASCÓN: As long as they don't interfere with the judge's powers directly. If the parties shift the burden of proof and consider that some evidence is not admissible, it is likely that the judge's powers are being encroached upon.

Bibliography

CALVINHO, G., *Carga de la prueba*, Buenos Aires: Astrea, 2016, pp. 8–10, 76–80, *passim*.

DAMAŠKA, M. R., *Evidence Law Adrift*, New Haven: Yale University Press, 1997, p. 145.

FAVALLI, D. (ed.), *The Sense and Non-Sense of Guidelines, Rules and other Para-Regulatory Texts in International Arbitration*, Huntington: Juris, 2015.

FERNÁNDEZ ARROYO, D. P., 'Soft Law and Arbitral Procedure: A Conditioned but Inescapable Couple', *European International Arbitration Review*, 7:2, 2018, pp. 71–86.

GASCÓN, F., STÜRNER, M., 'Access to Information and Evidence in the ELI/UNIDROIT European Rules on Civil Procedure: Some Fundamental Aspects', *Uniform Law Review (Revue de droit uniforme)*, 2019, pp. 14–41.

JOLOWICZ, J. A., *On Civil Procedure*, Cambridge: Cambridge University Press, 2000, pp. 205–221.

KAUFMANN-KOHLER, G., 'Soft Law in International Arbitration: Codification and Normativity', *Journal of International Dispute Settlement*, 1:2, 2010, pp. 1–17.

NEWMAN, L. W., RADINE, M. J. (eds.), *Soft Law in International Arbitration*, Huntington: Juris, 2014.

PARK, W. W., 'The Procedural Soft Law of International Arbitration', in MISTELIS, L. A., LEW, J. D. M. (eds.), *Pervasive Problems in International Arbitration*, Alphen aan den Rijn: Kluwer, 2006, pp. 141–154.

PETROCHILOS, G., *Procedural Law in International Arbitration*, Oxford: Oxford University Press, 2004, pp. 174–176, 214–223.

ROJAS, J. A., 'La prueba en el arbitraje. Interpretación de las Reglas IBA en el arbitraje internacional', in IIDP-IAPL, *La prueba en el proceso / Evidence in the Process*, Barcelona: Atelier, 2018, pp. 583–594.

STORME, M., *Study on the Approximation of the Laws and Rules of the Member States Concerning Certain Aspects of the Procedure for Civil Litigation* (final report), Dordrecht, 1994.

STÜRNER, M., 'Evaluation of Evidence and Standard of Proof in the ELI/UNIDROIT European Rules of Civil Procedure', in TICHÝ, L. (ed.), *Standard of Proof in Europe*, Tübingen: Mohr Siebeck, 2019, pp. 273–286.

Stürner, M., 'The ELI/UNIDROIT European Rules of Civil Procedure: Access to Information and Evidence', in Gascón, F., Hess, B. (eds.), *The Future of the European Law of Civil Procedure – Coordination or Harmonisation?*, Antwerp: Intersentia, 2020, pp. 205–222.

Stürner, R., 'The Principles of Transnational Civil Procedure: An Introduction to Their Basic Conceptions', *RabelsZ*, 69:2, 2005, pp. 201–254.

Trocker, N., 'From ALI-UNIDROIT Principles to Common European Rules on Access to Information and Evidence? A Preliminary Outlook and Some Suggestions', *Uniform Law Review* (*Revue de droit uniforme*), 19:2, 2014, pp. 239–291.

CHAPTER 7

Provisional and Protective Measures

Marco de Benito, Javier Gilsanz, Fernando de la Mata[†], *and Jaime Vegas*

The Rules would have been incomplete without a chapter on provisional measures. Comparative research shows the lack of uniformity: while some jurisdictions provide a detailed regulation, others leave it to the courts to develop this field on a case-by-case basis.

The main obstacle that legislators face in regulating provisional measures is the difficulty of establishing common standards and requirements. The aim and content of each provisional measure, as well as its proportionality, depend on the characteristics of a particular category of dispute and often simply on the facts of the case. Disputes relating to contract law, competition law, intellectual property or data protection require different solutions. There is therefore always a risk of falling into one of two extremes: either making the regulation too general or developing a set of discrete and probably redundant measures that lack the desired coherence. The Rules have sought to establish useful standards without going into excessive generalisation or detail.

 | DOI:10.1163/9789004533257_008

DE LA MATA: Our working group went through two phases. The first involved two speakers representing two different points of view: Gilles Cuniberti, professor of private international law at the University of Luxembourg, and Neil Andrews, professor of procedural law at the University of Cambridge. For different reasons, Neil and Gilles didn't participate in the second phase of the working group. They passed the baton to a new team led by Xandra Kramer, and new members were added. A few of us had been involved from the outset and therefore provided some continuity to the group.

The first question we had to address was whether to adopt the ALI-UNIDROIT Principles of Transnational Civil Procedure as a starting point, closely following their structure and content, or to create a new set of rules that would appear more distinctly European. Both approaches are valid, of course. In the end, as did other working groups, we decided to rely on the ALI-UNIDROIT Principles. In our case, the relevant provision was Principle 8:

> 8. *Provisional and protective measures*
>
> 8.1 The court may grant provisional relief when necessary to preserve the ability to grant effective relief by final judgment or to maintain or otherwise regulate the status quo. Provisional measures are governed by the principle of proportionality.
>
> 8.2 A court may order provisional relief without notice only upon urgent necessity and preponderance of considerations of fairness. The applicant must fully disclose facts and legal issues of which the court properly should be aware. A person against whom *ex parte* relief is directed must have the opportunity at the earliest practicable time to respond concerning the appropriateness of the relief.
>
> 8.3 An applicant for provisional relief should ordinarily be liable for compensation of a person against whom the relief is issued if the court thereafter determines that the relief should not have been granted. In appropriate circumstances, the court must require the applicant for provisional relief to post a bond or formally to assume a duty of compensation.

As we can see, this Principle includes three basic standards: on function and proportionality (8.1); on without-notice measures (8.2); and on damages and security (8.3).

The group then considered the various and diverse national approaches to the issue in Europe. Furthermore, the European Account Preservation Order Regulation,[1] the Intellectual Property Directive,[2] and the case law on the subject in relation to Brussels I Regulation before and after its recast[3] were examined in detail. Finally, we consulted soft law sources, including the UNCITRAL Model Law on International Commercial Arbitration,[4] the Helsinki Principles,[5] and, finally, the Storme Report.[6]

GILSANZ: Most of those sources are easy to identify and manage. National regimes are probably the exception. European regimes may be more diverse than we think.

DE LA MATA: I was surprised by the diversity of approaches. Provisional measures that are common in one country are considered unacceptable in another. European jurisdictions even differ on what provisional measures are, on how to define and conceptualise them. And we were all aware that our answers to these questions would determine the outcome. In this context, we held a meeting at the Max Planck Institute in Luxembourg, where Gilles Cuniberti led the discussion, explaining and ultimately convincing us that the only viable approach, the only one that would allow us to move forward in a neutral or aseptic way, was a strictly functional one. The consensus we reached on this approach, and our sincere desire to maintain it in subsequent discussions, helped us to avoid many problems.

---

1 Regulation (EU) 655/2014 of the European Parliament and of the Council of 15 May 2014 establishing a European Account Preservation Order procedure to facilitate cross-border debt recovery in civil and commercial matters.

2 Directive 2001/29/EC of the European Parliament and of the Council of 22 May 2001 on the harmonisation of certain aspects of copyright and related rights in the information society.

3 Council Regulation (EC) № 44/2001 of 22 December 2000 on jurisdiction and the recognition and enforcement of judgments in civil and commercial matters; Regulation (EU) 1215/2012 of the European Parliament and of the Council of 12 December 2012 on jurisdiction and the recognition and enforcement of judgments in civil and commercial matters (recast).

4 UNCITRAL Model Law on International Commercial Arbitration, adopted on 21 June 1985 and amended on 7 July 2006 (Arts. 17 to 17G).

5 Principles on provisional and protective measures, adopted by the International Law Association (ILA) in Helsinki in 1996.

6 STORME, M., *Study on the Approximation of the Laws and Rules of the Member States Concerning Certain Aspects of the Procedure for Civil Litigation* (final report), Dordrecht, 1994, Art. 10.

GILSANZ: The functional approach is evident from the designation that you chose, 'provisional and protective measures'.

DE LA MATA: We adhered to an almost venerable tradition, as it had already been established in the Brussels Convention 1968 as 'provisional, including protective, measures'.[7] In my opinion, the term does not refer to two clearly defined concepts, namely provisional measures on the one hand and protective measures on the other. Rather, it is generic and all-encompassing.[8]

GILSANZ: I suppose that the same approach explains the broad and merely descriptive definition of what these measures are in Rule 184:

> Rule 184. *Provisional and protective measures*
>
> (1) A provisional or protective measure is any temporary order that has one or more of the following functions:
>
> (a) to ensure or promote effective enforcement of final decisions concerning the substance of the proceedings, whether or not the underlying claim is pecuniary, including securing assets and obtaining or preserving information concerning a debtor and his assets; or
>
> (b) to preserve the opportunity for a complete and satisfactory determination of the proceedings, including securing evidence relevant to the merits or preventing its destruction or concealment; or
>
> (c) to preserve the existence and value of goods or other assets which form or will form the subject-matter of proceedings (pending or otherwise); or
>
> (d) to prevent harm from being suffered, to prevent further harm, or to regulate disputed issues, pending final judgment.

---

7 Brussels Convention on jurisdiction and the enforcement of judgments in civil and commercial matters, signed on 27 September 1968. Section 9. *Provisional, including protective, measures.* Art. 24. Application may be made to the courts of a Contracting State for such provisional, including protective, measures as may be available under the law of that State, even if, under this Convention, the courts of another Contracting State have jurisdiction as to the substance of the matter.

8 DE BENITO, M., 'Las medidas cautelares en las Reglas europeas de proceso civil', in GARCÍA MARRERO, J. (coord.), *Medidas cautelares y diligencias preliminares*, Cizur Menor: Aranzadi, 2021, pp. 691–710, at 695.

DE LA MATA: The distinguishing feature here is the temporary nature of the measures.[9] The provision begins by defining a provisional or protective measure as 'any temporary order' that – by way of predicate or specification only – 'has one or more of the following functions'. These functions are descriptive, but this doesn't mean that the enumeration was easy. On the contrary, we devoted several meetings and conferences to this single provision. Only once we had agreed on Rule 184 were we able to proceed with the rest of the project.

GILSANZ: What was the next challenge you faced?

DE LA MATA: The very understanding of how the four functions could work in practice!

The first function, safeguarding the possibility of an effective enforcement of the decision that may be rendered in the principal proceeding, didn't present difficulties; at least to me as a Spanish lawyer, as this is the primary function of provisional measures in Spanish law.[10] However, when we came to the clause that says 'including securing assets and obtaining or preserving information concerning a debtor and his assets', certain questions arose. What kind of information are we 'obtaining or preserving'? The fact that the debt may or may not be monetary, doesn't it overly broaden the types of situations in which the information thus 'obtained' may be made accessible to the counterparty?

The second function, the preservation of evidence that may be relevant in the main proceedings, is completely out of place in the way we systematise things in Spain, where this is only a necessary function of a comprehensive regulation of evidence rather than a 'provisional measure' as such. But apart from that, it's a fairly straightforward provision. That is not to say that there was no lively debate. For example, we had an intense debate about whether an *ante causam*, pre-commencement applicant should be obliged to commence proceedings within a certain period of time, particularly in relation to this possibility of securing evidence.

The third function, preserving the assets at issue in the main proceedings, may seem to be subsumed by the first function, ensuring effective enforcement, almost like a subtype serving the same purpose. What does

9 DE BENITO, M., 'Las medidas cautelares en las Reglas europeas de proceso civil', in GARCÍA MARRERO, J. (coord.), *Medidas cautelares y diligencias preliminares*, Cizur Menor: Aranzadi, 2021, pp. 691–710, at 695.

10 LEC, Art. 726.1, 1.ª

the third function add? And why do we find 'pending or otherwise' in brackets at the end? Just to include pre-commencement applications? Isn't this covered by the previous phrase 'which form or will form the subject-matter of proceedings'?

The fourth function has two sub-functions. The first sub-function, which we can call anticipatory, is to prevent harm by anticipating the content of what is sought in the main proceeding, which makes it possible to obtain provisionally what would be obtained definitively with a favourable judgment; for example, the cessation of anticompetitive conduct, the supply of goods or services, the facilitation of access to premises or even interim payments. The second sub-function, which we can call regulatory, consists in regulating the issues at stake by ordering the parties to do or not to do something to maintain things in a certain *statu quo*.

GILSANZ: This might raise some questions from the point of view of the suitability or appropriateness of the measure, which is introduced just after the above enumeration of purposes:

> Rule 184. *Provisional and protective measures*
>
> (2) A provisional or protective measure ordered should be suitable for its purpose.

DE LA MATA: This provision is certainly broad in its scope and doesn't provide any guidance on how to assess the connection that must exist between the relief sought in the main proceeding and the content of the specific measure sought. The suitability requirement is merely stated, not regulated.

GILSANZ: This brings us to another traditional feature of provisional remedies: instrumentality. Provisional remedies are a means to an end, never an end in themselves. This requirement of instrumentality is manifested, *inter alia*, in Rule 188(2): if proceedings are not instituted after a measure has been sought and obtained *ante causam*, before the commencement of the proceedings, it 'shall lapse'.

DE LA MATA: The temporary nature of these measures is an inherent aspect of their instrumentality. To remain in place, they require the existence of a main proceeding, whether current or future. Therefore, not only 'shall' the measures 'lapse' if proceedings are not initiated, but also when a final judgment is rendered in the main proceeding. This 'lapse' means that the measure will not be specifically lifted by the court but will cease being effective automatically. Naturally, the court can subsequently confirm, either on its own initiative or at the request of a party, that the measure has indeed 'lapsed' and is no longer in force.[11]

GILSANZ: Among several measures that are equally suitable and effective, the one that is least burdensome or harmful to the other party must be chosen: this is the requirement of proportionality.

> Rule 185. *Proportionality of provisional and protective measures*
>
> (1) A provisional and protective measure should impose the least burden on the respondent.
>
> (2) The court must ensure that the measure's effects are not disproportionate to the interests it is asked to protect.

DE LA MATA: One expression of this is the possibility given to the respondent in Rule 187(1) to offer appropriate security – even in the form of a formal undertaking, as the official commentary makes clear –[12] in lieu of the measure requested or already granted. And the same idea, together with the essential variability of the measures – always adopted *rebus sic stantibus* – is reflected in Rule 189, which allows the defendant to request the court to modify, suspend or revoke them if circumstances change.

But what I find most interesting in this provision is paragraph 2, which links this requirement to the idea of proportionality. In a way, the requirement to prefer the least burdensome measure is presented as a particular manifestation of the principle of proportionality, which is generally enshrined in Rules 5(1) and 6.

GILSANZ: I am also struck by the fact that the requirement for security from the applicant appears to be at the discretion of the judge, which means that it may not be required at all:

---

11 DE BENITO, M., 'Las medidas cautelares en las Reglas europeas de proceso civil', in GARCÍA MARRERO, J. (coord.), *Medidas cautelares y diligencias preliminares*, Cizur Menor: Aranzadi, 2021, pp. 691–710, at 708.

12 Rule 187, comment 1.

> Rule 187. *Security*
>
> (2) As a condition of granting or continuing a provisional or protective measure the applicant may, depending on the circumstances, be required to provide appropriate security.

This recalls injunctive relief in US civil procedure, a subject on which I wrote my doctoral thesis.[13] According to the American Federal Rules of Civil Procedure, there the judge can exercise considerable discretion to moderate or even waive security.[14] And not only depending on the applicant's lack of financial means, but also on what is called the 'balance of hardships' – whether the adoption of the measure may lead to an 'injustice' –, which also points to an idea of proportionality.[15]

As in the US, surely this relativisation of the security requirement is tempered by the objective responsibility to which applicants are subject in accordance with Rule 190:

> Rule 190. *Applicant liability*
>
> (1) If a provisional or protective measure is set aside, lapses, or if the proceedings are dismissed on procedural grounds or on their merits, the applicant must compensate the respondent for such loss or damage caused by the measure.

DE LA MATA: I like this provision because it encourages us to be careful and rigorous about the question of damages. We should consider security, as many arbitral tribunals do, as a kind of provisional or protective measure. Parties suffering from the measure argue that if the measure is subsequently revoked, the claimant will not have the means to adequately compensate for the damage suffered. Courts, on the other hand, tend to treat the guarantee as automatic and apply rules of thumb to determine its amount. Rarely is there a rigorous analysis of what the damages might be while the case is pending. Expert testimony would be required to determine the heads and figures of damages with any degree of accuracy, and this is rarely provided at the outset.

---

13 GILSANZ, J., *El proceso civil estadounidense. La tutela judicial cautelar*, Cizur Menor: Aranzadi, 2010.

14 See Rule 65 of the American Federal Rules of Civil Procedure.

15 See GILSANZ, J., *El proceso civil estadounidense. La tutela judicial cautelar*, Cizur Menor: Aranzadi, 2010, pp. 114 ff.

GILSANZ: If I may be permitted a brief foray into the first article of the special part, I'd also like to mention Rule 192, which distinguishes between classic attachments of property – with or without a duty of custody – and asset restraining orders which simply prevent the defendant from disposing of his property. The former, to which we are more used to in Spain, is a decision *in rem*, whereas the latter, known in common law jurisdictions as a Mareva injunction or a freezing order, is what they call *in personam*.[16] Even US lawyers are realising the many problems posed by this type of personal orders. Following the Grupo Mexicano de Desarrollo, S.A. v. Alliance Bond Fund, Inc. case before the Supreme Court,[17] Rule 65 of the Federal Rules of Civil Procedure, on injunctions and restraining orders, tightened the requirements so that, in cases where the main proceeding involves a monetary claim, it is no longer possible to obtain an *in personam* order to preserve the defendant's assets. The US seems to be moving slowly towards *in rem* attachments, while the EU is opening the door to *in personam* orders.

The idea of cooperation that is ingrained in the Rules' litigation model, and which gives us even a pale reflection of the vigorous enforcement of contempt of court that exists in England and common law countries in general, probably has a lot to do with this.

DE LA MATA: In common law countries, as far as I know, the instruments to ensure the effectiveness of provisional measures go far beyond economic sanctions.

GILSANZ: Indeed, in states such as New York, non-compliance can even lead to imprisonment.[18] Thus, there are many more powerful elements that are brought to bear through the contempt of court order to ensure compliance with the injunction.[19]

DE LA MATA: I wonder whether we have the mechanisms to ensure that these *in personam* measures are complied with.

---

16 See NEWMAN, L. W., BURROWS, M., *The Practice of International Litigation*, Huntington: Juris, 2013, part II, pp. 13–20.

17 527 US 308 (1999), available at https://www.oyez.org/cases/1998/98-231.

18 See SIEGEL, D. D., CONNORS, P. M., *New York Practice. Injunction*, Eagan: West, 2022, pp. 596–606.

19 See FISS, O., RENDLEMAN, D., *Injunctions*, Eagan: Foundation Press, 1984, pp. 889–940.

VEGAS: There are some measures in place, such as orders to provisionally cease in or refrain from an activity.[20] These might take the form of a *prohibición de disponer*, a prohibition to dispose, an old institution that is foreseen in our civil code.[21] However, this is sanctioned only with nullity of the transaction,[22] hence specific additional sanctions must be established for such a measure to work effectively.

In any case, it would be difficult to justify in Spain why this seemingly more invasive and, in principle, less effective measure of indirect sanctions should be chosen instead of simply seizing the assets and leaving the person alone. Legal culture would make its voice heard in such a delicate situation. The demand for the least burdensome measure would do the rest to lift such a measure.

GILSANZ: I've also noted other aspects of the Rules' regime of provisional measures that do not necessarily fit within the scope of provisional measures in Spain. Jaime, you were part of the legal team that, under the direction of Andrés DE LA OLIVA, was involved in the drafting of the Spanish civil procedure law 2000. What are your views on the ELI-UNIDROIT Rules from this comparative perspective?

VEGAS: The civil procedure law 2000 replaced the civil procedure law 1881, which had become outdated and required modernisation. Indeed, the Law was already outdated from its inception; it was born old, as it were. The Law was based on the old *solemnis ordo judiciorum*, which served as the prototype for Romano-canonical procedure. Consequently, it appeared to be more oriented towards the past than the future.[23]

The Law did not even mention provisional measures, let alone regulate them. Some measures that are now understood as provisional were introduced later, but in an uncertain, fragmented, and even discordant manner regarding pre-commencement measures, requirements, and so forth.

20 LEC, Art. 727, 7.ª

21 *Código civil*, Art. 785.2.

22 *Código civil*, Art. 6.3.

23 See generally DE LA OLIVA, A., 'Sobre la Ley 1/2000, de 7 de enero, de Enjuiciamiento Civil. Criterios inspiradores e innovaciones principales', in *Tribunales de justicia*, 2-2000, pp. 127–142; see also VEGAS, J., 'La reforma procesal civil española: criterios inspiradores y principales innovaciones de la Ley de Enjuiciamiento Civil de 2000', in DE LA OLIVA, A., PALOMO, D. (coords.), *Proceso civil. Hacia una nueva Justicia civil*, Santiago de Chile: Editorial Jurídica de Chile, 2007, pp. 1–21.

Consequently, it was possible to apply for the same measure under different regimes.[24]

The first step was to explicitly acknowledge provisional measures as one of three types of judicial measures mentioned on the opening page of the law. These three types can be further delineated as follows: firstly, declaratory relief, which encompasses three sub-types: mere declarations, orders of performance, and judicial modification of legal relations; secondly, enforcement; and thirdly, provisional measures.[25]

In contrast to the Rules, which define provisional and protective measures by reference to their temporary nature, we identified the defining feature as the function of safeguarding an effective relief in the main proceeding. This will, in most cases, mean ensuring future enforcement. In Spain, provisional measures must be 'aimed exclusively at guaranteeing the effectiveness of the relief that may be granted in a possible favourable judgement' to ensure that this judgement 'cannot be prevented or hampered by situations occurring while the principal proceeding is still pending'.[26]

At the time, there was a debate as to whether anticipatory interim measures had a place in our legal system.[27] It was established that measures designed to anticipate relief are available,[28] provided that the objective is to safeguard an effective relief in the main proceeding.[29] However, the legal definition refers to the possibility of temporarily granting claimants something 'similar' to what they seek in the main proceeding, rather than 'identical'.[30] Consequently, it is questionable whether an interim payment, as regulated in Rules 200 and 201, could be ordered if the claimant seeks monetary relief in the main proceeding. The Rules extend beyond the scope of

---

24 Carreras, J., 'Las medidas cautelares del artículo 1428 de la Ley de Enjuiciamiento Civil', in *Estudios de Derecho Procesal* (with Fenech, M.), Barcelona: Bosch, 1962, pp. 563–591.

25 LEC, Art. 5.

26 LEC, Art. 726.1, 1.ª

27 See Ortells, M., 'Sobre las medidas cautelares indeterminadas del artículo 1428 de la Ley de Enjuiciamiento Civil', *Diario La Ley*, 1989, 1, pp. 959 ff., reproduced in Picó, J. (coord.), *La evolución del Derecho procesal a la luz de 'Justicia': 40 años de historia*, Barcelona: Bosch, 2021, pp. 605–635; Calderón, M. P., *Las medidas cautelares indeterminadas en el proceso civil*, Madrid: Civitas, 1992, pp. 58 ff.

28 LEC, Art. 726.2.

29 See Díez-Picazo, I., 'Art. 726', in de la Oliva, A., Díez-Picazo, I., Vegas, J., Banacloche, J., *Comentarios a la Ley de Enjuiciamiento Civil*, Madrid: Civitas, 2001, pp. 1220–1221.

30 See Fernández-Ballesteros, M. Á., *La ejecución forzosa y las medidas cautelares en la nueva Ley de Enjuiciamiento Civil*, Madrid: Iurgium, 2001, pp. 688–691.

what was anticipated for the Spanish system, as the possibility of interim payment orders was not foreseen.

A further distinction can be observed in the way the procedures for the adoption, opposition, modification, and lifting of provisional measures are described in the Spanish law and the Rules. While the former provides a unified account,[31] the latter addresses each measure separately.

DE LA MATA: Yes, the chapter on provisional and protective measures is divided into two main sections (leaving aside the very few questions of private international law at the end of the chapter): a general part (Section 1, Rules 184 to 191) and a special part (Section 2, Rules 192 to 201). As is always the case with this legislative drafting technique,[32] the general part includes rules applicable, in principle, to all types of measures, and the special part contains rules applicable only to certain types of measures. As you point out, the general part doesn't include requirements that, in Spain, we find to be applicable to all types of measures.

DE BENITO: Like Jaime, I missed these common general requirements. No precautionary measure can be adopted without the applicant proving, even indirectly or *prima facie*, the reality of his right, thus allowing the court to assess the plausibility of the claim brought in the main proceeding. Also, by definition, there must be some kind and degree of risk that justifies such an invasive decision without the safeguards of a fully-fledged declaratory procedure. As it turns out, both requirements – traditionally known as *fumus boni juris* and *periculum in mora* – are reflected in one way or another in the way the Rules regulate each of the four different measures that they've chosen to address.

This is the case, as far as *fumus boni juris* is concerned, for asset preservation orders:

> Rule 193. *Criteria for awarding asset preservation orders*
>
> A party seeking an order under Rule 192 must show that:
>
> (a) their claim for relief has a good chance of succeeding on its substantive merits, …

31 LEC, Art. 728.

32 See MERRYMAN, J. H., PÉREZ-PERDOMO, R., *The Civil Law Tradition. An Introduction to the Legal Systems of Europe and Latin America*, Redwood City: Stanford University Press, 2018, pp. 68–79.

As well as regulatory measures:

> Rule 197. *Criteria for awarding a regulatory measure*
>
> A party seeking an order under Rule 196 must show:
>
> (a) it has a good chance of succeeding in the proceedings; ...

The same applies to the only anticipatory measure that is regulated, the interim payment order:

> Rule 201. *Criteria for awarding an interim payment*
>
> (1) An applicant seeking an order under Rule 200 must show that:
>
> (a) the defendant has admitted that they are liable to pay a monetary sum to the applicant, or the applicant has obtained a final judgment on liability, or it is highly likely that the applicant will obtain at least the amount sought in a final judgment; ...

Finally, the *fumus* requirement is also present in evidence preservation orders:

> Rule 199. *Criteria for awarding an evidence preservation measure*
>
> A party seeking an evidence preservation order must show that: ...
>
> (b) if the order requires access to a party or non-party's property the applicant has a strong *prima facie* case in respect of the merits of the applicant's claim or proposed claim for relief.

DE LA MATA: The question is, do we have only one standard regarding the *prima facie* assessment of the likelihood of success in the merits or different levels of likelihood and different nuances of success? Do we really have only one *fumus*, or distinct and gradually established *fumi*?

DE BENITO: The same can be said about *periculum in mora*. The commentary stresses that, except for the special provisions for advance payments, 'urgency is not a specific requirement'.[33] However, the expression shouldn't be understood today as referring literally to delay, to urgency, but to any situation of risk of ineffectiveness of the proceeding or the judgement. Without a concrete danger to be averted, all precautionary protection is

33 Rule 184, comment 1.

meaningless. Rather than just another requirement, it constitutes its *raison d'être*.[34] As might be expected, the word 'urgency' appears in Rule 138(4) when regulating judgments in default: 'the court may grant, in case of urgency, any provisional or protective measures'.

A review of the special part reveals that the necessity of a risk, a *periculum*, is a constant factor in all cases. For example, in asset preservation orders:

> Rule 193. *Criteria for awarding asset preservation orders*
>
> A party seeking an order under Rule 192 must show that: ...
>
> (b) it is likely that, without such an order, enforcement of a final judgment against the respondent will be impossible or exceedingly difficult.

And in regulatory measures, although in this case with a subtle interplay of copulative and disjunctive conjunctions:

> Rule 197. *Criteria for awarding a regulatory measure*
>
> A party seeking an order under Rule 196 must show:
>
> (a) it has a good chance of succeeding in the proceedings; or
>
> where there is a significant risk that damages to the respondent will not be capable of providing adequate compensation for any interference with their rights if the proceedings are dismissed, that there is a very strong possibility that the applicant will succeed in the proceedings; ...

In the interim payment order, the *mora* manifests itself in the strict meaning of 'delay' and therefore urgency:

> Rule 201. *Criteria for awarding an interim payment*
>
> (1) An applicant seeking an order under Rule 200 must show that: ...
>
> (b) they are in urgent need of payment by the defendant.

34 Díez-Picazo, I., 'Las medidas cautelares' (reviewed and updated by Gascón, F.), en *Curso de Derecho Procesal Civil II, Parte especial* (with de la Oliva, A., Vegas, J.), Madrid: Editorial Universitaria Ramón Areces, 2016, pp. 517–539, at p. 521.

Finally, this requirement is also present in evidence preservation orders:

> Rule 199. *Criteria for awarding an evidence preservation measure*
>
> A party seeking an evidence preservation order must show that:
>
> (a) there is a real risk that unless the order is made the evidence will not be available for determining the substantive proceedings on their merits; ...

The reiteration of the two ideas, the *fumus* and the *periculum*, prompts the question of whether it would not have been preferable to place them systematically, as universal requirements, in the general part.

DE LA MATA: Only if we assume, again, that there is a single standard of risk instead of different degrees of risk; a single *periculum*, and not rather different and gradually configured *pericula*.

DE BENITO: Rule 191 supports your suggestion. For interim payments, the possibility of imposing sanctions is ruled out:

> Rule 191. *Sanctions for non-compliance*
>
> Except in respect of interim payments, where there is noncompliance with a provisional or protective measure the court may impose a sanction under Rule 27, as appropriate.

This is a curious provision. Sanctions are a technique that is found throughout the Rules. Any obligation of the parties is subject to sanctions of a considerable variety of forms, as set out in Rules 27, 99, 104, and 110. However, the application of these interim payment orders is so restricted that the mere possibility of imposing a sanction on those who won't pay is directly excluded.

DE LA MATA: The commentary indicates that, in systems that permit interim payment orders, their issuance is frequently subject to more rigorous criteria than those applied to other types of measures. For example, where the defendant has admitted liability or the claimant has obtained a favourable judgment on liability, but only the *quantum* of damages remains to be determined.[35]

---

35 Rule 200, comment 4.

DE BENITO: The key issue is thus the unnamed or atypical measures. There are in fact more than four standard measures.

DE LA MATA: You're right. As I said at the outset, 'any temporary order' that fulfils one or more of the legally relevant functions (Rule 184) can be validly applied for and granted. There is no doubt that the Rules provide for a *numerus apertus*, not a *numerus clausus*: an open, not a closed list of measures.

GILSANZ: And unnamed or atypical measures are far from uncommon in practice.

DE BENITO: A general part that doesn't regulate common requirements inevitably leaves atypical measures completely unregulated. What do we do when we are faced with a request for one of these measures? Do we apply a kind of induction of the requirements common to the other four, as we have just outlined regarding *fumus* and *periculum*? Wouldn't that betray the idea of including specific requirements? On the other hand, as I said, isn't a certain measure of *periculum* inherent in precautionary measures, whatever form they take, and should therefore always be required, even if it is not expressly stated?

Maybe the general part of this chapter is intentionally silent? If we use deductive reasoning, we can make a syllogism: only the rules in the general part of the chapter apply to unregulated measures; these rules fail to mention anything equivalent to *fumus* and *periculum*; *ergo*, *fumus* and *periculum* don't apply to unregulated measures. This *argumentum e silentio* suggests that the regulation of each of the four discrete measures in the special part is justified by their specificities, so it can't be extended to other types of measures.

And yet, what prevents us from resorting to *analogy* with the typical measure that most closely resembles our atypical measure?

GILSANZ: Even without a general part, case law would find its way either by construction or by analogy. I'm probably more used to a more decentralised system. In the US, each federal circuit has different requirements, for example, in relation to injunctions. They coexist perfectly with this fragmentary reality without the need to have a well-structured general part. There are even issues that are supplemented by references to state legislation. For instance, Rule 64 of the Federal Rules of Civil Procedure, which is about seizing people or property, is supported by state legislation. Judges are flexible and aware of these rules and practices. For instance, one judge will identify four specific requirements for their circuit, while another will identify three, and so on. The system relies on the work of the courts to complete itself.

DE BENITO: In civil law countries, the balance between the most abstract and general rules possible and the more nuanced work of case law in the interpretation of those rules is also at the core of the system.[36] Portalis' *Discours preliminaire* comes to mind:

> A code, however complete it may seem, is no sooner finished than thousands of unexpected questions present themselves to the magistrate. For these laws, once drafted, remain as written. Men, on the other hand, never rest. They are always moving; and this movement, which never ceases and whose effects are variously modified by circumstances, continually produces some new fact, some new outcome.
>
> Many things are therefore necessarily left to the authority of custom, to the discussion of learned men, to the arbitration of judges.[37]

Regarding the further systemic impact of case law, I recall the words of the eminent Spanish jurist GÓMEZ DE LA SERNA, who, two decades after the definitive establishment of a cassation appeal in Spain, observed:

> Are there today as many doubts on positive law as before this period? No, because case law is increasingly equal in the different parts of the Monarchy; because the unity of case law, by completing the unity of

36 See VARANO, V., BARSOTTI, V., *La tradizione giuridica occidentale. Testo e materiali per un confront* civil law common law, Turin: Giappichelli, 2014, pp. 187–192.

37 '*Un code, quelque complet qu'il puisse paraître, n'est pas plutôt achevé, que mille question inattendues viennent s'offrir aux magistrats. Car les lois une fois rédigées demeurent telles qu'elles ont été écrites. Les hommes, au contraire, ne se reposent jamais ; ils agissent toujours : et ce mouvement, qui ne s'arrête pas, et dont les effets sont diversement modifiés par les circonstances, produit, à chaque instant, quelque combinaison nouvelle, quelque nouveau fait, quelque résultat nouveau. Une foule de choses sont donc nécessairement abandonnées à l'empire de l'usage, à la discussion des hommes instruits, à l'arbitrage des juges.*' PORTALIS, J. E. M., *Discours préliminaire du premier projet de Code civil*, originally *Motifs et discours prononcés lors de la publication du Code civil. Discours prononcé le 21 janvier 1801 et le Code civil promulgué le 21 mars 1804*, Bordeaux: Confluences, 2004, in English (recently) as *Preliminary Address*, Ottawa: The International Cooperation Group, Department of Justice of Canada, 2004, both versions available at https://www.justice.gc.ca/eng/rp-pr/csj-sjc/ilp-pji/code/index.html.

> [positive] law, ends up bringing about the unity of the law [legal system].[38]

Indeed, even in the absence of abstract and general rules, and with technically imperfect laws, the relevant role of legal doctrine in civil law countries allows shortcomings and contradictions to be resolved based on intellectual persuasion and personal authority rather than power, as a remote remnant of the duality of *auctoritas* and *potestas* so characteristic of Roman law.[39]

However, a good general rule that there must always be a likelihood of success on the merits would clarify the picture and make the process easier.

Vegas: The interpretative tools in question can facilitate the implementation of a more diverse array of anticipatory measures. To illustrate, the Spanish Law provides a non-exhaustive list of typical measures, including the suspension of disputed corporate agreements.[40] This measure is simultaneously regulatory and anticipatory in nature and could therefore serve as a reference point for analogy.[41]

This leads me to another point for reflection. While detailed civil procedure regulation has its advantages, it also has its disadvantages. It is irrelevant whether we employ an inductive or an analogical approach; the courts must always adapt and accommodate the requirements in question. It seems reasonable to assume that they do so with common sense.

---

38 '*Existen hoy tantas dudas sobre derecho constituido como antes de este período? No, porque la jurisprudencia va siendo igual en las diferentes partes de la monarquía; porque la unidad de la jurisprudencia, completando la unidad de la ley, concluye por producir la unidad del derecho*': Pedro Gómez de la Serna at the Royal Academy of Jurisprudence and Legislation, 1855, in Lorente, M., Martínez, F., Solla, M. J., *Historia legal de la justicia en España (1810–1978)*, Madrid: Iustel, 2012, p. 207, reproduced at de Benito, M., 'Back in Focus: Case Selection Standards in the Spanish Supreme Court', in Bravo, P. (coord.), *Supreme Courts Under Pressure. Controlling Caseload in the Administration of Civil Justice*, Cham: Springer, 2021, pp. 49–71, at 52.

39 On the role of legal doctrine in civil law, see Merryman, J. H., Pérez-Perdomo, R., *The Civil Law Tradition. An Introduction to the Legal Systems of Europe and Latin America*, Redwood City: Stanford University Press, 2018, pp. 56–67; or Varano, V., Barsotti, V., *La tradizione giuridica occidentale. Testo e materiali per un confront* civil law common law, Turin: Giappichelli, 2014, pp. 191–192. On the *auctoritas* and *potestas* duality, see d'Ors, Á., *Derecho privado romano*, Pamplona: eunsa, 2008, § 29.

40 lec, Art. 727,10.ª

41 Vegas, J., 'Posesión de los bienes litigiosos, medidas cautelares y ejecución provisional', in Gómez, J. L., Barona, S., Calderón, M. P. (coords.), *El Derecho Procesal español del siglo xx a golpe de tango.* Liber amicorum *en homenaje a Juan Montero Aroca*, Valencia: Tirant lo Blanch, 2012, pp. 907–925, at 916–919.

GILSANZ: I agree with Jaime. There's room in our legal system for more regulatory and anticipatory measures than we're currently seeing in our case law.

VEGAS: It is possible that the relatively low number of anticipatory orders requested in Spain is a consequence of a lack of familiarity with this legal instrument. The extensive list of measures permitted by the Law allows lawyers to be creative[42] and innovative in their approach, enabling them to request measures that address the risk in a unique way, as each case they face is, in essence, unique. In such cases, reference to the Rules can be decisive. The Rules can be used to demonstrate alternative approaches to legal practice, thereby gradually improving the legal culture of our courts.

DE LA MATA: I like the point about creative lawyers. Without creative lawyers, who can offer their own opinions and be criticised by judges and clients, we will never get anywhere. Until someone resurrected the *rebus sic stantibus* rule by invoking the UNIDROIT Principles,[43] the *rebus* was dormant. And already in the first or second Supreme Court ruling on *rebus sic stantibus*, the UNIDROIT Principles were mentioned. Let's also invoke the Rules without fear!

DE BENITO: '*Quodcumque volueritis petetis et fiet vobis*':[44] 'ask whatever you wish, and it will be done into you'. Each of us will see in the solitude of our own chambers, with the care and skill that comes from years or decades in the profession, and the conviction that we are fighting to uphold the law in each individual case,[45] how to convince the court of the application of the most sensible and appropriate requirements for the injunctive relief we seek.

---

42 See VARANO, V., BARSOTTI, V., *La tradizione giuridica occidentale. Testo e materiali per un confronto* civil law common law, Turin: Giappichelli, 2014, pp. 187–192.

43 UNIDROIT Principles of International Commercial Contracts, 2016 edition. See VENEZIANO, A., FINAZZI AGRÒ, E., 'The Use of the UNIDROIT Principles in Order to Interpret or Supplement National Law: An Italian Perspective', in GALIZZI, P., ROJAS ELGUETA, G., VENEZIANO, A., *The Multiple Uses of the UNIDROIT Principles of International Commercial Contracts: Theory and Practice*, Milan: Giuffrè, 2020, pp. 5–16.

44 John, 15–7.

45 VON JHERING, R., *Der Kampf ums Recht*, Frankfurt: Klostermann, 1872; in English *The Struggle for Law*, Chicago: Callaghan, 1879.

I think we sometimes overstate the reluctance of judges to engage in meaningful legal debate. Sometimes we have a bit of an unjustified lack of confidence in judges. This is often unfair, and always sad. Let's follow Calamandrei's example and, despite the challenges and limitations of our justice systems, sing a heartfelt 'eulogy of judges'![46]

Bibliography

CALAMANDREI, P., *Elogio dei giudici scritto da un avvocato*, Florence: Le Monnier, 1935–1959; more recently in Milan: Ponte alle Grazie, 1999; in English, *Eulogy of Judges*, Clark: The Lawbook Exchange, 2011 (reprint of the first American edition).

CALDERÓN, M. P., *Las medidas cautelares indeterminadas en el proceso civil*, Madrid: Civitas, 1992.

CARRERAS, J., 'Las medidas cautelares del artículo 1428 de la Ley de Enjuiciamiento Civil', in *Estudios de Derecho Procesal* (with FENECH, M.), Barcelona: Bosch, 1962, pp. 563–591.

COQUILLETTE, D. R., JOSEPH, G. P., VAIRO, G. M., VARNER, C. D., *Moore's Federal Practice: Civil*, New York: Matthew Bender, 2023.

DE BENITO, M., 'Back in Focus: Case Selection Standards in the Spanish Supreme Court,' in BRAVO, P. (COORD.), *Supreme Courts Under Pressure. Controlling Caseload in the Administration of Civil Justice*, Cham: Springer, 2021, pp. 49–71.

DE BENITO, M., 'Las medidas cautelares en las Reglas europeas de proceso civil', in GARCÍA MARRERO, J.(coord.), *Medidas cautelares y diligencias preliminares*, Cizur Menor: Aranzadi, 2021, pp. 691–710.

DE LA OLIVA, A., 'Sobre la Ley 1/2000, de 7 de enero, de Enjuiciamiento Civil. Criterios inspiradores e innovaciones principales', in *Tribunales de justicia*, 2-2000, pp. 127–142.

DÍEZ-PICAZO, I., 'Art. 726', in DE LA OLIVA, A., DÍEZ-PICAZO, I., VEGAS, J., BANACLOCHE, J., *Comentarios a la Ley de Enjuiciamiento Civil*, Madrid: Civitas, 2001, pp. 1220–1221.

DÍEZ-PICAZO, I., 'Las medidas cautelares' (reviewed and updated by GASCÓN, F.), en *Curso de Derecho Procesal Civil II, Parte especial* (with DE LA OLIVA, A., VEGAS, J.), Madrid: Editorial Universitaria Ramón Areces, 2016, pp. 517–539.

46 CALAMANDREI, P., *Elogio dei giudici scritto da un avvocato*, Florence: Le Monnier, 1935–1959; more recently in Milan: Ponte alle Grazie, 1999; in English, *Eulogy of Judges*, Clark: The Lawbook Exchange, 2011 (reprint of the first American edition).

D'ORS, Á., *Derecho privado romano*, Pamplona: EUNSA, 2008.

FERNÁNDEZ-BALLESTEROS, M. Á., *La ejecución forzosa y las medidas cautelares en la nueva Ley de Enjuiciamiento Civil*, Madrid: Iurgium, 2001, pp. 688–691.

FISS, O., RENDLEMAN, D., *Injunctions*, Eagan: Foundation Press, 1984.

GILSANZ, J., *El proceso civil estadounidense. La tutela judicial cautelar*, Cizur Menor: Aranzadi, 2010.

LORENTE, M., MARTÍNEZ, F., SOLLA, M. J., *Historia legal de la justicia en España (1810–1978)*, Madrid: Iustel, 2012.

MERRYMAN, J. H., PÉREZ-PERDOMO, R., *The Civil Law Tradition. An Introduction to the Legal Systems of Europe and Latin America*, Redwood City: Stanford University Press, 2018.

NEWMAN, L. W., BURROWS, M., *The Practice of International Litigation*, Huntington: Juris, 2013.

ORTELLS, M., 'Sobre las medidas cautelares indeterminadas del artículo 1428 de la Ley de Enjuiciamiento Civil', *Diario La Ley*, 1989, 1, pp. 959 ff., reproduced in PICÓ, J. (coord.), *La evolución del Derecho procesal a la luz de 'Justicia': 40 años de historia*, Barcelona: Bosch, 2021, pp. 605–635.

PORTALIS, J. E. M., *Discours préliminaire du premier projet de Code civil*, originally *Motifs et discours prononcés lors de la publication du Code civil. Discours prononcé le 21 janvier 1801 et le Code civil promulgué le 21 mars 1804*, Bordeaux: Confluences, 2004, in English (recently) as *Preliminary Address*, Ottawa: The International Cooperation Group, Department of Justice of Canada, 2004, both versions available at https://www.justice.gc.ca/eng/rp-pr/csj-sjc/ilp-pji/code/index.html.

STORME, M., *Study on the Approximation of the Laws and Rules of the Member States Concerning Certain Aspects of the Procedure for Civil Litigation* (final report), Dordrecht, 1994.

VARANO, V., BARSOTTI, V., *La tradizione giuridica occidentale. Testo e materiali per un confronto* civil law common law, Turin: Giappichelli, 2014.

VEGAS, J., 'La reforma procesal civil española: criterios inspiradores y principales innovaciones de la Ley de Enjuiciamiento Civil de 2000', in DE LA OLIVA, A., PALOMO, D. (coords.), *Proceso civil. Hacia una nueva Justicia civil*, Santiago de Chile: Editorial Jurídica de Chile, 2007, pp. 1–21.

VEGAS, J., 'Posesión de los bienes litigiosos, medidas cautelares y ejecución provisional', in GÓMEZ, J. L., BARONA, S., CALDERÓN, M. P. (coords.), *El Derecho Procesal español del siglo XX a golpe de tango.* Liber amicorum *en homenaje a Juan Montero Aroca*, Valencia: Tirant lo Blanch, 2012, pp. 907–925.

VENEZIANO, A., FINAZZI AGRÒ, E., 'The Use of the UNIDROIT Principles in Order to Interpret or Supplement National Law: An Italian Perspective', in GALIZZI, P., ROJAS ELGUETA, G., VENEZIANO, A., *The Multiple Uses of the UNIDROIT*

Principles of International Commercial Contracts: Theory and Practice, Milan: Giuffrè, 2020, pp. 5–16.

von Jhering, R., *Der Kampf ums Recht*, Frankfurt: Klostermann, 1872; in English *The Struggle for Law*, Chicago: Callaghan, 1879.

Wright, C. A., Miller. A. R., *et al.*, *Federal Practice and Procedure, Wright & Miller*, Eagan: West, 2023.

CHAPTER 8

Collective Proceedings

Marco Gradi, Elisabetta Silvestri, Ianika Tzankova, and Stefaan Voet

The issue of collective redress represents a significant challenge, with considerable scope for improvement. This mechanism, which has its roots in English law but was originally utilised in the US, has, for a considerable period of time, not received the attention it merits in Europe. This kind of procedure is closely linked with consumer protection, particularly in complex actions against corporate giants, both in terms of substantive and procedural law. Indeed, the efficacy of consumer or tort law is contingent upon the availability of appropriate procedural mechanisms, which in turn challenge commonly accepted ideas on core aspects of civil procedure, such as party autonomy and individual damage calculation.

The Rules seek to address the regulatory immaturity by proposing harmonisation measures that could inform future European and national legislation.

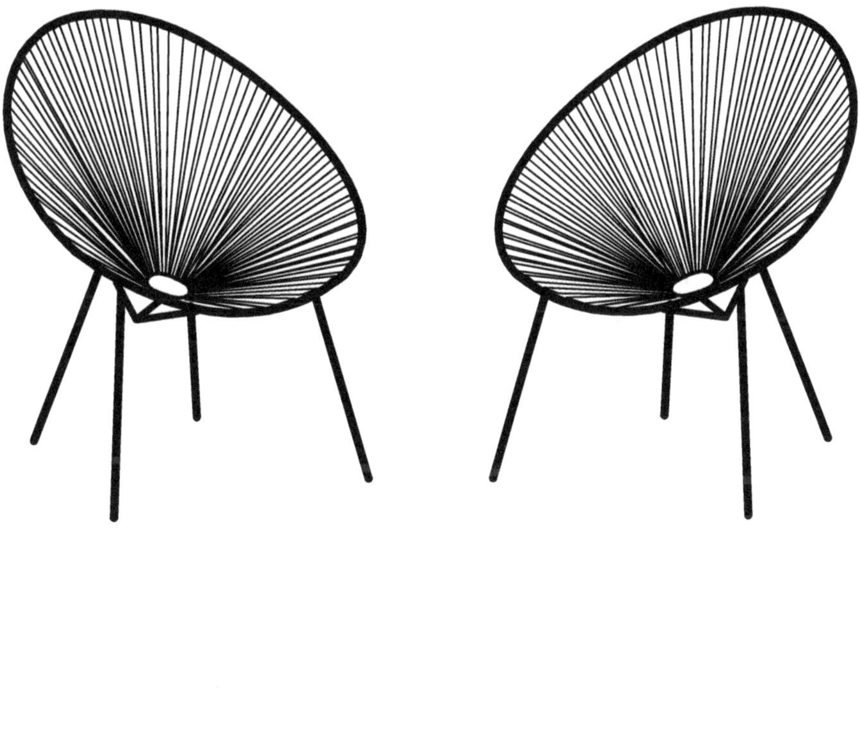

 | DOI:10.1163/9789004533257_009

VOET: The ALI-UNIDROIT Principles of Transnational Civil Procedure didn't deal in depth with the subject of parties to proceedings. The subsequent ELI-UNIDROIT project, with its ambition to go into more detail, aimed to introduce a more general framework regarding parties to civil proceedings: capacity, standing, joinder, intervention, etc.

Later, the scope of the ELI-UNIDROIT project was extended to include collective redress. At that time, some countries within the EU were establishing collective redress mechanisms, and EU legislators and policy-makers were paying increasing attention to this trend. As a result, the working group dealing with parties was also given the task of drafting a set of model rules on collective redress.

TZANKOVA: The issue was seen as politically sensitive and there was debate about whether it should be included at all. Some of us argued that it would be strange not to have collective redress in the Rules. Fortunately, the project leadership took the long view and decided to include it in the project. In my view, excluding collective redress would have had a negative impact on the credibility of the project.

VOET: The working group responsible for this section was diverse. We had academics who had written on the subject and practitioners who had experience in dealing with collective proceedings. Most of them had a civil law background, including the two co-editors, Emmanuel Jeuland and Astrid Stadler, Istvan Varga, and ourselves; only one, Vincent Smith, had a common law background. We discussed and drafted the articles in English and then translated them into French. In the process, many subtle but important legal points emerged.

TZANKOVA: This collaborative process of co-creation was truly inspiring. We had a number of face-to-face meetings where we discussed drafts that we had exchanged beforehand.

VOET: The idea wasn't to look for the lowest common denominator of all collective redress regimes in the EU Member States. Rather, the basic idea was to look at what was going on in these different countries and see what was working and what was not, while at the same time looking at some of the decisions taken by the EU institutions on the building blocks of collective redress mechanisms. All this was our most immediate source of inspiration.

TZANKOVA: In a book we wrote at the time,[1] we outlined a basis for this section of the rules. The book is interesting because we did not always feel that we had enough room to manoeuvre in the project: all the rules had to be written in a uniform way and in a certain format that was also consistent with the final products of the other working groups. In fact, our initial proposal was considered to be too detailed and to overlap to some extent with the rules on parties. We felt that there was much more to be said and we provided further explanation for some decisions that might have been seen as controversial compared to the approach of the EU institutions on some issues. We also didn't have the final version of the Consumer Collective Redress Directive at the time of writing.[2] We thought that our work and research could be useful to the EU institutions and to policymakers in the Member States who are dealing with the implementation of the Directive.

VOET: We noticed that the main concern of the EU legislature was to set up a basic regulatory framework that allowed Member States to allow for collective settlements. Therefore, a lot of attention was paid to collective settlements in the Rules. More specifically, Rules 221 to 226 focus on collective settlement pending a collective redress procedure, in which the court approves or rejects a settlement. However, there's also attention paid to the mechanisms for collective settlement outside collective proceedings, as exemplified in Rules 229 to 232.

TZANKOVA: The question of terminology deserves a special mention.

VOET: A pretty confusing set of terms has been used during these years: collective actions, class actions, group actions, collective redress. To avoid confusion, we tried to draft the articles in English, avoiding English terms that are closely related to specific procedural instruments or phrases that may be too loaded with connotations.

SILVESTRI: A key issue in collective redress revolves around the types of redress available. Under the Directive, both injunctive measures and redress measures can be sought:

---

1 STADLER, A., JEULAND, E., SMITH, V. (eds.), *Collective and Mass Litigation in Europe. Model Rules for Effective Dispute Resolution*, Cheltenham: Edward Elgar, 2020.

2 Directive (EU) 2020/1828 of the European Parliament and of the Council of 25 November 2020 on representative actions for the protection of the collective interests of consumers and repealing Directive 2009/22/EC.

Article 8. *Injunctive measures*

1. Member States shall ensure that injunctive measures referred to in point (a) of Article 7(4) are available in the form of:

(a) a provisional measure to cease a practice or, where appropriate, to prohibit a practice, where that practice has been deemed to constitute an infringement as referred to in Article 2(1);

(b) a definitive measure to cease a practice or, where appropriate, to prohibit a practice, where that practice has been found to constitute an infringement as referred to in Article 2(1).

Article 9. *Redress measures*

1. A redress measure shall require a trader to provide consumers concerned with remedies such as compensation, repair, replacement, price reduction, contract termination or reimbursement of the price paid, as appropriate and as available under Union or national law.

This system of remedies, combined with other questionable and obscure provisions, makes it difficult to decipher whether EU regulators intended to create a class action with a European flavour or a peculiar hybrid.

In particular, I have doubts about the injunctive measures that 'qualified entities' may seek under Article 8 of the Directive, which we have just mentioned. In my view, the Directive overlooks one of the main problems with collective injunctions: the effective enforcement of cease and desist orders. In some jurisdictions (and certainly in my own, Italy), this type of enforcement can be difficult to achieve. I understand that the emphasis of the Directive is on compensatory collective redress. Even so, I wonder whether there are specific reasons for the scant provisions regulating injunctive measures and the absence of any reference to their enforcement:

Rule 204. *Scope of application*

1. The Rules in Part XI, Section 1 apply to orders, known as collective interest injunction, made by a court, which direct any person to cease any conduct or behaviour that is infringing the law.

2. A collective interest injunction cannot be made on an interim basis under Part X of these Rules.

Rule 205. *Entitlement to apply for a collective interest injunction*

1. Any entity authorised under national law to bring actions in the collective interest may apply for a collective interest injunction that requires the cessation of any infringement of the law.

2. Where appropriate the court may order additional measures such as the publication of its decision with a view to eliminating the continuing effects of the infringement.

Rule 206. *Effect of collective interest injunctions*

A collective interest injunction binds the defendant in all future proceedings.

TZANKOVA: Another concern that comes to mind in relation to injunctions is that there has been very little cross-border activity by designated entities under the previous Injunctions Directive.[3] Is this an indication of the level of cross-border activity under the Directive, particularly in relation to collective redress?

VOET: It's true that we focused mainly on the controversial issue of compensatory collective redress. But you're right: in the Netherlands, there's a well-functioning injunction mechanism that works well. I think the potential of such an instrument for Europe is perhaps a little underestimated, because everyone's thinking about compensatory collective redress; everyone's thinking about the money, the big pot of gold that the defendant will pay to the representative claimants. People get blinded by that.

SILVESTRI: There's also no mention of collective actions for declaratory relief. In the absence of monetary compensation, there is no incentive to bring collective actions. Nevertheless, declaratory relief 'may have enormous significance when rights claims are pursued against institutions'.[4] It might have been beneficial to include a general rule at the outset of Part XI stating that the same remedies that are available in ordinary individual civil actions

---

3 Directive 2009/22/EC of the European Parliament and of the Council of 23 April 2009 on injunctions for the protection of consumers' interests.

4 HENSLER, D., 'Foreword', in FITZPATRICK, B. T., THOMAS, R. S. (eds.), *The Cambridge Handbook of Class Actions. An International Survey*, Cambridge: Cambridge University Press, 2021, p. XXIX.

are also available in collective proceedings, including declaratory, injunctive, monetary, and other forms of relief.

VOET: You're probably right.

TZANKOVA: Let us now turn our attention to another crucial matter: the legal status of the parties involved. This is of great importance in any litigation process, but it is of particular significance here, as we must ensure that the victims are the direct beneficiaries of the litigation.

There are two basic approaches to the issue: the individual and the institutional claimant model. In the individual claimant model, it is always a member of the group who acts as the group representative. In the institutional claimant model, it is an institution, normally a non-profit organisation, that is authorised by some state entity to act as a lead claimant on behalf of the victims.[5] The individual claimant model is the predominant approach in common law jurisdictions, such as the US and the UK. However, it is also found in a few civil law jurisdictions, including Denmark, Sweden, and Bulgaria. In most other EU Member States, the institutional claimant model is the preferred approach.[6]

Institutional claimants can be categorised into two groups: governmental or state-funded entities, and those that are privately funded, typically through membership fees. Examples of such entities include consumer or investor associations, private foundations, and the Dutch *Stichting*, which is one of the most well-known cases of a temporary entity set up for a specific collective claim.

In designing the Rules, we decided to take this diversity as a starting point and not to take sides by excluding any of these realities *a priori*. While the general choice for the institutional claimant model is clear, especially in the form of private non-profit organisations, we recognise that there may be other options to consider. The individual claimant model is somewhat controversial in Europe due to potential conflicts of interest and agency issues. However, upon closer examination, it becomes evident that these issues are present in both models. Naturally, this is inherent in any agent-principal relationship; it is neither unusual nor extraordinary. The key

5 STÖHR, A., 'The Implementation of Collective Redress: A Comparative Approach', *German Law Journal*, 21, 2020, pp. 1610–1624.

6 For a comparative overview, see FAIRGRIEVE, D., HOWELLS, G., 'Collective Redress Procedures: European Debates', *International & Comparative Law Quarterly*, 58-2, 2009, pp. 379–409.

point is that the nature of these agency issues differs depending on which of the two models we follow.[7]

With regard to the individual claimant model, there is a substantial body of academic, empirical, socio-legal, legal, and economic literature, primarily from the US and Canada, on the potential agency issues associated with this model and how to address them in practice, in case law, and in legislation.[8] In contrast, with regard to the institutional claimant model, there is a paucity of knowledge regarding the nature of these agency issues, let alone how to address them.

Furthermore, there is a lack of critical debate about our own institutional claimant model, with the assumption that it is superior to the individual claimant model.

VOET: I'm curious to know if you share this view.

TZANKOVA: My view is that making such assumptions is misplaced, and that questions of superiority are also misplaced here. There is still much to be learned about how different types of institutional claimants perform in practice, as they all have their own specific potential agency issues.

VOET: The question of standing is directly related to questions of funding, because it has a lot to do with the financial capacity of the entity or person bringing the claim. In Belgium, for example, we have an institutional claimant – an 'ideological plaint iff' –[9] that is nothing more than a consumer association; however, it is the only one that has the financial capacity to bring this costly type of procedure. It doesn't matter how beautiful your procedural framework is if you don't have the funding and financing rules in place to make it work.[10]

The issue of who initiates a collective redress procedure is inextricably linked to the financing and funding of these mechanisms. It's surprising that

7 STIER, B., TZANKOVA, I. N., 'The Culture of Collective Litigation: A Comparative Analysis', in HENSLER, D., HODGES, CH., TZANKOVA, I., *Class Actions in Context*, Cheltenham: Edward Elgar, 2016, pp. 23–50, at 36–40.

8 STÖHR, A., 'The Implementation of Collective Redress: A Comparative Approach', *German Law Journal*, 21, 2020, pp. 1610–1624.

9 MORABITO, V., 'Ideological Plaintiffs and Class Actions: An Australian Perspective', *University of British Columbia Law Review*, 34–2, 2001, pp. 459–514; MULHERON, R., *The Class Action in Common Law Legal Systems. A Comparative Perspective*, Oxford: Hart, 2004, pp. 304, 308–309, *passim*.

10 See TZANKOVA, I., 'Funding of Mass Disputes: Lessons from the Netherlands', *Journal of Law, Economics & Policy*, 8(3), 2012, pp. 549–591.

the EU legislator didn't focus on this aspect more. Many of these legislators, both at the Belgian and EU levels, seem to assume that the procedure will be financed and paid for in the same way as individual litigation. This assumption is erroneous because in collective redress there is a triangular relationship between defendant, representative, and the represented group.

SILVESTRI: This is true in several jurisdictions, and certainly in my own, Italy, where the question of adequate funding remains unresolved, although the new rules on collective redress, placed at the end of the code of civil procedure, have made some timid attempts to change the situation.[11] Third-party funding arrangements can be of paramount – and equally controversial – relevance as far as collective actions are concerned. Indeed, in Italy, third-party funding of litigation in general and with specific reference to collective proceedings is a much debated topic, although an adequate legislative framework hasn't yet been created.[12]

VOET: Funding is the elephant in the room. Everyone knows it is there, but it doesn't get the positive attention it deserves.

SILVESTRI: As you said, it's a common misconception that these two types of litigation, individual and collective, follow the same procedural rules and raise the same issues. A specific example of the different dynamics of the two types of litigation can be observed in Rule 209(d), which stipulates that lawyers and legal professionals in general, with the sole exception of 'legal academics',[13] cannot be 'qualified claimants'. At first, this seemed somewhat unusual. However, upon reflection, I believe I've grasped the rationale behind this choice. If the claimant is a lawyer who also acts as class counsel, his interest in obtaining the most favourable compensation for the class may depend exclusively on his interest in maximising his own legal fees.

---

11 Arts. 840-*bis* to 840-*sexiesdecies*. For an overview of the main features of these rules, see SILVESTRI, E., 'Rebooting Italian Class Actions', in UZELAC, A., VOET, S. (eds.), *Class Actions in Europe. Holy Grail or Wrong Trail?*, Cham: Springer, 2021, pp. 201–213.

12 AMARO, R., AZAR-BAUD, F. M. J., CORNELOUP, F. S., FAUVARQUE-COSSON F. B., JAULT-SESEKE, F. F., *Collective redress in the Member States of the European Union Policy: Study*, European Parliament, 2018, available at https://www.europarl.europa.eu/RegData/etudes/STUD/2018/608829/IPOL_STU(2018)608829_EN.pdf, pp. 90–91; KRAMER, X., TILLEMA, I., 'The Funding of Collective Redress by Entrepreneurial Parties: The EU and Dutch Context', *Revista Ítalo-Española de Derecho Procesal*, 2, 2020, p. 165–181.

13 Rule 209, comment 7.

The conflict of interest is inevitable. And, as the commentary to the Rule makes clear, conflicts of interest should be avoided to the extent that they 'might have an influence on the claimant's conduct of the collective proceeding, or any negotiation in, or settlement of, such proceedings'.[14]

VOET: The working group reached a consensus that the lawyer shouldn't act as a representative. The same is true in the US, although it could be argued that, through the individual class member, the lawyer and class counsel can bring claims. The potential implications of this approach are open to question. In the European context, the concept of giving standing to an individual, let alone a class action lawyer, was already a controversial one.

TZANKOVA: In addition, we did not find many examples concerning individual class members; and I do not think we saw a model where the lead representative claimant was a lawyer.

SILVESTRI: The pressing issue may revolve around an individual class member who happens to be a lawyer.

TZANKOVA: But then that is different, because the individual is acting in their own capacity as a group member, e. g., as a consumer. I do not think the Rules necessarily exclude that possibility.

SILVESTRI: After all, we're all consumers.

VOET: Another question is also whether not only individual class members or a non-profit association, but also governmental bodies – e. g., an *Ombudsman* – should be admitted as potential qualified claimants. The Directive expressly allows for this.[15] In Belgium, we have the Consumer Mediation Service, which is the residual ADR entity that was created after the 2013 Directive on consumer ADR.[16] It is a consumer ombudsman, partly public, partly private, and has the capacity to bring a class action, but only in order

14 Rule 209, comment 3.

15 Directive 2020/1828, Art. 4(7).

16 Directive 2013/11/EU of the European Parliament and of the Council of 21 May 2013 on alternative dispute resolution for consumer disputes and amending Regulation (EC) 2006/2004 and Directive 2009/22/EC (Directive on consumer ADR).

to obtain a collective settlement. If a settlement cannot be reached, another entity has to take over the procedure.

An example of this happened recently when the Consumer Mediation Service brought a class action for the first time. However, the Court of Appeal in Brussels dismissed the case, stating that the Service was not adequate to bring the case.[17] Personally, I have a lot of problems with this decision. Certainly, it's another possibility beyond the two options: the institutional and the individual claimant. But it's also something that the Directive allows.

TZANKOVA: As far as the two models are concerned, in the Directive we can observe a split between the approaches to the institutional model in the context of national collective actions compared to the context of cross-border collective actions.

VOET: It should be noted that the definition of cross-border collective actions is specific to the Directive. It has a different meaning than one would expect on a purely linguistic level. According to the Directive, cross-border collective actions are actions that an organisation brings before the court of a Member State other than the one in which the organisation was originally established. As such, it has nothing to do with the nature of the action, but rather with the origin of the organisation bringing the action.

TZANKOVA: Having clarified this, only institutional claimants can act as representatives of a group and seek collective redress in other Member States. In addition, they must meet stricter criteria in accordance with Article 4. In Europe, we take a strict approach to the issue of standing when it comes to the design of collective redress.

When designing collective redress systems, policy makers always have a choice: some are more conservative, some more liberal. In the case of Europe, on the issue of standing for collective redress – as well as on the issues of opt-in and opt-out, certification, funding costs, etc. – we have opted for the most conservative feature. That could be a problem.

VOET: In reality, as mentioned earlier, there is no solid evidence that qualified claimants actually bring these cross-border proceedings. Policy makers

17 Brussels Court of Appeal 14 April 2021, *Belgian Consumer Ombudsman Service v. six energy suppliers* (2019/AR/1763), *Mass Claims*, vol. 1, 2021, p. 140.

essentially added another layer to the existing framework, allowing these qualified claimants to bring class actions for compensatory damages. Initially, the distinction between national and cross-border actions was not so important. The European Commission received a lot of criticism for this at the time, especially from Germany.

As a result, they introduced some important changes. For cross-border actions, as Ianika has said, Article 4 of the Directive provides for some serious qualification requirements in terms of transparency:

> Article 4. *Qualified entities*
>
> 3. Member States shall designate an entity as referred to in paragraph 2 that has made a request for designation as a qualified entity for the purpose of bringing cross-border representative actions if that entity complies with all of the following criteria:
>
> a) it is a legal person that is constituted in accordance with the national law of the Member State of its designation and can demonstrate 12 months of actual public activity in the protection of consumer interests prior to its request for designation;
>
> b) its statutory purpose demonstrates that it has a legitimate interest in protecting consumer interests as provided for in the provisions of Union law referred to in Annex I;
>
> c) it has a non-profit-making character;
>
> d) it is not the subject of insolvency proceedings and is not declared insolvent;
>
> e) it is independent and not influenced by persons other than consumers, in particular by traders, who have an economic interest in the bringing of any representative action, including in the event of funding by third parties, and, to that end, has established procedures to prevent such influence as well as to prevent conflicts of interest between itself, its funding providers and the interests of consumers;
>
> f) it makes publicly available in plain and intelligible language by any appropriate means, in particular on its website, information that demonstrates that the entity complies with the criteria listed in points (a) to (e) and information about the sources of its funding in general, its organisational, management and membership structure, its statutory purpose and its activities.

As such, entities wishing to bring a cross-border collective action have to comply with these strict standards. As for domestic collective actions – and this makes sense in light of the principle of subsidiarity –, the Directive leaves it to the Member States to decide.

> Article 4. *Qualified entities*
>
> 4. Member States shall ensure that the criteria they use to designate an entity as a qualified entity for the purpose of bringing domestic representative actions are consistent with the objectives of this Directive in order to make the functioning of such representative actions effective and efficient.

All this means that we can have two types of qualified entities: those that can bring cross-border actions and those that are only recognised at national level, perhaps with lower standards. I don't think this is desirable.

TZANKOVA: And then there is the certification requirement. On the organisation's side, they may think: 'we have finally done it, we have fulfilled all these requirements, so now we can pursue the action and continue the substantive debate'. In reality, they haven't achieved it yet. In the Netherlands, the certification phase must be passed. Once an entity has met all the criteria for standing, it does not automatically mean that it can proceed with the class action to discuss the substantive dispute. Standing and certification are not necessarily the same thing. This seems to have been somewhat difficult to grasp for policy-makers in Member States with less experience of class actions.

VOET: One of the problems is that the Directive doesn't pay enough attention to cross-border issues, which have already been raised in connection with Dutch cases, such as Shell and Converium.[18]

TZANKOVA: We have to take a couple of steps back to understand the Dutch situation. In the Netherlands, the possibility of class actions has existed since 1994, on the basis of the civil code.[19] From that year onwards,

18 On international jurisdiction and recognition and enforcement issues, see PORETTI, P., 'Collective Redress in the European Union: Current Issues and Future Outlook', *EU and Member States: Legal and Economic Issues*, 3, 2019, pp. 339–362.

19 *Burgerlijk Wetboek* (Dutch civil code), Art. 3: 305a.

interest groups could bring civil actions on behalf of a group of victims. However, there was one important restriction: they could not claim monetary compensation. In practice, this meant that, if the claim was successful, individual victims had to initiate separate proceedings to establish the causal link between the harm they suffered and the harmful event alleged in the class action.

In the absence of a proper collective action for damages and in the aftermath of the financial crisis, the civil courts have been flooded with individual victims in a number of cases, putting enormous pressure on the judicial system. In response to this, a law on the collective settlement of mass tort claims (WCAM, according to its Dutch title) was introduced in 2005. Under WCAM, the claimant could settle with the defendant on behalf of the group; individual victims could opt out of the settlement and initiate individual proceedings. However, the basic structure was maintained: it was still not possible to claim compensation in collective proceedings: the claim for damages still had to be brought by individual victims.

Hence, the WCAM failed to offer a solution to the significant pressure on the judicial system caused by mass damage cases, and it was therefore considered necessary to introduce a new law on collective proceedings (WCAMCA), in force as of 1 January 2020. Now claimants can finally seek monetary compensation; but they can do so as long as the claim is sufficiently related to the Dutch legal sphere: for example, if the majority of the victims reside in the Netherlands; or if the defendant has its place of business in the Netherlands; or if the harmful event took place in the Netherlands. We call this the 'scope rule'.

The Shell and Converium cases[20] to which you refer, Stefaan, were made under the WCAM regime, not under the new WCAMCA rules; however, the two laws maintain a different jurisdictional treatment of settlements and claims. This seems to me problematic and undesirable. The basic procedural rules – not only on jurisdiction, but also on standing and other elements – should be the same whether settlement or litigation is involved. WCAMCA has not really remedied this discrepancy. What we have now is a much more restrictive jurisdictional regime in the context of collective

20 On these cases, see Mucha, J., 'Consumer Protection in Practice: A Transnational Comparative Account of Collective Redress Mechanisms (Part Two: The Dutch and the English Approaches)', *Humanities and Social Sciences*, 28–1, 2021, pp. 73–87, at 77. See also US Chamber Institute of Commerce for Legal Reform, *Collective Redress in Netherlands*, 2012, available at https://instituteforlegalreform.com/wp-content/uploads/2020/10/Collective_Redress_Netherlands.pdf, pp. 14–16.

proceedings. All this has to do with this 'scope rule', with all the strict jurisdictional requirements of connection to the Dutch scope. For example, the mere domicile of a holding company in the Netherlands as a defendant is not sufficient, according to the legislative history of the law, to establish the jurisdiction of the Dutch courts.

Now, some of us – including non-Dutch colleagues – believe that the Dutch rule on scope contravenes all the European rules on jurisdiction because it introduces a *de facto* extra-jurisdictional rule or, in effect, a *forum non conveniens* rule. It is known as a certification requirement, but, of course, labelling something differently does not change its nature. This anomalous situation can be explained by strong pressure from Dutch companies, worried that the Netherlands would attract many cases against Dutch companies from other EU countries. A restrictive scope rule was therefore the only way to pass this law. The Dutch government argued that the scope rule doesn't apply to individual actions: it may deprive victims of the collective action device, but not of the individual claims, and therefore it wasn't incompatible with EU jurisdiction rules.

Be as it may, the disturbing disparity between the rules on jurisdiction in the context of either settlement or litigation is all still out there.

Sooner or later, we all know that there will be an appeal to the Court of Justice of the EU to check whether this scope rule is in line with European rules on jurisdiction.

Voet: Still, if you look at the abundant case law you have there, the Netherlands is perhaps one step ahead of Europe. Many countries are aligning their rules with those of the Netherlands: Belgium and Slovenia, for example. We will soon see how this evolves once all Member States have implemented the Directive. Much of the impact this may have on jurisdictions will then depend, I think, on the interpretation and applicability by national supreme courts and, ultimately, the Luxembourg court. In cross-border cases, that is the most important issue. Ultimately, as Ianika says, we will have to wait for a uniform interpretation by the Court of Justice of the EU.

Gradi: This leads me to pose a more general question. Is it necessary for an implementation of the Directive to establish an effective system of collective redress, or is it sufficient to set minimum requirements, leaving the remainder to the discretion of national legislatures and courts?

Voet: The bar that the Directive has set is very low – this was already the case with the 2013 Recommendation and continues in the 2018 implementation report.[21] Of course, they will have to implement the Directive; but in the course and evolution of what happens in the legislative process, I think the bar is low. The question of qualified claimants is a good example. The qualification criteria for national class actions are very low. All in all, I don't think the Directive brings much new.

TZANKOVA: You are raising, Marco, a very interesting question; a classic question about European harmonisation. That is, the choice between harmonisation or letting everyone do what they think is best. While I am typically a supporter of diversity in all possible senses, I am a bit more nuanced when it comes to collective redress. I believe that common starting points, however minimal, are a good start and a positive force. One of the reasons is that we are seeing parallel actions emerging now that more EU Member States have their own regimes. If they are too diverse, how do we compare which one has been seised first? How can we do that if they are so different? So I think we will have a lot of additional problems of this kind, if we are too divergent and too different.[22]

GRADI: I agree that the Directive is a minimum. In some cases, however, there are some points that may require further reflection by national legislators. I'm thinking of the effects of *res judicata* against non-parties to the Directive. Each national legislature will have to reflect again on this. Even in Italy, the legislation is very new, so it is not yet implemented. I believe this is a time for reflection, and it's likely that any other draft will provide an important model for comparison.

SILVESTRI: That's an interesting issue: the problem of the *ultra vires* effect of *res judicata*, the extension of the binding effects of a final decision – which is rendered *inter alios*, among other parties – to non-parties.

---

21 Report from the Commission to the European Parliament, the Council, and the European Economic and Social Committee on the implementation of the Commission Recommendation of 11 June 2013 on common principles for injunctive and compensatory collective redress mechanisms in the Member States concerning violations of rights granted under Union law (2013/396/EU).

22 See TOUW, N., TZANKOVA, I., 'Parallel Actions in Cross-Border Mass Claims in the EU: A (Comparative) Lawyer's Paradise?', *Nederlands Internationaal Privaatrecht*, 9, 2023, pp. 9–30.

GRADI: Indeed, a classic issue in civil procedure. The *ultra vires* effect of *res judicata* is a practical and effective device. But it pays the price of imposing a remedy on persons who have not had the opportunity to exercise their procedural rights in the proceedings.[23] From the perspective of general theory, there are three possible solutions to this problem.

Firstly, the final judgment entailing binding effects on non-parties can be adopted only in particular cases. For example, it could bind non-parties in cases where they have been informed of the existence of the procedure, and have subsequently been allowed to participate on a voluntary basis, but waive the right to do so: a kind of potential participation.[24] In other cases, it binds non-parties if they have been represented in the procedure by a party that has actively participated on their behalf: a kind of fictitious participation.

Secondly, the final judgment can be binding on non-parties, but giving them the possibility – and the burden – to prove the injustice of the decision. In the previous solution, non-parties had no means to complain about the injustice of the decision. Here they do.

Thirdly, the final judgment may be considered as evidence in any subsequent proceedings involving non-parties; in other words, the judgment rendered *inter alios* may be disputed by the parties and freely assessed by the court in any subsequent proceedings involving non-parties.[25]

SILVESTRI: It's clear that the problems of *ultra vires* effects of *res judicata* present particular obstacles for collective proceedings, where it is impossible to guarantee the effective participation of all individuals concerned. Furthermore, it would be illogical to restrict the impact of the decision solely to those who actively engage in the proceedings.

GRADI: Both the ELI-UNIDROIT Rules and the EU Directive address this issue, offering different solutions that are useful to compare.

According to the Rules, the final judgment binds all parties – the qualified claimant and the defendant – but also the members of the group. This

---

23 FAIRGRIEVE, D., HOWELLS, G., 'Collective Redress Procedures: European Debates', *International & Comparative Law Quarterly*, 58-2, 2009, pp. 379–409, at 400.

24 See AMARO, R., AZAR-BAUD, F. M. J., CORNELOUP, F. S., FAUVARQUE-COSSON, F. B., JAULT-SESEKE, F. F., *Collective Redress in the Member States of the European Union Policy: Study*, 2018, p. 239.

25 See PORETTI, P., 'Collective Redress in the European Union: Current Issues and Future Outlook', *EU and Member States: Legal and Economic Issues*, 3, 2019, p. 357.

extends to those who have joined the proceedings through the opt-in mechanism, as well as to those included by court order if they have not opted out of the proceedings. In other words, group members who have expressly or tacitly joined the collective proceedings are bound by the collective decision and cannot challenge its content – positive or negative – in other proceedings. This applies, I insist, even if they are not formally part of the collective procedure. Rather, there is a kind of presumption of fictitious participation through the qualified claimant, who expressly or tacitly represents the group members acting on their behalf. After all, this stems from the very essence of collective proceedings:

> Rule 207. *Collective proceedings*
>
> Collective proceedings are proceedings brought by a qualified claimant on behalf of a group of persons who it is alleged are affected by an event giving rise to a mass harm, but where those persons, known as group members, are not parties to the action.

SILVESTRI: As you said, something similar happens with collective settlement agreements.

GRADI: Yes, and the *ultra vires* effect of the settlement or judgment can concern both the existence and the amount of compensation to be paid by the defendant. In the latter case, this also extends to the total amount of the compensable damages and the criteria for division of compensation between each member of the group. Rules 222 and 228 regulate the amount and content of compensation, while Rule 206 mentions the possible existence of infringement of relations by the defendant, but with specific reference to the collective interest injunctions. In the official comment to Rule 206, it's expressly stated that it would be appropriate for individuals to benefit from collective interest injunction. As such, in any future proceeding they should be able to rely on a finding that the defendant violated the law.

SILVESTRI: Do you believe that this benefit could also be extended to individuals who haven't joined a collective compensation procedure through the opt-in or opt-out mechanisms?

GRADI: I do. In this context, the violation of the defendant is certain, as a prerequisite for the collective compensation. While it's true that a qualified claimant doesn't represent these individuals, there's no violation of their right of action and defence because they themselves invoke an effect of collective decision in the context of an individual action. On the contrary, the defendant can't challenge such a decision since they've already had the opportunity to defend themselves on the issue in the whole active procedure. Of course, such extension can't be invoked with reference to the amount of compensation, which the individuals must demonstrate in each single action.

TZANKOVA: The solutions adopted by the Directive are different. Indeed, Article 15 stated that the final decision concerning the existence of the infringement harming collective interest can be used by all parties as evidence in the context of any other action. Here, only a probative value of the judgment, which is obtained *inter alios*, is recognised.

GRADI: Moreover, it's true that the EU legislation doesn't clearly specify whether these effects apply to individuals who haven't joined the collective action. However, the Directive does speak about third parties generally, so I think it'd be applicable for all individuals. Of course, it remains that individuals can only benefit from the ascertainment of the violation, but not from the compensation decided in the collective decision.

The problems with the binding effects of collective settlement agreements are obviously different. Both the ELI-UNIDROIT project and the EU Directive, first, make a court approval of the decision necessary. In the EU Directive, approval by an administrative authority is also possible. Either way, the important thing is public approval. Disapproval, on the other hand, requires that the unfairness of the agreement is verified. The Rules appear more precise on this point:

> Rule 225. *Approved settlements in opt-in actions*
>
> An approved settlement binds all group members who have opted-in at the time the order approving the settlement is made.
>
> Rule 226. *Approved settlements in opt-out proceedings*
>
> An approved settlement binds all group members unless they have opted-out of the collective proceedings at the time the order approving the settlement is made.

As indicated in the commentary, it wouldn't be appropriate to offer the opportunity to opt in later.[26] This would undermine the incentive for a group member to opt in earlier and reduce the amount of the settlement due to those members who originally opted in. The same would apply to the opt-out mechanism: it's inappropriate to allow an opt-out after settlement.

TZANKOVA: The problem, in my view, is the limited possibility of challenging the collective agreement in the event of unfairness. I guess that is the price you are willing to pay for finality.

GRADI: It seems that this option is left only to individuals who choose to exercise the opt-in or opt-out mechanism, with the solution applicable even if the collective agreement is reached outside a collective proceeding. Rule 232 addresses this situation:

> Rule 232. *Approval order and opt-in/opt-out procedure*
>
> The court must approve the proposed collective settlement on the basis of Rule 224.
>
> (a) If the court does not approve the proposed collective settlement it must give its reasons for refusing to approve it, and must remit the agreement to the parties.
>
> (b) The court must advertise the approved settlement in accordance with Rule 219(2), give information on whether the settlement shall become binding based on an opt-in or opt-out procedure, and fix a period of at least three months for the group members to opt-in or opt-out. The court shall decide to whom and how the notification to opt-in or to opt-out shall be given. If the terms of the settlement require a fixed number or percentage of group members to accept the settlement this must also be communicated clearly.
>
> (c) After the period fixed for opt-in or opt-out notifications and, where applicable, if the necessary number or percentage of group members have opted-in or have not opted-out, the court shall declare the approved settlement binding. Otherwise the court shall declare that the approval proceedings have been terminated without a binding settlement.

26 Rule 225, comment 2.

(d) An approved settlement shall bind all of the persons who have opted-in to the settlement or who have not opted-out of the settlement.

On the one hand, the members of the group are not explicitly recognised as having the power to challenge the collective agreement approved by the court, despite any objections that may be raised. On the other hand, the qualified claimants don't seem to have this power either, since they themselves have agreed to the terms of the agreement.

We could consider an adaptation of national law to allow an extraordinary right of appeal for those members of the group who object to the approval but do not want to be excluded from the collective agreement. Indeed, opting out of a collective agreement seems costly for an individual who may not be able to bring an individual action.

TZANKOVA: Another, perhaps more manageable, option that could lead to good qualitative results for the whole class is a system of professional objectors whose role would be to critically assess the settlement and draw the court's attention to possible points of contention.

Enough food for thought!

Bibliography

AMARO, R., AZAR-BAUD, F. M. J., CORNELOUP, F. S., FAUVARQUE-COSSON F. B., JAULT-SESEKE, F. F., *Collective Redress in the Member States of the European Union Policy: Study*, European Parliament, 2018, available at https://www.europarl.europa.eu/RegData/etudes/STUD/2018/608829/IPOL_STU(2018)608829_EN.pdf.

FAIRGRIEVE, D., HOWELLS, G., 'Collective Redress Procedures: European Debates', *International & Comparative Law Quarterly*, 58-2, 2009, pp. 379–409.

HENSLER, D., 'Foreword', in FITZPATRICK, B. T., THOMAS, R. S. (eds.), *The Cambridge Handbook of Class Actions. An International Survey*, Cambridge: Cambridge University Press, 2021.

KRAMER, X., TILLEMA, I., 'The Funding of Collective Redress by Entrepreneurial Parties: The EU and Dutch Context', *Revista Ítalo-Española de Derecho Procesal*, 2, 2020, pp. 165–181.

MORABITO, V., 'Ideological Plaintiffs and Class Actions: An Australian Perspective', *University of British Columbia Law Review*, 34-2, 2001, pp. 459–514.

MUCHA, J., 'Consumer Protection in Practice: A Transnational Comparative Account of Collective Redress Mechanisms (Part Two: The Dutch and the English Approaches)', *Humanities and Social Sciences*, 28-1, 2021, pp. 73–87.

MULHERON, R., *The Class Action in Common Law Legal Systems. A Comparative Perspective*, Oxford: Hart, 2004.

PORETTI, P., 'Collective Redress in the European Union: Current Issues and Future Outlook', *EU and Member States: Legal and Economic Issues*, 3, 2019, pp. 339–362.

SILVESTRI, E., 'Rebooting Italian Class Actions', in UZELAC, A., VOET, S. (eds.), *Class Actions in Europe. Holy Grail or Wrong Trail?*, Cham: Springer, 2021, pp. 201–213.

STADLER, A., JEULAND, E., SMITH, V. (eds.), *Collective and Mass Litigation in Europe. Model Rules for Effective Dispute Resolution*, Cheltenham: Edward Elgar, 2020.

STIER, B., TZANKOVA, I. N., 'The Culture of Collective Litigation: A Comparative Analysis', in HENSLER, D., HODGES, CH., TZANKOVA, I., *Class Actions in Context*, Cheltenham: Edward Elgar, 2016, pp. 23–50.

STÖHR, A., 'The Implementation of Collective Redress – A Comparative Approach', *German Law Journal*, 21, 2020, pp. 1606–1624.

TOUW, N., TZANKOVA, I., 'Parallel Actions in Cross-Border Mass Claims in the EU: A (Comparative) Lawyer's Paradise?', *Nederlands Internationaal Privaatrecht*, 9, 2023, pp. 9–30.

TZANKOVA, I., 'Funding of Mass Disputes: Lessons from the Netherlands', *Journal of Law, Economics & Policy*, 8(3), 2012, pp. 549–591.

US CHAMBER INSTITUTE OF COMMERCE FOR LEGAL REFORM, *Collective Redress in Netherlands*, 2012, available at https://instituteforlegalreform.com/wp-content/uploads/2020/10/Collective_Redress_Netherlands.pdf, pp. 14–16.

UZELAC, A., VOET, S. (eds.), *Class Actions in Europe. Holy Grail or Wrong Trail?*, Cham: Springer, 2021.

CHAPTER 9

Costs and Funding

Albert Henke, Paul Oberhammer, and Eva Storskrubb

Litigation costs and funding are typically regarded as relatively minor, ancillary aspects of civil procedure. Nevertheless, they have the potential to have far-reaching consequences. Both are of critical importance in determining access to justice, procedural strategies, and case dispositions. The recovery of costs can represent a significant proportion of the economic interest. Third-party funding, however, can act as a valuable resource in expensive litigation, facilitating the bringing of meritorious cases and decreasing financial losses.

The Rules propose an integral regulation of these issues, including the scope of court discretion to set costs to be recovered as well as the level of disclosure considered necessary for the adequate functioning of third-party funded litigation.

 | DOI:10.1163/9789004533257_010

HENKE: Matters regarding costs can be complex and controversial.

STORSKRUBB: That's why we made sure to get these rules out to a wider audience for feedback. We shared them with observers and people in other working groups, the structure group, and the advisory board for the Rules project.

Also, we know that the official commentary is an important part of the Rules. This is especially true when it comes to costs, because it shows what our working group was thinking when we wrote the Rules.

HENKE: It's all good reason. This part of the Rules shows how the European process has changed since the original EU treaties. At the time, we didn't even think about harmonising civil procedure. All that was discussed was the principles of equivalence and effectiveness. And now, we're looking at harmonising legal costs, which goes beyond the specific procedural regulation to touch upon tradition, cultural background, court organisation, and the regulation of the legal profession.

STORSKRUBB: After all, litigation costs have an impact on the internal market. They create procedural incentives or disincentives. They affect procedural behaviour and litigation strategies.

HENKE: Yes, absolutely. Comparative studies demonstrate the impact of applicable rules on the allocation and amount of recoverable costs on a party's strategy.[1]

To illustrate, the cost shift does not provide an increase in resources to an impecunious party. However, it might represent a sort of deterrent for a wealthy party from spending large sums on his case, thereby encouraging rational behaviours.

Conversely, when costs are shifted, the *recoverability gap* between the costs that the winner receives and the actual expenditure might affect the parties' decisions on whether or not to take judicial action.

1 See REIMANN, M., 'Cost and Fee Allocation in Civil Procedure: A Synthesis', in REIMANN, M. (ed.), *Cost and Fee Allocation in Civil Procedure: A Comparative Study*, Cham: Springer, 2012, pp. 20–22; O'REILLY, M., 'The Harmonisation of Costs Practices in International Arbitration: The Search for the Holy Grail', in BETANCOURT, J. C. (ed.), *Defining Issues in International Arbitration. Celebrating 100 Years of the Chartered Institute of Arbitrators*, Oxford: Oxford University Press, 2016, p. 272.

For instance, Directive 2004/48/EC ('Enforcement of intellectual property rights') stipulates that the loser shall pay the winner's costs in full. Based on the assumption that all Member States had a 100% cost shifting rule, the implementation of this rule in some EU jurisdictions has resulted in a decline in the number of IP injunction claims. This is because claimants were concerned that they would face an unacceptable risk if they lost the case. Consequently, the implementation of the Directive has in some instances resulted in an unintended consequence. This is due to a lack of consideration for the detailed operation of a national cost-shifting rule.

The strategic behaviours linked to the regulation on costs also depend on the amounts at stake and on the importance of the case. When the amounts at stake are high or the issue of little importance, the loser pays principle encourages potential claimants with a strong case to take legal action, whereas the American rule tends to dissuade them from doing so. Conversely, when the sums at stake are low or the issue important, the loser pays principle tends to dissuade claimants with a weaker case from taking legal action, when they would have been encouraged to do so by the American rule.

STORSKRUBB: Also, historically, costs have been one of the most immediate factors affecting access to justice.

HENKE: The connection between the rules on the allocation and determination of legal costs and the fundamental right of access to justice is undeniable.[2]

STORSKRUBB: And I'm not talking about only attorneys' fees, although this is usually the most relevant chapter of costs. Often the combined costs of court fees, experts' fees, and ancillary costs such as travel costs and indemnities to witnesses – the aggregate costs of both parties – are considered by litigants almost as part of the *actual* amount in dispute, of the whole economic interest at stake. In low-value civil claims (and sometimes when the value is not so low), the combined legal cost sum can even exceed the amount in dispute.

2 See GRAMATIKOV, M., BARENDRECHT, M., LAXMINARAYAN, M., VERDONSCHOT, J. H., KLAMING, L., VAN ZEELAND, C., *A Handbook for Measuring the Costs and Quality of Access to Justice*, Apeldoorn, Antwerp: Maklu, 2009; FARROW, T. C. W., JACOBS, L. (eds.), *The Justice Crisis. The Cost and Value of Accessing Law*, Vancouver: UBC Press, 2021.

HENKE: In low-value claims or claims that are not complex, the cost is relatively predictable in terms of the amount of fees and the proportion that should be recoverable. This makes it easier to manage. However, in larger commercial disputes, legal costs are less predictable, which makes it more difficult for the prospective litigant to manage their costs. This also affects access to justice.

Another issue from this standpoint is transparency regarding the criteria used to determine court fees and, generally, to inspire court decisions on attorneys' fees.

STORSKRUBB: The reality is that cost rules are closely linked to sensitive political choices regarding the funding of the justice system and the organisation and regulation of the legal profession. Even within European jurisdictions, there are quite divergent political choices in these matters. The equally diverging rules on costs are in part a function of these underlying political choices.

HENKE: It is accurate to say that, in relation to court organisation, the answers to the question of who deals with the costs, or whether the matter is in the hands of a judge or a clerk, or whether this issue is dealt with as part of ordinary proceedings or through special, separate proceedings, vary considerably from jurisdiction to jurisdiction.

STORSKRUBB: Bearing that reality in mind, within the working group we soon agreed that we should limit ourselves to provide a basic legal framework on costs. Some of the Rules are more detailed than others in the entire text of the Rules; the ones on costs are among the less detailed.

HENKE: Within that general approach, how did you draft the articles? Given that they're more of a framework than a detailed regulation, does that mean the court has a lot of leeway to rule on these matters?

STORSKRUBB: Not necessarily; but we did opt for a cost regime that places ample discretion in the hands of the decision maker, be it a judge or a clerk or another officer within the court organisation.

The general rules on costs can be read in Rules 239 to 241. Firstly, a mandate to determine costs in any event:

> Rule 239. *Decision on costs*
>
> (1) A court rendering a final judgment or terminating the proceedings in any other way shall determine which party is required to reimburse the other party or parties' costs of the proceedings, unless the parties have agreed otherwise. ...

Then, a general 'reasonable and proportionate' standard:

> Rule 239. *Decision on costs*
>
> (1) ... Any recovery of costs shall be limited to those that are reasonable and proportionate.

A standard that is reiterated when clarifying the scope and amount of costs:

> Rule 240. *Scope and amount of costs*
>
> (1) Parties may seek to recover the costs of the proceedings, in particular
>
> (a) reasonable and proportionate costs of their legal representation in the proceedings,
>
> (b) court and other fees such as those of court-appointed experts, interpreters, court reporters etc.,
>
> (c) other reasonable financial outlays resulting from the conduct of the proceedings, such as costs of party-appointed experts, travel expenses, and fees for the service of documents.
>
> (2) Costs under Rule 240(1) may also include costs reasonably incurred for the preparation of proceedings before they were commenced.
>
> (3) Parties may only recover costs which they have reasonably and proportionately incurred for the conduct of the proceedings, taking into account the amount in dispute, the nature and complexity of the issues, [and] the significance of the case for the parties.
>
> ...

Then the Rules go on to set forth the main criteria for the allocation of costs:

Rule 241. *General rule*

(1) When determining upon which party the obligation to reimburse costs shall be placed under Rule 239, the court shall take into account the circumstances of the specific proceedings, in particular whether and to what extent the parties' claims were successful.

(2) The court may also take into account the parties' conduct, in particular, whether and to what extent they acted in good faith and contributed to the fair, efficient and speedy resolution of the dispute.

As we can see, the parameters we proposed include the outcome of the case in a very broad sense, which includes not only who prevailed in the debate but also the circumstances of the case and the conduct of the parties, particularly if they acted in good faith and complied with their cooperation duties.[3] We went for what we call in the commentary the 'European rule' – loser pays – as opposed to the 'American rule' – each party should cover its own costs.[4] The European rule tends to reduce litigation costs; aims at compensating prevailing litigants in line with their substantive rights; discourages frivolous lawsuits; and facilitates access to justice.[5]

However, success shouldn't be the only factor. Costs are also powerful tools to promote compliance with some of the leitmotifs of the Rules: the cooperation principle, which applies to the parties' expected conduct in the first place (Rules 2 and 3); the necessary proportionality of the proceedings (Rule 6), sanctions (Rule 7), and costs (Rule 8). Here we find the same 'reasonable and proportionate' standard:

Rule 8. *Proportionality of costs*

Costs of proceedings should, in so far as possible, be reasonable and proportionate to the amount in dispute, the nature and complexity of

3 SMITH, V., 'Costs and Funding', in STADLER, A., SMITH, V., GASCÓN, F. (eds.), *European Rules of Civil Procedure. A Commentary on the ELI/UNIDROIT Model Rules*, Cheltenham: Edward Elgar, 2023, pp. 632–669, at 646–648.

4 SMITH, V., 'Costs and Funding', in STADLER, A., SMITH, V., GASCÓN, F. (eds.), *European Rules of Civil Procedure. A Commentary on the ELI/UNIDROIT Model Rules*, Cheltenham: Edward Elgar, 2023, pp. 632–669, at 645.

5 REIMANN, M., 'Cost and Fee Allocation in Civil Procedure: A Synthesis', in REIMANN, M. (ed.), *Cost and Fee Allocation in Civil Procedure: A Comparative Study*, Cham: Springer, 2012, p. 20.

> the particular proceedings, their importance for the parties and the public interest.

To sum up, the decision-maker enjoys broad discretion when it comes to costs; but the Rules do provide a general direction as to the allocation and amount of costs.

HENKE: What does the concept of proportionality mean in terms of costs? Is proportionality an effective tool for handling costs? Rule 5(1) places particular emphasis on proportionality *as a general principle*, designed to govern the entire dispute resolution process. In contrast, in most legal systems, proportionality is referred to as an important aspect of procedural law *in specific circumstances* only. These include simplified procedures in small claim proceedings, evidence-taking (to ensure that the least complex and least costly method is used), and provisional measures.

STORSKRUBB: In my jurisdiction, we do not have tariffs. Therefore, different cases and circumstances require different solutions. I believe that we must rely on the judges or clerks in charge to set standards and create good practices and an appropriate direction. In addition to the applicable bar deontological rules and the duties by which attorneys must abide, case law and practice will provide the key to understanding how proportionality must develop.

HENKE: Could this approach also be applied in jurisdictions where tariffs are predetermined by the legislature, at least regarding court costs?

STORSKRUBB: In the Rules we said that even if we have tariffs on the amount of costs locally, the costs that can be awarded should still be 'reasonable and proportionate':

> Rule 240. *Scope and amount of costs*
>
> (4) Where national law specify tariffs for the recovery of certain fees (such as, where relevant, court fees and fees for the parties' legal representation, for experts, and interpreters), any award of costs should nevertheless be consistent with the Rules of this Part.

HENKE: This general and insistent recourse to undetermined notions such as 'reasonability' and 'proportionality' might be problematic. Proportionality, in particular, is a very problematic general principle. Proportionality to what? In this context, what should the cost be proportionate to? To the amount in dispute? To the amount of work carried out by the lawyers? To the amount of work carried out by the court?

It's worth noting the differences between the German and English systems of the fixed-tariff procedure. Each has its own rationale, which could be jeopardised by an overriding proportionality requirement. For instance, the shifting of costs on a tariff basis provides a degree of predictability, although it does not necessarily ensure proportionality. An *ex ante* control of costs, like the one in force in Germany, makes it easier to predict costs, but it doesn't necessarily mean that costs will be allocated in a proportional way. On the other hand, an *ex post* control, which is a kind of soft control based on court discretion, like in England, doesn't necessarily keep costs under control. This is especially true in larger commercial disputes, where lawyers' fees can quickly spiral out of control unless there are pre-established limits.

STORSKRUBB: None of the two approaches is without peril. However, once we admit the parties' conduct into the pool of criteria to allocate costs, it's almost unavoidable to let go of any predetermined criteria.

HENKE: Possibly.

STORSKRUBB: The working groups that worked on that were very interested in the obligation of the parties to work for the efficient and speedy resolution of the dispute, and how the parties work towards a settlement. In the official commentary, we read that we don't have a rule in the cost part of the Rules on specific behaviour concerning how parties behave in relation to mediation or settlement.

HENKE: Even though, as we said earlier, cost can be used to orient the behaviour of all parties involved, also in this context. In Germany, for example, there are rules that allow partial recovery of costs in case of settlement.

STORSKRUBB: An interesting hint that we give in our commentary is that some EU Member States (though not many) have specific rules on, for example, if one party gives a settlement offer, and the other party is then less successful in the outcome, how such a settlement offer should impact the costs of the dispute. We didn't come up with a special rule for that. Settlement offers compared to the outcome might be a relevant factor, but it's not the only one. It's not straightforward either – there are so many factors, both internal and external, that can affect settlement conversations![6] For this reason, we didn't want to impose a rule based on that. Anyway, in the general part of our Rules there is already the idea that the parties should try to settle the dispute early on. If it seems relevant in a particular case, this idea should be applied.

HENKE: What about legal aid? I only find an article on such a classic and important aspect of access to justice:

> Rule 244. *Legal aid*
>
> (1) Parties are entitled to legal aid, as provided by national law, if their right of access to justice and to a fair trial so requires.
>
> (2) Such legal aid should be sufficient to cover reasonable and proportionate legal representation where legal provisions, the complexity of the case, or the vulnerability of a party so require.

STORSKRUBB: It's not a minor issue to say that legal aid should be provided. Although we don't go into the financial details in the Rules, legal aid is a primary source of funding. The way we phrased the very broad and general rule of legal aid is by giving a hint that we think that parties that are vulnerable, or don't have legal means and don't have sufficient means to cover their costs, should of course be entitled to legal aid. The legal aid should be sufficient to cover – once again – 'reasonable and proportionate' costs of legal representation.

HENKE: It's worth looking at this in the context of a growing trend towards privatising many aspects of the justice system. One reason third-party funding is so successful is that public funding, like legal aid, is becoming less relevant or less practicable. Also, the original design of these mechanisms has shown that they have some flaws. It's in this process of privatising justice that we can really see the diminishing importance of legal aid and the growing use of alternative funding methods, such as third-party funding.

---

6 ICC ARBITRATION AND ADR COMMISSION, 'Decisions on Costs in International Arbitration', *ICC Dispute Resolution Bulletin*, 2, 2015., pp. 17–18; SMITH, V., 'Costs and Funding', in STADLER, A., SMITH, V., GASCÓN, F. (eds.), *European Rules of Civil Procedure. A Commentary on the ELI/UNIDROIT Model Rules*, Cheltenham: Edward Elgar, 2023, pp. 632–669, at 638.

OBERHAMMER: The emergence of alternative means of funding is not a negative phenomenon. If you look at current sources of law, however, third-party funding seems to be something suspicious or even dangerous. The 2013 European Commission recommendation on common principles for injunctive and compensatory collective redress mechanisms concerning violations of rights granted under EU law[7] was quite clear in that respect. Paragraph 15 of that recommendation reads as follows:

> The court should be allowed to stay the proceedings if in the case of use of financial resources provided by the third party:
>
> a) there is a conflict of interest between the third party and the claiming party and its members;
>
> b) the third party has insufficient resources in order to meet its financial commitments to the claimant party initiating the collective redress procedure;
>
> c) the claimant party has insufficient resources to meet any adverse costs should the collective redress procedure fail.

The same rather cautious approach is reflected in the 2020 European Directive on representative actions for the protection of the collective interests of consumers.[8] Let me quote Article 10, Section 1:

> Article 10. *Funding of representative actions for redress measures*
>
> 1. Member States shall ensure that, where a representative action for redress measures is funded by a third party, insofar as allowed in accordance with national law, conflicts of interests are prevented and that funding by third parties that have an economic interest in the bringing or the outcome of the representative action for redress measures does not divert the representative action away from the protection of the collective interests of consumers.

---

7 Commission Recommendation of 11 June 2013 on common principles for injunctive and compensatory collective redress mechanisms in the Member States concerning violations of rights granted under Union law (2013/396/EU).

8 Directive (EU) 2020/1828 of the European Parliament and the Council of 25 November 2020 on representative actions for the protection of the collective interests of consumers and repealing Directive 2009/22/EC.

This guideline is then specified in Section 2:

> 2. For the purposes of paragraph 1, Member States shall in particular ensure that:
>
> (a) the decisions of qualified entities in the context of a representative action, including decisions on settlement, are not unduly influenced by a third party in a manner that would be detrimental to the collective interests of the consumers concerned by the representative action;
>
> (b) the representative action is not brought against a defendant that is a competitor of the funding provider or against a defendant on which the funding provider is dependent.

Section 3 of this Article 10 goes on to say:

> 3. Member States shall ensure that courts or administrative authorities in representative actions for redress measures are empowered to assess compliance with paragraphs 1 and 2 in cases where any justified doubts arise with respect to such compliance. To that end, qualified entities shall disclose to the court or administrative authority a financial overview that lists sources of funds used to support the representative action.

Finally, Section 4 states, to ensure compliance with paragraphs 1 and 2, the courts are empowered to take quite harsh 'appropriate measures':

> 4. Member States shall ensure that, for the purposes of paragraphs 1 and 2, courts or administrative authorities are empowered to take appropriate measures, such as requiring the qualified entity to refuse or make changes in respect of the relevant funding and, if necessary, rejecting the legal standing of the qualified entity in a specific representative action. If the legal standing of the qualified entity is rejected in a specific representative action, that rejection shall not affect the rights of the consumers concerned by that representative action.

HENKE: International arbitration institutions also appear to have some reservations about third-party funding.

OBERHAMMER: Yes, for example, the 2021 ICC Arbitration Rules, in the chapter on the arbitral tribunal:

> Article 11. *General provisions*
>
> 7. In order to assist prospective arbitrators and arbitrators in complying with their duties under Articles 11(2) and 11(3), each party must promptly inform the Secretariat, the arbitral tribunal and the other parties, of the existence and identity of any non-party which has entered into an arrangement for the funding of claims or defences and under which it has an economic interest in the outcome of the arbitration.

This article is referring to the duties under Articles 11(2) and 11(3) of the ICC rules. These duties are the arbitrator's duties to disclose all relevant facts that might play a role in the assessment, whether they're impartial and independent to serve as an arbitrator in a specific case:

> Article 11. *General provisions*
>
> 2. Before appointment or confirmation, a prospective arbitrator shall sign a statement of acceptance, availability, impartiality and independence. The prospective arbitrator shall disclose in writing to the Secretariat any facts or circumstances which might be of such a nature as to call into question the arbitrator's independence in the eyes of the parties, as well as any circumstances that could give rise to reasonable doubts as to the arbitrator's impartiality. The Secretariat shall provide such information to the parties in writing and fix a time limit for any comments from them.
>
> 3. An arbitrator shall immediately disclose in writing to the Secretariat and to the parties any facts or circumstances of a similar nature to those referred to in Article 11(2) concerning the arbitrator's impartiality or independence which may arise during the arbitration.

The ICC has addressed a very relevant issue of third-party funding, probably the only thing that should matter when it comes to drafting general rules in the field of civil procedure. In arbitration, it is important to know the funder in the background, as this is relevant for the arbitrator's conflict check. One should not serve as a regular house arbitrator for one funder, and one should not work on cases of a funder, or work as an expert for a funder, and sit as arbitrator and proceedings funded by the same funder at the same time, without a least disclosing this connection.[9]

This doesn't apply to state court judges, though. In most places, judges cannot be attorneys at the same time. In jurisdictions where judges can be attorneys at the same time, where they can render other legal services, such as legal opinions, this might be a problem. If you think that impartiality issues resulting from such activities are an overall problem, then you should resolve this simply by prohibiting such practices. This has nothing to do with third-party funding.

STORSKRUB: The EU legislator certainly advocates a more intense intervention in this regard.

OBERHAMMER: Indeed, the concern of the European institutions extends far beyond disclosure based on independence and impartiality reasons. The Directive requires that conflicts of interest and funding by third parties with an interest in the outcome of the representative action be prevented.

In this context, the 2020 European Directive on representative actions for the protection of the collective interests of consumers also hypothesises about situations where the decisions of qualified entities, including settlement decisions, are unduly influenced by a third party in a manner that will be detrimental to the collective interests of the consumers. It even goes so far as to *fantasise* about situations where the representative action is brought against the defendant that is a competitor of the funding provider. To prevent such situations, the Directive provides for the court to investigate, and to some extent police, third-party funding. The wording of the Directive suggests that this might even go so far that this results in court decisions to the detriment of the claimant, because such claimants might be denied standing to sue in these collective redress proceedings based on defects in the third-party funding arrangement.

To sum up, it looks like the EU legislator thinks that third-party funding is a very dangerous thing.

HENKE: Is it not?

9 TIRADO, J., MEAGHER, D. R., GUPTA, A., 'The Costs and Funding of International Arbitration', in BETANCOURT, J. C. (ed.), *Defining Issues in International Arbitration. Celebrating 100 Years of the Chartered Institute of Arbitrators*, Oxford: Oxford University Press, 2016, p. 291.

OBERHAMMER: It's not out of the question that some funders could be engaging in abusive practices. But this should be a matter for financial market regulation and supervision, not civil procedural law.[10] I believe this is the key message; and is exactly the approach of the Rules – although the final wording and the explanatory commentary were much less straightforward than originally intended and drafted.

HENKE: I see your point, but even though it shouldn't be *primarily* a civil procedural law issue, the latter is inevitably affected by the regime that governs the third-party funding mechanism. For this reason, some precautions were included in the Rules.

OBERHAMMER: Project leaders insisted on the need to include a few caveats concerning third-party funding, for instance the following:

> Rule 245. *Third-party funding and success fees*
>
> (2) Such a third party funding arrangement must be in accordance with applicable law and must not provide for inadequate compensation for the funder or enable the funder to exercise any undue influence on the conduct of the proceedings.

In turn, the Rules also contain some positive news for third-party funding, which is missed in the two EU sources of law that I mentioned earlier. Firstly, success fee arrangements with the funder or counsel are licit:

> Rule 245. *Third-party funding and success fees*
>
> (3) Parties may enter into success fee arrangements with counsel or a third party funder. Such arrangements must nevertheless be consistent with applicable law, the parties' access to fair legal representation and the integrity of the proceedings.

10 On the polemics on the regulation of third-party funders as financial service providers or legal service providers, see: CORDINA, A., STORSKRUBB, E., 'The Future Regulation of Third-Party Funding in Europe', *Nederlands-Vlaams tijdschrift voor mediation en conflictmanagement Aflevering*, 26-2, 2022, pp. 1–8. On the debate about the definition of the third-party funding, see ICCA-QUEEN MARY TASK FORCE, 'Report on Third-Party Funding in International Arbitration', *ICCA Reports*, 4, 2018, pp. 46–55.

Secondly, the Rules warn against the potential abuse of concerns about the funding arrangement to cast shadows of doubt on the merits of the funded claim. The provision reads as follows:

> Rule 245. *Third-party funding and success fees*
>
> (4) A violation of the requirements of Rule 245(1), (2) and (3) does not constitute a defence against the claim of the party availing itself of third party funding or a success fee arrangement.

Storskrubb: The article suggests the possibility of resorting to the decision on costs to sanction any irregularity in that regard, leaving the merits untouched:

> ... But, having made its decision on the claim, the court may ask for details of fee arrangements with a third party or counsel relevant for the instance at stake, and, upon consultation with the parties, it may take into account any disregard of applicable law or lacking fairness of the arrangement when it renders the final decision on costs determining the part of the claimant's costs to be reimbursed.

Oberhammer: Clearly not the brainchild of the cost group, but rather of the project leaders...

Storskrubb: The rules on collective redress are even more sceptical of third-party funding. According to Rule 237:

> Rule 237. *Third party funding*
>
> (1) A qualified claimant may use third-party litigation funding.
>
> (2) Rule 245 applies to any such third-party funding agreement. A court may, however, require a qualified claimant to disclose the details of any such funding agreement relevant for the instance at stake to the court and, in so far as appropriate, to the parties.

Oberhammer: This is contrary to the confidentiality of the funding agreements stipulated in Rule 245(1). I find this particularly unfortunate because, while in individual proceedings third-party funding is the exception, it is the rule in collective redress proceedings. In such proceedings, the consumer's access to justice is often only possible thanks to third-party funding arrangements. Rules providing strict disclosure obligations of third-party funding arrangements allow for tactics aimed at sabotaging the consumer's access to justice.

HENKE: Why are so many people so concerned with third-party funding, then?

OBERHAMMER: In the past, nobody was concerned about where a party got the money for litigation from. Some degree of financial leverage through debt or equity has been around for centuries. More recently, companies have begun to use dedicated lines of credit with financiers to mitigate the impact of litigation on their balance sheets; there are companies where litigation is an everyday reality. The courts don't ask about that. Courts don't ask whether the parent company or other group companies are funding the litigation, or whether someone is running their business on a bank loan or equity contributions from investors (and who those investors are), or whether you have legal expenses insurance, or whether you just have rich parents who will pay for the litigation. Nobody ever asks that.

Suddenly, the source of a party's funding becomes the subject of disclosure obligations and discussions, and even legal consequences, to the extent that the legal standing of that party could be challenged based on objections to third-party funding arrangements and disclosure obligations – both to the court and to the other parties. Now the legislators are saying that you must disclose to your opponent aspects that are an essential part of the strategic background to your litigation. I suspect that this is not the result of experience of actual problems, but rather the result of very successful lobbying and PR work by consultants and defendants.

HENKE: I can't quite agree. Concerns about third-party funding are not entirely unfounded. In recent decades, we have witnessed rather epochal changes, characterised by a shift in economic, political, institutional and judicial governance, towards an increasingly distinctly supranational dimension, with expropriation of powers and controls at the local or national level. The civil justice system has progressively lost its autonomy, becoming increasingly instrumentalised under the yoke of an overwhelming imperative of economic, financial, and market efficiency, to the needs of productivity and competitiveness of the system considered as a whole (as demonstrated by the recent waves of civil justice reforms at the continental level). This raises questions about who is really in control, who is ultimately responsible, who really exercises influence on the most relevant decision-making processes.

Similar questions arise in the context of judicial (or arbitration) proceedings. The economic and contractual imbalance between the funder and the funded party raises difficult questions. Who is the *real* party to the proceedings? Who makes the critical decisions (appointment of the lawyer, choice of procedural strategies, acceptance of a settlement proposal) in the context of a dispute? The issue of conflicts of interest (between the funder and the adjudicatory body, between the funder and the lawyer, between the funder and the counterparty of the funded party, etc.) is also crucial.[11]

In sum, it seems clear to me that this issue cannot be safely left to the financial markets or regulatory authorities.

STORSKRUBB: Speaking with Carlota Ucín, a brilliant researcher at Rotterdam, she said that the right question to ask is *who* we are protecting and what *values* are we safeguarding by setting out the disclosure duty. I totally agree with her.

OBERHAMMER: Me too. It is the key question. You might also ask, *who* is granted remedies under this legislation? I believe that the Directive is heading in the wrong direction in that respect. Article 10(4) might even create a basis for objections by the defendant in case of problems arising from the funding arrangement.

> Article 10. *Funding of representative actions for redress measures*
>
> 4. Member States shall ensure that, for the purposes of paragraphs 1 and 2, courts or administrative authorities are empowered to take appropriate measures, such as requiring the qualified entity to refuse or make changes in respect of the relevant funding and, if necessary, rejecting the legal standing of the qualified entity in a specific representative action. If the legal standing of the qualified entity is rejected in a

11 See SAULNIER, J., KORONTHALYOVA, I, MÜLLER, K., 'Responsible Private Funding of Litigation. European Added Value Assessment', European Parliament, 2021, available at https://www.europarl.europa.eu/RegData/etudes/STUD/2021/662612/EPRS_STU(2021)662612_EN.pdf, as well as the ensuing European Parliament Resolution of 13 September 2022 with recommendations to the Commission on responsible private funding of litigation (2020/2130(INL)), 'Responsible Private Funding of Litigation', available at https://www.europarl.europa.eu/doceo/document/TA-9-2022-0308_EN.pdf.

specific representative action, that rejection shall not affect the rights of the consumers concerned by that representative action.

Therefore, in the future, respondents will try to obtain as much information as possible about the funding arrangements. This will allow them to better understand the strategy and limitations of the funding and be better prepared to defend themselves. If they find something that isn't in line with court practice, their first line of defence will be to deny the qualified entity legal standing because of the improper funding arrangement.

This is absolutely the wrong approach because it is to the detriment of the consumers who are supposed to be protected. The last sentence of that paragraph says that this doesn't affect consumer rights, only the standing of the qualified entity. But the qualified entity is there to commence and pursue these proceedings on behalf of consumers!

So, EU law allows defendants to raise objections against the very parties these provisions are designed to protect. If you want to protect the right party, you must protect consumers in collective redress mechanisms from exploitation. That's why I said it should be done in relation to financial markets.

HENKE: Thinking about it the other way around, could potential defendants in collective redress lawsuits be subject to exploitation themselves?

OBERHAMMER: While it's conceivable, I haven't seen any factual evidence of this happening on a significant scale – at least, not in German-speaking countries.

Most funders finance one in ten of the proposals they receive because the other nine are not promising enough. Financing such litigation isn't unfair vis-à-vis the respondents. They ignore speculative, *junk* proceedings, and invest only in solid cases where they have some winning expectation.[12]

Have we ever been concerned that rich people and well-funded companies use their money to manipulate the administration of justice by hiring

12 ICCA-QUEEN MARY TASK FORCE, 'Report on Third-Party Funding in International Arbitration', *ICCA Reports*, 4, 2018, p. 31; '… when third-party funding contracts are admissible, however, they facilitate strong cases much more than weak ones' from AVRAHAM, R., WICKELGREN, A. L., 'Third-Party Litigation Funding with Informative Signals', *Journal of Law & Economics*, 61–4, 2018, pp. 637–675, at 642. See also HARRINGTON, W. J., 'Champerty, Usury, and Third-Party Litigation Funding', *The Brief*, 49–2, 2020, pp. 54–64.

excellent lawyers and bringing high-risk cases? But now that poor parties also have access to such funds, do we suddenly have a concern that this might be abusive? It does not seem honest. We should be glad that where legal aid is inadequate – and, as Albert points out, increasingly difficult to obtain – the market, has come up with a Plan B. This is an opportunity for legal proceedings to take place on a level playing field.

HENKE: To be honest, I don't see this mechanism as an alternative to legal aid.[13] Most funders don't use legal action to foster access to justice but – legitimately, for goodness' sake – to push their own financial goals, to fight their own battles. As you said, Paul, only one in ten of the proposals that funders receive are financed. The other nine don't seem to be promising enough. To put it another way, funders only invest in cases where they have a reasonable expectation of success. Legal aid, on the other hand, was traditionally designed to support those who are unable to afford legal representation to exercise their rights. It was never intended to be dependent on the prospects of success.

I agree that defendants shouldn't have an unfair strategic advantage because of the disclosure of third-party funding agreements. But in some cases, disclosure is useful in revealing the level of autonomy enjoyed by the funded party and potential conflicts of interest between all the actors involved. There are cases where the funder wields so much control that it should be considered a *real* party, with all the procedural consequences.[14]

It's not enough to have a lawyer present to guarantee a fair and due process. After all, lawyers are often paid by the funder, so they have a clear incentive – even if they comply with the rules of the profession – to create a direct link with the funder to secure compensation.[15]

STORSKRUBB: The issues of attorney-to-client loyalty and conflict of interest have existed long before the advent of formal third-party funding

13 CAPPELLETTI, M., 'The Emergence of a Modern Theme', in CAPPELLETTI, M., GORDLEY, J., JOHNSON, E., *Towards Equal Justice. A Comparative Study of Legal Aid in Modern Societies (Texts and Materials)*, Milan: Giuffrè, 1975, pp. 6–16; on the critics of the burden to bring 'the sound case' to obtain legal aid, see p. 42.

14 HARRINGTON, W. J., 'Champerty, Usury, and Third-Party Litigation Funding', *The Brief*, 49-2, 2020, pp. 54–64.

15 TIRADO, J., MEAGHER, D. R., GUPTA, A., 'The Costs and Funding of International Arbitration', in BETANCOURT, J. C. (ed.), *Defining Issues in International Arbitration. Celebrating 100 Years of the Chartered Institute of Arbitrators*, Oxford: Oxford University Press, 2016, p. 290.

arrangements. For example, trade unions funding disputes relating to employees. Those kinds of problems should be regulated by the bar ethical rules, or the deontological rules. I can't see that they can be regulated in another manner because the standards guiding the attorney-client relationship are already defined.

OBERHAMMER: The best example of third-party involvement, both now and before the advent of third-party funding, is the insurance industry. The insurance company is almost always in the background in liability cases, suggesting which lawyers to engage yet actually paying the opposing party's settlement. And yet no one has ever said that the *evil* insurance companies should be treated as the real parties to a dispute. Companies that run their business on bank loans and are involved in litigation sometimes must report to the bank what the outcome might be, whether there will be an inflow of money as a result, and so on. That's business.

HENKE: Regarding the insurer, there are mechanisms in place that allow them to become the *real* or *direct* party in disputes involving the insured party. Article 1917 (2) of the Italian civil code, for instance, states that the insurer has the right, upon communication to the insured, to pay the compensation due directly to the injured third party, and is obliged to pay directly if the insured requests it.

OBERHAMMER: If you look at it from a liberal perspective, it's a new kind of financial service. Normally, a liberal economy only prohibits services on the market in cases where it's proven that they are harmful. That's because there are constitutional limits to prohibiting the exercise of my freedom to have a new product on the market.

It isn't a coincidence that many companies in the third-party funding market are private equity firms, funded by people who have some money to invest in interesting ventures. This is what's currently happening, so why should we be barred from creating such a service due to some opaque considerations that, in some cases, it might be detrimental? If you prohibit all business activities that might be detrimental in some remote cases, then car production might be a much better candidate for prohibition than the third-party funding of proceedings.

HENKE: Certainly. However, to guarantee the autonomy granted to individuals and the freedom of economic initiative typical of a market economy, states have always provided dispute resolution mechanisms with *public* profiles (if not from the strictly structural and organisational point of view, at least in terms of the goals and objectives pursued). These mechanisms are informed by the principles of due process, such as the requirements of independence and impartiality of the adjudicatory body with respect to the dispute and the subjects involved in it. In this context, business can flourish and grow to the extent that there are limits, guarantees, and values which cannot be traced back to it or be swallowed up by it.

This is precisely the concept of civil justice autonomy to which I previously referred. In recent decades, we have observed the privatisation of numerous functions that were previously the exclusive domain of the state. This has resulted in the reduction of many political, administrative, and economic institutions to mere shells, with power and prerogatives often being removed and often externally directed. The phenomenon of third-party funding, which has seen explosive growth in recent years in certain jurisdictions, presents a similar risk to civil justice.

In short, there is a fear of a progressive privatisation of justice, influenced by business interests, and bent to its logic.

OBERHAMMER: Without meaning to, we started talking about civil procedure and ended up in an intense discussion about the role of the state and civil society.

HENKE: The world is changing so fast! Forgive me if I'm attached to the world of yesterday and a little afraid of the world of tomorrow!

Bibliography

AVRAHAM, R., WICKELGREN, A. L., 'Third-Party Litigation Funding with Informative Signals', *Journal of Law & Economics*, 61-4, 2018, pp. 637–675.

CAPPELLETTI, M., 'The Emergence of a Modern Theme', in CAPPELLETTI, M., GORDLEY, J., JOHNSON, E., *Towards Equal Justice. A Comparative Study of Legal Aid in Modern Societies* (*Texts and Materials*), Milan: Giuffrè, 1975, pp. 6 ff.

CORDINA, A., STORSKRUBB, E., 'The Future Regulation of Third-Party Funding in Europe', *Nederlands-Vlaams tijdschrift voor mediation en conflictmanagement Aflevering*, 26-2, 2022, pp. 1–8.

FARROW, T. C. W., JACOBS, L. (eds.), *The Justice Crisis. The Cost and Value of Accessing Law*, Vancouver: UBC Press, 2021.

Gramatikov, M., Barendrecht, M., Laxminarayan, M., Verdonschot, J. H., Klaming, L., van Zeeland, C., *A Handbook for Measuring the Costs and Quality of Access to Justice*, Apeldoorn, Antwerp: Maklu, 2009.

Harrington, W. J., 'Champerty, Usury, and Third-Party Litigation Funding', *The Brief*, 49-2, 2020, pp. 54–64.

ICC Arbitration and ADR Commission, 'Decisions on Costs in International Arbitration', *ICC Dispute Resolution Bulletin*, 2, 2015.

O'Reilly, M., 'The Harmonisation of Costs Practices in International Arbitration: The Search for the Holy Grail', in Betancourt, J. C. (ed.), *Defining Issues in International Arbitration. Celebrating 100 Years of the Chartered Institute of Arbitrators*, Oxford: Oxford University Press, 2016.

Reimann, M., 'Cost and Fee Allocation in Civil Procedure: A Synthesis', in Reimann, M. (ed.), *Cost and Fee Allocation in Civil Procedure: A Comparative Study*, Cham: Springer, 2012.

ICCA-Queen Mary Task Force, 'Report on Third-Party Funding in International Arbitration', *ICCA Reports*, 4, 2018.

Saulnier, J., Koronthalyova, I, Müller, K., 'Responsible Private Funding of Litigation. European Added Value Assessment', European Parliament, 2021, available at https://www.europarl.europa.eu/RegData/etudes/STUD/2021/662612/EPRS_STU(2021)662612_EN.pdf.

Smith, V., 'Costs and Funding', in Stadler, A., Smith, V., Gascón, F. (eds.), *European Rules of Civil Procedure. A Commentary on the ELI/UNIDROIT Model Rules*, Cheltenham: Edward Elgar, 2023, pp. 632–669.

Tirado, J., Meagher, D. R., Gupta, A., 'The Costs and Funding of International Arbitration', in Betancourt, J. C. (ed.), *Defining Issues in International Arbitration. Celebrating 100 Years of the Chartered Institute of Arbitrators*, Oxford: Oxford University Press, 2016.

CHAPTER 10

Judgments, *Lis Pendens*, *Res Judicata*

Christoph Kern, Enrique Vallines, Tanja Domej, and Jesús Loma

The act of rendering judgment represents one of the most pivotal moments within the legal process. In light of this, the Rules offer a series of provisions pertaining to judgments.

The Rules recommend a certain structure in judgments to facilitate the comprehension and the private and public scrutiny of the judge's rationale and decision. Of particular importance is the guidance provided regarding the regime of default judgments.

Another area addressed by the Rules is the impact of judgments, with a particular focus on their finality. In this regard, the Rules propose what are considered the optimal approaches to the scope of lis pendens and res judicata. These concepts are designed to prevent irreconcilable or contradictory judgments from emerging.

 | DOI:10.1163/9789004533257_011

KERN: As a member of the working group on judgments, and the co-reporter together with Chiara Besso, I would like to start by drawing your attention to some of the most relevant provisions of the general part of this section of the Rules.

Let's start with Rule 130, on the different types of judgments:[1]

> Rule 130. *Types of judgment*
>
> (1) The court may give
>
> (a) a final judgment, which is a judgment deciding the whole of a claim for relief;
>
> (b) a judgment deciding part of a claim for relief (a partial judgment);
>
> (c) where more than one claim for relief is made, a final judgment deciding one or more, but not all, of the claims for relief;
>
> (d) a judgment on preliminary procedural issues or on specific legal issues on the merits (see Rule 66);
>
> (e) a judgment in default.
>
> (2) Where the court gives a judgment that does not decide the whole of a claim for relief, the proceedings continue in respect of such parts for which judgment has not been given. If the court's judgment on a part of the claim for relief, on a procedural issue, or on legal issues on the merits is subject to appeal the court may exercise its discretion whether to continue or stay the proceedings according to the circumstances of the case.

This initial provision appears to be relatively straightforward. However, within the working group, there were robust discussions surrounding the concept of partial judgments. In certain legal systems, judgments must be comprehensive, which has led to the perception that partial judgments are a *contradictio in terminis*.

Additionally, the distinction between partial judgments and judgments on specific legal issues on the merits was challenging to define within the working group. These two classifications, *vertical* and *horizontal* if you will, were not immediately apparent to some of us.

---

1 See, e.g., MURRAY, P. L., STÜRNER, R., *German Civil Justice*, Durham: Carolina Academic Press, 2004, p. 356.

LOMA: I'm not sure I grasp these distinctions, which don't exist in my jurisdiction.

KERN: A partial judgment is final only in regard to a specific aspect of the claim. For instance, if a claimant, following an accident, claims both damages resulting from medical treatment (*damnum emergens*) and loss of earnings resulting from his inability to carry out his trade (*lucrum cessans*), there may be a partial judgment on the damnum and a subsequent partial judgment on the *lucrum*.

LOMA: Can we therefore speak of partial judgments simply as consecutive or juxtaposed final decisions?

KERN: I believe that would be an accurate definition.

LOMA: We often see bifurcation of proceedings in international arbitration.[2] Would that be an example?

KERN: Depending on the reason for the bifurcation. Preliminary rulings on jurisdiction, a possibility that exists in most European countries, receive specific treatment in the Rules, as judgments on preliminary procedural requirements are subject to independent appeal in accordance with Rule 66 (2). Preliminary rulings on responsibility and later rulings on *quantum* would also be considered not as partial judgments, but as something slightly different: judgments on specific legal issues on the merits.

LOMA: What would be the difference with partial judgments in those two examples?

KERN: The difference is that both judgments on preliminary procedural requirements and judgments on specific legal issues on the merits leave the

2 See ICC COMMISSION ON ARBITRATION AND ADR, *Effective Management of Arbitration. A Guide for In-House Counsel and Other Party Representatives*, Paris: ICC, 2017, available at https://iccwbo.org/news-publications/arbitration-adr-rules-and-tools/effective-management-of-arbitration-a-guide-for-in-house-counsel-and-other-party-representatives/, p. 11. For an empiric approach, see GREENWOOD, L., 'Does Bifurcation Really Promote Efficiency?', *Journal of International Arbitration*, 28–2, 2011, pp. 105–111; GREENWOOD, L., 'Revisiting Bifurcation and Efficiency in International Arbitration Proceedings', *Journal of International Arbitration*, 36–4, 2019, pp. 421–429.

case unresolved. They are specifically regulated in Rule 66 (perhaps somewhat hidden):

> Rule 66. *Judgments on preliminary procedural issues or on legal issues on the merits*
>
> (1) The court on its own motion or on the application of a party may give a judgment
>
> (a) deciding a preliminary procedural issue, or
>
> (b) deciding a legal issue on the merits.

LOMA: I think I understand what you're saying. In Spain, we admit exceptionally, for very specific cases, that liquidation of *quantum* is left for the enforcement phase.[3] It's not two separate and consecutive judgments, but one that doesn't fully resolve the claim because it needs to be further specified.

KERN: Exactly. In the working group we considered that Spanish type of *sentencias*.

LOMA: Rule 130 concludes with a reference to default judgments.

KERN: This was another issue that was extensively discussed in the working group. In certain legal systems, only failure to appear at the initial hearing can be the basis for a default judgment.[4] However, under the Rules, a party is in default if it has failed to attend the most recent hearing, even if it has attended all previous hearings.[5]

LOMA: That's a tough way to get lawyers and parties to show up for hearings.

3 LEC, Art. 219(3). See IGLESIAS, S., *La sentencia en el proceso civil*, Madrid: Dykinson, 2015.

4 See KERN C. A., 'Harmonisation of the Rules on Judgments and Appeals in Europe: A Few Remarks from the Inside', in GASCÓN, F., HESS, B. (eds.), *The Future of the European Law of Civil Procedure. Coordination or Harmonisation?*, Cambridge: Intersentia, 2020, pp. 223–240, at 226.

5 KERN, C. A., 'General Rules on Judgments' in STADLER, A., SMITH, V., GASCÓN, F. (eds.), *European Rules of Civil Procedure. A Commentary on the ELI/UNIDROIT Model Rules*, Cheltenham: Edward Elgar, 2023, pp. 380 ff., at 397, 400.

KERN: The approach is certainly more rigorous than what is typically seen in some jurisdictions. In Italy, as my Italian co-rapporteur, Chiara Besso, explained, lawyers only make sure they appear at the first hearing and often do not appear at subsequent hearings. This is because there is no default judgment for failing to appear at subsequent hearings. If a party does not appear at a subsequent hearing, the hearing is adjourned, and the case continues. The Rules opted for a stricter approach.

LOMA: Probably as an expression of the principle of cooperation, which is so strongly encouraged in the Rules.

DOMEJ: Another interesting issue is how default judgments can be challenged.

KERN: The application to set aside judgments by default is subject to several requirements set out in the Rules. In Germany, a default judgment can always be set aside at the request of the defaulting party, without the need to state reasons.[6] According to Rule 139(b), setting aside a default judgment is only possible if the defaulting party was not responsible or if the default is excusable. This was inspired by the new Swiss code of civil procedure, Tanja.[7]

DOMEJ: Overall, the default judgment provisions of the Rules appear to be much stricter than those of the Swiss code. If I understand the Rules correctly on this point, it is not even possible to lodge an ordinary appeal, for example, on the grounds that the court erred in its application of the law. I find this quite extraordinary.

KERN: You are correct. The Swiss code of civil procedure is merely a model for this limitation: setting aside requires that the defaulting party is not responsible or the default is excusable. It is not a model for the entire section.

Default judgments are a highly complex issue. Perhaps the outcome of the discussions of the working group is more restrictive than what we had in mind when we drafted it. In the event that the court makes an error in

---

6 ZPO, §§ 338, 340.

7 Swiss CPC, Art. 148(1). See KERN, C. A., 'General Rules on Judgments', in STADLER, A., SMITH, V., GASCÓN, F. (eds.), *European Rules of Civil Procedure. A Commentary on the ELI/UNIDROIT Model Rules*, Cheltenham: Edward Elgar, 2023, p. 415.

the law, the default judgment cannot be challenged unless it can be proven that the party was not at fault.

DOMEJ: Very strict indeed.

KERN: The approach is undoubtedly more rigorous than the German approach. In Germany, it is relatively straightforward to set aside a judgment in which the law is misapplied, as there is no requirement to state the reasons for the default. The Rules present a more challenging scenario. In some jurisdictions, where attendance at hearings and meeting deadlines can be difficult due to various reasons, this may be perceived as overly strict. It is possible that these default judgment provisions may not be universally welcomed.

DOMEJ: Another issue that hasn't been raised yet regarding default judgments is which court has the jurisdiction to set them aside.

KERN: My proposal was that the same court that handed down the default judgment would have jurisdiction to set it aside.[8] However, some members of our working group noted that this may not be a viable option. The first instance courts of many countries lack the necessary resources – judges, staff, and time – to deal with all default judgment cases.

It is important to consider the organisation of the courts when approaching annulment based on default. This issue has not yet been addressed because it affects structural aspects of the legal system, deeply ingrained traditions, and complex budgetary issues.[9] Consequently, there is a possibility of disagreement and friction regarding the provisions in the Rules concerning judgments by default.

DOMEJ: I concur. The situation under the Rules is fraught with risk in this regard. If a lawyer fails to appear for a hearing and the court rules on the

---

8 See KERN, C. A., 'Harmonisation of the Rules on Judgments and Appeals in Europe: A Few Remarks from the Inside', in GASCÓN, F., HESS, B. (eds.), *The Future of the European Law of Civil Procedure. Coordination or Harmonisation?* Cambridge: Intersentia, 2020, pp. pp. 223–240, at 226–227.

9 KERN, C. A., 'Harmonisation of the Rules on Judgments and Appeals in Europe: A Few Remarks from the Inside', in GASCÓN, F., HESS, B. (eds.), *The Future of the European Law of Civil Procedure. Coordination or Harmonisation?*, Cambridge: Intersentia, 2020, pp. 223–240, at 229.

subject matter of the hearing – potentially through a partial judgment –, the party may lose that part of the dispute and be barred from raising those issues again. The lawyer is ultimately responsible for this outcome.

LOMA: Professional liability could always be lurking in the background.

KERN: That's perhaps why this issue has provoked a somewhat lively discussion.

DOMEJ: Furthermore, the relationship between this approach and the goal of procedural economy is not straightforward. According to the Rules, it is mandatory to attend and defend the case, even if you do not believe it is worthwhile, in order to prevent potential repercussions in the future. I am uncertain if this is the optimal solution. In this context, there may be merit to a more limited concept of *res judicata*.

When drafting procedural rules, it is important to consider not only the purely legal situation, but also the factual likelihood that there will be a second litigation after some of these issues have already been decided. A default judgment can have serious consequences, so a reasonable party will do much to prevent it. However, a default judgment is often a very quick and straightforward way to settle a dispute.

In short, I believe that it may be excessive to penalise default judgments so heavily.

KERN: In terms of procedural economy, it is not always the case that a stricter regulation will result in fewer cases. In fact, it may lead to more cases than before.

LOMA: I'm wondering if there's any data on how often motions are filed to set aside judgments by default. If it doesn't happen very often, it probably won't slow down the proceedings much.

KERN: At least in Germany, it happens quite often.[10] In 2021, local courts (*Amtsgerichte*) issued 151,522 default judgments, compared to 205,625 ordinary judgments, and district courts (*Landgerichte*) issued 26,388 default

---

10 See *Statistisches Bundesamt, Fachserie* 10, *Reihe* 2.1: *Rechtspflege Zivilgerichte*, 2022, pp. 38 ff., 48 ff.

judgments, compared to 135,958 ordinary judgments. I'm not sure if there is data in Switzerland.

DOMEJ: It looks like the rules in Switzerland are a little different from what we have in the Rules. In Switzerland, when a default judgment is rendered, the court looks at any written or oral statements submitted by the party that is in default. It also has to take evidence about the facts alleged by the non-defaulting party; the non-defaulting party's factual assertions are not considered to be admitted.

This approach to default judgments differs from that outlined in the German code of civil procedure. Swiss default judgments are contradictory judgments. They are similar to (though not identical with) the German 'decision based on the record as it stands' (*Entscheidung nach Aktenlage*), rather than the judgment by default (*Versäumnisurteil*).

In Switzerland, the ordinary appeals are available against default judgments. The rules on new allegations and evidence at the appellate stage typically prevent a party that was in default at first instance from introducing new facts or evidence. However, if the court made an error in the law, the party can successfully appeal a default judgment.

I am unaware of any data on the number of default judgments handed down in Switzerland and the number that are appealed, with the outcome being either successful or unsuccessful. These judgments are not treated as a special category.

LOMA: Rule 130 mentions final and partial judgments, judgments on preliminary procedural issues, judgments on specific legal issues on the merits, and judgments in default. I'm missing one type of judgment: summary judgments.[11] Are they regulated elsewhere in the Rules?

KERN: You will not find any reference to 'summary judgments' as such in the Rules. At the beginning, some participants in the project were fascinated by the idea of summary judgments, and there was a clear indication that our working group should draft a provision on summary judgments. During the drafting process, however, it became clear that the idea of summary judgments was far from established in comparative terms, so the idea of a

11 See MAXEINER, J. R., *Failures of American Civil Justice in International Perspective*, Cambridge: Cambridge University Press, 2011, pp. 158–159.

rule entitled 'summary judgment' was abandoned.[12] In the end, however, Rule 65 (again somewhat hidden) on 'early final judgments' was included:

> Rule 65. *Early final judgments*
>
> (1) The court, on its own motion or on the application of a party, may give an early final judgment upon simplified proceedings.
>
> (2) In an early final judgment the court may
>
> (a) determine that it lacks jurisdiction or competence to adjudicate the dispute or whether the claim is inadmissible due to a failure to comply with other procedural requirements; or
>
> (b) give a final judgment or a judgment on part of the claim for relief by only deciding questions of law based on non-contested facts, or on the basis that there has been a failure by the parties to assert necessary and relevant facts timeously, or there has been a failure to proffer necessary means of evidence timeously; or
>
> (c) give a judgment upon the withdrawal of a claim, whether that was permitted or consented to, or upon an admission by the defendant.

LOMA: Is it really the same thing?

KERN: What is a summary judgment, anyway? During the discussions, we all understood the role of summary judgments in traditional common law proceedings, as we find them in the US in particular, simply as final judgments rendered by the court prior to trial by jury.[13] In civil procedural systems,[14] where the taking of evidence is not so markedly concentrated in an evidentiary hearing and the coexistence of a judge and jury is unknown, an anticipated judgment is hardly surprising.[15] Therefore, we included a

12 KERN, C. A., 'Harmonisation of the Rules on Judgments and Appeals in Europe: A Few Remarks from the Inside', in GASCÓN, F., HESS, B. (eds.), *The Future of the European Law of Civil Procedure. Coordination or Harmonisation?*, Cambridge: Intersentia, 2020, pp. 223–238, at 231.

13 See MAXEINER, J. R., *Failures of American Civil Justice in International Perspective*, Cambridge University Press, 2011, pp. 130–131).

14 See, e.g., CHASE, O. G., HERSHKOFF, H., SILBERMAN, L., SORABJI, J., STÜRNER, R., TANIGUCHI, Y., VARANO, V. (eds.), *Civil Litigation in Comparative Context*, Eagan: West, 2017, pp. 278–291.

15 See KERN, C. A., 'Harmonisation of the Rules on Judgments and Appeals in Europe: A Few Remarks from the Inside', in GASCÓN, F., HESS, B. (eds.), *The Future of the*

provision on early final judgments. These judgments are 'early' in that they are rendered without a full evidentiary hearing, as is the case whenever the dispute is not factual but purely legal.

LOMA: Do such early judgments enjoy the full effects of *res judicata*?

KERN: Early final judgments are as final as later final judgments.

LOMA: I wanted to ask you about the 'legitimate interest' of the claimant, which is mentioned among the contents and requirements of judgments in Rules 132 and 133:

> Rule 132. *Contents of judgments*
>
> (2) The court may only grant a declaratory judgment, including a negative declaratory judgment, if the claimant can establish that they have a legitimate interest in obtaining the declaration sought.
>
> Rule 133. *Procedural requirements of judgments on the merits*
>
> The court may only give a judgment on the merits when it is satisfied that
>
> (e) the claimant has a legitimate interest to commence the proceedings on its claim for relief;

KERN: Rule 132(2) refers only to declaratory relief. Therefore, the legitimate interest at stake here is the legitimate interest in obtaining a declaratory judgment. Most jurisdictions have a filter in place to avoid an overwhelming number of merely declaratory actions – whether positive or negative – on issues that shouldn't require judicial adjudication.[16] Many neighbour disputes over noise and garden plants are essentially declaratory actions and shouldn't reasonably be taken to court.

European Law of Civil Procedure. Coordination or Harmonisation?, Cambridge: Intersentia, 2020, pp. 223–238, at 231.

16 For France, see, e.g., ZSCHUNKE, U., 'L'intérêt à agir: Action déclaratoire et interdiction de l'action populaire', in SCHULZE, G., (ed.), *Europäisches Privatrecht in Vielfalt geeint. Der modernisierte Zivilprozess in Europa*, Munich: Sellier, 2014, pp. 41–56, at 49 ff. For Switzerland, see CPC, Art. 88, 59(2)(a), and Tribunal Fédéral Suisse, judgment of 16 January 2015, case 4A_414/2014, BGE 141 III 68, 71 ff. For Germany, see ZPO, § 256(1), and MURRAY, P. L., STÜRNER, R., *German Civil Justice*, Durham: Carolina Academic Press, 2004, p. 196.

LOMA: And can the defendant or even the court claim a lack of legitimate interest to request early termination of the proceedings, to file motions to strike out? Bear in mind that Rule 133 doesn't limit this requirement to merely declaratory claims.

KERN: In Germany, a legitimate interest is required, but this is practically irrelevant in most situations. Anyone asserting a right can do so in court, with only a few exceptions: the insolvency administrator instead of the debtor, the estate executor instead of the heir, and a few others.[17] Even if law students were to file a lawsuit for ten euros just to see how civil procedure works, it would be very difficult for the judge to dismiss the case and say that there is no legitimate interest. Unless the case is obviously and completely fabricated, a court should not be able to dismiss the case.

I do not believe that legitimate interest should be a ground for dismissal of a regular claim. Rather, it should be seen as a filter for merely abusive actions, for example excessive declaratory actions.

It is true that legitimate interest is also mentioned in other parts of the Rules; not only Rule 133 on the requirements of judgments, but also Rule 40 on voluntary intervention ('anyone who has a legitimate interest in one or more parties succeeding in proceedings may intervene in support of their claim or defence') and Rule 153 on appeals (one must show 'a legal interest in a judgment' to lodge an appeal).

DOMEJ: The situation in Switzerland is comparable to that in Germany. In addition to the declaratory action, there are instances where a legitimate interest can be a factor. As stated in the Rules and commentaries, there is sometimes confusion as to whether the existence of a legitimate interest is a question of procedural or substantive law. This question arises in actions for declaratory relief, but also in negative performance claims, where the claimant requests that the court prohibit the defendant from taking a specific action.

Provisional and protective measures are similar in that the party must sometimes prove that there is a risk, a *periculum* of something jeopardizing the effectiveness of the future judgment.

---

17 See, e.g., ROSENBERG, L., SCHWAB, K. H., GOTTWALD, P., *Zivilprozesssrecht*, Munich: Beck, 2018, § 46, numbers 5 ff.

VALLINES: In Spain, the concept of legitimate interest – as in the case of the related but different concept of legal standing to sue and be sued (*legitimación*) – is generally considered a substantive issue that is closely related to the merits.[18] Accordingly, issues related to legitimate interest will generally be discussed during the main proceedings and decided in the final judgment.

It is worth noting that there is an exception to this general rule. If there are supervening circumstances that show that the claimant no longer holds 'a legitimate interest to be granted the judicial relief sought', the court may bring the proceedings to an end via an early final order.[19] This exception to the general rule demonstrates that Spanish law is cautious about the legal nature and the most appropriate moment to deal with issues related to the legitimate interest or legal standing of the parties.

In contrast, anticipating the decision would be possible under the Rules. Rule 133(e) states that the question of whether the claimant holds a 'legitimate interest to commence the proceedings on its claim for relief' is deemed to be procedural rather than substantive in nature. As such, it may be decided either in an early final judgment under Rule 65(2)(a) or in a preliminary judgment under Rule 66(1)(a). An early final judgment would be appropriate if the legitimate interest is absent, and a preliminary judgment would be in place if the legitimate interest exists.

However, even if the legitimate interest were to be considered, as in Spain, as substantive rather than procedural, it could be argued that an anticipated decision would still be available via Rules 65(2)(b) or 66(1)(b). As previously mentioned, the court has the authority to bifurcate proceedings and address a question of substantive law at an early stage. In accordance with Rules 49(7), (6) and (3), the court may determine 'the separation of questions', 'the order in which issues will be tried', the 'type and form of the procedure', and, if necessary, the need to deal with separate questions in 'early decisions'.

This does not imply that the concept of legitimate interest as a matter of procedural or substantive law is without further consequence. For instance,

18 See generally SÁNCHEZ, B., *La sustitución procesal: análisis crítico*, unpublished doctoral dissertation, Complutense University of Madrid, 2016, available at https://hdl.handle.net/20.500.14352/22304, pp. 223–296. *Pro*, DE LA OLIVA, A., 'Art. 10', in DE LA OLIVA, A., DÍEZ-PICAZO, I., VEGAS, J., BANACLOCHE, J., *Comentarios a la Ley de Enjuiciamiento Civil*, Madrid: Civitas, 2001, pp. 92–98. *Contra*, MONTERO, J., *De la legitimación en el proceso civil*, Barcelona: Bosch, 2006.

19 LEC, Art. 22. See GASCÓN, F., *La terminación anticipada del proceso por desaparición sobrevenida del interés*, Madrid: Civitas, 2003.

in Spain, judgments on substantive matters are *res judicata*, whereas judgments on procedural matters are not.[20] However, in the Rules, this should not be a problem as judgments on either substantive or procedural issues have the same effect of *res judicata*. A decision on whether a legitimate interest exists will, in any case, be *res judicata* under Rule 147(1).[21]

KERN: This brings me to another issue. As a prerequisite for a judgment on the merits, and in addition to the claimant's legitimate interest, Rule 133 requires that 'the cause of action between the parties is not *res judicata*' and that 'there are no pending proceedings involving the same parties and the same cause of action in another court' (*lis pendens*). Unlike in some common law jurisdictions and historically in French[22] and Italian[23] law, parallel proceedings are prevented as much as possible. The Rules on *lis pendens* essentially follow this approach, which is the approach taken by Brussels I bis[24] and the case law of the Court of Justice of the EU.[25]

DOMEJ: Traditionally, in many jurisdictions, *lis pendens* and *res judicata* have been regarded as parallel concepts. It is often said that *res judicata* is a kind of continuation of *lis pendens*, or that *lis pendens* is an anticipation of *res judicata*. At EU level, however, this is no longer the case. The concepts of *res judicata* and *lis pendens* have been largely dissociated. The case law of the ECJ has extended the scope of *lis pendens* to the extent that it now goes well beyond the traditional scope of *res judicata* in most jurisdictions.

---

20 See, e.g., DE LA OLIVA, A., *Curso de Derecho Procesal Civil II. Parte Especial*, Madrid: Ramón Areces, 2016, pp. 329 ff.

21 See BRUNS, A., 'Effect of Judgments: Res Judicata', and VALLINES, E., 'Proceedings before a Final Hearing and Final Hearing', both in STADLER, A., SMITH, V., GASCÓN, F. (eds.), *European Rules of Civil Procedure. A Commentary on the ELI/UNIDROIT Model Rules*, Cheltenham: Edward Elgar, 2023, pp. 420 and 370, 375, respectively.

22 *Cour de cassation, Civ. 1ère*, 1 December 1969, *Anciens établ. Valla et Richard*, Clunet 97 (1970), 707, 708; see HOLLEAUX, D., 'La litispendance internationale', *Travaux du Comité français de droit international privé*, 32–34, 1974, pp. 203–230; overturned by *Cour de cassation, Civ. 1ère*, 26 November 1974, *Société Miniera di Fragne*, Clunet 102 (1975), 108, 109.

23 CPC, Art. 3, in the wording given by Legge 31 May 1995, Article 7, n. 218, *Riforma del sistema italiano di diritto internazionale privato.*

24 EU Regulation 1215/2012 of the European Parliament and of the Council of 12 December 2012 on jurisdiction and the recognition and enforcement of judgments in civil and commercial matters (recast).

25 See, e.g., *Cartier parfums-lunettes SAS, Aya Corporate Solutions assurances SA v. Ziegler France SA et al.*, Judgment of 27 February 2014, case 1/13, ECLI:EU:C:2014:109, para. 40.

KERN: The *Kernpunkttheorie*.

DOMEJ: Yes. The name of this doctrine comes from the term *Kernpunkt* appearing in the German language version of the *Gubisch v. Palumbo* judgment.[26] This is the judgment in which the ECJ laid down the principles governing the scope of *lis pendens* in European civil proceedings. *Kernpunkt* means core question or core point, the issue that lies at the heart of the matter. The Gubisch judgment states that the same issue must be at the heart of both actions.

This is a broad concept of *lis pendens*, as it doesn't require that the claims asserted in the two proceedings are completely identical or mirror images of each other. In this way, the ECJ has created a very powerful mechanism to prevent irreconcilable judgments and to concentrate closely related claims before the same court.

KERN: Indeed, this broad concept of *lis pendens* also encompasses claims that traditionally, at least in German-speaking jurisdictions, would have been considered as related but not identical claims.

DOMEJ: Consequently, the concept of cause of action for the purposes of *lis pendens* is not identical to the concept of cause of action for the purposes of *res judicata*. This was a deliberate decision, which is explained in the introductory remarks to the section on the effects of pendency and judgments. The commentary points out the following:

> The effect of a broad conception of the cause of action is much more drastic *ex-post* than *ex-ante*. In the pre-commencement phase of proceedings, the parties are still able to adapt their procedural conception to secure the full concentration of their dispute with one court in contrast to the situation after rendition of the judgment, where the parties may be surprised by somewhat unclear and not always foreseeable consequences. Whereas the European Court of Justice's conception has developed clear contours over the last few decades in respect of *lis pendens*, the situation in respect of *res judicata* remains unclear and underdeveloped.

26 *Gubisch Maschinenfabrik KG v. Giulio Palumbo*, Judgment of 8 December 1987, case 144/86, ECLI:EU:C:1987:528.

I am not entirely convinced that this concept of *lis pendens* always leads to simple and predictable answers. But it is true that, in the EU context, *lis pendens* is much more developed than *res judicata*. A European doctrine of *res judicata* has only recently begun to emerge in the case law of the ECJ in the Gothaer case[27] of 2012 (unless we count the case law on irreconcilable judgments as a kind of beginning of a doctrine of *res judicata*). Meanwhile, the case of *Gubisch v. Palumbo*, which formed the basis for the European *lis pendens* doctrine, was decided over three decades ago, in 1987.

VALLINES: It is important to note that the Rules apply the European *lis pendens* doctrine not only for cross-border but also domestic cases.[28]

DOMEJ: The Swiss Federal Tribunal has also adopted such a solution.[29] And it tends not to cause major problems. There is something to be said for an approach that treats domestic and cross-border cases equally, unless there are good reasons for treating them differently. From the point of view of avoiding irreconcilable judgments and fragmentation of litigation, I think a broad concept of *lis pendens* is a good thing. Of course, practical problems may arise where it is not possible to bring all the claims before the court first seised because that court does not have jurisdiction over both or all the claims. In this case, a broad concept could risk denying justice unless creative solutions are found.

The Rules deal with such situations in a slightly different way from Brussels I bis because, in addition to stay and dismissal, the Rules provide for the possibility of referring the case to the court first seised and consolidating it there. If that is not possible, the court second seised does not necessarily have to dismiss or decline jurisdiction; it can stay the proceedings. I am still not sure that this is a perfect solution in all situations and that the strict priority principle is necessarily appropriate in all situations. But it is a step forward compared to what the Brussels I bis Regulation offers us.

---

27 *Gothaer Allgemeine Versicherung AG and Others v. Samskip GmbH*, Judgment of 15 November 2012, case 456/11, ECLI:EU:C:2012:719.

28 GASCÓN, F., SCHUMANN, G., 'The Rules on *Lis Pendens* and on *Res Judicata* in the ELI/UNIDROIT Model European Rules of Civil Procedure', *Ius Dictum*, 5, 2021, pp. 15–29, at 17–20.

29 *Tribunal Fédéral Suisse*, judgment of 8 May 2002, case 4C.385/2001, BGE 128 III 284; Judgment of 15 May 2012, case 5A_423/2011, BGE 138 III 570.

LOMA: Why don't we now examine the issue of *res judicata* in the Rules in more detail?

VALLINES: Disputes must come to an end. Once a dispute has reached that end because there is no further possibility of appeal, the result must be respected, and the dispute should not be reopened. In this sense, Rule 147 gives *res judicata* effect to almost any kind of judgment that cannot be appealed:

> Rule 147. *Types of judgment that become* res judicata
>
> (1) Final judgments, including partial judgments, default judgments, and judgments that decide procedural issues or issues on the merits are *res judicata*.
>
> Rule 148. *Judgments that are* res judicata
>
> A judgment is *res judicata* when ordinary means of recourse are not or are no longer available.

There is only one exception, mentioned in Rule 147(2):

> Rule 147. *Types of judgment that become* res judicata
>
> (2) Provisional measures do not have *res judicata* effects on the merits of the issues in dispute in proceedings.

In other words, no decision on provisional measures is binding when it comes to deciding the merits of the case in the final judgment. However, prior to that final judgment and in the context of further proceedings seeking to modify the provisional measures adopted, it can be argued that an unappealable final decision on provisional measures is indeed *res judicata*: any application for modification of the decision on provisional measures should be rejected on the basis of *res judicata* as long as the circumstances that led to that decision still exist.[30]

---

30 BRUNS, A., 'Effect of Judgments: Res Judicata' in STADLER, A., SMITH, V., GASCÓN, F. (eds.), *European Rules of Civil Procedure. A Commentary on the ELI/UNIDROIT Model Rules*, Cheltenham: Edward Elgar, 2023, p. 421; GASCÓN, F., SCHUMANN, G., 'The Rules on *Lis Pendens* and on *Res Judicata* in the ELI/UNIDROIT Model European Rules Of Civil Procedure', *Ius Dictum*, 5, 2021, pp. 15–29, at 21.

DOMEJ: Immediately after these general statements, a world of difficult questions arises. One of them concerns the material scope of *res judicata*.[31]

VALLINES: Rule 149 provides a comprehensive answer to that question. Essentially, any decision included in any judgment will be *res judicata*, regardless of whether the decision is included in the operative part or in the reasoning part of the judgment.

In paragraph 1, there is something that may sound familiar to a German scholar:[32] that *res judicata* encompasses whatever the court decides on the claim for relief.

> Rule 149. *Material scope of* res judicata
>
> (1) The material scope of *res judicata* is determined by reference to the claims for relief in the parties' pleadings, including amendments, as decided by the court's judgment.

This decision on the claim is normally contained in the operative part of the judgment. There is a consensus that the decision contained in the operative part becomes *res judicata* and has this binding effect in subsequent proceedings between the same parties.

Paragraph 2 is probably the most interesting part of Rule 149:

> Rule 149. *Material scope of* res judicata
>
> (2) *Res judicata* also covers necessary and incidental legal issues that are explicitly decided in a judgment where parties to subsequent proceedings are the same as those in the proceedings determined by the prior judgment and where the court that gave that judgment could decide those legal issues.

In other words, any explicit (not merely implicit) decision on a point of law (not a point of fact)[33] that is considered 'necessary and incidental' to decide on the claim for relief – i.e., a decision which is a 'necessary legal

---

31 See, e.g., MURRAY, P. L., STÜRNER, R., *German Civil Justice*, Durham: Academic Press, 2004, pp. 357–360.

32 See ZPO, § 322(1).

33 The exclusion of decisions on questions of fact from the scope of *res judicata* reflects the French and German traditions. See BRUNS., A., 'Effect of Judgments: Res Judicata', in STADLER, A., SMITH, V., GASCÓN, F. (eds.), *European Rules of Civil Procedure. A*

step to the conclusion of proceedings', one of 'its logical antecedents' –[34] will also be considered part of the material scope of *res judicata.*

Furthermore, the decision will be binding in any subsequent proceedings between the same parties (Rule 151) if the court had jurisdiction to decide on the issue and regardless of whether the decision is included in the operative part of the judgment or in its reasoning.

The official commentary cites the example of a claimant seeking damages for breach of contract, but the contract's validity is disputed during the proceedings. Even if the court's decision on the contract's validity is not reflected in the operative part of the judgment, it is still binding. It is considered an explicit decision on a legal question that is 'necessary and incidental' to decide on the claim:[35]

> This Rule only relates to legal relationships and issues, not to facts as facts by themselves cannot be the subject of a judicial declaration covered by *res judicata.* Incidental and necessary legal issues are the necessary legal steps to the conclusion of proceedings, its logical antecedents; the decision on the claim depends upon them. For example: the claimant claims for damages on the ground of a contract; the existence and the validity of the contract are incidental and necessary legal issues to be decided if there is a disagreement on them between the parties. ... *No distinction is to be made in this regard* [the application of Rule 149(2)] *between the operative part of the judgment and its reasons.*[36]

LOMA: An allegation of nullity is typically an affirmative defence. Other typical affirmative defences would be prescription or set-off. Would the same approach be taken for all of them? Are all decisions on defences raised by the defendant *res judicata*?

VALLINES: Paragraphs 3 and 4 of Rule 149 only mention one of those defences, namely set-off:

Commentary on the ELI/UNIDROIT Model Rules, Cheltenham: Edward Elgar, 2023, pp. 423–424, 425.

34 Rule 149, comment 2.

35 Rule 149, comment 2.

36 Rule 149, comment 2 (emphasis added).

Rule 149. *Material scope of* res judicata

(3) *Res judicata* also applies where a defendant brings a defence based on set-off and

(a) the claim and that defence are upheld by the court, or

(b) the claim is admitted and the defence of set-off is rejected.

(4) Where a claim is rejected on grounds other than set-off, so that the court does not decide the set-off defence, only the judgment on the claim becomes *res judicata*.

According to the maxim *unius inclusio, alterius exclusio* (the inclusion of one thing imples the exclusion of another), when one or more things of a class are explicitly mentioned in a statute, others of the same class are excluded. Consequently, if the legal text (Rule 149) has considered only one defence (set-off) as *res judicata*, it would not be unreasonable to conclude that it must have intended to exclude the other defences.

However, in my view, this interpretation would be excessively formalistic. The specific reference to set-off may be explained for other reasons. The Rules may have been designed to emphasise that any actual decision on set-off, regardless of whether set-off was raised as a defence or as a counterclaim, is covered by *res judicata*. This would prevent the same creditor from attempting to collect the same debt twice. From this perspective, there would be no reason to interpret Rule 149(3) and (4) as establishing a limitation to the scope of *res judicata*.

The provisions of Rule 149 illustrate how the Rules favour the establishment of *res judicata* in relation to any legal decisions taken by a court in a final and unappealable judgment, including all decisions on the defences raised by the defendant.

Rule 149(2) may also be relevant in support of this interpretation. It could be argued that the decisions on the defences raised by the defendant relate to 'legal issues' that are 'necessary and incidental' to the decision on the claim. If the defendant has raised an affirmative defence, the court must rule on it in order to rule on the claim. Let's consider the *exceptio non adimpleti contractus*, the defence of unperformed contract. The claimant demands performance of obligation A, but the defendant asserts that the claimant should have fulfilled reciprocal obligation B first. To resolve this dispute, the court must determine the validity of this defence. This could be considered a legal issue that is 'necessary and incidental' and thus fall within the material scope of *res judicata* under Rule 149(2).

LOMA: After all, as Rule 23(1) clarifies, 'the scope of the dispute is determined by the claims and defences of the parties in the pleadings, including amendments'.

VALLINES: Yes, but Rule 23 is more complex. Paragraph 1 outlines the *scope of the dispute*, which encompasses both 'claims and defences'. Paragraph 2, however, seems to refer to a different concept, what we might call the *scope of the decision*. This would cover 'only' the 'relief claimed', as Rule 23(2) emphasises:

> Rule 23. *Scope*
>
> (1) The scope of the dispute is determined by the claims and defences of the parties in the pleadings, including amendments.
>
> (2) The court must decide on, and only on, the relief claimed.

Looking at Rule 23(2), it would seem that the court must 'decide on, and only on', the claim stated by the claimant (the 'relief claimed'), irrespective of the scope of the dispute, which, according to Rule 23(1), includes both 'claims and defences'. In other words, Rule 23(2) would appear to suggest that the court may, at its discretion, avoid deciding on the defences raised by the defendant as long as it actually decides on the claim formulated by the claimant.

This would be consistent with a view of *res judicata* that is limited to the operative part, since it is in the operative part that an actual decision on the claim is made. It would also lead to the view that the decisions on the defences, if any, should not be considered to be covered by *res judicata*.

Reading the commentary, however, it is clear that this is not what the drafters of Rule 23 intended. Commenting on Rule 23(1), the drafters argue that the 'scope of the dispute' – 'determined by the claims *and defences* of the parties in the pleadings' – is considered to dictate 'the *obligatory* contents of the court's decision'.[37] In other words, it is 'obligatory' to decide on the entire 'scope of the dispute': on all the claims brought by the claimant and all the defences raised by the defendant. This means that, in the end, the *scope of the dispute* and the *scope of the decision* coincide. The court is obliged to give an answer to every claim and every defence.

---

37 Rule 23, comment 1.

The only nuance would be if the claimant or the defendant had raised a particular claim or defence 'in the alternative' and the claim or defence that was raised first was finally upheld by the court. In this situation, the claim or defence raised in the alternative may indeed be left without a decision by the court.

Consequently, Rule 23(2) does not permit the court to leave the defendant without a decision on all or some of his defences. If the defendant has requested a decision on a defence, that decision is due under Rule 23(1).

LOMA: Probably this builds on the assumption that, upon the introduction of a defence, the defendant is also 'claiming' a particular 'relief' in terms of requesting that the court issues a judgment dismissing the claim formulated by the defendant.

However, such a broad understanding of the expression 'relief claimed' in Rule 23(2) would seem to contradict the official commentary, as it refers to the claim for relief 'as formulated by the claimant'.[38]

VALLINES: I must concede that there is an apparent mismatch here. To resolve this, it would be beneficial to differentiate between a positive and a negative mandate in Rule 23.

The positive rule is that the tribunal must decide on both the claims and the defences, in line with our previous discussions.

The negative rule entails three prohibitions, which are clearly outlined in the commentary.[39] First, 'the court is not permitted to change the formulation of the claims or defences of its own motion'. Second, the court 'may not grant something other than that which was claimed' (a decision *extra petita* is prohibited). Third, 'the court is also not authorised to grant more than sued for, even if this could be done in accordance with the substantive law applicable to the case' (a decision *ultra petita* is not allowed).

In conclusion, Rule 23(1) requires the court to rule on *all* claims and defences, and Rule 23(2) requires the court to rule *exclusively* on those claims and defences.

This interpretation of Rule 23 provides an additional argument in favour of considering all affirmative defences within the scope of *res judicata* and in favour of considering set-off as simply one defence among other possible defences to which Rule 149 applies. In my view, if all defences are part of

---

38 Rule 23, comment 2.

39 Rule 23, comment 2.

the scope of the dispute and the scope of the decision under Rule 23, then the decisions on those defences are also *res judicata* under Rule 149.

DOMEJ: The construction is elegant, but an objection might be raised regarding set-off. A claim asserted by way of set-off may arise from a legal relationship that has no bearing with the main claim. Following your interpretation, all preliminary issues related to this completely different claim would necessarily acquire the binding force of *res judicata*. This would be a significant and probably excessive extension of the principle. It is uncertain whether this question was fully recognised and discussed within the group.

VALLINES: Tanja, you are concerned that under the current wording of Rule 149, any 'necessary and incidental legal issues' connected to a set-off that has nothing to do with the main claim could be considered to fall within the scope of *res judicata*. Am I correct?

DOMEJ: I would suggest that this is not an entirely implausible interpretation, given the wording of the provision:

> Rule 149. *Material scope of* res judicata
>
> (3) *Res judicata* also applies where a defendant brings a defence based on set-off and
>
> (a) the claim and that defence are upheld by the court, or
>
> (b) the claim is admitted and the defence of set-off is rejected.
>
> (4) Where a claim is rejected on grounds other than set-off, so that the court does not decide the set-off defence, only the judgment on the claim becomes *res judicata*.

Both the German and Austrian codes of civil procedure include a similar set-off rule.[40] The Swiss code doesn't, but Swiss doctrine subscribes to the same approach.[41] In my understanding, this rule is normally meant to expand the scope of *res judicata* in systems where *res judicata* does not normally cover 'necessary and incidental legal issues'.

---

40 For Germany, see ZPO, § 322(2); for Austria, see ZPO, § 411(1).

41 See WEBER, P., OBERHAMMER, P., in OBERHAMMER, P., DOMEJ, T., HAAS, U. (eds.), *Kurzkommentar Schweizerische Zivilprozessordnung*, Basel: Helbing Lichtenhahn, 2021, § 236, para. 50.

Like you, I wonder why such a rule is necessary when we already have the first two paragraphs:

> Rule 149. *Material scope of* res judicata
>
> (1) The material scope of *res judicata* is determined by reference to the claims for relief in the parties' pleadings, including amendments, as decided by the court's judgment.
>
> (2) *Res judicata* also covers necessary and incidental legal issues that are explicitly decided in a judgment where parties to subsequent proceedings are the same as those in the proceedings determined by the prior judgment and where the court that gave that judgment could decide those legal issues.

VALLINES: Probably for the avoidance of doubt.

LOMA: Another thing to think about is whether *res judicata* can cover issues that weren't explicitly decided.

VALLINES: That's a very interesting question. Can *res judicata* extend beyond the *actual* scope of the decision? In other words, is there a *virtual* scope of *res judicata*?

To answer that question, it's worth starting by recalling the principle of concentration of legal and factual issues, enshrined in Rule 22:

> Rule 22. *Concentration of legal and factual issues*
>
> (1) Parties must bring all the legal and factual elements in support of, or in objection to, a claim for relief that arise out of the same cause of action in one single proceeding.
>
> (2) Non-compliance with Rule 22(1) renders proceedings on the same claim for relief arising out of the same cause of action inadmissible.

DOMEJ: We must differentiate. According to Rule 149(2), *res judicata* only extends to 'necessary and incidental legal issues that are explicitly decided in a judgment.' However, I believe this only refers to what we would call the *Bindungswirkung* (the *positive* or binding effect of *res judicata* on subsequent proceedings). If the discussion is limited to the question of whether an action should be prevented or allowed to continue because it has already been decided (the purely *negative* function of *res judicata*),[42] I agree that we must also consider any allegations that could have been raised in the first action.

While Rule 149 does not explicitly state this, it follows necessarily from Rule 22, as Enrique correctly pointed out, and the commentary on Rule 149 also states.

LOMA: You can't just *save* some defences for later in case you need them in any other future dispute about the same issue.

VALLINES: Any *virtual* rather than *actual* scope of *res judicata* would be derived from Rule 22 rather than from Rule 149. In the Spanish code, it is explicitly stated that any missing factual or legal grounds that could have been alleged will be deemed to be covered by *lis pendens* and *res judicata* in any future proceedings on the same issue.[43]

LOMA: Those facts and legal arguments would then be considered as adjudicated, even though they were never really adjudicated.

VALLINES: The Rules do this, in a way. If you attempt to initiate a new proceeding based on facts or legal arguments that you failed to present in support of the initial action, then your claim will be inadmissible. There is, thus, a certain fiction that those facts or legal arguments were considered and adjudicated.

It has been argued that Rule 22 has 'a direct effect on the material scope of *res judicata*' in terms of 'all the legal and factual elements in support of a claim for relief falling within the material scope of the *res judicata* irrespective of whether they were alleged by the claimant or not'.[44] The truth is, however, that the missing factual and legal elements were never actually adjudicated.

For this reason, it would be more logical to say that Rule 22 is simply a provision that requires all questions of fact and law to be concentrated and that failure to comply with this provision will have consequences. This

42 See MURRAY, P. L., STÜRNER, R., *German Civil Justice*, Durham: Carolina Academic Press, 2004, pp. 360–361.

43 LEC, Art. 400.

44 GASCÓN, F., SCHUMANN, G., 'The Rules on *Lis Pendens* and on *Res Judicata* in the ELI/UNIDROIT Model European Rules of Civil Procedure', *Ius Dictum*, 5, 2021, pp. 15–29, pp. 23–24.

provision has no real connection with *res judicata*, which requires an actual court decision on a particular matter.

After all, unlike in the Spanish code, Rule 22 doesn't mention *res judicata*. Also, Rule 149 – which deals with the 'material scope of *res judicata*' – assumes that *res judicata* is always linked to a court decision. This is evident from its wording: 'as decided by the court's judgment' (paragraph 1); 'explicitly decided' (paragraph 2); 'upheld' or 'rejected' (paragraph 3); and 'decide' (paragraph 4).[45] The same approach – that *res judicata* requires an actual court decision – could, by the way, be found in the case law of the ECJ.[46]

LOMA: What are the practical implications of either of these theses?

VALLINES: In terms of the purely negative effect of *res judicata*,[47] based on the idea of *non bis in idem*[48] (literally, 'not twice in the same thing'), the consequences appear to be the same. Under both perspectives, parties are prevented from instituting a subsequent proceeding where they intend to raise factual or legal grounds that they ought to have raised in the first proceeding.

But let us now consider the positive or binding or prejudicial effect of *res judicata*.[49] This *Bindungswirkung*, which Tanja mentioned earlier, happens when the decision given in the first proceeding is taken as having already been decided for the purposes of a second proceeding with a related action.

LOMA: If a mother obtains a first judgment declaring someone to be the father of the child, then she can sue him for child support, because the first judgment is *positively* binding on the court hearing the second case.

---

45 CADIET, L., AMRANI-MEKKI, S., 'General Principles: Party Disposition and Principle of Party Autonomy', in STADLER, A., SMITH, V., GASCÓN, F. (eds.), *European Rules of Civil Procedure. A Commentary on the ELI/UNIDROIT Model Rules*, Cheltenham: Edward Elgar, 2023, pp. 35–60, at 42.

46 TURMO, A., 'A New Chapter in the Saga of National *Res Judicata* and the Effectiveness of EU Law: Confirming the Trend towards Increasing Encroachments upon Domestic Procedural Law', *EU Law Live*, 30 May 2022.

47 See DE LA OLIVA, A., *Objeto del proceso y cosa juzgada en el proceso civil*, Cizur Menor: Civitas, 2005, pp. 105–110.

48 HOVAGUIMIAN, P., 'The *Res Judicata* Effects of Foreign Judgments in Post-Award Proceedings: To Bind or Not to Bind?', *Journal of International Arbitration*, 34–1, 2017, pp. 79–106, at 80–82.

49 See DE LA OLIVA, A., *Objeto del proceso y cosa juzgada en el proceso civil*, Cizur Menor: Civitas, 2005, pp. 105–110.

VALLINES: That's a perfect example.

As previously discussed, in this case we are not dealing with *res judicata* under Rule 149, but with the burden to concentrate all elements of fact and law under Rule 22.

However, if we adopt the view that, under Rule 22, the non-raised elements may be considered *res judicata* under Rule 149, we must then consider whether those elements carry also the positive or binding effect of *res judicata*. To frame the question more provocatively: is it reasonable to attribute a *res judicata*-like binding effect to the fiction that there has been an adjudication on those missing (and actually non-adjudicated) elements?

Before we can answer, we must be aware that we should not only accept the fiction that there has been a decision on those factual and legal elements, but also the additional fiction that the fictitious decision had a particular content (the one that should positively bind any future courts). One could assume, for instance, that there has been an actual court decision *rejecting* the grounds that were not raised in the first proceeding.[50]

However, accepting this additional fiction would likely involve going a step too far in the use of a *fictio juris*. It also appears to be at odds with the wording of Rule 149, which, as discussed, seems to link *res judicata* with the existence of a real and actual court decision.

In conclusion, the factual and legal grounds not raised in the first proceeding don't appear to have a positive binding force on subsequent proceedings under the Rules.

KERN: The resolution of this complex and interesting discussion will depend on whether we take a narrow or broad concept of the material scope of the *Bindungswirkung* of *res judicata*. In other words, whether only the operative part of the decision counts or everything that could have been discussed.

In German scholarship, it is understood that the operative part of a decision will bind future courts, while everything outside this part will not.[51]

DOMEJ: In summary, there are issues with the concept of a virtual decision. In simpler terms, parties are (*negatively*) prevented from raising these issues at a later stage.

50 See VALLINES, E., *La preclusión en el proceso civil*, Madrid: Civitas, 2004, pp. 324–325.

51 See, e.g., ROSENBERG, L., SCHWAB, K. H., GOTTWALD, P., *Zivilprozesssrecht*, Munich: Beck, 2018, §§ 155–157.

Take enforcement proceedings, for example. Certain actions can be brought against enforcement proceedings, e.g. an application to discontinue enforcement proceedings or an application for a declaration that the claim does not exist. The question is whether you can raise issues in the enforcement proceedings that you could have raised in the first action. This is the situation where Rule 22 applies. That is something quite different and less problematic than the concept contained in Rule 149. And I think it is consistent with a narrow concept of *res judicata*.

KERN: Absolutely. At the enforcement stage, the debtor can always object that the claim has been satisfied, e.g. the debt has been paid, after the judgment has become *res judicata*. However, he would be precluded from raising any objection that he could have raised before the judgment. The debtor would not be able to bring any means of attack, defence, or review against the earlier, declaratory judgment.

If there are proceedings on another claim – that's when the concept of *res judicata* comes into play.

LOMA: The difference can be substantial. It's really important for litigants to know whether they're going to be facing what US lawyers call *issue preclusion* or *claim preclusion*.[52] While issue preclusion stops you from relitigating the issues that have already been litigated, claim preclusion stops you from relitigating all the issues of a claim. When we think about the idea of the burden of concentration, we're moving from issue preclusion to claim preclusion.

Keep in mind that we may be dealing with different claims from different titles or the same title, with potentially high legal costs. Parties might want to test the waters before they jump in headfirst. For example, can we start with a 1 million claim and, if successful, claim for the other 99 million?

DOMEJ: There was a lively debate in our working group about whether claim preclusion should be applied. The decision was against claim preclusion, as reflected in the commentary.[53] However, the commentary also states that if a partial claim is filed, it should be an explicit partial claim.[54]

---

52 See, e.g., CHASE O. G., HERSHKOFF, H., SILBERMAN, L., SORABJI, J., STÜRNER, R., TANIGUCHI, Y., VARANO, V. (eds.), *Civil Litigation in Comparative Context*, Eagan: West, 2017, pp. 438–451.

53 Rule 22, comment 2.

54 Rule 22, comment 2.

One distinction to be made is between issues that could have been litigated with respect to a claim that was actually brought and claims, including partial claims, that were not brought at all. The former is covered by Rule 22, while the latter is not covered by Rule 22 but potentially covered by Rule 149(2).

If the claimant does not specify the partial nature of the claim, the claim is a *hidden* partial claim (*verdeckte Teilklage*). Comment 2 on Rule 22 seems to suggest that the claimant must specify the partial nature of the claim, but I do not think that this is reflected in the Rules. In the German-speaking jurisdictions, the prevailing view now seems to be that hidden partial claims are allowed, i.e., the claimant is not required to make it explicit that the claim is only partial for subsequent additional claims to be admissible.[55]

Another query is whether it is possible to successfully file a new partial claim after a previous one was dismissed on the merits. Rule 149(2) seems to suggest that once you've tested the waters and it didn't work out, it's game over. This is also the view recently adopted by the Swiss Federal Tribunal.[56] In Germany, however, it is the prevailing opinion – not without controversy – that additional later claims are not precluded by an adverse judgment on the preceding partial claim.[57]

Bibliography

ALTHAMMER, C., in BORK, R., ROTH, H. (eds.), *Stein/Jonas Kommentar zur Zivilprozessordnung*, vol. 4, Tübingen: Mohr Siebeck, 2018.

55 For Germany, see Federal Supreme Court, judgment of 9 April 1997, case IV ZR 113/96, 135 BGHZ 178, 181 (1998); for Switzerland, see *Tribunal Fédéral Suisse*, judgment of 18 January 2012, case 4A_401/2011.

56 *Tribunal Fédéral Suisse*, judgment of 23 March 2021, case 4A_449/2020, BGE 147 III 345.

57 For further details on this debate, see ALTHAMMER, C., in BORK, R., ROTH, H. (eds.), *Stein/Jonas Kommentar zur Zivilprozessordnung*, vol. 4, Tübingen: Mohr Siebeck, 2018, § 322, at numbers 139 ff.; GOTTWALD, P., in KRÜGER, W., RAUSCHER, T., *Münchener Kommentar zur Zivilprozessordnung*, Munich: Beck, 2020, § 322, at numbers 129 ff.; LEIPOLD, D., 'Teilklagen und Rechtskraft', in BETTERMANN, K., WISCH, M. L., OTTO, H., SCHMIDT, K. (eds.), *Festschrift für Albrecht Zeuner*, Tübingen: Mohr Siebeck, 1994, pp. 431–449; MARBURGER, P., 'Rechtskraft und Präklusion bei der Teilklage im Zivilprozess', in FLUME, W., JAKOBS, H. H., PICKER, E., WILHELM, J. (eds.), *Gedächtnisschrift für Knobbe-Keuk*, Cologne: Otto Schmidt, 1997, pp. 187–200; OBERHAMMER, P., 'Wieder einmal: Rechtskraft bei Teilklagen', in BORK, R., HOEREN, T., POHLMANN, P. (eds.), *Festschrift für Helmut Kollhosser*, Karlsruhe: VVW, pp. 501–521.

Bruns, A., 'Effect of Judgments: *Res judicata*', in Stadler, A., Smith, V., Gascón, F. (eds.), *European Rules of Civil Procedure. A Commentary on the ELI/UNIDROIT Model Rules*, Cheltenham: Edward Elgar, 2023.

Cadiet, L., Amrani-Mekki, S., 'General Principles: Party Disposition and Principle of Party Autonomy', in Stadler, A., Smith, V., Gascón, F. (eds.), *European Rules of Civil Procedure. A Commentary on the ELI/UNIDROIT Model Rules*, Cheltenham: Edward Elgar, 2023, pp. 35–60.

Chase O. G., Hershkoff, H., Silberman, L., Sorabji, J., Stürner, R., Taniguchi, Y., Varano, V. (eds.), *Civil Litigation in Comparative Context*, Eagan: West, 2017.

de la Oliva, A., *Curso de Derecho Procesal Civil II. Parte Especial*, Madrid: Editorial Universitaria Ramón Areces, 2016.

de la Oliva, A., *Objeto del proceso y cosa juzgada en el proceso civil*, Cizur Menor: Civitas, 2005.

de la Oliva, A., 'Art. 10', in de la Oliva, A., Díez-Picazo, I., Vegas, J., Banacloche, J., *Comentarios a la Ley de Enjuiciamiento Civil*, Madrid: Civitas, 2001, pp. 92–98.

Gascón, F., Schumann, G., 'The Rules on *Lis Pendens* and on *Res Judicata* in the ELI/UNIDROIT Model European Rules of Civil Procedure', *Ius Dictum*, 5, 2021, pp. 15–29.

Gottwald, P., in Krüger, W., Rauscher, T., *Münchener Kommentar zur Zivilprozessordnung*, Munich: Beck, 2020.

Holleaux, D., 'La litispendance internationale', *Travaux du Comité français de droit international privé*, 32–34, 1974, pp. 203–230.

Hovaguimian, P., 'The *Res judicata* Effects of Foreign Judgments in Post-Award Proceedings: To Bind or Not to Bind?', *Journal of International Arbitration*, 34–1, 2017, pp. 79–106.

Iglesias, S., *La sentencia en el proceso civil*, Madrid: Dykinson, 2015.

Kern, C. A., 'Harmonisation of the Rules on Judgments and Appeals in Europe: A Few Remarks from the Inside', in Gascón, F., Hess, B. (eds.), *The Future of the European Law of Civil Procedure. Coordination or Harmonisation?*, Cambridge: Intersentia, 2020, pp. 223–240.

Leipold, D., 'Teilklagen und Rechtskraft', in Bettermann, K., Wisch, M. L., H., Schmidt, K. (eds.), *Festschrift für Albrecht Zeuner*, Tübingen: Mohr Siebeck, 1994, pp. 431–449.

Marburger, P., 'Rechtskraft und Präklusion bei der Teilklage im Zivilprozess', in Flume, W., Jakobs, H. H., Picker, E., Wilhelm, J. (eds.), *Gedächtnisschrift für Knobbe-Keuk*, Cologne: Otto Schmidt, 1997, pp. 187–200.

Maxeiner, J. R., *Failures of American Civil Justice in International Perspective*, Cambridge: Cambridge University Press, 2011.

MONTERO, J., *De la legitimación en el proceso civil*, Barcelona: Bosch, 2006.

MURRAY, P. L., STÜRNER, R., *German Civil Justice*, Durham: Carolina Academic Press, 2004.

OBERHAMMER, P., 'Wieder einmal: Rechtskraft bei Teilklagen', in BORK, R., HOEREN, T., POHLMANN, P. (eds.), *Festschrift für Helmut Kollhosser*, Karlsruhe: VVW, pp. 501–521.

ROSENBERG, L., SCHWAB, K. H., GOTTWALD, P., *Zivilprozesssrecht*, Munich: Beck, 2018.

SÁNCHEZ, B., *La sustitución procesal: análisis crítico*, unpublished doctoral dissertation, Complutense University of Madrid, 2016, available at https://hdl.handle.net/20.500.14352/22304.

TURMO, A., 'A New Chapter in the Saga of National *Res Judicata* and the Effectiveness of EU Law: Confirming the Trend towards Increasing Encroachments upon Domestic Procedural Law', *EU Law Live*, 30 May 2022.

VALLINES, E., 'Proceedings Before a Final Hearing and Final Hearing', in STADLER, A., SMITH, V., GASCÓN, F. (eds.), *European Rules of Civil Procedure. A Commentary on the ELI/UNIDROIT Model Rules*, Cheltenham: Edward Elgar, 2023.

VALLINES, E., *La preclusión en el proceso civil*, Madrid: Civitas, 2004.

WEBER, P., OBERHAMMER, P., in OBERHAMMER, P., DOMEJ, T., HAAS, U. (eds.), *Kurzkommentar Schweizerische Zivilprozessordnung*, Basel: Helbing Lichtenhahn, 2021.

ZSCHUNKE, U., 'L'intérêt à agir: Action déclaratoire et interdiction de l'action populaire', in SCHULZE, G. (ed.), *Europäisches Privatrecht in Vielfalt geeint. Der modernisierte Zivilprozess in Europa*, Munich: Sellier, 2014.

CHAPTER 11

Appeals

Marco de Benito, Frédérique Ferrand, and Christoph Kern

Every legal system has been engaged in a long-lasting debate on the opportunities to review cases and the standards of access to the appellate process. The central issue is posed as a question: which types of access restrictions and which scope of review serve to maintain equilibrium between fundamental rights and public interests. The responses to this question exhibit considerable diversity. There is no uniform solution regarding the function of appellate justice, the grounds for granting access to appeal, or the consideration of factual and legal issues.

Aware of this diversity, the Rules propose a particular approach to the transfer of cases from the initial to the final decision. This approach considers the advantages and disadvantages of entry requirements, the scope of review of appellate courts, and the functions of last resort courts in each legal system.

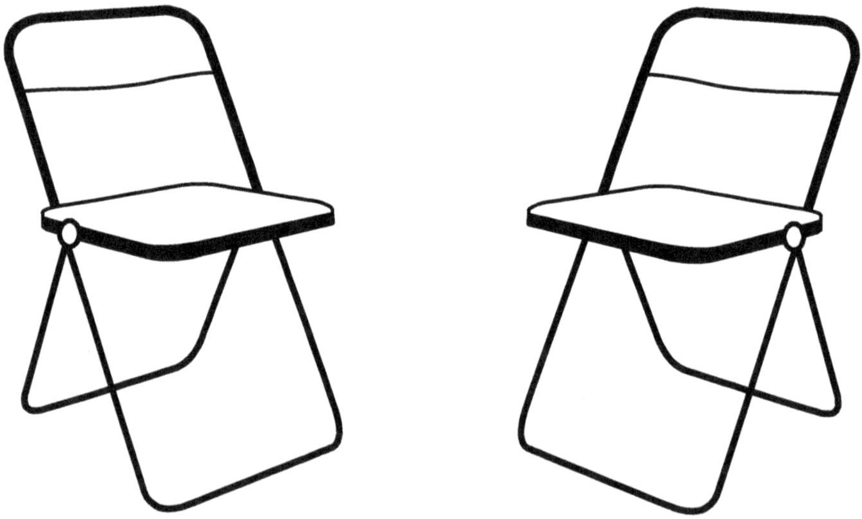

 | DOI:10.1163/9789004533257_012

FERRAND: The working group on means of review was one of the last to be set up within the ELI-UNIDROIT Model Rules project. At the beginning, I had the impression that most of the members of the steering committee – and some colleagues, including myself – thought it would be extremely difficult to draw up uniform European rules on means of review.[1]

I acted as an expert in the working group for the ALI-UNIDROIT Principles of Transnational Civil Procedure. I remember a meeting in the early 2000s in the beautiful Villa Aldobrandini, the Roman headquarters of UNIDROIT. When we started to discuss the means of review, a lively, even heated discussion ensued. It was a very sensitive subject, and we couldn't reach a general compromise.

We reached a compromise on the immediate enforceability of first instance judgments as a rule, with some exceptions where enforcement can be stayed 'in the interest of justice':

> Principle 26. *Immediate enforceability of judgments*
>
> 1. The final judgment of the first-instance court ordinarily should be immediately enforceable.
>
> 2. The first-instance court or the appellate court, on its own motion or motion of a party, may in the interest of justice stay enforcement of the judgment pending appeal.
>
> 3. Security may be required from the appellant as a condition of granting a stay or from the respondent as a condition of denying a stay.

This was, in my view, a balanced solution between the interests of the creditor, who had won at first instance, and those of the debtor, who could have a fair chance of winning his case on appeal.

KERN: We reproduced this provision, almost *verbatim*, in the ELI-UNIDROIT Rules:

1 See JUNILLON, J., 'Le projet ALI-UNIDROIT, vue critique d'un praticien du droit', and MOUSSA, T., 'Le projet ALI-UNIDROIT, vue critique d'un magistrat', both in FERRAND, F. (dir.), *La procédure civile mondiale modélisée*, Paris: EJT, 2004, pp. 40 ff. and 54 ff. respectively. See also KERN, C. A., 'Harmonisation of the Rules on Judgments and Appeals in Europe – A Few Remarks from the Inside', in GASCÓN, F., HESS, B. (eds.), *The Future of the European Law of Civil Procedure. Coordination or Harmonisation?*, Cambridge: Intersentia, 2020, pp. 223–238.

Rule 162. *Provisional enforcement*

(1) Unless otherwise provided for, final judgment and any appellate court judgments are enforceable immediately regardless of whether an appeal has been commenced by filing a notice of appeal.

(2) An appellant may apply to the appellate court to stay enforcement if they have filed a notice of appeal and enforcement is manifestly excessive.

(3) Security may be required from an appellant as a condition of granting a stay or from a respondent as a condition of refusing to grant a stay.

FERRAND: We had a very clear model to follow on that point. However, when we look at the provision that dealt specifically with appeals in the ALI-UNIDROIT Principles, we find that it doesn't provide for a uniform solution at all: it merely refers to the law of the forum.

Rule 27. *Appeal*

27.1 Appellate review should be available on substantially the same terms as other judgments under the law of the forum. . . .

Referring the issue to the law of the forum is hardly an impressive achievement when drafting transnational principles. In fact, I'd say this provision was a real admission of failure, because we could not find an agreement between, on the one hand, the common law principles of finality and exceptionality of access to appeal and, on the other hand, the continental view of access to appeal as a natural step that can almost be taken for granted. As a result, when we started working for the ELI-UNIDROIT Rules, we couldn't really take the ALI-UNIDROIT Principles as a starting point.

DE BENITO: The configuration of appeals is not simply a matter of procedural choices; it also depends on the organisation of the courts in each country. This may have been a further complicating factor.

FERRAND: That's a fundamental consideration. Keep in mind that the different organisation of the courts is linked to the different level of quality of first instance decisions. You can't compare, for example, a first instance trial in England – which perhaps lasts a few days with the hearing of witnesses and experts – with a hearing in a French court where, over the morning or afternoon, dozens of cases are called. It was difficult to find a solution that was in line with how justice works in such different jurisdictions.

DE BENITO: The contrast is even more pronounced when considering the US,[2] as was the case with the ALI-UNIDROIT Principles. I can appreciate why a harmonised principle couldn't be achieved at that time.

FERRAND: Consequently, the draft ELI-UNIDROIT Rules project began and evolved with the issue of appeals left out. However, when most of the chapters were finished, the members of the structure group and the steering committee realised that it wasn't appropriate to present such an all-encompassing regulation, almost a model code, without a single word on appeals. That's why ours was one of the last groups to be created. The inevitable sense of urgency that ensued also explains the small, executive size of the team, consisting of only four members: Christoph Kern, Fernando Gascón, Magne Strandberg, and myself, all of us members of other previous working groups.[3] Time was short, the subject matter was difficult, and we struggled to find solutions.

DE BENITO: Well, you managed to put together a pretty comprehensive set of rules on the subject, despite the restrictions. Let's take a quick look at them, shall we?

KERN: The 'general part' consists of only two articles. The first recognises a 'right to appeal':

> Rule 153. *Right of appeal or to seek recourse*
>
> Where a party, or exceptionally a non-party, has a legal interest in a judgment, subject to the provisions in this Part, they may appeal from, or rely on other types of recourse against, it.

In our draft, the heading of this article was 'legal interest', which captures the idea more accurately since not everyone always has a broad 'right of appeal'. The official commentary reflects this by calling 'legal interest' a

2 See CHASE, O. G., 'American Exceptionalism and Comparative Procedure', *American Journal of Comparative Law*, 50, 2002, pp. 277–301.

3 KERN, C. A., 'Means of Review in the ELI/UNIDROIT Model European Rules of Civil Procedure', *Zeitschrift für Zivilprozess International*, 25, 2020, pp. 287–303, at 288–289.

'general criterion for legal standing' and pointing out its function as 'a continuous test that must be fulfilled at every stage of litigation'. In the appeal context, this is defined as a 'legitimate need to challenge' the decision.[4]

The second rule of the general part is the rule on 'waiver of right to appeal':

> Rule 154. *Waiver of right to appeal or to seek recourse*
>
> (1) A party may waive their right of appeal or to seek recourse. Waiver must be informed and express. Waiver may be given to the court in writing before or during a court hearing, or given orally in a court hearing.
>
> (2) Waiver may be effected before a first instance judgment or other decision or a first appeal judgment is made. Such a waiver may only be made where it is agreed by all the parties.
>
> (3) Where a party is bringing or defending proceedings as a consumer, they cannot waive their right to appeal before judgment has been made.
>
> (4) All waivers must be recorded by the court in a judgment or other official record, if any.

As we can read in paragraph 2, waiver must be mutual, 'agreed by all the parties'. To waive the possibility to appeal while the proceedings are pending and the judgment hasn't yet been rendered means that neither party knows what it is waiving; hence, both must share the risk. One party may waive that 'right of appeal' only if the other party does the same. Only such a mutual waiver can have the serious effect of extinguishing the right to appeal.[5] This is a fair solution, in my opinion, although I wouldn't be surprised if it is not universally accepted.

---

4 Rule 153, comment 1. See also KERN, C. A., 'Means of Review in the ELI/UNIDROIT Model European Rules of Civil Procedure', *Zeitschrift für Zivilprozess International*, 25, 2020, pp. 287–303, at 291–292.

5 See KERN, C. A., 'Means of Review in the ELI/UNIDROIT Model European Rules of Civil Procedure', *Zeitschrift für Zivilprozess International*, 25, 2020, pp. 287–303, at 291–292; and KERN, C. A., 'Procedural Contracts in Germany', in CABRAL, A. P., NOGUEIRA, P. H. (eds.), *Negócios processuais*, Salvador: Jus Podivm, 2017, pp. 213, at 215 ff.

DE BENITO: I understand this right to waive an appeal as an expression of party autonomy *propter actionem*, as distinct from expressions of party autonomy *propter jurisdictionem* and *propter processum*.[6]

And I wonder whether all grounds of appeal should be waivable. What if the ground of appeal to be waived would have been based on a breach of an important procedural guarantee? Rules 169(2) and 174(2) speak of reversing a judgment for 'grave' or 'serious' 'procedural error'. Rules 172(1) and 174(1) provide for appeals 'to correct a violation of a fundamental right'. Making those grounds waivable in advance – wouldn't that open the door to the possibility of the court acting arbitrarily or carelessly?

If these grounds could be waived in advance, wouldn't that open the door to the court acting in an arbitrary or frivolous manner?

KERN: This is precisely what I meant to say about risk sharing between the parties. The risk is shared but the negative outcome is not necessarily so. The parties waive their right to appeal in advance knowing that one will eventually win and the other will lose. They even accept the possibility of a 'procedural error' or a 'violation of a fundamental right' to the detriment of only one of them, as you point out.

FERRAND: The general part you presented, Christoph, contains a remarkably concise regulation. In the draft that we presented to the structure group, however, the general part included a rule on withdrawal, a rule on extension of time limits, and a rule on representation by a lawyer. These provisions were eventually taken out of the general part on 'means of review' and put into a different section, which functions as a general part on 'appeals'. This creates a double 'general part', which introduces a further level of complexity in the structure.

KERN: Exactly. Part IX, 'Means of review', begins with Section 1, entitled 'General part'. Then there is Section 2, entitled 'Appeals', which contains rules on first appeals and second appeals. This is followed by Section 3, 'First appeals', and Section 4, 'Second appeals', with specific provisions on each of those appeals. The chapter is completed by Section 5, 'Review of

6 DE BENITO, M., 'La autonomía privada en el proceso civil: apuntes taxonómicos', in BANACLOCHE, J., GASCÓN, F. (eds.), *Logros y retos de la justicia civil en España*, Valencia: Tirant lo Blanch, 2022, pp. 251–262.

procedural error and miscellaneous Appeals', and Section 6, 'Extraordinary Recourse'.[7]

FERRAND: The issue arises from the fact that some of the provisions included in this 'general part of the special part' that is Section 2 distinguish between the first appeal and the second appeal. Consequently, they cannot be considered 'general' for all appeals. Section 2 may be understandable if the rules were identical, but in most cases they are not.

For instance, Rule 156, 'Time limits for appeals', stipulates that a notice of appeal must be filed within one month if it's a first appeal or within two months if it's a second appeal. Why then group all this together in a single Section 2 called 'Appeals', if we already have Sections 3 and 4 on first and second appeals?

Another example: Rule 157 deals only with the content of the notice and grounds for the first appeal. Then there is a separate rule, Article 158, which deals with the same issues but for the second appeal. And with a clearly different content in either case. In the first appeal it is possible to file two different briefs: the first with the notice of appeal and the second with the grounds of appeal (Rule 157); whereas in the second appeal, the notice of appeal and the grounds must be filed in a single document (Rule 158) – as the working group had originally proposed for both the first and second appeals, by the way.

KERN: The treatment of withdrawal – *ex post* withdrawal as opposed to *ex ante* waiver (Rule 154) – is also different: a party can withdraw a first appeal, but not a second appeal unless with the consent of the other party and the court.

> Rule 163. *Withdrawal*
>
> (1) A party that has commenced a first appeal can withdraw their appeal at any time.
>
> (2) A second appeal can only be withdrawn by a party with the consent of the other party and the court.

7 KERN, C. A., 'Means of Review in the ELI/UNIDROIT Model European Rules of Civil Procedure', *Zeitschrift für Zivilprozess International*, 25, 2020, pp. 287–303, at 293.

This is probably new for several legal systems – other legal systems already had a similar rule –,[8] but experience seems to suggest that such a rule is a good idea to avoid tactical withdrawals of a second appeal, which can be observed sometimes.

DE BENITO: I think this is a natural distinction to make, even if we ignore the issue of structure for a moment. Firstly, the idea of withdrawal as a bilateral act is already present in the Rules: the claimant may only terminate the proceeding 'with the defendant's consent' (Rule 56). Secondly, second appeals serve not only the *jus litigatoris*, the private interest of litigants, but even more so the *jus constitutionis*, the public interest in a clear and uniform development of the law.[9] The other party or the court, acting on behalf of this public interest, might legitimately want to see the point at issue settled by the higher court.

FERRAND: The same dual solution is found in the treatment of 'representation'. In the first appeal, represented by a lawyer 'may be required'; in the second appeal, representation by a lawyer is mandatory.

> Rule 164. *Representation in an appeal court*
>
> (1) If representation is not mandatory according to applicable law, a first appeal court may require a party to be represented by a lawyer if they are incapable of representing themselves in an understandable manner or if it is necessary for the proper administration of justice.
>
> (2) Parties must be represented by a lawyer in proceedings before a second appeal court.

(It is perhaps worth noting that in our draft, the draft that we presented to the structure group, the title of this provision was 'representation by a lawyer'; we felt that 'representation' wasn't as precise or intuitive.)

KERN: The working group considered the major problems that exist in England with *pro se* litigants and the ability of *pro se* litigants to defend their

8 See, e.g., German ZPO, § 565, second sentence.

9 See generally JOLOWICZ, J. A., 'Introduction: Recourse against Judgment in the European Union: A Comparative Survey', in JOLOWICZ, J. A., VAN RHEE, C. H. (eds.), *Civil Procedures in Europe: Recourse Against Judgements in the European Union*, vol. 2, Alphen aan den Rijn: Kluwer, pp. 1–11.

cases at first instance, but even more so at second and third instance (if we can call the third instance an *instance*).[10]

FERRAND: No doubt, each of these different solutions for the first and second appeals is fully justified. However, in terms of structure, to conclude our reasoning, Section 2 seems to me to be a little contrived. It gives the impression that there are common rules when most of them are not. In terms of legislative drafting technique, it isn't the best calibrated legal mechanism. Had it been in my power, I would have eliminated Section 2 and distributed these provisions between the special sections on first and second appeal.

The structure of the final text, which – I must insist – wasn't chosen by the working group, seems to reveal a political choice to make the European rules reflect a common law model, in which the appeal mechanism is always basically the same, rather than a civil law model, in which both appeals are conceived as completely different things. A common section with the title 'Appeals' necessarily mixes the two very different means of recourse that are '*appel*' and '*pourvoi*', '*Berufung*' and '*Revision*', '*apelación*' y '*casación*', the ordinary second instance and the limited final recourse to a supreme court. To be honest, I'm not very happy about it.

KERN: The working group tried to reach a compromise between the more open appellate system of the civil law tradition and the more restrictive common law conception of appeal. The consensus reached was strong and far-reaching. Possibly, the text that was finally adopted unintentionally reopened some of the culture clash that had been overcome during the drafting process.[11]

DE BENITO: I agree with Frédérique, and I'd go even further. What concerns me is that below a certain *summa gravaminis*, a threshold value, the

10 See, e.g., CIVIL JUSTICE COUNCIL, 'Access to Justice for Litigants in Person (or Self-Represented Litigants)', 2011; THE JUDICIAL WORKING GROUP ON LITIGANTS IN PERSON, 'Report', 2013, p. 3, 6 ff.; LORD CHIEF JUSTICE, 'Report', 2016, p. 19; all three reports available at judiciary.gov.uk. See also ZUCKERMAN, A. A. S., 'No Justice Without Lawyers – The Myth of an Inquisitorial Solution', *Civil Justice Quarterly*, 33-2014, pp. 355–374; SORABJI, J., 'Austerity's Effect on English Civil Justice', *Erasmus Law Review*, 8-2015, 4, pp. 159–173, at 164 ff.

11 See STÜRNER, R., 'The ELI / UNIDROIT Model European Rules of Civil Procedure. An Introduction to Their Basic Conceptions', *RabelsZ*, 86, 2022, pp. 421–472, at 455, 456, 469.

Regulation sets up the first appeal as if it were an appeal of last resort to a supreme court.

Rule 166. *Right to appeal*

(1) A party has a right to appeal against a first instance judgment if

(a) the value of the appealed claim exceeds [the value of the appealed claim as determined by applicable law, for instance twice the average monthly wage in the forum State] or

(b) the appeal court grants permission to appeal based on the contents of the notice and reasons for appeal.

(2) In deciding whether to grant permission to appeal, the appeal court shall take the following into account

(a) whether the legal issue in dispute is of fundamental significance, or

(b) the further development of the law, or the public interest in securing uniform adjudication require an appellate decision, or

(c) fundamental procedural requirements have been violated.

Firstly, this provision gives the first appellate court a lot of leeway to grant or deny leave to appeal. Secondly, it requires the parties and the first court of appeal to use filtering standards that are open to interpretation, like the standards used in some countries for final appeals to supreme courts and even constitutional courts – such as the grounds of assessment of *interés casacional* and *especial trascendencia constitucional* in Spain – rather than the ordinary first appeals to intermediate courts.[12] In reality, in the Rules, the grounds for the first appeal are basically the same as those for the second, just expressed differently:

Rule 172. *Right to a second appeal*

(1) A party may only appeal from a first appeal judgment if such an appeal is necessary to

(a) correct a violation of a fundamental right,

---

12 de Benito, M., 'Back in Focus: Case Selection Standards in the Spanish Supreme Court,' in Bravo, P., van Rhee, C. H. (eds.), *Supreme Courts Under Pressure. Controlling Caseload in the Administration of Civil Justice*, Cham: Springer, pp. 49–71.

(b) secure uniformity in the law,

(c) decide a fundamental question which is not limited to the case at issue, or

(d) develop the law.

Leaving aside the problems of interpretation that divergent wordings of the same idea always cause in legislative technique, the crucial point here is that this system blurs the identity of each of the two appeals by replicating – and *duplicating* – the filtering technique of the last remedy in the first appeal.

KERN: Both provisions are inspired by the German ZPO:[13]

§ 511. *Appeal available as a remedy*

(4) The court of first instance shall admit an appeal in cases in which:

1. The legal matter is of fundamental significance or wherever the further development of the law or the interests in ensuring uniform adjudication require a decision to be handed down by the court of appeal, and wherever

2. The judgment does not adversely affect the party by an amount higher than 600 euros.

§ 543. *Admission to appeal*

(2) An appeal on points of law is to be admitted if:

1. The legal matter is of fundamental significance, or

2. The further development of the law or the interests in ensuring uniform adjudication require a decision to be handed down by the court hearing the appeal on points of law.

FERRAND: One of the main justifications for this system, which departs drastically from the French conception of both the first and the second

13 See generally MURRAY, P. L., STÜRNER, R., *German Civil Justice*, Durham: Carolina Academic Press, 2004, pp. 373–386 (*Berufung*) and 386–399 (*Revision*).

appeal, is that the Rules aim here not to 'undermine public confidence in the civil justice system' by 'devaluing the status of first instance proceedings'.[14]

DE BENITO: I understand and share the need to foster public confidence in first instance justice.[15] From many points of view, the first instance is the critical moment of the legal process. However, the Rules already reflect this choice throughout the text. Confidence in the individual judges, in the lawyers, in the parties themselves, and the personal responsibility of each of these actors of civil justice – in a word, trust in first instance civil justice – is rooted in the very litigation model of the Rules.

The Rules begin by expecting parties and counsel to cooperate loyally 'to promote the fair, efficient, and speedy resolution of the dispute' (Rule 2) under the judges' sense of prudence and initiative (Rule 4) in the exercise of the broad powers that the Rules place in their hands (Rule 49).

First instance judgments are then provisionally enforced (Rule 162(1)). Even the fact that security 'may be required' but is not necessarily required to apply for provisional enforcement (Rule 162(3)) suggests reliance on the first instance.

A very open second instance wouldn't be compatible with the system's reliance on the first instance. But in the Rules, appeal 'shall be by review, not a *de novo* hearing', as the penultimate version of Rule 155 used to read. 'In general, the relief sought is limited by what was claimed or defended at first instance' (Rule 167(2)). Similarly, the pleadings and evidence are limited to what could have been pleaded or proven at first instance (Rule 168).

Finally, we have the legal certainty provided by case law emanating from the supreme courts (Rule 172). If case law effectively serves to clarify, unify, supplement, and develop the law, then it provides the ultimate systemic feedback to reinforce the centrepiece of the entire legal process: the application of the law *juxta allegata et probata*, in accordance with the

14 Rule 166, comment 1.

15 See, on a recent reform aimed at reinforcing public confidence in first-instance civil justice, DE LA OLIVA, A., 'Spanish Civil Procedure Act 2000: Flying over Common and Civil Law traditions', in WALKER, J., CHASE, O. G. (eds.), *Common Law, Civil Law and the Future of Categories*, Markham: LexisNexis, 2010, pp. 63–74. Regarding the need to strengthen the first instance in France with more resources and experienced judges, see SAUVÉ, J. M., *et al.*, 'Rendre justice aux citoyens. Rapport du comité des États généraux de la justice (octobre 2021-avril 2022)', 2022, available at https://medias.vie-publique.fr/data_storage_s3/rapport/pdf/285620.pdf.

allegations and evidence presented. And this climax occurs primarily in the first instance.

In summary, is there a genuine risk in the general litigation model of the Rules of a 'devaluation of the status of first instance proceedings' that would 'undermine public confidence in the civil justice system'? Why, then, do we need to duplicate and extend to first appellate courts what is simply intended to unify or develop the law at the top of the judicial pyramid? Are we prepared to have a multitude of regional courts engaged in the 'development of the law' and the 'securing of uniform adjudication' within their respective territories? How could the system work without infusing even a drop or two of *stare decisis*, without incorporating some degree of precedent setting by lower courts?

KERN: I'll answer with another question: why should lower courts not be involved in achieving uniform application of the law? After all, they are perhaps even better placed than national supreme courts to develop the law could, because they are closer to the low value cases of ordinary citizens. Relying on them for the development of the law could yield better results than a leapfrog appeal to the relevant supreme court. It allows low-value cases to have the same quality of justice without the same level of cost and complication. It is a compromise that balances the hard definition of a value threshold.

What your concerns show, in any case, is that everything in the system is intertwined. If we touch the access and scope of the first appeal, it can have consequences for the design of the whole procedural system. I agree with that.

FERRAND: I understand that this is a controversial choice. Indeed, we discussed a lot about this interplay between appeals to higher and lower courts during our meetings. The key point in this respect is the value threshold. A party can always appeal if the amount in dispute exceeds a certain threshold. The threshold is therefore, in practice, the centre of gravity of the first appeal. There are simply small value cases that raise important questions of law, and we must ensure that they can be channelled to higher courts.

KERN: If you accept that the value threshold applies to the first appeal at all, then you either exclude low value cases from access to the highest court or you need some filtering technique. It's only a matter of logic to have similar criteria in both appeals, in Rules 166(2) and 172.

DE BENITO: Your argument is persuasive. Yes, probably *summa gravaminis* and filtering standards go hand in hand. The question, then, is at what figure to set the threshold. The German threshold you mentioned, Christoph, of 600 euros, seems reasonable from the point of view of access to justice, to appellate justice in this case. However, the Rules allow for a higher figure: twice the average monthly salary means that the threshold will always exceed 600 euros and can go up to almost 5,000 euros in some countries.

FERRAND: In France, the value threshold is set precisely at 5,000 euros.[16] And it is an absolute requirement, as we do not have the option of the open standards. Simply put, small value cases don't benefit from the possibility of an ordinary appeal; only a direct or leapfrog *pourvoi en cassation* is available.

DE BENITO: An alternative approach would be to eliminate the value threshold entirely and rely on the relatively limited scope of the second appeal in terms of claims, facts, and evidence. It may be possible to generate a similar volume of appeals without requiring intermediate appellate courts to perform the delicate legal operations associated with the application of open-ended and potentially discretionary rules.

KERN: One of our main concerns was to avoid or at least control the overloading of the appellate courts. Appellate courts should focus on the most important cases. Is the amount in dispute a good indicator of the importance of a case? Comparative law suggests that it is. Indeed, some European legal systems are much more restrictive than the Rules.

As for the delicate task of applying the open standards, the Rules expect a lot from judges, as well as from parties and lawyers, as you pointed out earlier. It isn't easy to be a judge under these Rules. You must give advice and opinions. You must think about the consequences of individual cases in the development of the law. It is not easy. But nobody said it should be!

DE BENITO: Regarding procedure, I note that the Rules don't favour either submitting the entire notice of appeal at once, with a full statement of grounds, or a two-stage process where first a notice of appeal is filed and then the grounds are set out in a separate document.

16 Regarding the *Tribunal judiciaire,* see Art. R. 211-3-24 of the French judicial code (*Code de l'organisation judiciaire*).

Rule 157. *Contents of the notice of and reasons for appeal – first appeal*

(1) A notice of appeal for a first appeal must state that an appeal is being commenced and must identify the judgment subject to the appeal. It may also provide reasons for the appeal. Reasons for the appeal if not set out in the notice of appeal should be set out in a separate document.

Is the leeway left to the appellant or to the court?

FERRAND: In France, we have a two-stage process for any first appeal. The appellant has one month from the notification of the first instance judgment to file a notice of appeal, and then three months to file the full brief with the legal grounds.[17] This reflects the reality that a simple notice of appeal can be time-consuming. In the Rules, the pleading must be filed within one month of service of the judgment (Rule 156(1)) and the full pleading *may* be filed within an additional month (Rule 157(3)), at the discretion of the appellant, as I understand the provision. Moreover, the additional month is 'unless the court orders otherwise', thus giving some room for discussion by the parties and decision by the judge.

KERN: Personally, I'd prefer to first clarify as soon as possible whether or not there will be an appeal, as happens in Germany as well,[18] rather than waiting two months to file (or receive, if we take the appellee's perspective) both the notice and the grounds of appeal. However, I understand that this aspect depends very much on national traditions and the mentality of the lawyers and courts involved. What we did in the Rules regarding the first appeal is, in effect, to leave it to the appellant to decide according to the circumstances and the complexity of the case, and perhaps also simply according to the agendas of the party and counsel. Ultimately, the specific time limit for filing the full brief in the first appeal is subject to the discretion of the court; in practice, this provision is likely to be used more to extend the time limit than to shorten it.

DE BENITO: It is surprising that the time limit for lodging a first appeal is treated more flexibly and may end up being longer than the time limit for

17 CPC, Arts. 902 and 908. See FERRAND, F., 'Appel: délais de l'appel', in *Répertoire de procédure civile Dalloz*, 2022, §§ 7 ff.

18 German ZPO, §§ 517–520.

lodging a second appeal, which must always be lodged within two months of the notification of the judgment, with no room for court discretion (Rule 156(2)). Second appeals are naturally more difficult and take longer to draft properly. It is worth noting that second appeal briefs typically involve two complex legal operations. Firstly, it is necessary to demonstrate that the limited grounds for the admissibility of the second appeal exist in the case:

> Rule 172. *Right to a second appeal*
>
> (1) A party may only appeal from a first appeal judgment if such an appeal is necessary to
>
> (a) correct a violation of a fundamental right,
>
> (b) secure uniformity in the law,
>
> (c) decide a fundamental question which is not limited to the case at issue, or
>
> (d) develop the law.

Secondly, it is essential to clarify the legal issue at stake, as second appeals in the Rules clearly focus on questions of law rather than questions of fact:

> Rule 174. *Scope of appellate review – second appeal*
>
> (1) Within the relief sought, as far as admissible, the second appeal court's review shall encompass
>
> (a) the interpretation and application of the law in the first appeal judgment;
>
> (b) the legality of the proceedings in the first appeal court, provided that the appellant challenged the error complained about immediately before that court.

And we all know that explaining a *quæstio juris*, particularly with the nuance and depth required by a supreme court, is often more challenging than providing a different version of a *quæstio facti*.

Could it be, in conclusion, that the official commentary is a little too optimistic when it refers to the 'more limited scope of second appeals'?[19]

19 Rules 155 and 156, comment 3.

KERN: You're right. Actually, the German *Revision* is filed in two steps, with some judicial discretion over the time limits.[20] However, everyone in the working group agreed that we need a more consistent and stricter approach in this case. Second appeals should be few and far between, and only for important cases. That's why we decided not to give lawyers any reason to file an appeal brief before they've looked closely at the judgment to see if they can make a second appeal. We also thought about the fact that in some countries, only a few lawyers are allowed to file second appeals and to appear in front of the court of second appeal.[21]

Bibliography

CHASE, O. G., 'American Exceptionalism and Comparative Procedure', *American Journal of Comparative Law*, 50, 2002, pp. 277–301.

DE BENITO, M., 'Back in Focus: Case Selection Standards in the Spanish Supreme Court,' in BRAVO, P., VAN RHEE, C. H. (eds.), *Supreme Courts Under Pressure. Controlling Caseload in the Administration of Civil Justice*, Cham: Springer, pp. 49–71.

DE BENITO, M., 'La autonomía privada en el proceso civil: apuntes taxonómicos', in BANACLOCHE, J., GASCÓN, F. (eds.), *Logros y retos de la justicia civil en España*, Valencia: Tirant lo Blanch, 2022, pp. 251–262.

DE LA OLIVA, A., 'Spanish Civil Procedure Act 2000: Flying over Common and Civil Law traditions', in WALKER, J., CHASE, O. G. (eds.), *Common Law, Civil Law and the Future of Categories*, Markham: LexisNexis, 2010, pp. 63–74.

FERRAND, F., 'Appel: délais de l'appel', in *Répertoire de procédure civile Dalloz*, 2022.

JOLOWICZ, J. A., 'Introduction: Recourse against Judgment in the European Union: A Comparative Survey', in JOLOWICZ, J. A., VAN RHEE, C. H. (eds.), *Civil Procedures in Europe: Recourse Against Judgements in the European Union*, vol. 2, Alphen aan den Rijn: Kluwer, pp. 1–11.

JUNILLON, J., 'Le projet ALI-UNIDROIT, vue critique d'un praticien du droit', in FERRAND, F. (dir.), *La procédure civile mondiale modélisée*, Paris: EJT, 2004, pp. 40 ff.

KERN, C. A., 'Harmonisation of the Rules on Judgments and Appeals in Europe – A Few Remarks from the Inside', in GASCÓN, F., HESS, B. (eds.), *The Future of the*

20 German ZPO, §§ 542–551.

21 KERN, C. A., 'Means of Review in the ELI/UNIDROIT Model European Rules of Civil Procedure', *Zeitschrift für Zivilprozess International*, 25, 2020, pp. 287–303, at 294–295.

European Law of Civil Procedure. Coordination or Harmonisation?, Cambridge: Intersentia, 2020, pp. 223–238.

KERN, C. A., 'Means of Review in the ELI/UNIDROIT Model European Rules of Civil Procedure', *Zeitschrift für Zivilprozess International*, 25, 2020, pp. 287–303.

KERN, C. A., 'Procedural Contracts in Germany', in CABRAL, A. P., NOGUEIRA, P. H. (eds.), *Negócios processuais*, Salvador: Jus Podivm, 2017, pp. 213 ff.

MOUSSA, T., 'Le projet ALI-UNIDROIT, vue critique d'un magistrat', in FERRAND, F. (dir.), *La procédure civile mondiale modélisée*, Paris: EJT, 2004, pp. 54 ff.

MURRAY, P. L., STÜRNER, R., *German Civil Justice*, Durham: Carolina Academic Press, 2004.

SAUVÉ, J. M., *et al.*, 'Rendre justice aux citoyens. Rapport du comité des États généraux de la justice (octobre 2021-avril 2022)', 2022.

SORABJI, J., 'Austerity's Effect on English Civil Justice', *Erasmus Law Review*, 8-2015, 4, pp. 159–173.

STÜRNER, R., 'The ELI / UNIDROIT Model European Rules of Civil Procedure. An Introduction to Their Basic Conceptions', *RabelsZ*, 86, 2022, pp. 421–472.

ZUCKERMAN, A. A. S., 'No Justice Without Lawyers – The Myth of an Inquisitorial Solution', *Civil Justice Quarterly*, 33–2014, pp. 355–374.

CHAPTER 12

Translation

Marco de Benito and Emmanuel Jeuland

The study of law is primarily a study of texts, such as statutes and judgments. Consequently, law and language are inextricably linked. Legal language always reflects the distinctive characteristics of the legal system and preserves the traces of centuries of history. Therefore, a good legal translation requires more than a good knowledge of vocabulary and drafting skills.

The translation of the Rules, which are not themselves written in standard legal English, must at least aim to convey their original ideas and spirit into another language, which is itself filled with the ideas and spirit of an age-old and complex system of national civil procedure. In turn, having the Rules formulated in different languages will reveal a wealth of unexpected ideas, associations, viewpoints, and shades of meaning, thus underscoring and multiplying their inspirational power.

DE BENITO: Translation is a branch of philology. And philology, 'linguistics', is one of the great sciences. We lawyers are at best modest amateurs in it. We must openly admit this.

 | DOI:10.1163/9789004533257_013

The thing is, however, that the use of the term 'philology' as a cultism to designate the 'science of language', 'linguistics', only appeared in the 18th century and is therefore relatively recent in all our languages. But it has a much older meaning, less scientific but closer to the original meaning of the Greek lexemes that worm the word. The term philology is derived from the Greek φιλολογία (*philología*), from the terms φίλος (*phílos*), meaning 'love, affection, loved, beloved, dear, friend', and λόγος (*lógos*), meaning 'word, articulation, reason'.

With this meaning, it was already used in Rome to designate not something *scientific* (an utterly anachronic paradigm) but simply the 'fondness and care for letters' (Cicero) or the 'care in the selection of words' (Seneca).

The word 'philologist' even appears as a synonym for 'advocate' or 'rhetor', evoking the classical *vir bonus dicendi peritus* definition.

From this more casual, more vulgar perspective, most of us lawyers are, to some extent, 'philologists'. '*Nos enim ita philologi sumus*', Cicero wrote to a friend.[1] Some have even suggested that the study of law is a study of texts, not facts – of *verba*, not *facta* –, and that it belongs to the humanities, not the social sciences.[2]

Nothing other than this 'care in the selection of words' is what I wished, with the utmost modesty, for the Rules in Spanish.

Emmanuel, you had a slightly different task, since the French version of the Rules is one of the two original versions, and it was drafted in parallel to the English original.

JEULAND: Yes, but the challenges this posed, since most of the discussion took place in English, had much in common with the general problems and challenges of translation and specifically legal translation.

Let's think. What goals does legal translation have? I would summarise that it implies an adaptation of a norm or legally relevant text that can adequately convey its message.[3]

It is not always evident even for lawyers, but one legal language is applicable only to one legal system, not necessarily to all the legal systems using

1 Letter to Marcus Quintus VIII, *mense Maio a.u.c.* 699, available at https://www.thelatinlibrary.com/cicero/fratrem2.shtml.

2 D'ORS, Á., *Nueva introducción al estudio del derecho*, Madrid: Civitas, 1999, pp. 18–20.

3 MOUSOURAKIS, G., *Comparative Law and Legal Traditions. Historical and Contemporary Perspectives*, Cham: Springer, 2019, p. 109.

the same language (English, French, Spanish are used by numerous countries, but terminology differs sometimes).[4]

DE BENITO: Although a standard or canon of learned legal Spanish does exist, the specific nuances of legal Spanish do vary depending on the Spanish-speaking jurisdiction in question.

JEULAND: The content, scope, and context of the legal text in question must firstly be grasped, understood, *interpreted* by the translator in as much depth and detail as possible. Consequently, the operation is one of comparative law. The connection between legal translation, legal interpretation, and comparative law is substantial and intertwined.[5]

DE BENITO: Like Roman pontifices – the Latin term for priest, *pontifex*, seems to come from *pontes facere*, building bridges –, any legal translator wants to build a bridge between legal systems, each of which operates with a specific language. On this side of the stream, the translator must first interpret the text in its 'con-text'; then decode it from the legal system in which it operates as an active element; and then re-encode it to be understood in the new context on the other side of the stream.[6]

To get a reliable translation, we need to look beyond the four corners of a text[7] and think in terms of a comparatist or, to be more accurate, a structuralist perspective – a dynamic, structural law-in-action perspective.[8]

4 DE GROOT, G.-R., 'Legal Translation', in SMITS, J. M. (ed.), *Elgar Encyclopedia on Comparative Law*, Cheltenham: Edward Elgar, 2012, pp. 538–549, at 538.

5 See CURRAN, V. G., 'Comparative Law and Language', in REIMANN, M., ZIMMERMANN, R. (eds.), *The Oxford Handbook of Comparative Law*, Oxford: Oxford University Press, 2019, pp. 682–710, at 686.

6 See CURRAN, V. G., 'Comparative Law and Language', in REIMANN, M., ZIMMERMANN, R. (eds.), *The Oxford Handbook of Comparative Law*, Oxford: Oxford University Press, 2019, pp. 682–710, at 686; MOUSOURAKIS, G., *Comparative Law and Legal Traditions. Historical and Contemporary Perspectives*, Cham: Springer, 2019, p. 109.

7 GASCÓN, F., 'Traducción jurídica y sistemas procesales: algunas reflexiones acerca de las características de los procesos civiles en los sistemas de derecho continental', in *Seminarios Complutenses de Derecho Romano: Revista Complutense de Derecho Romano y Tradición Romanística*, 28 (2015), pp. 417–434, at 422.

8 HUSA, J., *Interdisciplinary Comparative Law. Rubbing Shoulders with the Neighbours or Standing Alone in a Crowd*, Cheltenham: Edward Elgar, 2022, p. 52.; ENGBERG, J., 'Comparative Law for Legal Translation: Through Multiple Perspectives to Multidimensional Knowledge', *International Journal for the Semiotics of Law*, 33:2 (2020), pp. 263–282, at 270.

JEULAND: The challenge is that the source and the target texts should be equal in meaning and should lead to the same interpretation and application in practice.[9] The new language version should not be wider or narrower than the original.[10] It can happen that, in the name of interpretation and adaptation, translators end up trying to improve the law a little.[11]

DE BENITO: To improve it a little, of course, by adding our own views to the content or even just the drafting.

JEULAND: Noble aims can have unintended consequences. For example, we may be tempted to make an ambiguous rule more precise, maybe forgetting that the original ambiguity may have been intentional, perhaps as a point of compromise between different visions or even conflicting interests.[12] As a result, the rule is distorted, 'lost in translation'.

DE BENITO: So, we must put aside our own inner Tribonian or Portalis and accept the rule as it is.

JEULAND: Moderation or even modesty should be borne in mind as a maxim.

DE BENITO: The French version was developed alongside the English one as amid the very *travaux préparatoires*. That closeness, that simultaneity probably avoided many translating issues. The Spanish version was necessarily one step farther from those *travaux*.

JEULAND: Possibly, but the challenge has always been present, even during the discussion of the English and French originals. The same self-restraint,

---

9 ŠARCEVIC, S., 'Legal Translation and Translation Theory: A Receiver-oriented Approach', paper presented at *La traduction juridique: Histoire, theorie(s) et pratique / Legal Translation: History, Theory/ies, Practice*, Bern/Geneva: ASTTI/ETI, 2000, available at https://www.tradulex.com/Actes2000/sarcevic.pdf, p. 5.

10 DE GROOT, G.-R., 'Legal Translation', in SMITS, J. M. (ed.), *Elgar Encyclopedia on Comparative Law*, Cheltenham: Edward Elgar, 2012, pp. 538–549, at 540.

11 ŠARCEVIC, S., 'Legal Translation and Translation Theory: A Receiver-Oriented Approach', paper presented at *La traduction juridique: Histoire, theorie(s) et pratique / Legal Translation: History, Theory/ies, Practice*, Bern/Geneva: ASTTI/ETI, 2000, available at https://www.tradulex.com/Actes2000/sarcevic.pdf, p. 5.

12 PRIETO, F., 'International and Supranational Law in Translation: From Multilingual Lawmaking to Adjudication', *The Translator*, 20:3 (2014), pp. 313–331, at 322.

the same rigor or modesty was needed to make sure that the rule says what it intends to say.

DE BENITO: One of the principal themes of structuralist theory is the concept of function. As comparatists, we'll seek for functional equivalence in the specific structure of a legal system.

JEULAND: Correct. The source text and the target text should lead to the same function, that is, their interpretation and application in practice. By comparing the similarities and differences in the role and effect of *prima facie* analogous legal institutions, we can draw conclusions about their functional equivalency.[13]

DE BENITO: And functional equivalency is often in the antipodes of literal equivalency. It is more about *transcreation* – re-creating a text for a specific target audience, going beyond a faithful word-for-word copying.[14] Here the choice between poor translation and good adaptation is evident.[15]

JEULAND: Because legal translation is full of *faux amis*. In fact, it is typical for legal systems to use structurally different institutions to achieve the same result; think of common law 'estoppel' and civil law '*venire contra factum proprium*' or 'abuse of rights' doctrines.

DE BENITO: It goes without saying that a translator can't just translate words literally. This isn't just a principle that applies to legal translation. Translators of poetry, or fiction literature, have always emphasised that the target text should express the same energy, emotions, even rhythm and colour; and an excessive insistence on literal fidelity will not necessarily create the same effect in another language. Blind copying from dictionaries ignores the peculiarities of language and threatens to deteriorate the text.

---

13 DE GROOT, G.-R., VAN LAER, C. J. P., 'The Dubious Quality of Legal Dictionaries', *International Journal of Legal Information*, 34:1 (2006), pp. 65–84, at 68; DULLION, V., 'Droit comparé pour traducteurs: de la théorie à la didactique de la traduction juridique', *International Journal for Semiotics of Law*, 28:1 (2015), pp. 91–106, at 96.

14 HUSA, J., *Interdisciplinary Comparative Law. Rubbing Shoulders with the Neighbours or Standing Alone in a Crowd*, Cheltenham: Edward Elgar, 2022, p. 53.

15 DURO, M. 'Ordenamientos jurídicos y traducción (common law y civil law)', in DURO, M., MARTÍNEZ, A. B., SAN GINÉS, P. (eds.), *Introducción a la traducción jurídica y jurada (inglés-español). Orientaciones doctrinales y metodológicas*, Granada: Comares, 1997, pp. 41–59, at 58.

Any translation, whether a foreign language or foreign law, is an act of comparison of systems and contexts.[16]

JEULAND: However, whereas in literature obtaining the same *impression* will sometimes suffice,[17] in legal translation we must exercise greater caution, not only because we are dealing with mandates, which require a high degree of certainty in their meaning, but because the similarity of institutions can be incomplete and misleading. For example: can we translate the common law 'trust' as '*fiducie*' in French? Or, even more generally, 'property' into '*propriété*', simply considering the dense semantic residue historically attached to each of these words?[18]

DE BENITO: An interdisciplinary approach is beneficial in this regard. For instance, semiotics posits the use of a conceptual frame, comprising 'slots' and 'fillers', namely structure and content. Effective communication hinges on the alignment of frames with those of the interlocutor. The frame approach differs from lexical approaches in that it focuses on universal concepts and offers new insights.[19] I find this method particularly effective as it allows us to deconstruct and then reconstruct the concept in a way that is aligned with the mentality of another culture.

Take arbitration cases involving arbitration clauses in Russian, for instance. This is a good example of how a word-for-word translation can have the opposite legal effect. There are a few cases where the term 'arbitration tribunal' has been translated into Russian as Арбитражный суд

16 See CURRAN, V. G., 'Comparative Law and Language', in REIMANN, M., ZIMMERMANN, R. (eds.), *The Oxford Handbook of Comparative Law*, Oxford: Oxford University Press, 2019, pp. 685–686; MONJEAN-DECAUDIN, S., POPINEAU-LAUVRAY, J., 'How to Apply Comparative Law to Legal Translation. A New Juritraductological Approach to the Translation of Legal Texts", in BIEL, L., ENGBERG, J., MARTÍN, R., SOSONI, V. (eds.), *Research Methods in Legal Translation and Interpreting. Crossing Methodological Boundaries*, London: Routledge, 2019, pp. 115–129.

17 See BOCQUET, C., *La traduction juridique. Fondement et méthode*, New Leuven: De Boeck, 2008; MONJEAN-DECAUDIN, S., *Traité de juritraductologie: Épistémologie et méthodologie de la traduction juridique*, Villeneuve d'Ascq: Septentrion, 2022.

18 PASQUAU, M., 'Las peculiaridades del lenguaje jurídico desde la perspectiva del jurista', in DURO, M., MARTÍNEZ, A. B., SAN GINÉS, P. (eds.), *Introducción a la traducción jurídica y jurada (inglés-español). Orientaciones doctrinales y metodológicas*, Granada: Comares, 1997, pp. 9–23, at 21.

19 ENGBERG, J., 'Comparative Law for Legal Translation: Through Multiple Perspectives to Multidimensional Knowledge', *International Journal for the Semiotics of Law*, 33:2 (2020), pp. 263–282, at 271.

(*arbitrazhniy sud*), which is a state court that deals with commercial disputes. This special terminology is a result of the unique nature of socialist arbitration institutions, which were part of the government system. Even though the word арбитражный (*arbitrazhniy*) is correctly translated as 'arbitration', the legal effect of the clauses is the opposite: in English, people are required to submit their disputes to arbitration, while in Russian, a state court is given the jurisdiction to hear the case. In a recent case, a New York court, after a detailed comparison, admitted that the English version was 'awkward'.[20] The parties used similar 'slots' without realizing they had different 'fillers'.

JEULAND: You never know where you come across *le faux ami du traducteur*. Indeed, this knowledge is hardly accessible without comparative research.

DE BENITO: Furthermore, the operation is incomplete without even an aspiration to respect and not sacrifice what we might call *idiomaticity*, the elusive style or genius of each language.[21]

JEULAND: From the times of Stendhal reading the *Code Napoléon* to *take the tone*, French writers and legislators are traditionally concerned with style. Frédérique Ferrand, Loïc Cadiet, and I also were stylistically conscious. Loïc was very influential on this point. We wanted to ensure that the French version was not only legally accurate, but also offered some of that clarity and elegance that we find and love in our language.

DE BENITO: We also aimed to ensure that the translated rules sounded natural and coherent in Spanish. We opted for a straightforward and unadorned style, aiming for a level of simplicity and clarity that would be familiar to native Spanish speakers. A *castizo* Spanish, if you like, to use

20 *LaRubInt Corp. v. Joint Stock Company Studio Soyuzmultfilm*, case № 22-cv-4461 (HG) (E.D.N.Y. Apr. 20, 2023). See also the award of the International Commercial Arbitration Court for Russian Chamber of Commerce (ICAC) 06.09.2002 № 217/2001. See also POPKOVA, E. M., 'Arbitrazh vs Arbitration: Terminology Traps in the Russian-English Translation of the Russian Judiciary System', *Philological Sciences at MGIMO Collection of Scientific Papers*, 61:46 (2011), pp. 98–109.

21 PRIETO, F., 'International and Supranational Law in Translation: From Multilingual Lawmaking to Adjudication', *The Translator*, 20:3 (2014), pp. 313–331, at 322.

the words of the *Real Academia Española*: 'Said of the language: without a mixture of voices or strange turns of phrase'.[22] *Voices* and *turns of phrase* – that is, words and sentence structures, the overall flow and rhythm of speech.

And we found that the plain and natural voice is often the most technically appropriate. For instance, '*pedir*' is used to designate the *petitum*, which, along with the *causa petendi*, identifies the action and thus defines the subject matter of the proceedings (Rule 22).[23]

Regarding the *turns of phrase*, our objective was to ensure that the discourse flowed naturally in Spanish. This entailed occasionally rearranging the phrase to achieve a more natural sound for a Spanish audience, as exemplified by Rule 38:

> Rule 38. *Necessary joinder of parties*
>
> (1) A proceeding must be brought by or against parties jointly where either the joint nature of the legal right or the substantive law requires a judgment to bind all of the joined parties in the same terms.
>
> Artículo 38. *Litisconsorcio necesario*
>
> 1. Cuando, por el carácter indivisible del derecho o por exigencia de una norma sustantiva, la sentencia hubiera de afectar a varios sujetos de forma conjunta, deberán todos ellos demandar o ser demandados conjuntamente.

In certain instances, it was necessary to combine multiple sentences into a single unit to maintain continuity, as the Spanish period tends to be longer than the English one.

> Rule 26. *Applicable law*
>
> (2) The court must determine the correct legal basis for its decision. This includes matters determined on the basis of foreign law. It may only do so having provided the parties a reasonable opportunity to present their arguments on the applicable law.

---

22 3. '*Dicho del lenguaje: sin mezcla de voces ni giros extraños*'.

23 LEC, Art. 399.

> Artículo 26. *Fundamentos de derecho*
>
> 2. El tribunal determinará las normas de derecho aplicables, incluyendo, en su caso, normas de derecho extranjero, y siempre asegurándose de que las partes hayan tenido oportunidad de formular sus alegaciones al respecto.

JEULAND: We carried out a similar exercise and often found inspiration in the French *Code civil* and the *Code de procédure civile* when it came to style choices.

> Rule 42. *Third-party notice*
>
> (1) A party may give any person notice of the dispute if, in the event of that party's claim or defence being unsuccessful, they might have a claim against or be subject to a claim by that person.
>
> Article 42. *Intervention forcée*
>
> 1) Une partie peut mettre en cause un tiers si, dans l'hypothèse où sa demande serait jugée mal fondée ou ses moyens de défense rejetés, un litige pourrait survenir entre cette partie et ce tiers.
>
> Rule 46. *Litigation capacity*
>
> (1) A non-resident's litigation capacity shall be assessed according to the law of their habitual residence or their citizenship.
>
> Article 46. *Capacité à agir en justice*
>
> 1) La capacité à agir en justice d'une personne ne résidant pas dans l'État du juge saisi est vérifiée selon la loi de l'État de sa résidence habituelle ou de sa nationalité.

DE BENITO: We did the same with the Spanish *Código civil* and the *Ley de enjuiciamiento civil*. Also, we often checked the *Código Procesal Civil Modelo para Iberoamérica*[24] to make sure we didn't make too many exceptions to the canon or standard Spanish legal language. Legal Spanish is part of the common heritage of all Spanish-speaking nations. The European nature of the Model Rules should not make the Spanish version any less universally Hispanic, something like a local *Spanish of Spain*.

---

24 Código Procesal Civil Modelo para Iberoamérica.

We even allowed ourselves to be playfully guided by memories and resonances (we'd say '*concordancias*' to mirror a famous work by a great Spanish jurist from the 19th century).[25] For instance, we liked to switch out the English full stop with a Spanish semicolon followed by 'but not' ('*pero no*'), a structure that shows up at least sixteen times in the *Código civil*.[26] For instance, Rule 27(1):

Rule 27. *Sanctions for non-compliance with rules and court orders*

(1) The court shall disregard factual allegations, modifications of claims and defences, and offers of evidence that are introduced later than permitted by these rules or by court orders, including those concerning amendment. Preclusion does not apply if the court could have taken notice of the party's failure or mistake and itself failed to raise with the parties whether they wished to seek an amendment or relief from sanction.

Artículo 27. *Sanciones por inobservancia de normas procesales y resoluciones judiciales*

1. El tribunal inadmitirá cualesquiera alegaciones de hecho, modificaciones de las pretensiones o proposiciones de prueba formuladas fuera del plazo previsto en estas Reglas u otorgado por el tribunal; pero no operará la preclusión si el tribunal, habiendo tenido conocimiento a tiempo del retraso al que se exponía una parte, se abstuvo de invitarla a subsanarlo.

---

25 García Goyena, F., *Concordancias, motivos y comentarios del Código civil español*, Madrid: Sociedad Tipográfico-Editorial, 1852.

26 Some of those articles that most directly affect civil procedure include: 1813. *Se puede transigir sobre la acción civil proveniente de un delito*; pero no *por eso se extinguirá la acción pública para la imposición de la pena legal.* 1816. *La transacción tiene para las partes la autoridad de la cosa juzgada*; pero no *procederá la vía de apremio sino tratándose del cumplimiento de la transacción judicial.* 1825. *Puede también prestarse fianza en garantía de deudas futuras, cuyo importe no sea aún conocido*; pero no *se podrá reclamar contra el fiador hasta que la deuda sea líquida.* 1912. *El deudor puede solicitar judicialmente de sus acreedores quita y espera de sus deudas, o cualquiera de las dos cosas*; pero no *producirá efectos jurídicos el ejercicio de este derecho sino en los casos y en la forma previstos en la Ley de Enjuiciamiento Civil.* 1935. *Las personas con capacidad para enajenar pueden renunciar la prescripción ganada*; pero no *el derecho de prescribir para lo sucesivo.* 1975. *La interrupción de la prescripción contra el deudor principal por reclamación judicial de la deuda, surte efecto también contra su fiador*; pero no *perjudicará a éste la que se produzca por reclamaciones extrajudiciales del acreedor o reconocimientos privados del deudor.*

Also compare the original and the translation of Rule 140(2):

> Rule 140. *Time limit to apply to set aside a default judgment*
>
> (2) The court may extend the time limit under Rule 140(1) where the defendant can show good reason for their non-compliance. No application to set aside can, however, be brought more than one year and, in cross-border cases, two years after the default judgment was entered.
>
> Artículo 140. *Plazo para solicitar la rescisión de la sentencia en rebeldía*
>
> 2. El tribunal podrá prorrogar el plazo del apartado anterior si acredita el demandado razón legítima que le hubiese impedido actuar; pero no cabrá rescisión transcurrido un año, o dos en situaciones transfronterizas, desde la fecha en que se hubiera dictado la sentencia en rebeldía.

The same with 'to do or not to do something' (Rule 132), '*hacer o no hacer alguna cosa*'. This immediately brings us back to Article 1088 of the *Código civil*,[27] where we find this 'some thing' ('*alguna cosa*'), which is just so simple and elegant.

In any case, as previously stated, the French version introduced an additional layer of complexity, as the project required ongoing adaptation. I am interested in learning more about that process.

JEULAND: That is correct. The French version presented a unique challenge: while the project's working language was English, there was also a need for an official French version to be produced alongside the English one. In several groups, colleagues worked in languages other than English. For instance, Frédérique Ferrand worked in German, Italian, English, and French. In the groups I was in, we worked in English and then in French towards the end of the project, with one of the final meetings dedicated to the French version. At this meeting, we explored how the French version compared to the English version, which often resulted in changes to the English version. This enhanced the quality of the result.

This semi-bilingual drafting process may enable legal reformers to draw inspiration from both versions and develop a superior rule by integrating the insights from both.

---

27 Spanish CC, Art. 1088: *Toda obligación consiste en dar, hacer o no hacer alguna cosa.*

The philosopher Walter Benjamin said that the truth of translation lies not in the target or original language, but somewhere in between.[28] Even in this situation, there isn't really an *original* language, because we use both languages at almost the same time. It's fair to say that English was the main working language. But French, as a second language, improved the English version, and vice versa.

DE BENITO: We did keep an eye on the French original to really understand the nuances of certain provisions. An example is Rule 93:

> Rule 93. *Admission by a failure to challenge evidence*
>
> The court may take a party's unjustified failure to make a timely response to an opposing party's contention as a sufficient basis for considering that contention to be admitted or accepted. ...

We needed to read this provision in French, which translates 'failure to challenge evidence' as '*défaut de contestation*', to reach the proper Spanish translation:

> Article 93. *Admission par défaut de contestation*
>
> Le juge peut décider que l'absence injustifiée de réponse en temps utile d'une partie à une allégation de la partie adverse constitue un fondement suffisant pour considérer cette allégation comme admise ou acceptée. Préalablement, le juge informe la partie qu'il envisage de tirer une telle conclusion et lui donne la possibilité de faire valoir ses observations.
>
> Artículo 93. *Admisión por ausencia de impugnación de hechos*
>
> Si, alegado un hecho, la parte contraria se abstuviera injustificadamente de impugnarlo en tiempo y forma, el tribunal podrá tenerlo por admitido. Si estuviese valorando proceder de ese modo, lo hará saber a la parte, asegurándose de que pueda formular alegaciones.

JEULAND: That exemplifies my point perfectly.

---

28 BENJAMIN, W., 'Die Aufgabe des Übersetzers", preface to BAUDELAIRE, C., *Tableaux parisiens*, Heidelberg: Richard Weissbach, 1923; English translation by RENDALL, S., as 'The Translator's Task', *TTR: traduction, terminologie, rédaction*, 10:2 (1997), pp. 151–165, available at https://german.yale.edu/sites/default/files/benjamin_translators_task.pdf.

DE BENITO: What type of difficulties did you encounter during that semi-bilingual drafting process?

JEULAND: I can provide three practical examples related to the specific quirks of legislative drafting, untranslatable words, and the issue of English words that designate two realities or similar but not entirely coincident realities in French.

DE BENITO: Sounds interesting. Let's start with the quirks of legislative drafting.

JEULAND: For example, how to translate 'shall' or 'must'. We had two English colleagues: one was in favour of 'shall', the other preferred 'must'. After a lot of back and forth, they decided that 'must' sounded more modern. In French, when used in a legislative context, the present tense of the given verb is sufficient to render a sentence into a command or directive.

Another example is the word 'rules'. Should we translate this with '*règle*', which is the exact equivalent of 'rule', or by '*article*'? After consideration, we decided to use '*article*' because it is universally used in French legislation.

DE BENITO: We also went for '*artículo*'. It's more in line with Spanish tradition and seems more accurate too, as it distinguishes the external, conventional divisions of a legal text from the *regulæ juris* that they may contain.

(Just as a side note, 'article' is also used by English lawyers, at least since the time of Jeremy Bentham. The word 'article' also appears in the normative production of the EU, ELI, UNIDROIT, UNCITRAL, the Hague Conference on Private International Law, etc., in English.)

We even went a step further and translated the 'Parts' and the 'Sections' in which the Rules are divided as '*Capítulos*' and '*Títulos*', the usual manner to refer to the subdivisions of a piece of legislation in Spanish – in either side of the Atlantic.

JEULAND: Then there is the use of the plural or singular. There are words that are singular in English, but plural in French, and vice versa. For example, 'information' in English and '*informations*' in French; 'proceedings' in English and '*procédure*'; '*instance*', or '*action*' in French.[29]

---

29 JEULAND, E., LALANI, S., 'Action', in *Lexicographical Research in Civil Procedure*, Paris: IRJS, 2017.

Also challenging was the translation of words such as 'fair opportunity' or 'reasonable'. In the English version, these words appear quite frequently, reflecting a looser approach to the structure of the proceedings, which can't always be adequately captured in French. This explains why the word 'reasonable' appears thirty-two times in the English version (including the derivatives 'unreasonable', 'reasonably' and 'unreasonably'), but only twenty-three times in the French version (including the derivatives '*raisonnablement*' and '*déraisonnablement*').

Let's take Rule 11:

> Rule 11. *Fair opportunity to present claim and defence*
>
> The court must manage proceedings to ensure that parties have a fair opportunity to present their case and evidence, ...
>
> Article 11. *Présentation des demandes et moyens de défense*
>
> Le juge administre la procédure de manière à ce que les parties aient une possibilité équitable de présenter leur affaire et leurs preuves, ...

You will see that 'fair opportunity' is not translated in the title, while we have '*le juge administre*' instead of 'manage', and '*la procédure*' instead of the plural 'proceedings'. Finally, we translated 'fair opportunity' as '*possibilité équitable*'.

DE BENITO: We translated 'fair' as '*justo*' in that case in both the title and the provision:

> Artículo 11. *Justa oportunidad de formular pretensiones y defensas*
>
> El tribunal administrará el procedimiento de modo que las partes tengan justa oportunidad de formular alegaciones y aportar pruebas ...

JEULAND: The untransferable genius of each language!

DE BENITO: Let's move on to the second challenge you mentioned: the issue of untranslatable words.[30]

---

30 CASSIN, B. (dir.), *Vocabulaire européen des philosophies : Dictionnaire des intraduisibles*, Paris: Seuil, 2004; English translation by APTER, E., LEZRA, J., WOOD, M. (eds.), *Dictionary of Untranslatables: A Philosophical Lexicon*, Princeton: Princeton University Press, 2015. See also LEGRAND, P., 'Issues in the Translatability of Law', in BERMANN, S.,

JEULAND: The introduction of foreign terms should be allowed sparingly and only as a last resort, de Groot argues. We followed this approach to avoid transforming the French version into 'a collection of foreign-language words glued together by prepositions, adverbs and verbs from the target language'.[31] For example, we refused to import 'discovery' or 'disclosure'. The same goes for 'case management', which lies at the heart of the system, and which we felt obliged to translate in different ways depending on the context, such as '*mise en état*', '*management*', '*gestion*', '*administration*', or '*gestion de l'instance*'. For example:

> Rule 4. *Role of the court – the general case management duty*
>
> The court is responsible for active and effective case management. ...
>
> Article 4. *Office du juge*
>
> Il appartient au juge d'assurer la conduite active et effective de l'instance. ...

In the title, '*office du juge*' sidesteps the general case management duty; in the actual provision, case management became '*la conduite de l'instance*'.

DE BENITO: I like the word 'office', like the original Latin '*officium*'. In Spanish, however, it'd have sounded awkward. We chose '*deberes*' instead, in plural. Regarding 'case management', that central piece of the procedural model proposed by the Rules, we did the same as you: breaking it down into a periphrasis, '*gestionar e impulsar el proceso*', in an attempt at capturing the vast semantic field of 'case management' in English and in the Rules:

> Artículo 4. *Deberes del tribunal. Deber general de gestión e impulso procesal*
>
> Es responsabilidad del tribunal gestionar e impulsar el proceso de modo activo y eficaz, ...

JEULAND: The third example I wanted to look at concerns English words that have several translations in French. For example, 'service' can be translated in French as '*notification*' and '*signification*'. In the 1965 Hague

WOOD, M. (eds.), *Nation, language, and the Ethics of Translation*, Princeton: Princeton University Press, 2005; and LEGRAND, P., 'European Legal Systems Are Not Converging', *International and Comparative Law Quarterly*, 45:1 (1996), pp. 52–81.

31 DE GROOT, G.-R., 'Legal Translation', in SMITS, J. M. (ed.), *Elgar Encyclopedia on Comparative Law*, Cheltenham: Edward Elgar, 2012, pp. 538–549, at 541.

Convention, we have 'service' in English and both '*notification et signification*' in French. '*Signification*' is limited to service by the *huissier* and, since we did not want to relate our rules to a profession, we stuck to the exact equivalent of 'service', which is '*notification*'. As for 'evidence' and 'proof', this was much easier as there is only one word, '*preuve*'.

A similar problem arises with words that share the same lexeme but have slightly different meanings. For example, 'action' and 'proceedings'. The English 'action' can be translated by '*procédure*' or '*action*' depending on the context, while 'proceedings' in English can sometimes be translated by '*action*' in French or by '*procédure*'. It was therefore a challenge to use these words in the Rules.

We had a particular problem with 'on behalf of', or the problem of 'representation'. In English, 'representation' and 'on behalf of' have a wider meaning than in French.

DE BENITO: The same happens in Spanish.

JEULAND: 'Representation' encompasses, for example, 'class action'. This is not really a matter of *representation* in civil countries, because the victims are not parties to the proceedings and therefore are not the represented party in the class action. This meant that the term 'on behalf of' could not be translated as 'represented' in French.

Moving on to the essential definition of 'collective proceedings'. 'Collective proceedings' are proceedings brought by a qualified claimant on behalf of a group of persons who, it's alleged, are affected by an event, but are not parties to the action.

Let's look at the translation of Rule 207:

> Rule 207. *Collective proceedings*
>
> Collective proceedings are proceedings brought by a qualified claimant on behalf of a group of persons who it is alleged are affected by an event giving rise to a mass harm, but where those persons, known as group members, are not parties to the action.
>
> Article 207. *Définition*
>
> Une action de groupe en réparation est une action exercée par un demandeur qualifié en lieu et place d'un groupe de personnes, identifiées comme les membres du groupe, victimes d'un dommage ayant pour cause commune un manquement de même nature. Ces personnes ne sont pas parties à la procédure.

So, we see '*une action de groupe*' instead of 'collective proceedings'; 'proceedings' is translated by '*action*'; and 'on behalf of' is '*en lieu et place*', which is not the expression of choice to translate a matter of representation. At the end of the rule, we translate 'not party to the action' with '*ne sont pas parties à la procédure*'. Again, 'action' is translated as '*procédure*'.

DE BENITO: It's a fun fact that where they say 'proceedings' and then 'action', you say '*action*' and then '*procédure*'! In Spanish, we managed to keep an equivalence between 'proceedings' and '*proceso*', although both terms are far from having perfect semantic correlation:

> Artículo 207. *Procesos colectivos*
>
> Se entiende por proceso colectivo todo proceso incoado por demandante habilitado en interés de un grupo de personas que, según se alega, se ven afectadas por un hecho del que se ha derivado un daño colectivo, pero no se constituyen en partes del proceso.

JEULAND: Finally, we turn to the concept of 'appeal'. In England, 'appeal' means any recourse, without limitation. In France, on the other hand, as in Italy, Belgium, the Netherlands, and other countries influenced by the Napoleonic codes, we have various recourses and then '*cassation*' – which can only be considered an 'appeal' in a more limited way than in English.

Then, when we had to translate 'second appeal', '*cassation*' came to mind initially, but it didn't seem to capture the meaning of the 'second appeal' accurately. Frédérique, Loïc, and I discussed this and decided to use the word '*pourvoi*'.

The English text is interesting because it reflects this dialectic:

> Rule 153. *Right of appeal or to seek recourse*
>
> Where a party, or exceptionally a non-party, has a legal interest in a judgment, subject to the provisions in this Part, they may appeal from, or rely on other types of recourse against, it.

This might seem a bit unusual for an English lawyer, as usually there's only an appeal or recourse. However, the paragraph is trying to reflect other European traditions where the appeal is the main recourse, although there may be other ways to challenge the decision.

In French, we translated 'appeal or to seek recourse' with '*voie de recours*', which is a kind of catch-all expression that also exists in Spanish and Italian to describe all the available recourses.

> Article 153. *Droit à une voie de recours*
>
> Une partie ou, à titre exceptionnel, un tiers, qui y a un intérêt juridique, peut exercer une voie de recours contre un jugement, conformément aux dispositions de la présente Partie.

DE BENITO: We struggled with appeals as well. In Spanish we almost intuitively distinguish between ordinary and extraordinary appeals; but both are clearly '*recursos*'. This was decisive to literally translate the 'first appeal' and the 'second appeal' as '*primer recurso*' and '*segundo recurso*'.

Since these terms are not the most expressive or graceful, we considered using a periphrasis such as '*recurso de primer grado*' and '*recurso de segundo grado*'. In fact, this would reflect the linguistic structure of a historical Spanish appeal, the '*recurso de segunda suplicación*', which was heard by the Royal and Supreme Council of the Indies, seated in Madrid, against rulings handed down by way of appeal by the highest court of the relevant American viceroyalty or captaincy.

At the end, however, we went for '*primer recurso*' and '*segundo recurso*', which have the virtue, after all, of reflecting the relatively schematic nature of the Rules as a model law.

JEULAND: That exercise of looking for inspiration in legal history is a perfect example of why we should preserve the use of several languages in European legislative drafting.[32] That is our richness, and I hope that this project will be a model for that as well.

DE BENITO: Speaking of history, what about the use of Latin in legal English and in our own languages? Latin is a fundamental part of the rich English legal tradition, as it is on the continent. But sometimes Latin expressions there have taken on a meaning of their own – a meaning that's perfectly correct on *that* side of the Channel, but which doesn't quite fit in with the semantic field of the same Latin word on *this* side of the Channel.

32 See ROBERTSON, C. D., *Multilingual Law. A Framework for Analysis and Understanding*, London: Routledge, 2018; OST, F., *Traduire. Défense et illustration du multilinguisme*, Paris: Fayard, 2009.

Thus, what in *English legal Latin* is called '*inter partes*' or '*ex parte*' (literally, 'from a party' or 'between the parties') is better expressed in *Spanish legal Latin* as '*inaudita parte debitoris*', '*inaudita altera parte*', or simply '*inaudita parte*' ('the other party having been heard' or 'not having been heard').

Moreover, the expression '*inter partes*' ('between the parties') is not free from ambiguity, as it seems to be widely used in Europe in the sphere of private, not procedural law, to refer to the relative effect of contracts between the contracting parties, as opposed to property and in rem securities, which are opposable *erga omnes* ('towards everyone').

The *English legal Latin* terminology comes possibly from a domestic development of these terms in the history of English law. But Latin is an essential part of the common legal heritage of Europe: if used at all, the more widely accepted terminology coming from the *jus commune* should prevail over national usages.

In only one case did we introduce a Latin expression that was not in the English text: '*recurso per saltum*' to translate 'leapfrog appeal', which would've been a somewhat exotic literal translation for a Spanish ear.

JEULAND: It's a fascinating question, and a bit of a paradox because in French law (which has its roots in Roman law), you don't see many Latin expressions. This goes back to the Villers-Cotterêts ordinance of 1539, which prohibited vernacular languages and Latin in the courts. At the time, the aim was to impose the French language (spoken only in central France, around Paris) as the *lingua franca*. Thus, when the English Rules use '*ex parte*' (Rules 50 and 186), '*ex officio*' (Rules 33 and 63) or '*res judicata*' (Rules 133, 148, 149, etc.), the French version refers successively to '*parties non entendues*', '*pouvoir d'office*', and '*autorité de chose jugée*'.

DE BENITO: Let's fast-forward from the past to the future, when we've already translated the Rules into three, ten, fifteen different languages, even though English and French remain the original versions. Will that enrich or hinder interpretation?

JEULAND: To answer this, it may be useful to look at the experience of multilingual legal systems, such as Switzerland or Canada, and, of course, the EU with its twenty-four official languages.[33] All of these contribute to

33 Bulgarian, Croatian, Czech, Danish, Dutch, English, Estonian, Finnish, French, German, Greek, Hungarian, Irish, Italian, Latvian, Lithuanian, Maltese, Polish, Portuguese, Romanian, Slovak, Slovenian, Spanish, and Swedish.

clarifying the meaning of the text and must be considered while interpreting and applying the law.[34]

No language can fully capture the full range of meanings and nuances in the world. When different language versions are available, they give us a better understanding of the core message. The experience of multilingual states shows that even the clearest text can't fully capture the content of a legal provision.[35]

DE BENITO: This approach is known as the Augustinian interpretation method: the use of multiple versions of the same law to gain insight into its intended meaning and prevailing logic. The term refers to the method developed by the bishop of Hippo in the fourth century, which involved comparing several translations when interpreting Scripture.[36]

The ECJ applies the Augustinian method when faced with a difficult issue of interpretation: to seek to unveil the *mens legis*, the intention of the legislator, by considering at least a selection of the twenty-four authentic versions of EU legislation:

> It must be borne in mind that community legislation is drafted in several languages and that the different language versions are all equally authentic. An interpretation of a provision of community law thus involves a comparison of the different language versions.[37]

---

34 See ŠARCEVIC, S., 'Legal Translation and Translation Theory: a Receiver-Oriented Approach', paper presented in *La traduction juridique: Histoire, theorie(s) et pratique / Legal Translation: History, Theory/ies, Practice,* Bern, Geneva: ASTTI/ETI, available at https://www.tradulex.com/Actes2000/sarcevic.pdf, p. 5; PICHONNAZ, P., 'Legal Interpretation in Multilingual States: An Opportunity', *Journal of Comparative Law,* 124:12 (2017), pp. 124–141, p. 130; DEVINAT, M., PICHONNAZ, P., 'L'égalité des langues officielles devant les cours suprêmes: regards croisés sur le droit canadien et le droit suisse', *Revue de Droit Suisse,* 136:1 (2017), pp. 271–288, at 276.

35 PICHONNAZ, P., 'Challenging Textual Interpretation in Multilingual Legal Systems', *French Journal of Legal Policy,* 1:1 (2023), pp. 4–5.; PICHONNAZ, P., 'Legal Interpretation in Multilingual States: An Opportunity', *Journal of Comparative Law,* 124:12 (2017), pp. 124–141, at 133.

36 SOLAN, L. M., 'The Interpretation of Multilingual Statutes by the European Court of Justice', *Brooklin Journal International Law,* 34:2 (2009), pp. 277–301, at 281. See also SOLAN, L. M., 'Interpreting Multilingual Laws: Some Costs and Benefits', in KJAER, A. L., LAM, J. (eds.), *Language and Legal Interpretation in International Law,* Oxford: Oxford University Press, 2022, pp. 131–151, at 133. See also HUSA, J., *Interdisciplinary Comparative Law. Rubbing Shoulders with the Neighbours or Standing Alone in a Crowd,* Cheltenham: Edward Elgar, 2022, p. 72.

37 *CILFIT and Lanificio di Gavardo SpA v. Ministry of Health,* Judgment of the Court of 6 October 1982, case 283/81, ECLI:EU:C:1982:335, para. 18.

JEULAND: To accomplish this, it is vital to break free from the constraints of the predefined hierarchy of interpretation methods (literal, systematic, historical, teleological, comparative) and embrace a 'pragmatic pluralism of methods'.[38]

DE BENITO: Look how multilingual contracts are interpreted: even though the UNIDROIT Principles of International Commercial Contracts establish a hierarchy of methods, with a residual solution, authors take these rules *cum mica salis* and call for flexibility in the choice of methods.[39]

JEULAND: After all, multilingual interpretation naturally gives centre stage to teleological analysis and makes it more difficult to take advantage of 'linguistic accidence' and even 'language-shopping'.[40] The content of a legal provision cannot depend on the language version of the same law.[41]

DE BENITO: In Wittgenstein's words, '*die Grenzen meiner Sprache bedeuten die Grenzen meiner Welt*', 'the limits of my language mean the limits of my world'.[42] Let's break down the limits of our legal languages and thus expand the limits of our legal world!

---

38 PICHONNAZ, P., 'Challenging Textual Interpretation in Multilingual Legal Systems', *French Journal of Legal Policy*, 1 (2023), pp. 1–12, at 5, 9.

39 VOGENAUER, S. (ed.), *Commentary on the UNIDROIT Principles of International Commercial Contracts* (PICC), Oxford: Oxford University Press, 2015, p. 608; HERBOTS, J. H., 'Interpretation of Contracts', in SMITS, J. M. (ed.), *Elgar Encyclopedia on Comparative Law*, Cheltenham: Edward Elgar, 2012, pp. 421–448, at 431; PICHONNAZ, P., 'Legal Interpretation in Multilingual States: An Opportunity', *Journal of Comparative Law*, 124:12 (2017), pp. 124–141, at 139–140.

40 SOLAN, L. M., 'Interpreting multilingual laws: some costs and benefits' in KJAER, A. L., LAM, J. (eds.), *Language and Legal Interpretation in International Law*, Oxford: Oxford University Press, 2022, pp. 131–151, at 140–144.

41 DYRDA, A., GIZBERT-STUDNICKI, T., 'Do Legal Concepts Travel?' in KJAER, A. L., LAM, J. (eds.), *Language and Legal Interpretation in International Law*, Oxford: Oxford University Press, 2022, pp. 50–64, at 61.

42 WITTGENSTEIN, L., *Tractatus Logico-Philosophicus* (translated by OGDEN, C. K.), London: Kegan Paul, Trench, Trubner & Co.; New York: Harcourt, Brace & Co., 1922, para. 5.6, at 74.

Bibliography

BENJAMIN, W., 'Die Aufgabe des Übersetzers", preface to BAUDELAIRE, C., *Tableaux parisiens*, Heidelberg: Richard Weissbach, 1923; English translation by RENDALL, S., as 'The Translator's Task', *TTR: traduction, terminologie, rédaction*, 10:2 (1997), pp. 151–165, available at https://german.yale.edu/sites/default/files/benjamin_translators_task.pdf.

BOCQUET, C., *La traduction juridique. Fondement et méthode*, New Leuven: De Boeck, 2008.

CASSIN, B. (dir.), *Vocabulaire européen des philosophies: Dictionnaire des intraduisibles*, Paris: Seuil, 2004; English translation by APTER, E., LEZRA, J., WOOD, M. (eds.), *Dictionary of Untranslatables: A Philosophical Lexicon*, Princeton: Princeton University Press, 2015.

DE GROOT, G.-R., 'Legal Translation', in SMITS, J. M. (ed.), *Elgar Encyclopedia on Comparative Law*, Cheltenham: Edward Elgar, 2012.

DE GROOT, G.-R., VAN LAER, C. J. P., 'The Dubious Quality of Legal Dictionaries', *International Journal of Legal Information*, 34:1 (2006), pp. 65–84.

DEVINAT, M., PICHONNAZ, P., 'L'égalité des langues officielles devant les cours suprêmes: regards croisés sur le droit canadien et le droit suisse', *Revue de droit Suisse*, 136:1 (2017), pp. 271–288.

D'ORS, Á., *Nueva introducción al estudio del derecho*, Madrid: Civitas, 1999.

DULLION, V., 'Droit comparé pour traducteurs: de la théorie a` la didactique de la traduction juridique', *International Journal for Semiotics of Law*, 28:1 (2015), pp. 91–106.

DURO, M., 'Ordenamientos jurídicos y traducción (common law y civil law)', in DURO, M., MARTÍNEZ, A. B., SAN GINÉS, P. (eds.), *Introducción a la traducción jurídica y jurada (inglés-español). Orientaciones doctrinales y metodológicas*, Granada: Comares, 1997, pp. 41–59.

DYRDA, A., GIZBERT-STUDNICKI, T., 'Do Legal Concepts Travel?' in KJAER, A. L., LAM, J. (eds.), *Language and Legal Interpretation in International Law*, Oxford: Oxford University Press, 2022, pp. 50–64.

ENGBERG, J., 'Comparative Law for Legal Translation: Through Multiple Perspectives to Multidimensional Knowledge', *The International Journal for the Semiotics of Law*, 33:2, 2020, pp. 263–282.

GARCÍA GOYENA, F., *Concordancias, motivos y comentarios del Código civil español*, Madrid: Sociedad Tipográfico-Editorial, 1852.

GASCÓN, F., 'Traducción jurídica y sistemas procesales: algunas reflexiones acerca de las características de los procesos civiles en los sistemas de derecho continental', in *Seminarios Complutenses de Derecho Romano: Revista Complutense de Derecho Romano y Tradición Romanística*, 28 (2015), pp. 417–434.

GROSSWALD CURRAN, V., 'Comparative Law and Language', in REIMANN, M., ZIMMERMANN, R. (eds.), *The Oxford Handbook of Comparative Law*, Oxford: Oxford University Press, 2019, pp. 682–710.

HERBOTS, J. H., 'Interpretation of Contracts', in SMITS, J. M. (ed.), *Elgar Encyclopedia on Comparative Law*, Cheltenham: Edward Elgar, 2012, pp. 421–448.

HUSA. J., *Interdisciplinary Comparative Law. Rubbing Shoulders with the Neighbours or Standing Alone in a Crowd*, Cheltenham: Edward Elgar, 2022.

JEULAND, E., LALANI, S., *Lexicographical Research in Civil Procedure*, Paris: IRJS, 2017.

LEGRAND, P., 'Issues in the Translatability of Law", in BERMANN, S., WOOD, M. (eds.), *Nation, Language, and the Ethics of Translation*, Princeton: Princeton University Press, 2005.

LEGRAND, P., 'European Legal Systems Are Not Converging', *International and Comparative Law Quarterly*, 45:1 (1996), pp. 52–81.

MONJEAN-DECAUDIN, S., *Traité de juritraductologie: Épistémologie et méthodologie de la traduction juridique*, Villeneuve d'Ascq: Septentrion, 2022.

MONJEAN-DECAUDIN, S., POPINEAU-LAUVRAY, J., 'How to Apply Comparative Law to Legal Translation. A New Juritraductological Approach to the Translation of Legal Texts', in BIEL, L., ENGBERG, J., MARTÍN, R., SOSONI, V. (eds.), *Research Methods in Legal Translation and Interpreting. Crossing Methodological Boundaries*, London: Routledge, 2019, pp. 115–129.

MOUSOURAKIS, G., *Comparative Law and Legal Traditions. Historical and Contemporary Perspectives*, Cham: Springer, 2019.

OST, F., *Traduire. Défense et illustration du multilinguisme*, Paris: Fayard, 2009.

PASQUAU, M., 'Las peculiaridades del lenguaje jurídico desde la perspectiva del jurista', in DURO, M., MARTÍNEZ, A. B., SAN GINÉS, P. (eds.), *Introducción a la traducción jurídica y jurada (inglés-español). Orientaciones doctrinales y metodológicas*, Granada: Comares, 1997, pp. 9–23.

PICHONNAZ, P., 'Challenging Textual Interpretation in Multilingual Legal Systems', *French Journal of Legal Policy*, 1 (2023), pp. 1–12.

PICHONNAZ, P., 'Legal Interpretation in Multilingual States: An Opportunity', *Journal of Comparative Law*, 124:12 (2017), pp. 124–141.

POPKOVA, E. M., 'Arbitrazh vs Arbitration: Terminology Traps in the Russian-English Translation of the Russian Judiciary System', *Philological Sciences at MGIMO Collection of Scientific Papers*, 61:46 (2011), pp. 98–109.

PRIETO, F., 'International and Supranational Law in Translation: From Multilingual Lawmaking to Adjudication', *The Translator*, 20:3 (2014), pp. 313–331.

ROBERTSON, C. D., 'Legislative Drafting in English for Non-Native Speakers: Some Do's and Don'ts (With Reference to EU Legislation)', *ESP Across Cultures*, 7

(2010), special issue: GOTTI, M., WILLIAMS, C. (eds.), *Legal English Across Cultures*, pp. 147–163.

ROBERTSON, C. D., *Multilingual Law. A Framework for Analysis and Understanding*, London: Routledge, 2018.

ŠARCEVIC, S., 'Legal Translation and Translation Theory: A Receiver-Oriented Approach', in *La traduction juridique: Histoire, theorie(s) et pratique / Legal Translation: History, Theory/ies, Practice*, Bern, Geneva: ASTTI/ETI, 2000, available at: https://www.tradulex.com/Actes2000/sarcevic.pdf.

SOLAN, L. M., 'The Interpretation of Multilingual Statutes by the European Court of Justice', *Brooklyn Journal International Law*, 34:2 (2009), pp. 277–301.

SOLAN, L. M., 'Interpreting Multilingual Laws: Some Costs and Benefits', in Kjaer, A. L., Lam, J. (eds.), *Language and Legal Interpretation in International Law*, Oxford: Oxford University Press, 2022, pp. 131–151.

VOGENAUER, S. (ed.), *Commentary on the UNIDROIT Principles of International Commercial Contracts (PICC)*, Oxford: Oxford University Press, 2015.

WITTGENSTEIN, L., *Tractatus Logico-Philosophicus* (translated by OGDEN, C. K.), London: Kegan Paul, Trench, Trubner & Co.; New York: Harcourt, Brace & Co., 1922.

CHAPTER 13

Where from Here?

Paolo Biavati, Marco de Benito, Frédérique Ferrand, and Burkhard Hess

The Rules project has resulted in the ambitious and multifunctional set of provisions on a multitude of core procedural issues. However, the publication of the Rules, a soft law instrument, marks just a beginning. The effective incorporation of the Rules into legal reform initiatives, everyday legal practice, and legal discourse constitutes an even greater challenge.

DE BENITO: We have been discussing different aspects of the Rules: case management, party autonomy, evidence, judgments, appeals, etc. After having gone through these in some detail, I thought I'd ask just one question: where do we go from here?

HESS: Every time I look at the Rules, I find them different from other pieces of model legislation. Why?

Firstly, they were elaborated in a very interesting way by different groups and teams applying comparative methods. In a way, the internationality

 | DOI:10.1163/9789004533257_014

of the different groups ensured a truly comparative approach to civil procedure.

Secondly, codifications of civil procedure are usually national codifications: they are drafted and discussed in a national context and are made for national courts. Of course, there may also be some provisions addressing cross-border issues. However, what makes the Rules so special is that they address both domestic and cross-border proceedings in an integrated manner.

Thirdly, the Rules have great potential for integrating information technology. They allow proceedings to be conducted entirely by electronic means. The importance of this current development cannot be overestimated.[1] Since the corona crisis, we have seen how the courts have taken a big step towards electronic proceedings.[2] This is possible within the framework of the Rules. Rule 18(4) indicates that whenever a full and comprehensive electronic conduct of the proceedings is possible, case management conferences may be conducted electronically, and evidentiary hearings may also be performed by videoconference.

> Rule 18. *Oral and written proceedings*
>
> (4) In so far as appropriate, proceedings may be conducted using any available means of information and communication technology.

The use of electronic services has been envisaged, perhaps not as a first alternative, but as a very important way of informing and communicating with the parties. This also entails the obligation for lawyers to provide electronic addresses and to make electronic service possible. The same applies to the taking of evidence. Here, too, we have the possibility of using video and electronic communication techniques and of questioning witnesses by videoconference.

This is a very interesting development, which could even facilitate the creation of specific, electronic procedures in cross-border cases.[3] The

---

1 See Themeli, E., 'The Frontiers of Digital Justice in Europe', in Kramer, X., Hoevenaars, J., Kas, B., Themeli, E. (eds.), *Frontiers in Civil Justice. Privatisation, Monetisation and Digitisation*, Cheltenham: Edward Elgar, 2022, pp. 102–120. See also Stürner, R., 'The ELI / UNIDROIT Model European Rules of Civil Procedure. An Introduction to Their Basic Conceptions', *RabelsZ*, 86, 2022, pp. 421–472, at 469–471.

2 Krans, B., Nylund, A., *Civil Courts Coping with Covid-19*, The Hague: Eleven, 2021.

3 See Kramer, X., 'Digitising Access to Justice: The Next Steps in the Digitalisation of Judicial Cooperation in Europe', *Revista General de Derecho Europeo*, 56, 2022, pp. 1–9.

perspective that the EU – the European lawmaker – could adopt in cross-border contexts is that distance is a major obstacle. In this case, there could be an opportunity to arrive at a specific and authentic European cross-border procedure based on information technology, where the parties do not need to meet in person – at least not as a rule. I would strongly recommend going in this direction because we are already partly there. The platform established by the Commission has been very successful in cross-border cases, especially when considering online dispute resolution inside and outside the courts.

So, where we go from here? Let's try to set up a European electronic civil procedure for cross-border commercial cases based on these Model Rules.

BIAVATI: The Rules were written by scholars who gathered their best ideas and experiences. However, if we were to adapt them to our legal system, we would have to confront the tangible reality of judges and lawyers and their assumptions and preconceptions. We may all sit around a table sharing the same ideas on civil procedure in Europe, but we must not assume that all these ideas will be well received by the concrete actors of civil justice.[4] For example, the Rules do not recognise the principle of *nemo contra se edere tenetur*, which is deeply rooted in Italian legal culture. The Rules are important to improve ideas, but then they must come to life.

There is another serious difficulty in adopting the Rules in one way or another. In Italy we are working on a reform of civil procedure. Our aim is to improve the effectiveness of civil justice and we often take inspiration from the Rules to translate the framework law – we have written a *legge delega* – into an appropriate articulated text. We can use at least some of them. Remo Caponi pointed out how interesting the provisions on joint applications and agreements on applicable law are.[5] They could be well accepted in Italy. However, we are not totally changing our judicial organisation. And this is key. We could take the most technically perfect code, and have it enacted in Italy or elsewhere, but it wouldn't necessarily improve

4 See, e.g., GASCÓN, F., 'Comparative Perspectives in Procedural Law: Some Remarks and Proposals', in CADIET, L., HESS, B. REQUEJO, M., *Approaches to Procedural Law. The Pluralism of Methods*, Baden-Baden: Nomos, 2017, pp. 15 ff. In Italian, see generally DONDI, A., ANSANELLI, V., COMOGLIO, P., *Processi civili in evoluzione. Una prospettiva comparata*, Milan: Giuffrè, 2015.

5 See CAPONI, R., 'Le regole del modello europee ELI-UNIDROIT sullo sfondo della riforma italiana del processo civile', *Rivista trimestrale di diritto e procedura civile*, 3-2022, pp. 717 ff.

the reality of civil justice. Procedure and organisation go hand in hand and at the same time pose completely different challenges.

The difficulties multiply considering all European judicial systems. We may have an excellent basis for unitary legislation, such as the Rules, yet organisational and even constitutional diversity raises an almost insurmountable obstacle to its practical application.

Perhaps we could start working on finding some general models of judicial organisation, as difficult as that may seem. An e-justice organisation, like the one proposed by Burkhard, could overcome some of the organisational differences. But, again, only in part.

In short, where should we go from here? We should consider bringing together traditional judicial organisations and systems in Europe.[6]

FERRAND: I fully agree with Paolo. The Rules in themselves are inevitably *disembodied*. Legal transplant often requires some sort of adaptation to the local terrain.[7]

I remember what happened in France, when comparative materials were used selectively and opportunistically to promote filtering of access to the *Cour de cassation*.[8] The justices of the Court were very interested in importing the German model of selective appeal. The report, written by a former minister of justice, concluded that such a selective appeal would not fit the French legal culture because 'the French legal community has a very special relationship with the law and with the equality of litigants before the law'.[9] Indeed, it would have created a great deal of tension, since a selection of

6 See, *inter alia*, QUESADA, P. M., *El principio de efectividad del Derecho de la Unión Europea y su impacto en el Derecho procesal nacional*, Madrid: Iustel, 2019. See also BIAVATI, P., *Europa e processo civile. Metodi e prospettive*, Turin: Giappichelli, 2003.

7 See FERRAND, F., 'Faut-il s'adapter ? De l'avenir du procès civil : reddition ou résistance ?', *International Journal of Procedural Law*, 2-2020, pp. 253–280, also in English 'On the Future of Civil Procedure – Should One Adapt or Resist?', in MIKI, K. (ed.), *Technology, the Global Economy and Other New Challenges for Civil Justice*, Brussels: Intersentia, 2021, pp. 17–44. On the goals of comparative law and the importance of cultural traditions, see LEGRAND, P., *Le droit comparé*, Paris: PUF, 2016.

8 See COUR DE CASSATION, 'Rapport de la Commission de réflexion sur la réforme de la Cour de cassation', 2017; COUR DE CASSATION, 'Rapport de mission de la Commission chargée, dans la cadre de la mise en œuvre de la réforme de la Cour de cassation, de l'élaboration d'un projet de dispositif opérationnel de filtrage des pourvois', 2018; both available at courdecassation.fr.

9 NALLET, H., *et al.*, 'Pour une réforme du pourvoi en matière civile', 30 September 2019, available at www.dalloz-actualite.fr/sites/dalloz-actualite.fr/files/resources/2019/11/nallet.pdf.

final appeals would have left decisions that do not comply with the law untouched; resulted in a breach of equality between citizens before the law and justice;[10] led to a decline in the quality of decisions on the merits rendered by lower courts; and increased the risk of regionalisation of justice.

This is one of the reasons why I am reluctant to support the European Model Rules in France, because it would benefit the promoters of this selective system of last resort appeals. Think of Rule 172:

> Rule 172. *Right to a second appeal*
>
> (1) A party may only appeal from a first appeal judgment if such an appeal is necessary to
>
> (a) correct a violation of a fundamental right,
>
> (b) secure uniformity in the law,
>
> (c) decide a fundamental question which is not limited to the case at issue, or
>
> (d) develop the law.
>
> (2) A second appeal court shall, on its own motion, assess whether the requirements of Rule 172(1) have been met.

This may seem very natural in some jurisdictions – not in France.

Of course, many provisions in the Rules are truly inspiring also in France: cooperation; proportionality; the overriding objective of a fair, efficient, and speedy resolution of the dispute; collective redress. Many of these will make their way into the legal discussion in France and elsewhere, including the EU institutions. In July 2017, the European Parliament approved a resolution on common standards in civil procedure,[11] without any remarkable

---

10 The French *Conseil constitutionnel* has insisted on the constitutional value of the principle of equality before the law and before the administration of justice, based on Arts. 6 and 16 of the Declaration of Human and Civic Rights of 26 August 1789 (to which the Preamble of the French Constitution refers). See, e.g., decisions of the *Conseil constitutionnel* of 20 January 2005, № 2004-510 DC, *Loi relative aux compétences du tribunal d'instance, de la juridiction de proximité et du tribunal de grande instance*; 21 March 2019, № 2019-778 DC, *Loi de programmation 2018–2022 et de réforme pour la justice* (para. 21); 20 September 2019, № 2019-801 QPC, *M. Jean-Claude F. [Notes d'audience établies par le greffier lors des débats devant le tribunal correctionnel]*, para. 8.

11 European Parliament resolution of 4 July 2017 with recommendations to the Commission on common minimum standards of civil procedure in the European Union.

success. The Model Rules have a brighter future because they are better structured, more comprehensive, clearer, and more solid in their approach to each topic.

As Burkhard said, one of the Rules' strongest points is their modernity. In ELI's tenth anniversary, Norel Rosner, legal and policy officer for Civil Justice at the EU Commission, said in his speech that the EU Commission had already been influenced by the Rules, for instance towards the recast of the Evidence Regulation[12] and the Service Regulation.[13] In which, by the way, also as Burkhard mentioned, a strong promotion of electronic means is evident at first glance. The lasting impact of the Model Rules will be in their modernity – in their open and prudent approach to modernity.

In any case, I don't believe that the European Commission, which showed interest in the drafting of the Rules and participated in several meetings with ELI and UNIDROIT, will suggest implementing the Regulation as such. Rather, they will be inspired by some very specific rules in the cross-border sphere. Keep in mind that the EU does not have the competence to draft or suggest regulations or directives at national level, hence their fragmented approach. Under the existing Treaties, EU procedural law will never resemble our essentially complete and consistent national codes of civil procedure.

Where do we go from here, then? In the short and medium term, we must strive for an open understanding of the meaning of fair adjudication and find the inspiration to – when necessary – reform and improve national and European procedural legal systems along the lines of the Rules.

---

12 Regulation (EU) 2020/1783 of the European Parliament and of the Council of 25 November 2020 on cooperation between the courts of the Member States in the taking of evidence in civil or commercial matters (taking of evidence) (recast).

13 Regulation (EU) 2020/1784 of the European Parliament and of the Council of 25 November 2020 on the service in the Member States of judicial and extrajudicial documents in civil or commercial matters (service of documents) (recast). See RASIA, C., 'Il nuovo regolamento Ue n. 1784 del 2020 sulle notifiche nel prisma della digitalizzazione della giustizia europea', *Rivista trimestrale di diritto e procedura civile*, 4-2021, pp. 1299 ff. See also SCHMITZ, M. (dir.), GIELEN, P., (coord.), *La signification des actes judiciaires et extrajudiciaires en Europe. Analyses, jurisprudences et perspectives du règlement UE № 2020/1784*, Brussels: Bruylant, 2022, in particular CRISTIAN, N., DRAGOS, S., HALDI, K., 'L'e-CODEX et la plateforme européenne de transmission des documents', pp. 105 ff.

HESS: Exactly. We cannot expect that, in a few years' time, litigation in Europe will be the same in, say, Stockholm, Paris, and Munich. That is not our goal. We have different national traditions, cultures, and judicial systems and this is our wealth. As Paolo said, the organisation of justice is important in this respect. To overcome shortcomings, we need to be more functional.

I have always appreciated and supported the idea of commercial courts.[14] The new commercial courts in Germany, particularly those in Stuttgart and Mannheim, are working effectively and innovatively. Commercial courts of this type are very competitive. I see an opportunity to adopt the Rules as a pioneering approach in European procedural law, based on the best practices of different countries.

There is a historical precedent. In Germany in the 1970s, procedural reform was based on the so-called Stuttgart model. This was a court in that city with innovative judges who had already been experimenting with the new procedures for several years before the legislature adopted them generally.

DE BENITO: You said that commercial courts are competitive. In fact, they compete with other commercial courts nationally and internationally.[15] Sometimes, especially in high value cases, they compete not only with other commercial courts but also with international arbitral tribunals,[16] which are also wonderful vantage points from which to contemplate and test procedural developments. Commercial courts and arbitral tribunals can enrich each other. In fact, they have been doing this discretely for some time. First, in the legal framework. The New York Convention[17] laid the cornerstone of the international circulation of awards. There was nothing similar in civil

---

14 See generally KRAMER, X., SORABJI, J. (eds.), *International Business Courts. A European and Global Perspective*, The Hague: Eleven, 2019; or BREKOULAKIS, S., DIMITROPOULOS, G. (eds.), *International Commercial Courts. The Future of Transnational Adjudication*, Cambridge: Cambridge University Press, 2022.

15 On competition between courts and civil justice systems, see WAGNER, G., 'The Dispute Resolution Market', *Buffalo Law Review*, 62, 2014, pp. 1085–1158. See also SORABJI, J., KRAMER, X., 'Introduction: The International Business of Courts', and THEMELI, E., 'International Commercial Courts Competition in Europe: A Litigation Competition Approach', both in KRAMER, X., SORABJI, J. (eds.), *International Business Courts. A European and Global Perspective*, The Hague: Eleven, 2019, pp. 1–20 and 273–296 respectively.

16 See BOOKMAN, P. K., 'The Adjudication Business', *Yale Journal of International Law*, 45, 2020, pp. 227–283, especially at 275–280.

17 Convention on the Recognition and Enforcement of Foreign Arbitral Awards, signed in New York on 10 June 1958.

procedure. However, the Hague Choice of Court Convention[18] and the Hague Judgments Convention[19] were recently adopted to facilitate the international circulation of judgments. In the meantime, the EU strengthened judicial cooperation to the extent that it abolished exequatur.[20] Second, commercial courts and arbitral tribunals can be mutually enriched through the harmonisation of procedural principles, rules, and practices. Arbitral harmonisation can be seen in the form of a wide variety of soft law instruments that offer non-binding regulation of relevant issues. Institutions such as UNCITRAL, ICCA, the ICC, and the IBA are particularly active and influential in this regard. As far as civil procedure is concerned, we have, among others, the ALI-UNIDROIT Principles of Transnational Civil Procedure, and now our ELI-UNIDROIT Model Rules. And the general procedural trends – an active adjudicator, the principle of cooperation, convergence in the main hearing model, balanced access to information and evidence – are strikingly similar in both fields.

HESS: It is certainly an engaging process, perhaps even an unlikely one given that the two worlds have long lived with their backs turned to each other.

DE BENITO: Indeed, state courts and arbitration tribunals both belong to the same 'legal system', as traditionally required for a decision to have *res judicata* effect.[21] Through this process of rapprochement, the legal system is slowly beginning to resemble a 'system' and, as such, is building what Nassim Nicolas Taleb would call *antifragility*.[22] This strikes me as a suggestive idea. A porcelain cup is *fragile* because it falls and breaks. A stone is *robust* because it does not vary and adapt to its surroundings. Something

18 HCCH Convention of 30 June 2005 on Choice of Court Agreements. It is already in force in the EU and the UK; and has been signed by the US.

19 HCCH Convention of 2 July 2019 on the Recognition and Enforcement of Foreign Judgments in Civil or Commercial Matters. Interestingly, it has so far been signed by, among others, Ukraine in 2020, the Russian Federation in 2021, and the US in 2022. Perhaps a happy coincidence that bodes well.

20 Regulation (EU) 1215/2012 of the European Parliament and of the Council of 12 December 2012 on jurisdiction and the recognition and enforcement of judgments in civil and commercial matters (recast).

21 DE LY, P., SHEPPARD, A., 'ILA Final Report on Res Judicata and Arbitration', *Arbitration International*, 25-2009, 1, pp. 67–82, at 73–76.

22 TALEB, N. N., *Antifragile. Things that Gain from Disorder*, New York: Random House, 2012.

antifragile goes one step further: it improves every time it falls. Decentralised competition within a system creates antifragility because it has the potential to improve the entire system – in this case, not this commercial court at the expense of that one, or commercial courts at the expense of arbitration tribunals, or vice versa, but the entire civil and commercial dispute resolution system. Competition therefore contributes to a fairer, more efficient, and faster resolution of civil and commercial disputes as a whole. This is good for the users, who in the end are the only ones who matter.

HESS: All those competitive instances have now the Rules to experiment, differentiate, and improve.

DE BENITO: The chapter on access to information and evidence comes to mind. In this respect, the Rules offer a more comprehensive, more cohesive, and more detailed regulation than the IBA Rules on the taking of evidence,[23] which are commonly referred to in arbitration. The Rules' regulation can be adopted to advantage in both fields.

BIAVATI: It is easier for any of us to play as a lawyer in international arbitration, anywhere in the world, than to play as a lawyer in another country, because the tools we use are basically the same.[24] The way of working in an arbitral tribunal remains the same, but the way of working in other tribunals is very different from one country to another. We have no organisation problems in arbitration because we work in the same way. There are differences, of course, but they are very few. For example, the UNCITRAL arbitration model instruments[25] can be applied in many countries, directly or after translation into different languages and codes.

The Rules can help to go down the road of better harmonisation. Specific procedural rules may differ, but it would be very important to achieve a

---

23 IBA Rules on the Taking of Evidence in International Arbitration, adopted by a resolution of 17 December 2020 of the Council of the International Bar Association.

24 See, among many, SALOMON, C. T., 'The Conduct of an International Arbitration: Do the Rules Make a Difference?', *Journal of International Arbitration*, 21:2, 2004, pp. 103–141; BERGER, B., 'Rights and Obligations of Arbitrators in the Deliberations', *ASA Bulletin*, 2013, 31-2, pp. 244–261; CONSOLO, C., *Problemi e soluzioni in tema di arbitrato. Riguardato da un giurista italiano teorico-pratico*, Milan: Wolters Kluwer, 2020, pp. 602 ff.

25 UNCITRAL Notes on Organizing Arbitral Proceedings, 1996 and 2016. UNCITRAL Arbitration Rules, 1976, 2010, and 2013. UNCITRAL Model Law on International Commercial Arbitration, 1985 and 2006.

common standard in proceedings:[26] for example, to follow the same steps, if not the same deadlines.

DE BENITO: That's interesting. The role of lawyers is far from being harmonised. Cultural assumptions and ethical obligations are not yet harmonised. It is not only the office and the judicial organisation that are different.

BIAVATI: That is the strength and beauty of the best-practice idea. Perhaps we should promote meetings with judges and bar associations to explain how cases can be handled in a way they are not used to. And start quoting the Rules in everyday litigation. The world is changing very fast. We must be optimistic.

FERRAND: I once had to offer my expertise in an international arbitration case about the scope of *res judicata*. No one knew the Rules. I decided to explain them and use them as a reinforcing argument. The Rules thus entered the legal debate in that case – and perhaps in others in the future.

DE BENITO: Sophisticated lawyers regularly do the same, as to the merits of their case, with the UNIDROIT Principles on international commercial contracts since their publication in 1994:[27]

> As amply demonstrated by the extensive body of case law and bibliographic references, … the UNIDROIT Principles continue to be well received generally and have not given rise in practice to any significant difficulties of application.

Can you imagine if, in a couple of decades, the same could be said of the Rules?

---

26 See, *inter alia*, PETROCHILOS, G., *Procedural Law in International Arbitration*, Oxford: Oxford University Press, 2004, p. 176; or RUBINO-SAMMARTANO, M., *International Arbitration Law and Practice*, Huntington: Juris, 2014, chapter 17, 'Applicable Procedural Law'.

27 UNIDROIT Principles of International Commercial Contracts, 2016 edition: Overview, Introduction, available at https://www.unidroit.org/instruments/commercial-contracts/unidroit-principles-2016/overview/. See VENEZIANO, A., FINAZZI AGRÒ, E., 'The Use of the UNIDROIT Principles in Order to Interpret or Supplement National Law: An Italian Perspective, in GALIZZI, P., ROJAS ELGUETA, G., VENEZIANO, A., *The Multiple Uses of the UNIDROIT Principles of International Commercial Contracts: Theory and Practice*, Milan: Giuffrè, 2020, pp. 5–16.

FERRAND: To that end, we should really promote a common training of lawyers, judges, academics, and policymakers, in the EU to start with. Otherwise, the Rules will remain, as I said, *disembodied*.

HESS: Colleagues from Latin America (Brazil, Argentina, Chile) have shown interest in this project and the possibilities of using it as reference for inspiration in their countries. Alan Uzelac told me the same recently about Eastern Europe. He has been active in projects in Montenegro and Serbia and testifies to this interest. It seems that in his country, Croatia, the Rules have set standards for proposed legal reform on procedural calendars and illegally obtained evidence. Chinese colleagues are also following the project closely.

BIAVATI: The Rules set a standard for reform that clearly transcends specific cross-border situations and offers nothing short of a model of *good* civil procedure.

DE BENITO: As such, among other things, they are also excellent teaching material. We can draw inspiration from the old *jus commune* to teach law – not only substantive law but also procedural law – as a common language with dialectal expressions. The Rules can be adopted as a leitmotif, thus providing students with a reference point from which to identify and verify the expression of this or that principle in the law and practice of certain jurisdictions. Like a musical theme with multiple variations, a dialogue can be established between the Rules and national laws.

BIAVATI: I couldn't agree more, Marco. Our Latin forefathers talked about taking aspects from different cultures and putting them together to create a complete whole. It is the idea of 'legal contamination' that is today realised in the dialogue between the great European courts, Luxembourg and Strasbourg, and the national superior and constitutional courts.[28] Perhaps this healthy contamination that takes place to better protect basic human rights

---

28 See JACOBS, F., 'Human Rights in the EU: The Role of the Court of Justice', *European Law Review*, 2001, pp. 331–341; HARPAZ, G., 'The European Court of Justice and its Relations with the European Court of Human Rights: The Quest for Enhanced Reliance, Coherence and Legitimacy', *Common Market Law Review*, 2009, pp. 105 ff.; GIANNITI, P., *Diritti fondamentali e giudice comune. Verso un sistema europeo di tutela integrata*, Rome: Aracne, 2022; BIAVATI, P., 'La tutela multilivelli dei diritti fondamentali: una bussola per l'Europa?', in BIAVATI, P. (ed.), *Giustizia senza confini. Studi offerti a Federico Carpi*, Bologna: Bononia University Press, 2012, pp. 33 ff.

can also improve the way civil proceedings are handled, for the higher goal of justice for all.

Bibliography

BERGER, B., 'Rights and Obligations of Arbitrators in the Deliberations', *ASA Bulletin*, 2013, 31–2, pp. 244–261.

BIAVATI, P., *Europa e processo civile. Metodi e prospettive*, Turin: Giappichelli, 2003.

BIAVATI, P., 'La tutela multilivelli dei diritti fondamentali: una bussola per l'Europa?', in BIAVATI, P. (ed.), *Giustizia senza confini. Studi offerti a Federico Carpi*, Bologna: Bononia University Press, 2012, pp. 33 ff.

BOOKMAN, P. K., 'The Adjudication Business', *Yale Journal of International Law*, 45, 2020, pp. 227–283.

BREKOULAKIS, S., DIMITROPOULOS, G. (eds.), *International Commercial Courts. The Future of Transnational Adjudication*, Cambridge: Cambridge University Press, 2022.

CAPONI, R., 'Le regole del modello europee ELI-UNIDROIT sullo sfondo della riforma italiana del processo civile', *Rivista trimestrale di diritto e procedura civile*, 3-2022, pp. 717 ff.

CONSOLO, C., *Problemi e soluzioni in tema di arbitrato. Riguardato da un giurista italiano teorico-pratico*, Milan: Wolters Kluwer, 2020.

DE LY, P., SHEPPARD, A., 'ILA Final Report on Res Judicata and Arbitration', *Arbitration International*, 25-2009, 1, pp. 67–82.

DONDI, A., ANSANELLI, V., COMOGLIO, P., *Processi civili in evoluzione. Una prospettiva comparata*, Milan: Giuffrè, 2015.

FERRAND, F., 'Faut-il s'adapter ? De l'avenir du procès civil : reddition ou résistance ?', *International Journal of Procedural Law*, 2-2020, pp. 253–280.

FERRAND, F., 'On the Future of Civil Procedure – Should One Adapt or Resist?', in MIKI, K. (ed.), *Technology, the Global Economy and Other New Challenges for Civil Justice*, Brussels: Intersentia, 2021, pp. 17–44.

GASCÓN, F., 'Comparative Perspectives in Procedural Law: Some Remarks and Proposals', in CADIET, L., HESS, B. REQUEJO, M., *Approaches to Procedural Law. The Pluralism of Methods*, Baden-Baden: Nomos, 2017, pp. 15 ff.

GIANNITI, P., *Diritti fondamentali e giudice comune. Verso un sistema europeo di tutela integrata*, Rome: Aracne, 2022.

HARPAZ, G., 'The European Court of Justice and its Relations with the European Court of Human Rights: The Quest for Enhanced Reliance, Coherence and Legitimacy', *Common Market Law Review*, 2009, pp. 105 ff.

Jacobs, F., 'Human Rights in the EU: The Role of the Court of Justice', *European Law Review*, 2001, pp. 331–341.

Kramer, X., 'Digitising Access to Justice: The Next Steps in the Digitalisation of Judicial Cooperation in Europe', *Revista General de Derecho Europeo*, 56, 2022, pp. 1–9.

Kramer, X., Sorabji, J. (eds.), *International Business Courts. A European and Global Perspective*, The Hague: Eleven, 2019.

Krans B., Nylund, A., *Civil Courts Coping with Covid-19*, The Hague: Eleven, 2021.

Legrand, P., *Le droit comparé*, Paris: PUF, 2016.

Nallet, H., *et al.*, 'Pour une réforme du pourvoi en matière civile', 30 September 2019, available at https://www.dalloz-actualite.fr/sites/dalloz-actualite.fr/files/resources/2019/11/nallet.pdf.

Petrochilos, G., *Procedural Law in International Arbitration*, Oxford: Oxford University Press, 2004.

Quesada, P. M., *El principio de efectividad del Derecho de la Unión Europea y su impacto en el Derecho procesal nacional*, Madrid: Iustel, 2019.

Rasia, C., 'Il nuovo regolamento Ue n. 1784 del 2020 sulle notifiche nel prisma della digitalizzazione della giustizia europea', *Rivista trimestrale di diritto e procedura civile*, 4-2021, pp. 1299 ff.

Rubino-Sammartano, M., *International Arbitration Law and Practice*, Huntington: Juris, 2014.

Salomon, C. T., 'The Conduct of an International Arbitration: Do the Rules Make a Difference?', *Journal of International Arbitration*, 21:2, 2004, pp. 103–141.

Schmitz, M. (dir.), Gielen, P., (coord.), *La signification des actes judiciaires et extrajudiciaires en Europe. Analyses, jurisprudences et perspectives du règlement UE № 2020/1784*, Brussels: Bruylant, 2022.

Sorabji, J., Kramer, X., 'Introduction: The International Business of Courts', in Kramer, X., Sorabji, J. (eds.), *International Business Courts. A European and Global Perspective*, The Hague: Eleven, 2019, pp. 1–20.

Stürner, R., 'The ELI / UNIDROIT Model European Rules of Civil Procedure. An Introduction to Their Basic Conceptions', *RabelsZ*, 86, 2022, pp. 421–472.

Taleb, N. N., *Antifragile. Things that Gain from Disorder*, New York: Random House, 2012.

Themeli, E., 'International Commercial Courts Competition in Europe: A Litigation Competition Approach', in Kramer, X., Sorabji, J. (eds.), *International Business Courts. A European and Global Perspective*, The Hague: Eleven, 2019, pp. 273–296.

Themeli, E., 'The Frontiers of Digital Justice in Europe', in Kramer, X., Hoevenaars, J., Kas, B., Themeli, E. (eds.), *Frontiers in Civil Justice. Privatisation, Monetisation and Digitisation*, Cheltenham: Edward Elgar, 2022, pp. 102–120.

VENEZIANO, A., FINAZZI AGRÒ, E., 'The Use of the UNIDROIT Principles in Order to Interpret or Supplement National Law: An Italian Perspective, in GALIZZI, P., ROJAS ELGUETA, G., VENEZIANO, A., *The Multiple Uses of the UNIDROIT Principles of International Commercial Contracts: Theory and Practice*, Milan: Giuffrè, 2020, pp. 5–16.

WAGNER, G., 'The Dispute Resolution Market', *Buffalo Law Review*, 62, 2014, pp. 1085–1158.

APPENDIX

ELI-UNIDROIT Model European Rules of Civil Procedure

Part 1 – General Provisions

Section 1 – Scope

Rule 1. Scope

(1) These Rules apply to the resolution of domestic and cross-border disputes in civil and commercial matters whatever the nature of the court.[1]

(2) These Rules do not apply to:

(a) the status or legal capacity of natural persons, rights in property arising out of a matrimonial relationship or out of a relationship deemed by the law applicable to such relationship to have comparable effects to marriage;

(b) bankruptcy, proceedings relating to the winding-up of insolvent companies or other legal persons, judicial arrangements, compositions and analogous proceedings;

(c) social security;

(d) arbitration;

(e) maintenance obligations arising from a family relationship, parentage, marriage or affinity;

(f) wills and succession, including maintenance obligations arising by reason of death.

(3) These Rules may also apply where incidental issues arise which fall within Rule 1(2), if the principal matter in dispute is within the scope of Rule 1(1).

1 Reproduced by kind permission of the European Law Institute (ELI) and the International Institute for the Unification of Private Law (UNIDROIT). The black letter version of the Rules is reproduced for ease of reference, in the knowledge that the Rules should be read and interpreted in the light of the explanatory commentary (see Preamble, § 22). The available language versions of the text can be found on the ELI and the UNIDROIT websites at https://www.europeanlawinstitute.eu/projects-publications/publications/eli-unidroit-model-european-rules-of-civil-procedure/ and https://www.unidroit.org/instruments/civil-procedure/eli-unidroit-rules/. The full text in English has been edited and published in book form as ELI, UNIDROIT, *ELI–UNIDROIT Model European Rules of Civil Procedure. From Transnational Principles to European Rules of Civil Procedure*, Oxford: Oxford University Press, 2021.

Section 2 – Principles

A Co-operation

Rule 2. General

Parties, their lawyers and the court must co-operate to promote the fair, efficient and speedy resolution of the dispute.

Rule 3. Role of the parties and their lawyers

Parties and their lawyers must:

(a) take reasonable and appropriate steps to settle disputes amicably;
(b) contribute to the proper management of the proceedings;
(c) present facts and evidence;
(d) assist the court in the determination of the facts and the applicable law;
(e) act in good faith and avoid procedural abuse when dealing with the court and other parties.

Rule 4. Role of the court – the general case management duty

The court is responsible for active and effective case management. The court must ensure that parties enjoy equal treatment. Throughout proceedings it shall monitor whether parties and their lawyers comply with their responsibilities under these Rules.

B Proportionality

Rule 5. Role of the court

(1) The court must ensure that the dispute resolution process is proportionate.

(2) In determining whether a process is proportionate the court must take account of the nature, importance and complexity of the particular case and of the need to give effect to its general management duty in all proceedings with due regard for the proper administration of justice.

Rule 6. Role of the parties and their lawyers

Parties and their lawyers must co-operate with the court to promote a proportionate dispute resolution process.

Rule 7. Proportionality of sanctions

Sanctions for breach of any of the rules must be proportionate to the seriousness of the matter involved and the harm caused and reflect the extent of participation and the degree to which the conduct was deliberate.

Rule 8. Proportionality of costs

Costs of proceedings should, in so far as possible, be reasonable and proportionate to the amount in dispute, the nature and complexity of the particular proceedings, their importance for the parties and the public interest.

C Settlement

Rule 9. Role of the parties and their lawyers

(1) Parties must co-operate in seeking to resolve their dispute consensually, both before and after proceedings begin.

(2) Lawyers must inform the parties about the availability of consensual dispute resolution methods, assist them in selecting the most suitable method, and, where appropriate, encourage its use. They must ensure that they use any mandatory method.

(3) Parties may ask the court to render a settlement agreement enforceable.

(4) When a consensual settlement as a whole cannot be reached, parties must take all reasonable opportunities to reduce the number of contested issues prior to adjudication.

Rule 10. Role of the court

(1) The court must facilitate settlement at any stage of the proceedings. Particularly, it must ensure that the parties consider settlement in the preparatory stage of proceedings and at case management conferences. If necessary for furthering the settlement process, it may order the parties to appear before it in person.

(2) The court must inform the parties about the availability of different types of settlement methods. It may suggest or recommend the use of specific consensual dispute resolution methods.

(3) The court may participate in settlement attempts and assist the parties in reaching a consensual resolution. It may also assist in drafting settlement agreements.

(4) Where a judge mediates during a settlement process and receives information in the absence of one of the parties, that judge must not decide the case.

D Right to Be Heard

Rule 11. Fair opportunity to present claim and defence

The court must manage proceedings to ensure that parties have a fair opportunity to present their case and evidence, to respond to their respective claims and defences and to any court orders or matters raised by the court.

Rule 12. Basis of court decisions

(1) In reaching any decision in proceedings the court must consider all factual, evidential, and legal issues advanced by the parties. Court decisions must specifically set out their reasoning concerning substantial issues.

(2) The court must not base its decisions on issues that parties have not had an opportunity to address.

Rule 13. Communications with the court

(1) The court must not communicate with a party in the absence of other parties. This prohibition does not apply to without-notice proceedings or to routine procedural administration.

(2) All communications by parties with the court must be provided to all other parties at the time when they are made to the court.

(3) When the court becomes aware of a failure to comply with the requirement in Rule 13(2), it must promptly provide the parties with the content of the communication.

E Representation and Assistance

Rule 14. Self-representation and mandatory representation

Except when legal representation is required by law, parties have a right to represent themselves in proceeding.

Rule 15. Representation and assistance in court

(1) Parties may engage a lawyer of their own choice. They may do so both when they choose to be, and when they are required by law to be, represented by a lawyer. This right includes the right to representation by a lawyer admitted to practice in the forum and to receive active assistance before the court from a lawyer admitted to practice elsewhere.

(2) Parties may, where the law permits it, be represented or assisted in court by an individual or organisation other than a lawyer.

(3) When representing or assisting a party the court must respect a lawyer's professional independence. This includes ensuring that lawyers are able to fulfil their duty of loyalty to their client and maintain client confidentiality.

Rule 16. Hearing parties

(1) Parties have the right to be heard in person by the court.

(2) The court may always hear parties in person.

F Oral, Written and Public Proceedings

Rule 17. Public proceedings

(1) Hearings and court decisions, including their reasoning, must, as a general rule, be public.

(2) The court may order the proceedings, or parts thereof, especially oral hearings and the taking of evidence, to be in private (in camera) for reasons of public policy, including national security, privacy, or professional secrets, including business confidentiality, or in the interests of the administration of justice. Where necessary the court may make suitable protective orders to maintain the privacy or confidentiality of hearings held or evidence taken in private.

(3) Judgments and their reasoning shall be accessible to the public to the extent that proceedings are open to the public. When hearings have been in private, publicity of the judgment may be limited to its operative part.
(4) Court files and records shall be publicly accessible at least to persons with a legal interest in them and to those making a legitimate inquiry.
(5) The identity of parties, witnesses and other natural persons mentioned in the judgment may be private where strictly necessary.

Rule 18. Oral and written proceedings

(1) Pleadings and applications must be presented initially in writing.
(2) The court may order parties to present oral argument and carry out the oral examination of witnesses or experts. Where a party requests it, the court must permit oral argument, and may permit oral examination.
(3) The court may order witnesses and experts to submit written statements.
(4) In so far as appropriate, proceedings may be conducted using any available means of information and communication technology.

G Languages, Interpretation and Translation

Rule 19. Language of the court

Proceedings, including documents and oral communications, must as a general rule be in a language of the court. The court may permit all or part of the proceedings to be conducted in other languages where doing that would not prejudice the parties or the right to a public hearing.

Rule 20. Interpretation and translation

(1) Interpretation or translation must be provided by the court to parties who are not sufficiently competent in the language used in the proceedings. The right to interpretation includes the right of parties with hearing or speech impediments to receive appropriate assistance. Such interpretation and translation shall ensure the proceedings are fair by enabling the parties to participate in them effectively.
(2) Where documents are translated, the parties may agree, or the court may order, that such translation be limited to such parts of the documents as necessary to ensure the proceedings are fair and that the parties are able to participate effectively in them.

Section 3 – Proceedings

A Commencement, Termination, Concentration and Scope

Rule 21. Commencement and termination

(1) Proceedings may only be instituted by a party. The court cannot institute proceedings on its own motion.
(2) Parties may terminate proceedings in whole or in part by withdrawal, admission of the claim or settlement.

Rule 22. Concentration of legal and factual issues

(1) Parties must bring all the legal and factual elements in support of, or in objection to, a claim for relief that arise out of the same cause of action in one single proceeding.

(2) Non-compliance with Rule 22(1) renders proceedings on the same claim for relief arising out of the same cause of action inadmissible. This preclusion does not apply if

(a) subsequent to the earlier proceeding, there has been a change in relevant facts on which judgment in those proceedings was based, or

(b) the non-compliant party has obtained or acquired a new right since judgment was given in the earlier proceeding.

Rule 23. Scope

(1) The scope of the dispute is determined by the claims and defences of the parties in the pleadings, including amendments.

(2) The court must decide on, and only on, the relief claimed.

B Facts, Evidence and Applicable Law

Rule 24. Facts

(1) The parties must put forward such facts as support their claim or defence. The court may invite the parties to clarify or supplement these facts.

(2) The court must not consider facts not introduced by the parties.

(3) The court may consider such facts not specifically addressed by a party but that are necessarily implied by matters of fact put forward by the parties or which are contained within the case file. It may only do so if they are relevant to a party's claim or defence and the parties have been given a reasonable opportunity to respond.

Rule 25. Evidence

(1) Each party is required to prove all the relevant facts supporting its case. Parties must offer evidence supporting their factual contentions. Substantive law determines the burden of proof.

(2) Each party has, in principle, a right to access all forms of relevant, non-privileged and reasonably identified evidence. In so far as appropriate, parties and non-parties must contribute to disclosure and production of evidence. It is not a basis of objection to such disclosure by a party that disclosure may favour the opponent or other parties.

(3) In so far as appropriate the court may invite the parties to supplement their offers of evidence. Exceptionally, it may take evidence on its own motion.

Rule 26. Applicable law

(1) While taking account of any applicable special provisions, the parties may present legal arguments supporting their claim or defence.

(2) The court must determine the correct legal basis for its decision. This includes matters determined on the basis of foreign law. It may only do so having provided the parties a reasonable opportunity to present their arguments on the applicable law.

(3) Where parties are free to dispose of their rights, they may agree on the legal basis of the claim or on specific issues in the claim. Such an agreement must be explicit and must, even if it was made before commencement of the proceedings, be set out in the pleadings. The agreement binds the court.

C Sanctions for Non-compliance and Relief from Sanctions

Rule 27. Sanctions for non-compliance with rules and court orders

(1) The court shall disregard factual allegations, modifications of claims and defences, and offers of evidence that are introduced later than permitted by these rules or by court orders, including those concerning amendment. Preclusion does not apply if the court could have taken notice of the party's failure or mistake and itself failed to raise with the parties whether they wished to seek an amendment or relief from sanction.

(2) As a general rule, the court may continue the proceedings and decide on the merits based on the facts and evidence available to it.

(3) The court may draw negative factual inferences, order a party or their lawyer to bear the costs of non-compliance, or in serious cases of non-compliance render an *astreinte*, an order for payment of a fine, administrative sanction as provided by national law, or hold the non-compliant party in contempt.

(4) In assessing the nature of any compensation or fine under this rule, the court may require payment on the following bases: a lump sum; an amount per period of breach; or, an amount per offence. In the latter two cases the amount may be subject to a maximum as determined by the court.

Rule 28. Relief from the consequences of procedural non-compliance

Where a sanction for non-compliance with a rule or court order has been imposed, the subject of the sanction may apply for relief from that sanction. In considering whether, on application by a party, to exercise its discretion to grant relief the court must take account of the need for proceedings to be conducted consistently with the principles of co-operation and proportionality.

Part II – Parties

Section 1 – General Part

Rule 29. The parties to proceedings

(1) Parties to civil proceedings are all the persons by and against whom the proceedings are brought.

(2) Anyone who has the capacity to hold a right under substantive law may be a party to civil proceedings.

Rule 30. Litigation capacity of natural persons

(1) Litigation capacity is the capacity to exercise rights in civil proceedings.
(2) Anyone who has the capacity to exercise rights or obligations in their own name under the substantive law shall be deemed to have litigation capacity.
(3) Anyone not within the scope of Rule 30(2) must be represented in proceedings by a representative according to the rules of the applicable law.

Rule 31. Representation of legal persons and other entities

Legal persons and other entities that are parties must exercise their rights through natural persons who are entitled to represent them according to the substantive law.

Rule 32. Proof of representation

The court may, at any time in the proceedings, order the representative to prove the existence or scope of their power to act.

Rule 33. Court review of its own motion (*ex officio* review)

The Court shall at all times ensure compliance with Rules 29 to 31 and make any appropriate order.

Rule 34. Persons entitled to bring proceedings

Persons with litigation capacity must bring proceedings in their own name and on the basis of their own substantive rights unless either these Rules or substantive law otherwise permit.

Rule 35. Public interest

A person who is authorised by law to act in the public interest, may act as a party or intervene in any proceedings.

Section 2 – Special Part

A Multiple Parties

1 *Joinder of Parties*

Rule 36. Voluntary joinder of parties

(1) Multiple parties may bring or defend claims in a single proceeding. They may do so if
   (a) their claims are closely connected, and
   (b) the court has jurisdiction with respect to all parties.
(2) The court may, where it is necessary for the purpose of properly managing the proceedings, order the claims to continue as separate proceedings.

(3) Each of the joined parties acts on their own account. Their actions or omissions in the proceedings shall not prejudice the other joined parties.

Rule 37. Consolidation of separate proceedings
The court may order the consolidation of separate proceedings pending before it to enable them to be managed properly in a single proceeding.

Rule 38. Necessary joinder of parties

(1) A proceeding must be brought by or against parties jointly where either the joint nature of the legal right or the substantive law requires a judgment to bind all of the joined parties in the same terms.

(2) A procedural act carried out by one or more of the joined parties shall affect all such parties.

(3) In the case of settlement, waiver of claim, or an admission, all the joined parties must consent to be bound by the act.

2 *Intervention and Third Parties*

Rule 39. Principal intervention
Anyone not a party to proceedings who claims a right in its subject matter, may bring a claim directly against one or more of the parties in the court, in which the dispute is pending at first instance or, if the Court so permits, on appeal.

Rule 40. Voluntary intervention in support of a party

(1) Anyone who has a legitimate interest in one or more parties succeeding in proceedings may intervene in support of their claim or defence. They may intervene at any time before the final hearing is concluded.

(2) The intervenor in support of a party may not object to any procedural step already taken in the proceeding. Intervenors may, however, take any procedural step that the party they support may take if this is not in conflict with any procedural step taken by that party.

Rule 41. Notice by voluntary intervenors

(1) Anyone seeking to participate in proceedings as an intervenor under the preceding Rules must make an application to the court. The application must state the basis on which intervention is sought. Notice of the application shall be given to the parties.

(2) The parties shall be heard concerning the proposed intervention. The court may order the applicant and the parties to attend an oral hearing.

(3) An application to intervene does not suspend the proceedings unless the court orders otherwise.

Rule 42. Third-party notice

(1) A party may give any person notice of the dispute if, in the event of that party's claim or defence being unsuccessful, they might have a claim against or be subject to a claim by that person.

(2) A person given notice under Rule 42(1) becomes a party to the proceedings unless the court, upon application, orders otherwise.

(3) The third-party notice must state the matter at issue and the reason why they have been given such notice.

Rule 43. *Amicus curiæ*

(1) Any natural or legal person, or other entity, may provide the court with submissions concerning important issues in proceedings with the consent of the court. The court may also invite such submissions.

(2) Before giving its consent, or inviting submissions, under Rule 42(1) the court must consult the parties.

B Substitution and Succession of Parties

Rule 44. Substitution and succession

(1) At any time after proceedings are commenced the court must permit the substitution or the succession of a party by another person where the law requires it.

(2) At any time after proceedings are commenced the court may permit the substitution or the succession of a party by another person if that is appropriate in the interest of the good administration of justice.

(3) Unless the court orders otherwise, the proceedings continue upon substitution or succession of a party from the position they had reached at the time substitution or succession was effected.

Section 3 – Cross-Border Issues

Rule 45. Capacity of foreign nationals to be a party

The capacity of foreign nationals or legal persons incorporated outside the forum State shall be assessed for foreign nationals according to the law of the country of their habitual residence or their citizenship, and for legal persons according to the law of the State of their incorporation.

Rule 46. Litigation capacity

(1) A non-resident's litigation capacity shall be assessed according to the law of their habitual residence or their citizenship.

(2) A non-resident who lacks capacity to conduct litigation under the law of their habitual residence or citizenship but has such capacity under the law of the forum State may take procedural steps in proceedings on their own behalf.

(3) A legal person, incorporated outside the forum State, shall have its litigation capacity assessed according to the law of the place of incorporation.

Part III – Case Management

Rule 47. Careful conduct of litigation by the parties

Parties must present their claims, defences, factual allegations and offers of evidence as early and completely as possible and as appropriate to the careful conduct of litigation in order to secure procedural expedition.

Rule 48. Court control of proceedings

At all stages of the proceedings the court must monitor whether parties and their lawyers comply with Rule 47 and any order made under Rule 49.

Rule 49. Means of case management

Where necessary for the proper management of proceedings, the court shall, in particular:

(1) encourage parties to take active steps to settle their dispute or parts of their dispute and, where appropriate, to use alternative dispute resolution methods;
(2) schedule case management conferences;
(3) determine the type and the form of the procedure;
(4) set a timetable or procedural calendar with deadlines for procedural steps to be taken by parties and/or their lawyers;
(5) limit the number and length of future submissions;
(6) determine the order in which issues should be tried and whether proceedings should be consolidated or separated;
(7) determine the separation of questions concerning jurisdiction, provisional measures and statutes of limitation for early decision upon special hearings;
(8) consider necessary amendments regarding the parties' proper representation, the consequences of changes related to the parties to litigation and the participation of third parties, intervenors, or other persons;
(9) consider amendments to the pleadings or offers of evidence in the light of the parties' contentions;
(10) require a party's appearance in person or require a party's representative, who should be fully informed of all matters relevant to the proceedings, to be present at a court hearing;
(11) address the availability, admissibility, form, disclosure and exchange of evidence and, if adequate to the state of proceedings,
 (a) determine the admissibility of evidence;
 (b) order the taking of evidence.

Rule 50. Case management orders

(1) The court may make any case management order on its own motion or on application of a party. When orders or decisions are made without prior consultation with the parties or on a without-notice (*ex parte*) basis, parties not previously heard may apply for the order or decision to be reconsidered at a hearing or on the basis of written submissions.

(2) If the parties agree on a case management measure the court shall not determine differently without good reason.
(3) The court may vary or revoke any case management order upon a party's or its own motion.

Part IV – Commencement of Proceedings

Section 1 – Pre-Commencement Procedural Duties

Rule 51. Duty to promote consensual resolution and effective management

(1) Before proceedings are issued, parties shall co-operate with each other in order to avoid unnecessary disputes and costs, to facilitate the early consensual resolution of their dispute and, where such a resolution is not possible, the proportionate management of future proceedings according to Rules 2–11 and 47–50.
(2) In order to further the general duty set out in Rule 51(1) parties may:
- (a) provide each other with concise details of their potential claims or defences;
- (b) clarify and, wherever possible, narrow the legal and factual issues in dispute; and
- (c) identify relevant evidence so as to facilitate effective and early assessment of the merits of their positions.

(3) Parties may also:
- (a) consider a possible timetable for proceedings;
- (b) estimate the potential cost of proceedings;
- (c) consider issues of limitation, jurisdiction, provisional measures, and of any other procedural matter.

Section 2 – Commencement and Pleadings

A Statement of Claim

Rule 52. Submission of the statement of claim

To commence proceedings the claimant must submit a statement of claim to the court, as provided in Rule 53. Notice shall be given as provided in Part VI.

Rule 53. Contents of the statement of claim

(1) The statement of claim must state, as a minimum, the designation of the specific court and of the parties, the relief sought and the grounds therefore.
(2) The statement of claim should:
- (a) state the relevant facts on which the claim is based in reasonable detail as to time, place, participants and events;
- (b) describe with sufficient specification the available means of evidence to be offered in support of factual allegations;

(c) refer to the legal grounds that support the claim, including foreign law, in a way that is sufficient to permit the court to determine the claim's legal validity;

(d) state the detailed remedy requested, including the monetary amount or the specified terms of any other remedy sought;

(e) allege compliance with any applicable condition precedent, according to applicable national law, to bringing the claim, such as parties having to engage in pre-commencement conciliation or mediation, or having to issue a formal demand concerning the subject matter of the dispute.

(3) If a claimant does not fully comply with the requirements of Rule 53(2), the court must invite the claimant to amend the statement of claim. If a claimant shows good cause why it is not possible to provide details of relevant facts or specify the means of evidence in their statement of claim but the statement of claim nevertheless demonstrates that there is plausible dispute on the merits, the court should give due regard to the possibility that relevant detailed facts will develop later in the course of the taking of evidence.

(4) Whenever possible, means of evidence on which a claimant relies, must be attached to the statement of claim, if feasible with a copy for the defendant and other parties.

(5) A claimant may apply, in their statement of claim, for access to evidence under the custody or control of a defendant or non-party and which are to be offered in support of the claimant's allegations.

(6) The claimant may respond in a statement of claim to the defendant's defence as known from any exchange of arguments before commencement of proceedings. In this case Rule 54 applies to this part of their statement of claim.

(7) If the claimant makes a third-party claim or cross-claim seeking relief from a third party or a co-claimant Rule 53 applies correspondingly.

Rule 54. Statement of defence and counterclaims

(1) A defendant must, within 30 consecutive days from the date of service of notice, respond to the claimant's statement of claim. In appropriate cases, the court may properly extend the time for answer by court order.

(2) Rule 53 concerning the details of statements of claims applies to the defendant's response.

(3) Any failure by a defendant, whether explicit or tacit to deny an allegation contained in the claimant's statement of claim may be considered an admission for the purpose of the proceeding and obviates proof thereof.

(4) A defendant must set out in their response to the claimant's statement of claim which allegations are admitted or contested. A contested allegation is one that is either denied, neither admitted nor denied, or for which an alternative statement of facts is alleged. Where the defendant can neither admit nor deny reasons must be given in the defence why that is the case.

(5) If a defendant relies on an affirmative defence, their response to the claimant's statement of claim must allege all facts sufficient to permit the court to determine the legal validity of the defence, and offer means of evidence in support of the factual allegations. Rules 53(2)(a)–(c), (3) and (4) applies. The claimant may answer affirmative defences.
(6) The defendant may state a counterclaim seeking relief from a claimant. The defendant may also state a claim against a co-defendant or a third party. Rule 53 applies. The parties so addressed must answer these claims as provided in the previous provisions.

Rule 55. Amendments to pleadings

(1) A party, upon showing good cause to the court and upon notice to other parties, has a right to amend its claims or defences when the amendment does not unreasonably delay the proceeding or otherwise result in injustice. In particular, amendments may be justified to take account of events occurring after those alleged in earlier pleadings, newly discovered facts or evidence that could not previously have been obtained through reasonable diligence, or new evidence obtained from the exchange of evidence.
(2) Permission to amend must be granted on such terms as are just, including, where necessary, adjournment or continuance, or compensation by an award of costs to another party.
(3) The amendment must be served on the opposing party who has 30 consecutive days in which to respond, or such time as the court may order.
(4) Any party may apply to the court for an order requiring another party to provide by amendment a more specific statement of that party's pleading on the ground that the challenged statement does not comply with the requirements of these Rules. Such a request temporarily suspends the duty to answer.

Rule 56. Withdrawal and admission of the claim

(1) With the defendant or defendants' consent, the claimant may terminate the proceeding or any part of it by complete or partial withdrawal of the claim without prejudice save as to costs. Unilateral withdrawal without prejudice is only permitted if made before the first hearing of the court. In any case the claimant shall bear the reasonable and adequate costs of other parties.
(2) A defendant may terminate the proceeding or any part of it by admission of the whole claim or a part of the claim. The claimant may thereafter file a request to obtain judgment.

B Joint Application for Party-Agreed-Proceedings

Rule 57. Contents of the joint application

(1) A joint application is a statement of claim in which parties jointly may submit to the court their agreement according to Rule 26, their respective claims and defences, the issues on which they disagree and which are to be determined by the court, and their respective arguments on those disputed issues.

(2) In order to be admissible, the joint application must contain:
- (a) the designation of the parties;
- (b) the designation of the court before which the proceedings are brought;
- (c) the relief sought, including the monetary amount or the specified terms of any other remedy sought; and
- (d) the relevant facts and the legal grounds, on which the action is based.

(3) A joint application must describe the available means of evidence to be offered in support of factual allegations. Whenever possible, such evidence must be attached to the application.

(4) It must be signed and dated by the parties.

Rule 58. Related agreements

In so far as procedural rules are subject to party disposition, parties may agree on any procedural matter, such as the jurisdiction of the court, provisional measures, and publicity of hearings (see Rule 26(3)).

Rule 59. Amendment

(1) Parties have a right to amend their joint application when the amendment does not unreasonably delay management of the proceedings. In particular, amendments may be justified in order to take account of events occurring after those alleged in earlier pleadings, or newly discovered facts or evidence that could not previously have been obtained through reasonable diligence.

(2) Amendments are only admissible upon agreement of the parties.

Rule 60. Termination of party-agreed-proceedings

Before party-agreed-proceedings are determined by the court, parties may terminate them or any part of them by complete or partial joint withdrawal.

Part V – Proceedings Preparatory to a Final Hearing

Rule 61. Case management hearings to prepare for the final hearing and determination

(1) To prepare for a final hearing, the court may hold an early case management hearing and if necessary further ones as the case progresses.

(2) Case management hearings may be held in person. If appropriate the court may proceed in written form or use any available electronic means of communication.

(3) In or immediately after a case management hearing, the court should, upon consultation with the parties: set a timetable or procedural calendar with

deadlines for parties to complete their procedural obligations; set the timetable for a final hearing; and, the possible date by which judgment will be given.
(4) Whenever appropriate, the court may provide parties with advice relevant to their preparation for the final hearing and judgment. Such advice should, in so far as possible, be given in the early case management hearing. Case management orders should be made in or immediately after the early case management hearing.

Rule 62. Means of case management during the pre-final hearing phase

(1) The court may use all the means of case management set out in Rules 49(1), (3)–(6).
(2) Appropriate measures for the disclosure of evidence and the taking of evidence before a final hearing are, particularly,
- (a) the production and mutual exchange of documents;
- (b) requests for written witness statements and their exchange;
- (c) the appointment of a court expert and expert conferences between a court-appointed expert and experts appointed by the parties, or between court-appointed experts;
- (d) requests for information from third parties, including public authorities;
- (e) personal inspection of evidence by the court.

Rule 63. The closing of preparatory proceedings

(1) As soon as the court is satisfied that both parties have had a reasonable opportunity to present their case during the preparatory proceedings and that it has had an opportunity to clarify issues and take any relevant evidence before the final hearing in accordance with Rule 62(2), it will close the proceedings and refer the case to the final hearing. Once the pre-final hearing phase of proceedings is closed, no further submissions, arguments or evidence are allowed, except as provided by Rule 63(2) and Rule 64(4).
(2) Only under very exceptional circumstances may the court, on its own motion (*ex officio*) or upon a party's well-founded application, permit further statements and submissions.

Rule 64. The final hearing

(1) In so far as practicable, the final hearing should be concentrated. A concentrated final hearing may be adapted to the use of electronic communication techniques.
(2) The final hearing must be before the judge or judges who are to give the final judgment.
(3) Ordinarily, the court should take oral evidence and evidence on those issues that are still matters of serious dispute between the parties.
(4) All relevant evidence not received by the court in the preparatory proceedings may be taken in the final hearing. New evidence not offered in the pleadings

or upon amendment in the preparatory stage may be admitted only if a party shows strong and overwhelming reasons for not having produced it earlier.

(5) The court must properly manage the final hearing according to Rules 48–49. In particular, it must

(a) determine the order in which issues shall be tried;

(b) require a party's appearance in person or require a party's representative, who should be fully-informed of all matters relevant to the proceedings, to be present at the hearing;

(c) order the taking of evidence.

(6) Documentary or other tangible evidence must have been disclosed to all other parties prior to the final hearing. Oral evidence may be taken only if notice has been given to all parties of the identity of the person to be examined and the substance of their intended evidence.

(7) Parties must have an opportunity to submit their final conclusions including statements on the results of evidence-taking.

Rule 65. Early final judgments

(1) The court, on its own motion or on the application of a party, may give an early final judgment upon simplified proceedings.

(2) In an early final judgment the court may

(a) determine that it lacks jurisdiction or competence to adjudicate the dispute or whether the claim is inadmissible due to a failure to comply with other procedural requirements; or

(b) give a final judgment or a judgment on part of the claim for relief by only deciding questions of law based on non-contested facts, or on the basis that there has been a failure by the parties to assert necessary and relevant facts timeously, or there has been a failure to proffer necessary means of evidence timeously; or

(c) give a judgment upon the withdrawal of a claim, whether that was permitted or consented to, or upon an admission by the defendant.

(3) Rules 61–64 and Part VIII of these Rules apply, as appropriate to an early final judgment.

Rule 66. Judgments on preliminary procedural issues or on legal issues on the merits

(1) The court on its own motion or on the application of a party may give a judgment

(a) deciding a preliminary procedural issue, or

(b) deciding a legal issue on the merits

(2) Rules 61–64 and Part VIII of these Rules apply, as appropriate to the issue to be determined under this Rule. Judgments on preliminary procedural requirements according to Rule 133 are subject to independent appeal.

Rule 67. Provisional measures and interim payment orders
The court may make any order for provisional measures according to Part x or for an interim payment as provided by Part x, Rules 199 and following.

Part vi – Service and Due Notice of Proceedings

Section 1 – General Part – Service, Due Notice and the Right to Be Heard

Rule 68. Service of documents and minimum content

(1) Statements of claim and any other procedural documents amending the relief sought or seeking new relief under Rule 55 should be served in accordance with Rules 74–78 and 80–81.

(2) The statement of claim or documents seeking to amend proceedings must comply with the requirements of Rules 53 and 55.

Rule 69. Information about the procedural steps necessary to contest the claim
The statement of claim must clearly state the following:

(a) the procedural requirements for contesting the claim, including where applicable: the time limit for contesting the claim; the time of any scheduled court hearing; the name and address of the court or other institution to which a response to the claim should be sent or before which to appear, and whether representation by a lawyer is mandatory; and

(b) the consequences of a failure to respond or to appear in court, in particular, where applicable, the possibility that a judgment may be entered against the defendant in default of responding to the claim and the liability for costs related to the court proceedings.

Rule 70. Where the defendant fails to enter an appearance
Where the defendant has not responded to the statement of claim or not appeared in court, default judgment shall only be given according to Rule 138(3).

Section 2 – Responsibility for and Methods of Service

A General Provisions

Rule 71. Responsibility for service

(1) Responsibility for service of documents lies with the court/parties.

(2) If responsibility lies with the court, upon application the court may entrust a party with service of documents if appropriate.

(3) Where responsibility lies with the parties the court retains supervisory control which may include the power to set aside service.

Rule 72. Applicability of rules

The following rules on service methods apply to the documents referred to in Rule 68 and to any other documents required to be served including court decisions.

Rule 73. Priority of methods guaranteeing receipt

Documents shall be served using a method that guarantees receipt (Rules 74–76). If such service is not possible, alternative service methods apply, as specified in Rule 78. Where the address for service is unknown or other methods of service have failed, methods of last resort, specified in Rule 80, may be used to effect service.

B Methods of Service

Rule 74. Service guaranteeing receipt

(1) Service guaranteeing receipt includes

(a) service by physical delivery attested to by an acknowledgement of receipt signed by the addressee or by a document signed by a court officer, bailiff, post officer or other competent person who effected the service stating that the addressee has accepted the document, and the date of the service;

(b) service via a designated electronic information system using appropriately high technical standards attested to by an acknowledgement of receipt that the system generates automatically where the addressee has a legal obligation to register with that system. Such an obligation shall be imposed on legal persons and on natural persons engaging in independent professional activities for disputes relating to their trade or profession;

(c) service by other electronic means if the addressee has previously and explicitly agreed to use this service method or is under a legal obligation to register an e-mail address for the purpose of service. Such service must be attested to by the addressee's acknowledgement of receipt, which must include the date of receipt, and which is returned by the addressee;

(d) postal service attested to by an acknowledgement of receipt, which must include the date of receipt, and which is signed and returned by the addressee.

(2) Where an acknowledgment of receipt, under Rule 74(1)(c) or (d), is not received within a designated time, service according to Rule 74(1)(a) or (b), if available, should be attempted before alternative service methods can be used.

Rule 75. Service on legal persons by physical delivery

If Rule 74(1)(a) or (d) applies, service on a statutory representative of a legal person can be effected at the business premises. Business premises include the principal place of business, the place of the legal person's statutory seat, the central administration, or a branch, agency or establishment if the dispute arises out of the activity of that branch, agency or establishment.

Rule 76. Service on representatives

(1) If a minor or a party that lacks legal capacity has a legal custodian or guardian, service on them is equivalent to service on the addressee.

(2) Service on a person nominated to receive service by the addressee is equivalent to service on the addressee.

Rule 77. Refusal to accept service

Service according to Rule 74(1)(a) also includes service attested to by a document signed by the competent person who effected the service and stating that the addressee refused to receive the document. The document must be deposited at a specified place for a certain period of time for the purpose of collection by the addressee who has been informed where and when to collect the document.

Rule 78. Alternative service methods

(1) If the addressee is not available for service according to Rule 74, the following alternative service methods effected by a court officer, bailiff, postal officer or other competent person are available

- (a) service at the addressee's home address on persons who are living in the same household as the addressee or are employed by the addressee, and who are able and willing to accept the document;
- (b) in the case of a self-employed addressee or a legal person, service at the addressee's business premises on persons who are employed by the addressee, and who are able and willing to accept the document;
- (c) depositing the document at a post office or with competent public authorities and placing written notification of that deposit in the addressee's mailbox. In such a case the notification must clearly identify the document as a court document, the date by which it must be collected, the place where it can be collected and the contact details of the relevant person effecting service. Service is only effected when the document is collected.

(2) Service according to Rule 78(1)(a) and(b) shall be attested to by:

- (a) a document signed by the competent person who effected service, indicating:
  - (i) the method of service used;
  - (ii) the date of service; and
  - (iii) the name of that person and their relationship to the addressee,

  or
- (b) an acknowledgement of receipt by the person served.

(3) Service according to Rule 78(1)(a) and (b) is not allowed if the recipient is the party opposing the addressee in the proceedings.

(4) Service according to Rule 78(1)(c) shall be attested to by:

- (a) a document signed by the competent person who effected service, indicating:

(i) the method of service used; and
(ii) the date of collection,

or

(b) an acknowledgement of receipt by the person served.

Rule 79. Service of documents during proceedings

(1) During proceedings, if a party is represented by a lawyer, service of documents may normally be effected on the lawyer or from lawyer-to-lawyer without Court intervention. Lawyers must provide an electronic address that can be used for service of documents.

(2) During proceedings, if a party is represented by a lawyer, they must notify the Court and any lawyer who represents other parties or intervenors of any change of postal or electronic address.

(3) During proceedings, parties must notify the court of any change of residence, of place of business or of their postal or electronic address.

Rule 80. Service methods of last resort

(1) If service by methods that guarantee receipt (Rules 74–77) or alternative service (Rule 78) is not possible because the addressee's address is unknown or service has otherwise failed, service of documents may be effected as follows:

(a) by publication of a notice to the addressee in a form provided for by law of the forum State, including publication in electronic registers accessible to the public, and

(b) by sending a notice to the addressee's last known address or e-mail address, if applicable.

(c) For the purpose of subparagraphs (a) and (b), notice means information which clearly states the character of the document to be served as a court document, the legal effect of the notification as effecting service, information as to where the addressee can collect the documents or copies thereof, and the date by which they have to be collected.

(2) The address is unknown if the Court or the party responsible for service has made every reasonable effort to discover the addressee's present address. Efforts to find the present address must be documented in the Court files.

(3) Service shall be deemed to be effected within two weeks after publication of the notice and after having sent the notice to the last known address or e-mail address, as applicable. If there is no last known address or e-mail address service shall be deemed to be effected within two weeks after publication of the notice.

Rule 81. Cure for defective service

If service of documents does not meet the requirements of Rules 74–79, such non-compliance will be cured if the addressee's conduct proves that they received the document to be served personally and in sufficient time for them to arrange their defence or in any other way respond as required by the nature of the document.

Section 3 – Cross-Border Issues

A In the European Union

Rule 82. Language requirements

(1) In the case of natural persons not engaging in independent professional activities the documents referred to in Rule 68 and the information referred to in Rule 69 must be in a language of the proceedings and, unless it is evident that the addressee understands the language of the forum, also in a language of the European Union Member State of the individual's habitual residence.
(2) In the case of legal persons the documents referred to in Rule 68 and the information referred to in Rule 69 must be in a language of the proceedings, and also the language of the legal person's principal place of business, its statutory seat or of the principal documents in the transaction.

Rule 83. Non-application of Rule 81

If service of documents does not comply with the language requirements of Rule 82, Rule 81 does not apply.

Rule 84. Modification of time periods

If the addressee is domiciled in a European Union Member State different from the forum State then the time periods provided in Rule 80(3) are four weeks instead of two weeks.

B Outside the European Union

Rule 85. General rule

The preceding rules also apply when the addressee has no domicile or habitual residence within the European Union, subject to Rule 86.

Rule 86. Relationship to the HCCH 1965 Service Convention

Where there is occasion to transmit a judicial or extra-judicial document for service outside the European Union, the application of the preceding rules is without prejudice to the application of the HCCH 1965 Service Convention.

Part VII – Access to Information and Evidence

Section 1 – General Part

A General Provisions on Evidence

Rule 87. Standard of proof

A contested issue of fact is proven when the court is reasonably convinced of its truth.

Rule 88. Matters not requiring positive evidence

(1) The following do not require positive evidence:

(a) admitted facts;

(b) uncontested facts;

(c) facts which are notorious to the court.

(2) The existence of facts can be presumed on the basis of other proven facts.

(3) When a party has possession or control of evidence concerning a relevant fact and that party, without justification, fails to produce it, the court may consider that relevant fact to be proven.

Rule 89. Relevance

(1) Relevant evidence is admissible.

(2) The court, whether of its own motion or on application by a party, shall exclude evidence that is irrelevant. Relevance is determined by the court by reference to the matters alleged in the parties' pleadings.

Rule 90. Illegally obtained evidence

(1) Except where Rule 90(2) applies, illegally obtained evidence must be excluded from the proceedings.

(2) Exceptionally, the court may admit illegally obtained evidence if it is the only way to establish the facts. In exercising its discretion to admit such evidence the court must take into account the behaviour of the other party or of non-parties and the gravity of the infringement.

Rule 91. Evidentiary privileges and immunities

(1) Effect should be given to privileges, immunities, and similar protections for all persons who are heard in order to provide information in a case or concerning the production of evidence or other information.

(2) In particular, evidence may not be elicited in violation of:

(a) the right of a spouse, partner equal to a spouse or close relative of a party to refuse testimony;

(b) the right of a person not to incriminate themselves;

(c) legal professional privilege, any other professional privilege, confidence, trade secrets and other similar interests as provided by law;

(d) confidentiality of communications in settlement negotiations unless the negotiations have occurred in a public hearing or overriding public interests so require;

(e) national security interests, State secrets or other equivalent public interest issues.

(3) The court should consider whether these protections justify a party's failure to disclose evidence or other information when deciding whether to draw adverse inferences or to impose sanctions.
(4) The court should recognise these protections when imposing sanctions on a party or non-party in order to compel disclosure of evidence or other information.
(5) A claim of privilege, immunity or other similar protection made with respect to a document shall describe it in sufficient detail to enable another party to challenge the claim.

B Management of Evidence

Rule 92. Management and presentation of evidence

(1) Whenever necessary and appropriate, the court must order the taking of relevant evidence offered by a party. Where the court makes such an order it may make case management orders concerning the sequence and timing of the production of evidence. The court may also make orders, where appropriate, concerning the form in which evidence will be produced. Rules 49(9) and (11), 50, 62, 64(3)–(6) and 107 apply.
(2) The court, while affording the parties an opportunity to respond, may suggest evidence not previously proposed by a party, which it considers may be relevant to an issue in dispute. If a party accepts such a suggestion, the court will order the taking of that evidence so that it may be offered in support of that party's contentions of fact and law.
(3) Exceptionally, the court may, while affording the parties an opportunity to respond, order the taking of evidence not previously proposed by a party.
(4) The court shall provide each party with a fair opportunity and adequate time to respond to evidence presented by another party or taken by the court.

Rule 93. Admission by a failure to challenge evidence

The court may take a party's unjustified failure to make a timely response to an opposing party's contention as a sufficient basis for considering that contention to be admitted or accepted. Before doing so the court must inform the party that it is considering drawing such a conclusion concerning the evidence and provide them with an opportunity to respond.

Rule 94. Early party identification of evidence

Parties must identify evidence which they intend to produce to support the factual allegations set out in their pleadings.

Rule 95. Notification of evidence

(1) Parties must make documentary or tangible evidence available to other parties.

(2) Parties may only propose witness evidence if notice is given to all other parties of the relevant witnesses' identity and the subject-matter of their proposed evidence.
(3) The court may direct that parties keep evidence of which they have been notified confidential.

Rule 96. Additional evidence after amendment
The court may, while affording the parties an opportunity to respond, permit or invite a party to clarify or amend their factual contentions and to offer additional evidence accordingly.

C Presentation and Evaluation of Evidence

Rule 97. Conduct of hearings where evidence is to be adduced
(1) Whenever appropriate, the court will hear and receive evidence directly at a hearing before the parties unless, exceptionally, it has authorised evidence to be taken by an individual authorised to act on its behalf or at another location.
(2) Any hearing where evidence is taken shall be video recorded, provided that the necessary technical equipment is available. The video recording must be kept under the court's direction.
(3) The taking of evidence, in hearings or in camera, can involve, where appropriate, the use of technology, such as videoconferencing or similar distance communication technologies.

Rule 98. Evaluation of evidence
The court will freely evaluate evidence.

Rule 99. Sanctions concerning evidence
The court, whether on its own motion or on application by a party, may impose sanctions under Rule 27 when:
(a) a person has unjustifiably failed to attend to give evidence or to answer proper questions, or to produce a document or other item of evidence;
(b) a person has otherwise obstructed the fair application of the rules concerning evidence.

Section 2 – Access to Evidence Orders

Rule 100. General framework
When making orders under the Rules in this Part the court will give effect to the following principles:
(a) as a general rule, each party should have access to all forms of relevant and non-privileged evidence;
(b) in response to a party's application, under Rule 101, seeking access to evidence, the court will, if the application is granted, direct the production of relevant, non-privileged, and sufficiently identified evidence held or controlled by

another party or, if necessary, by a non-party, even if such production might be adverse to that person's interests.

Rule 101. Application for access to evidence

(1) Subject to the considerations and procedure contained in these Rules, any claimant or defendant, or any prospective claimant who intends to commence proceedings, can apply to the court for an order securing access to relevant and non-privileged evidence held or controlled by other parties or non-parties.
(2) An application for an order securing access to evidence may include an application for the imposition of measures to protect or preserve evidence, including an application for provisional or protective measures under Part X.
(3) Material or information supplied under this rule only becomes evidence when it is formally introduced as such into the proceedings by a party or exceptionally by the court according to Rules 25(3), 92(2) and (3) and 107(2).

Rule 102. Relevant criteria where an application for access to evidence is made

(1) A party or prospective party applying for an order for access to evidence must

(a) identify, as accurately as possible in the light of the circumstances of the case, the specific sources of evidence to which access is sought, or alternatively

(b) identify closely defined categories of evidence by reference to their nature, content, or date.

(2) An application must satisfy the court of the plausibility of the merits of the applicant's claim or defence by demonstrating that

(a) the requested evidence is necessary for the proof or proposed proof of issues in dispute in proceedings or in contemplated proceedings;

(b) the applicant cannot otherwise gain access to this evidence without the court's assistance; and

(c) the nature and amount of evidence subject to the application is reasonable and proportionate. For this purpose the court will take into account the legitimate interests of all parties and all interested non-parties.

(3) If an application for access to evidence is made prior to the commencement of proceedings, the applicant must indicate with sufficient precision all elements necessary to enable the court to identify the claim for relief which the applicant intends to make.
(4) The court may not grant any application under this Rule which involves a vague, speculative, or unjustifiably wide-ranging search for information.

Rule 103. Confidential information

(1) The court shall consider whether an application under Rule 101 for access to evidence concerns or includes confidential information, especially in relation

to non-parties. In so doing, the court must have regard to all relevant rules concerning the protection of confidential information.

(2) Where necessary, in the light of the circumstances of the case, the court, amongst other things, may make an order for access to evidence containing confidential information adjusted in one or more of the following ways in order to protect the relevant interest in maintaining confidentiality

- (a) redacting relevant sensitive passages in documents;
- (b) conducting hearings *in camera*;
- (c) restricting the persons allowed to gain access to or inspect the proposed evidence;
- (d) instructing experts to produce a summary of the information in an aggregated or otherwise non-confidential form;
- (e) writing a non-confidential version of a judicial decision in which passages containing confidential data are deleted;
- (f) limiting access to certain sources of evidence to the representatives and lawyers of the parties and to experts who are subject to a duty of confidentiality.

Rule 104. Sanctions for breach of confidentiality

(1) If a person breaches any duty of confidentiality the aggrieved party may apply to the court for an order imposing one or more of the following sanctions

- (a) wholly or partially dismissing a party in breach's claim or defence, where the substantive proceedings are still pending;
- (b) declaring the party or other person in breach liable for damages and ordering payment of such compensation;
- (c) ordering the party in breach to pay the costs of the substantive proceedings irrespective of the outcome of those proceedings;
- (d) imposing on the party or the person in breach a fine appropriate to the breach;
- (e) imposing on the party's representative or representatives or the person in breach a fine appropriate to the breach.

(2) Any sanction imposed by the court under Rule 104(1) must be proportionate to the nature of the breach. In determining the proportionality of the sanction the court must take particular account of the fact that a breach occurred before proceedings on the merits were commenced, where that is the case.

Rule 105. Access to evidence held by public authorities

(1) Except where information is protected on public interest grounds, Government and other public agencies must comply with an order made under these Rules.

(2) Where a Government or public agency seeks to refuse access to evidence on public interest grounds, they must provide the court with a reasoned

explanation of the basis for their refusal and must satisfy the requirements set out in Rule 91(5).

Rule 106. Time of applications

(1) Applications for access to evidence may be made prior to the initiation of proceedings, in a statement of claim, or in pending proceedings.
(2) If an order has been made prior to the initiation of proceedings, where appropriate, the successful applicant may be required to initiate proceedings within a specified, reasonable, period of time. If the applicant fails to comply with this requirement the court may set aside the order, direct the return of any evidence supplied to the applicant further to the order, impose an appropriate sanction on the party in default, or make any other appropriate order.

Rule 107. The process for granting access orders

(1) The court shall determine an application for an order under Rule 101(1) for access to evidence according to Rule 50.
(2) Orders under Rule 101(1) may be made by the court on a without-notice basis in very exceptional cases only. Where it does so it must permit parties and affected non-parties to be heard at a with-notice hearing.
(3) If applications for access to evidence are made prior to the commencement of proceedings the court should ordinarily determine the application only after giving any affected party or non-party an opportunity to respond and make representations concerning the grant of the order, its scope and proposed implementation.
(4) The party or non-party from whom access to evidence is sought may apply for the grant of a different but no less effective form or method of access. Such an application must demonstrate that the proposed alternative will be less burdensome to the party to whom it is to provide access.

Rule 108. Costs and security

(1) The cost of implementing an order for access to evidence shall be borne by the applicant. Where appropriate the court may require the applicant to make an immediate payment of costs to a party or non-party against whom the order is made.
(2) The court may, upon the application of the person against whom an order for access to evidence is made, order security to be given by the party in whose favour the order is made. The order shall be for any predictable expense to be incurred in the implementation of that order. If security is required by the court, it must be provided before any order for access can be given effect.
(3) At the conclusion of the proceedings the court may determine the incidence of costs differently from the general rule.

Rule 109. Implementation

The court shall ensure that any such necessary and practical steps required to implement orders for access to evidence are implemented fairly and effectively. Such steps may include:

(a) issuing directions concerning the appropriate place and manner in which the order is to be carried out;

(b) directing that the applicant may be assisted by an expert; or

(c) by making any relevant order under Part X of these Rules.

Rule 110. Non-compliance with access orders

(1) The court may impose any one or more of the following sanctions upon any party or non-party who is subject to, and aware of, an order requiring the giving of access to evidence, and destroys or conceals such evidence, or otherwise renders it impossible to carry out the order successfully

(a) declaring as admitted the facts which form the subject-matter of the relevant order for access to sources of evidence;

(b) treating the defendant or prospective defendant as having impliedly conceded the basis or any relevant part of the claim which has been made or which was proposed by the applicant;

(c) imposing on the relevant respondent to the order (and in accordance with the relevant court's established disciplinary powers) an appropriate penalty per day of delay in implementing the order.

(2) An order made under Rule 110(1) must be proportionate to the nature of the non-compliance and may only be made on application of the party in whose favour the order requiring access to evidence was made.

(3) This Rule is without prejudice to any other sanctions or disciplinary procedural measures available to the court, including measures according to Rules 27 and 99.

Section 3 – Types of Evidence

A Documents

Rule 111. Documentary and electronic evidence

(1) Parties may offer any relevant document as evidence.

(2) Document means anything in which information is recorded or maintained in any form, including but not limited to paper or electronic form. Information may be recorded in writing, pictures, drawings, programmes, voice messages, or electronic data, including e-mail, social media, text or instant messages, metadata, or other technological means. It may be maintained electronically on, but not limited to, computer, portable electronic devices, cloud-based or other storage media.

(3) Documents that a party maintains in electronic form must ordinarily be submitted or produced in electronic form, unless the court orders otherwise.

(4) Parties may challenge the authenticity of any document submitted as evidence. In such a case, the court must order the parties to take such steps as are necessary to establish the document's authenticity.

Rule 112. Authentic instruments

(1) An authentic instrument is a document, which has either been formally drawn up or the authenticity of which has been certified by a public authority.
(2) Electronically recorded authentic instruments have the same probative force as those recorded on paper.

Rule 113. Documents: language and translation

(1) On the application of a party or on the court's own motion, any document shall be produced in or translated into a language of the court.
(2) Translation of lengthy or voluminous documents may be limited according to Rule 20(2).

B Testimonial Evidence

Rule 114. Witnesses of fact

(1) Subject to considerations of relevance, admissibility, case management and privilege or immunity, a party may present the evidence of any witness of fact.
(2) If a witness whose evidence satisfies the requirements of Rule 114(1) refuses to give evidence, whether in whole or in part, they can be ordered to do so by the court.
(3) A witness is under an obligation to tell the truth while giving their evidence. The court may require a witness to give their evidence under oath. The court may instruct the witness accordingly prior to the examination.

Rule 115. Witness evidence

(1) Ordinarily, witness evidence should be received orally. The court may, however and upon having received submissions from the parties on the issue, require that such evidence be given initially in writing. Such written evidence must be supplied to all other the parties in advance of the hearing where the witness is to give oral evidence. Oral evidence at a hearing may be limited to supplemental questioning following the presentation of a witness's written evidence.
(2) Each witness shall appear in person unless the court allows the use of video-conferencing or of similar technology with respect to that witness.
(3) A person giving evidence may be questioned first by the court or the party adducing their evidence. Where a witness has first been questioned by the court or by party other than the one adducing their evidence, that party must be given the opportunity to put supplemental questions directly to the witness.
(4) Parties may challenge the reliability of witness evidence.

Rule 116. Witnesses: language and translation

(1) Where a witness is not competent in an official language in which the proceeding is being, or may be, conducted interpretation or translation must be provided by the court.

(2) Where appropriate, and with the court's and parties' consent, a witness may testify in a language other than the official language of proceedings.

Rule 117. Witness statements

(1) A party may, with the court's consent, present a written statement of sworn testimony from any person. Such a statement must be in their own words and contain their testimony about relevant facts.

(2) The court, in its discretion, may consider such written statements as if they were made by oral testimony at a hearing before the court.

(3) A party may apply for an order requiring the personal appearance of the author of such a written statement before the court. Where such an order is made, the witness may be examined by way of supplemental questioning by the court or the opposing party.

C Examination of Parties

Rule 118. Examination of parties and consequences of refusal to respond

(1) The court may accord evidentiary effect to any statement made by a party that has been questioned before the court. Rule 114(3) applies correspondingly.

(2) Each party shall be given an opportunity to question their opponent in front of the court on relevant issues of fact.

(3) The court can draw relevant inferences if a party unjustifiably refuses to appear at a hearing or to answer any relevant question put to them by their opponent or by the court or refuses to swear an oath.

(4) If the party to be questioned is a legal person, it shall provide the identity of the natural person or persons who participated directly in the relevant course of events on its behalf, in order for them to be questioned, provided they can still be considered as a representative of that legal person. The court may draw relevant inferences if a legal person fails, without justification, to provide this information.

D Expert Evidence

Rule 119. Party-appointed experts

Parties may present expert evidence on any relevant issue for which such evidence is appropriate. They may do so through an expert of their choice.

Rule 120. Court-appointed experts

(1) The court may appoint one or more experts to give evidence on any relevant issue for which expert evidence is appropriate, including foreign law.

(2) Experts can be individuals or legal entities. In the case of legal entities at least one individual must assume responsibility for the expert's report.

(3) If the parties agree upon an expert, the court ordinarily should appoint that expert.

(4) Parties may object to the appointment of a court-appointed expert on grounds of bias. Where there is a reasonable apprehension of bias, the court must either, as relevant, refuse to appoint the expert, rescind their appointment or set aside their evidence in its entirety.

Rule 121. Instructions to court-appointed experts

(1) The court shall instruct experts concerning the issues on which they are to provide evidence. It should set reasonable time limits within which any such expert should submit their written report or reports.

(2) In an appropriate case, the court may extend or limit the scope of its instructions to an expert. It may also vary any time limit for submission by an expert of their report.

(3) The court must inform the parties of any orders given or varied under this Rule.

(4) Where a party objects to the nature or scope of instructions given by the court to an expert, it may apply to the court to vary those instructions.

Rule 122. Duties of experts

(1) An expert, whether appointed by the court or by a party, owes a duty to the court to present a full, objective and impartial assessment of the issue addressed.

(2) No expert may give evidence outside their field of expertise. An expert may also refuse to give evidence for the same reasons a witness may refuse to give evidence.

(3) An expert must not delegate their task to third parties unless authorised to do so by the court.

(4) Where an expert, without a reasonable explanation, fails to render their evidence within time limits set by the court, the court may impose appropriate sanctions.

Rule 123. Expert access to information

(1) Court-appointed experts should be provided with access to all relevant and non-privileged information necessary to enable them to prepare their written report.

(2) In particular, a court-appointed expert may ask a party to provide any information, to provide access to any documents, permit inspection of property or entry upon land for the purposes of inspection, to the extent that such are relevant and material to the proceedings.

(3) In appropriate circumstances, an expert may examine a person or have access to information derived from a physical or mental examination of that person.

Rule 124. Expert reports and oral evidence

(1) Expert evidence should ordinarily be given in the form of a written report. However, in simple cases, the court may order that expert evidence be given orally.

(2) An expert may give oral testimony to explain their written report either on the court's request or on the application of any party. Subject to any applicable legal provisions, such oral testimony may be given at a hearing or via any appropriate means of distance communication, such as, but not limited to, videoconferencing.

(3) The court may require an expert to give their evidence, whether that is in the form of a written report or by way of oral testimony, on oath.

(4) Where an expert gives oral testimony, parties may only ask the expert questions that are relevant to their report.

(5) If a party-appointed expert fails to appear when duly summoned to attend an oral hearing, and does so without a valid reason, the court may disregard that expert's written report.

Rule 125. Costs

(1) The fees and expenses of a court-appointed expert shall form part of the costs of the proceedings. The court may order that a party who applies for an expert to be appointed pay their fees in advance.

(2) The fees and expenses of a party-appointed expert shall only be recoverable from the other party if the court so orders.

E Judicial Inspection

Rule 126. Judicial inspection in general

(1) A party may apply for an order permitting the examination of persons or things. To facilitate such an examination the court may authorise access to evidence, including access to land or private premises. To ensure the adequacy of inspection, access may be subject to such conditions as the court considers just with regard to the special circumstances of the case and in accordance with applicable law.

(2) A party may apply for permission to carry out a physical or mental examination of a person. The court, in consultation with the parties, shall determine the timing and arrangements for such an examination.

(3) The court may inspect or require the inspection of evidence by a court-appointed or party-appointed expert, as it deems appropriate.

(4) Parties and their representatives may attend an inspection or examination ordered under this Rule, unless the court provides otherwise.

(5) In this Rule and in Rule 127(1), 'things' refers to any physical or electronic item, movable or immovable elements of such items.

Rule 127. Non-parties and judicial inspection

(1) The court may order non-parties to produce things for inspection by the court or a party.

(2) The provisions set in Section 2 of Part VII of these Rules apply to any order to be made or made under Rule 127(1).

Section 4 – Cross-Border Issues

A In the European Union

Rule 128. Cross-border evidence-taking within the European Union

(1) When evidence has to be taken in another European Union Member State and when access is needed to evidence located in another Member State, the court and the parties may rely on the provisions of Council Regulation (EC) No 1206/2001 of 28 May 2001 on cooperation between the courts of the Member States in the taking of evidence in civil or commercial matters.

(2) Without prejudice to the application of Council Regulation (EC) No 1206/2001 of 28 May 2001 on cooperation between the courts of the Member States in the taking of evidence in civil or commercial matters,

(a) the court may directly summon a witness residing in another Member State;

(b) the court may appoint an expert to submit a report, the preparation of which requires the undertaking of activities (inspection of persons or premises located) in another Member State;

(c) a party or non-party, to whom an order for access to evidence is addressed, and who is residing or domiciled in the Member State of the court, is under a duty to produce the required documents and evidence, even if they are located in a Member State different to the one of the court issuing the order;

(d) a court may address an order for access to evidence to prospective parties and to non-parties domiciled in another Member State.

B Outside the European Union

Rule 129. Cross-border evidence taking of outside the European Union

When evidence needs to be taken outside the European Union or when the addressee of an order for access to evidence has no domicile or habitual residence within the European Union, the court and the parties may rely on the provisions of the Convention on the Taking of Evidence Abroad in Civil or Commercial Matters (Hague Evidence Convention of 18 March 1970) or of other relevant international conventions.

Part VIII – Judgment, *Res Judicata* and *Lis Pendens*

Section 1 – General Part

Rule 130. Types of judgment

(1) The court may give

(a) a final judgment, which is a judgment deciding the whole of a claim for relief;

(b) a judgment deciding part of a claim for relief (a partial judgment);

(c) where more than one claim for relief is made, a final judgment deciding one or more, but not all, of the claims for relief;

(d) a judgment on preliminary procedural issues or on specific legal issues on the merits (see Rule 66);

(e) a judgment in default.

(2) Where the court gives a judgment that does not decide the whole of a claim for relief, the proceedings continue in respect of such parts for which judgment has not been given. If the court's judgment on a part of the claim for relief, on a procedural issue, or on legal issues on the merits is subject to appeal the court may exercise its discretion whether to continue or stay the proceedings according to the circumstances of the case.

Rule 131. Structure of a judgment

A judgment must contain

(a) the court's designation and composition;

(b) the place and date of the judgment;

(c) the names of the parties and, if applicable, of their lawyers;

(d) the relief claimed;

(e) the order of the court;

(f) the legal and factual grounds for the judgment;

(g) the signature of the judge or judges, if necessary;

(h) the signature of the court clerk, if necessary; and

(i) where relevant, information on formal requirements of any available means to challenge the decision.

Rule 132. Contents of judgments

(1) A judgment, depending on the nature of the relief claimed, may

(a) order a defendant to do or not to do something,

(b) create, alter or terminate a legal relationship,

(c) make a declaration of rights, or

(d) dismiss the claim for relief either on procedural grounds or where it determines it to be without merit.

(2) The court may only grant a declaratory judgment, including a negative declaratory judgment, if the claimant can establish that they have a legitimate interest in obtaining the declaration sought.

Rule 133. Procedural requirements of judgments on the merits

The court may only give a judgment on the merits when it is satisfied that

(a) the parties have litigation capacity according to Rules 29(2)–31, 34, 35, and 45–46;

(b) the court has subject matter and territorial jurisdiction;

(c) there are no pending proceedings involving the same parties and the same cause of action in another court unless an exception provided for in the Rules on *lis pendens* applies;

(d) the cause of action between the parties is not *res judicata*;

(e) the claimant has a legitimate interest to commence the proceedings on its claim for relief; and

(f) any other procedural requirement specified in these Rules is met.

Rule 134. Service of judgment

A judgment must be served on all parties by a method provided for in Part VI of these Rules.

Section 2 – Special Part

A Default Judgment

Rule 135. Entry of default judgment against a claimant

(1) The court must enter a default judgment dismissing proceedings where

- (a) a claimant has failed to appear at a hearing at which they were required to appear; and
- (b) a defendant has applied for default judgment to be entered.

(2) The court may not enter default judgment under this Rule on its own motion.

Rule 136. Entry of default judgment against a defendant

(1) The court must enter a default judgment against a defendant, where the defendant has

- (a) failed to reply to a statement of claim within the time limit for filing a defence, or
- (b) failed to appear at a hearing at which they were required to appear; and
- (c) a claimant has applied for default judgment to be entered.

(2) A court entering judgment on the application of a claimant shall

- (a) where the facts submitted by the claimant justify it on the merits, grant the relief sought, or
- (b) where the facts submitted by the claimant do not justify the grant of relief, dismiss the proceedings on the merits.

Rule 137. Default judgments on a part of a claim for relief or on one of several claims for relief

(1) The court may enter a default judgment on part of a claim for relief or on one of several claims for relief where

- (a) a party fails to appear at a hearing that is dedicated exclusively to that part of the claim, or to one of several claims, for relief, or
- (b) a defendant fails to reply to the statement of claim in respect of that part of the claim, or to one of several claims, for relief.

(2) Where the court is able to give, but has not yet given, judgment under Rule 130 on part of a claim for relief or on one of several claims for relief, and a party is in default, the court must

- (a) enter judgment on that part of a claim for relief or on one of several claims for relief, and
- (b) enter a default judgment in respect of the other part or parts of the claim for relief or other claims for relief.

Rule 138. Conditions precedent for granting a default judgment

(1) The Court may enter a default judgment on the basis of a party's failure to appear at a hearing only if

- (a) notice of the date and time of the hearing was served on that party by a method provided for by these Rules, and
- (b) the Court is satisfied that the period between service and the hearing was adequate.

(2) The Court may only enter a default judgment against a defendant for failing to reply to a statement of claim if

- (a) the statement of claim was served on the defendant by a method provided for by these Rules,
- (b) the time limit for filing a defence has expired, and
- (c) where no time limit was prescribed by the rules, service was effected in sufficient time to enable the defendant to arrange their defence.

(3) The court may enter a default judgment against a defendant even if no receipt of service has been submitted to the court if

- (a) no proof of any other kind has been received although reasonable efforts have been made to obtain evidence that the defendant actually received the documents instituting the proceedings, and
- (b) a period of time not less than three months, which is considered to be adequate by the court to enable the defendant to arrange their defence has elapsed since the date of service by a method provided for by these Rules.

(4) Notwithstanding Rules 138(3)(a) and (b), the court may grant, in case of urgency, any provisional or protective measures.

Rule 139. Application to set aside a default judgment

The party against whom a default judgment has been entered may apply to have the judgment set aside on the basis that

(a) any of the conditions precedent for entry of the default judgment were not met, or

(b) the party against whom the default judgment was entered was either not responsible for the default or the default was excusable.

Rule 140. Time limit to apply to set aside a default judgment

(1) An application to set aside must be made within 30 days of the date of service of the default judgment. In cross-border cases, the application must be made within 60 days of the date of the service of the default judgment.

(2) The court may extend the time limit under Rule 140(1) where the defendant can show good reason for their non-compliance. No application to set aside can, however, be brought more than one year and, in cross-border cases, two years after the default judgment was entered.

B Judicial Settlements

Rule 141. Judicial settlements

(1) When parties reach a consensual settlement of their dispute, either before or after proceedings have commenced or during proceedings, they may apply to the court to enter a decision giving effect to the agreement.

(2) A decision giving effect to the agreement shall not be entered if it is contrary to law or the court would not have the power to enter a judgment in the terms of the parties' agreement.

(3) If the court refuses to give effect to the settlement, any party to it can appeal from the refusal. The rules applicable to first appeals apply to such an appeal (See Part XI, Section 2).

Section 3 – Effects of Pendency and Judgments

A *Lis Pendens* and Related Actions

Rule 142. Pendency

(1) Where proceedings involving the same cause of action and between the same parties are brought in different courts, any court other than the court first seised shall of its own motion stay its proceedings until such time as the jurisdiction of the court first seised is established (the priority principle).

(2) Where Rule 142(1) applies, the court seised of the dispute may request any other court seised to provide it with information about the proceedings pending before it and the date on which it was seised in accordance with Rule 145. The court providing the information shall provide it the requesting court without delay.

(3) Where the jurisdiction of the court first seised is established, the court shall order parallel proceedings to be consolidated in accordance with Rule 146. Where proceedings have been consolidated, any court other than the court first

seised shall decline its jurisdiction in favour of that court. When the requirements for consolidation are not met any court other than the court first seised shall, as appropriate, stay or dismiss the proceedings.

Rule 143. Exceptions from the priority principle

(1) When the court second seised has exclusive jurisdiction, the court first seised must decline jurisdiction in favour of that court. In such a case the court that has exclusive jurisdiction must not stay its proceedings.

(2) Rule 143(1) does not apply when both courts have exclusive jurisdiction.

(3) Without prejudice to Rules protecting weaker parties and without prejudice to jurisdiction by appearance, where a court upon which an agreement confers exclusive jurisdiction is seised, any other court must stay proceedings until such time as the court seised on the basis of the agreement declares that it has no jurisdiction under it.

(4) Where the court designated in the agreement has established jurisdiction in accordance with the agreement, any other court shall decline jurisdiction in favour of that court.

Rule 144. Related proceedings

(1) Where related proceedings are pending in different courts, any court other than the court first seised may stay its proceedings.

(2) Where the proceeding in the court first seised is pending at first instance, any other court must also decline jurisdiction if the court first seised has consolidated proceedings according to Rule 146.

(3) For the purposes of this Rule, proceedings are deemed to be related where there is a relationship between the causes of action such that it would be in the interests of justice to determine them together.

Rule 145. Time at which a court is seised for the purposes of pendency and relatedness

(1) The court is deemed to be seised:

- (a) at the time when the statement of claim or an equivalent document is filed with the court, provided that the claimant has not subsequently failed to effect service on the defendant according to these Rules, or
- (b) if the statement of claim or an equivalent document has to be served before being filed with the court, at the time when it is received by an authority responsible for service, provided that the claimant has not subsequently failed to take steps required to file it with the court.

The authority responsible for service referred to Rule 145(1)(b) is the first authority that receives the documents to be served.

(2) Where a statement of claim is filed during proceedings it becomes pending at the time when it is invoked in the hearing or when it has been filed with the court or served on the other party.

(3) The court, or the authority responsible for service, referred to in Rule 145(1), shall note, respectively, the date the statement of claim or the equivalent document is filed, or the date of receipt of the documents to be served.

Rule 146. Consolidation of proceedings

(1) Where the jurisdiction of the court first seised is established, it may, upon application of one of the parties, order the consolidation of several sets of proceedings under Rules 142 and 144.

(2) The court first seised may only consolidate proceedings when it has jurisdiction to hear them and when such parallel proceedings are pending at the first instance.

(3) Before ordering consolidation the court shall hear the parties and communicate with any other courts seised.

(4) When the court first seised has assumed jurisdiction over the proceedings and has consolidated them, any other court must decline jurisdiction.

(5) Consolidation does not prejudice any procedural or substantive consequences of the filing or pendency of parallel proceedings.

(6) When consolidation is not possible in the court first seised, the court second seised may, on application of any party, consolidate the proceedings, as appropriate, under Rules 146(1)–(5).

B *Res Judicata*

Rule 147. Types of judgment that become *res judicata*

(1) Final judgments, including partial judgments, default judgments, and judgments that decide procedural issues or issues on the merits are *res judicata.*

(2) Provisional measures do not have *res judicata* effects on the merits of the issues in dispute in proceedings.

Rule 148. Judgments that are *res judicata*

A judgment is *res judicata* when ordinary means of recourse are not or are no longer available.

Rule 149. Material scope of *res judicata*

(1) The material scope of *res judicata* is determined by reference to the claims for relief in the parties' pleadings, including amendments, as decided by the court's judgment.

(2) *Res judicata* also covers necessary and incidental legal issues that are explicitly decided in a judgment where parties to subsequent proceedings are the same as those in the proceedings determined by the prior judgment and where the court that gave that judgment could decide those legal issues.

(3) *Res judicata* also applies where a defendant brings a defence based on set-off and

- (a) the claim and that defence are upheld by the court, or
- (b) the claim is admitted and the defence of set-off is rejected.

(4) Where a claim is rejected on grounds other than set-off, so that the court does not decide the set-off defence, only the judgment on the claim becomes *res judicata.*

Rule 150. Modification of judgments requiring periodical performance

(1) Where a judgment that has become *res judicata* requires periodic performance, on application by a party, the court may vary the judgment prospectively.
(2) A judgment may only be varied under this Rule where there is a substantial change of circumstances.

Rule 151. Persons bound by *res judicata*

Only parties to proceedings, the heirs and successors are bound by those parts of a judgment that are *res judicata.*

Rule 152. Court assessment of *res judicata* of its own motion (*ex officio*)

The court shall take *res judicata* into account of its own motion.

Part IX – Means of Review

Section 1 – General Part

Rule 153. Right of appeal or to seek recourse

Where a party, or exceptionally a non-party, has a legal interest in a judgment, subject to the provisions in this Part, they may appeal from, or rely on other types of recourse against, it.

Rule 154. Waiver of right to appeal or to seek recourse

(1) A party may waive their right of appeal or to seek recourse. Waiver must be informed and express. Waiver may be given to the court in writing before or during a court hearing, or given orally in a court hearing.
(2) Waiver may be effected before a first instance judgment or other decision or a first appeal judgment is made. Such a waiver may only be made where it is agreed by all the parties.
(3) Where a party is bringing or defending proceedings as a consumer, they cannot waive their right to appeal before judgment has been made.
(4) All waivers must be recorded by the court in a judgment or other official record, if any.

Section 2 – Appeals

Rule 155. Notice of appeal – General

(1) An appeal is commenced by way of filing a notice of appeal with the relevant court of Appeal.

(2) Upon being filed with the court, notice of appeal must be served on the respondent, in accordance with Part VI of these Rules.

Rule 156. Time limits for appeals

(1) For a first appeal, the notice must be filed with the court within one month of service of the judgment.

(2) For a second appeal, the notice must be filed with the court within two months of service of the judgment.

Rule 157. Contents of the notice of and reasons for appeal – First appeal

(1) A notice of appeal for a first appeal must state that an appeal is being commenced and must identify the judgment subject to the appeal. It may also provide reasons for the appeal. Reasons for the appeal if not set out in the notice of appeal should be set out in a separate document.

(2) The reasons for the appeal must specify

- (a) the relief sought;
- (b) the legal arguments, substantive and procedural, on which the appeal is based in respect of both its admissibility and substance;
- (c) if applicable, the grounds for which any evaluation of evidence was seriously wrong; and
- (d) if applicable, any new facts to be alleged and new means of evidence that will be introduced in the appeal, and the reasons why they ought to be admitted.

(3) Where reasons for the appeal are set out in a separate document from the notice of appeal they must be served within two months of service of the judgment, unless the court orders otherwise.

Rule 158. Contents of the notice of and reasons for appeal – Second appeal

(1) A notice of appeal for a second appeal must state that an appeal is being commenced and must identify the judgment subject to the appeal. It must also provide the reasons for the appeal.

(2) The reasons for the second appeal must contain:

- (a) the relief sought;
- (b) the legal arguments, procedural and substantive, on which the second appeal is based.

Rule 159. Response to the notice of appeal – General

(1) The respondent to an appeal must file with the court and serve on the appellant a reply to the notice of appeal (the reply) within two months of service of the notice of appeal, unless the court orders otherwise.

(2) The appellant must respond to the reply within two weeks of service, unless the court orders otherwise.

Rule 160. Contents of a respondent's reply

A reply may contain the following

(a) reasons why the appeal court should uphold the judgment subject to appeal; or

(b) notice of and reasons for appeal from the judgment subject to appeal, which seek to uphold the judgment for different reasons to those given in the judgment. Rule 157(2) and Rule 158(2) apply according to whether the reply concerns a first or second appeal.

Rule 161. Derivative appeals

(1) A party that has lost their right of appeal due to the expiry of the time limit for filing a notice of appeal in Rule 156(2), may appeal if another party (the appellant) appeals from the judgment.

(2) The party bringing a derivative appeal (a derivative appellant) must serve a Notice of Appeal. Rules 156–159 apply accordingly.

(3) A derivative appeal lapses if the appellant's appeal is not heard on its merits.

(4) A respondent to a derivative appeal must file a response to it. Rules 159-160 apply accordingly.

Rule 162. Provisional enforcement

(1) Unless otherwise provided for, final judgment and any appellate court judgments are enforceable immediately regardless of whether an appeal has been commenced by filing a notice of appeal.

(2) An appellant may apply to the appellate court to stay enforcement if they have filed a notice of appeal and enforcement is manifestly excessive.

(3) Security may be required from an appellant as a condition of granting a stay or from a respondent as a condition of refusing to grant a stay.

Rule 163. Withdrawal

(1) A party that has commenced a first appeal can withdraw their appeal at any time.

(2) A second appeal can only be withdrawn by a party with the consent of the other party and the court.

(3) A party that withdraws an appeal must bear the costs, including any court fees, incurred by other parties because of the appeal.

Rule 164. Representation in an appeal court

(1) If representation is not mandatory according to applicable law, a first appeal court may require a party to be represented by a lawyer if they are incapable of representing themselves in an understandable manner or if it is necessary for the proper administration of justice.

(2) Parties must be represented by a lawyer in proceedings before a second appeal court.

Rule 165. Extension of deadlines – non-domiciled parties

Where a party is not domiciled in the State whose court is seised of the proceedings, any time limit applicable to an appeal is extended by one month unless the court provides otherwise.

Section 3 – First Appeals

Rule 166. Right to appeal

(1) A party has a right to appeal against a first instance judgment if

- (a) the value of the appealed claim exceeds [the value of the appealed claim as determined by applicable law, for instance twice the average monthly wage in the forum State] or
- (b) the appeal court grants permission to appeal based on the contents of the notice and reasons for appeal.

(2) In deciding whether to grant permission to appeal, the appeal court shall take the following into account

- (a) whether the legal issue in dispute is of fundamental significance, or
- (b) the further development of the law, or the public interest in securing uniform adjudication require an appellate decision, or
- (c) fundamental procedural requirements have been violated.

(3) The appeal court shall, on its own motion, assess whether the requirements of Rules 166(1) and (2) have been met.

Rule 167. Scope of a first appeal

(1) A first appeal can be brought against the whole, or part, of a first instance judgment.

(2) In general, the relief sought is limited by what was claimed or defended at first instance.

(3) However, the relief sought may be broadened or amended within a first appeal if

- (a) all parties to the appeal consent, or
- (b) the court considers it appropriate for the proper administration of justice.

Rule 168. New facts and taking evidence

(1) Within the relief sought, the appellate court shall consider new facts alleged by the parties

- (a) in so far as those facts could not have been introduced before the first instance court, or
- (b) in so far as the first instance court failed to invite the parties to clarify or supplement facts that they had introduced to support their claim or defence under Rules 24(1) and 53(3).

(2) Within the relief sought, the appellate court shall take evidence offered by the parties only if

- (a) the evidence could not have been offered to the first instance court;

(b) the evidence was offered to the first instance court and was erroneously rejected or could not be taken for reasons outside the party's control; or

(c) the evidence concerns new facts admissible according to Rule 168(1).

Rule 169. Scope of appellate review – First appeal

(1) Within the relief sought, the appellate court's review shall encompass

(a) the application of the law in the judgment;

(b) the legality of the proceedings in the first instance court, provided that the appellant challenged the error complained about immediately before the first instance court if such challenge was possible;

(c) evaluation of the evidence if the appellate court determines that such a review is warranted in order to prevent serious injustice.

(2) The appellate court will reverse a first instance judgment for procedural error only if it potentially influenced the judgment or if it was so grave that such influence need not be proven.

Rule 170. First appeal court decisions

(1) In general, the appellate court shall decide the matter that forms the substance of the appeal.

(2) The appellate court may refer the matter back to the first instance court, if necessary, for it to decide the matter.

(3) If the parties to the appeal agree to it, the appellate court must decide the matter.

Rule 171. Contents of the first appeal court's judgment

In so far as it agrees with the first instance court's judgment, the appellate court's judgment may refer to the legal and factual grounds in that judgment. It may also set out its own reasons in its judgment. In the latter case, the appellate court is deemed to have adopted the legal and factual grounds of the first instance judgment which are not contrary to its own reasoning.

Section 4 – Second Appeals

Rule 172. Right to a second appeal

(1) A party may only appeal from a first appeal judgment if such an appeal is necessary to

(a) correct a violation of a fundamental right,

(b) secure uniformity in the law,

(c) decide a fundamental question which is not limited to the case at issue, or

(d) develop the law.

(2) A second appeal court shall, on its own motion, assess whether the requirements of Rule 172(1) have been met.

Rule 173. Scope of a second appeal

(1) A second appeal can be brought against the whole, or part, of a first appeal judgment.

(2) The relief sought is limited by what was claimed or defended in the first appeal.

Rule 174. Scope of appellate review – Second appeal

(1) Within the relief sought, as far as admissible, the second appeal court's review shall encompass

- (a) the interpretation and application of the law in the first appeal judgment;
- (b) the legality of the proceedings in the first appeal court, provided that the appellant challenged the error complained about immediately before that court.

(2) The second appeal court will reverse the first appeal judgment for a procedural error only if the procedural error has potentially influenced the judgment or if it was so serious that such influence need not be proven.

Rule 175. Second appeal court decisions

(1) The second appeal court shall determine the substantive issue before it if

- (a) it is to reverse the first appeal judgment having held that there had been a violation of the law, and
- (b) it has concluded that it can determine the issue.

(2) In all other circumstances, the second appeal court must refer the matter back to the first appeal court for it to finally determine the matter. In such a circumstance, the first appeal court is bound by the second appeal court's assessment of the law.

Rule 176. Contents of the second appeal court's judgment

A second appeal court must provide its own reasons in its judgment. If they are adequate, it may refer to the reasons given in the first appeal court's or the first instance court's judgment.

Rule 177. Leapfrog appeal

(1) Instead of a regular appeal to the first appeal court, an appeal may be brought directly to the second appeal court (a leapfrog appeal).

(2) A second appeal court may only grant permission to bring a leapfrog appeal if

- (a) an appellant applies directly to it to bring such an appeal, setting out its reasons why permission should be granted, and does so within the time limits applicable to a first appeal;
- (b) the appellant's application complies with Rule 158;
- (c) the requirements of Rule 172(1) are met.

(3) An appeal under this rule is deemed to be a second appeal, and the Rules applicable to second appeals apply accordingly.

Section 5 – Review of Procedural Error and Miscellaneous Appeals

Rule 178. Immediate review of procedural error

(1) If a party, or non-party affected by a procedural order, fails to challenge a procedural error that was caused by the court or another party immediately upon it being made, the error is waived.
(2) Rule 178(1) does not apply if a party acted carefully pursuant to the requirements of Rule 47 or if the rule affected is not subject to waiver by the parties. This Rule applies to non-parties *mutatis mutandis.*
(3) Upon objection and having heard the parties the court may render, revoke or vary court rulings. Rules 49 and 50 apply accordingly.

Rule 179. Separate appeal against the review of procedural orders by the court

(1) Unless otherwise provided for in Rule 179(2), a decision on a challenge to a procedural error cannot be made the subject of a separate appeal.
(2) A separate appeal is available against decisions made in respect of
- (a) a stay of proceedings;
- (b) the transfer of proceedings to another court;
- (c) security for costs;
- (d) the exclusion of a party from a hearing or the imposition of a fine on a party;
- (e) a refusal to disqualify a judge or court-appointed expert; and
- (f) if provided for in a specific rule.

(3) A separate appeal must be filed with the court within two weeks of notice of the decision.

Rule 180. Appeals against procedural decisions that affect non-parties

(1) A person who is not a party to litigation but directly affected by a procedural ruling given by the court has a right of appeal.
(2) The right of appeal must be exercised in accordance with Rule 179(3).

Section 6 – Extraordinary Recourse

Rule 181. Scope of an extraordinary motion for review

(1) An extraordinary motion for review re-opens proceedings that have otherwise been finally determined either at first instance or on appeal.
(2) Such a review may, if successful, rescind a judgment that has become *res judicata.* Where it does so the court will give case management directions for the future management of the proceedings.

Rule 182. Grounds for an extraordinary motion for review

(1) An extraordinary motion for review may only be brought against a judgment on the following grounds

(a) the court was wrongly constituted,

(b) a party's right to be heard was violated severely,

(c) a judgment was obtained by fraud or violence,

(d) after a judgment is issued, evidence that would have been decisive to it is recovered or obtained, and such evidence was not available prior to judgment being given due either to *force majeure* or improper conduct by the party in whose favour the judgment was made, or

(e) the European Court of Human Rights has ruled that the judgment given in national proceedings infringed any of the rights established in the European Convention for the Protection of Human Rights and Fundamental Freedoms and its Protocols, provided that the infringement, due to its nature and seriousness, entails persistent effects, which can only be stopped by means of such a review; however, in no case may the review affect rights acquired in good faith by third parties.

(2) The motion shall only be admissible under Rule 182(1)(a), (b) or (c) if the applicant was unable, without any fault on their behalf, to raise the ground on which they rely before the judgment that is to be subject to review became *res judicata.*

Rule 183. Time limits and withdrawal

(1) An application by a party for an extraordinary motion for review must be made within three months from the date on which that party became aware of the grounds for review.

(2) In no case may an application be made after ten years have elapsed from the time the judgment, which is to be the subject of such a review, has become *res judicata.*

(3) An extraordinary motion for review can be withdrawn at any time.

Part X – Provisional and Protective Measures

Section 1 – General Part

Rule 184. Provisional and protective measures

(1) A provisional or protective measure is any temporary order that has one or more of the following functions:

(a) to ensure or promote effective enforcement of final decisions concerning the substance of the proceedings, whether or not the underlying claim is pecuniary, including securing assets and obtaining or preserving information concerning a debtor and his assets; or

(b) to preserve the opportunity for a complete and satisfactory determination of the proceedings, including securing evidence relevant to the merits or preventing its destruction or concealment; or

(c) to preserve the existence and value of goods or other assets which form or will form the subject-matter of proceedings (pending or otherwise); or

(d) to prevent harm from being suffered, to prevent further harm, or to regulate disputed issues, pending final judgment.

(2) A provisional or protective measure ordered should be suitable for its purpose.

Rule 185. Proportionality of provisional and protective measures

(1) A provisional and protective measure should impose the least burden on the respondent.

(2) The court must ensure that the measure's effects are not disproportionate to the interests it is asked to protect.

Rule 186. Without-notice (*ex parte*) procedure

(1) The court may order a provisional or protective measure without-notice (*'ex parte'*) only if, in the circumstances, proceedings with-notice (*'inter partes'*) would frustrate the prospect of the applicant receiving effective protection of their interests.

(2) When granting an order without-notice the court must give the respondent an opportunity to be heard at the earliest possible time, that date to be specified in the order that was made without-notice. The respondent should be given notice of the order and of all the matters relied upon before the court to support it as soon as possible.

(3) An applicant must fully disclose to the court all facts and legal issues relevant to the court's decision whether to grant relief and, if so, on what terms.

(4) The court must make a prompt decision concerning any objection to the grant of a provisional or protective measure or its terms.

Rule 187. Security

(1) When assessing whether to grant or continue a provisional or protective measure the court may consider whether security can be provided by the respondent in lieu of the order.

(2) As a condition of granting or continuing a provisional or protective measure the applicant may, depending on the circumstances, be required to provide appropriate security.

(3) Security must not be required solely on the basis that the applicant or respondent is not a national or resident of the forum State.

Rule 188. Initiation of proceedings

(1) Where the applicant has been granted a provisional or protective measure before initiating proceedings under Rules 21(1), 53, such proceedings must be initiated before the date set by the court. Where the court does not set such a date or it is not otherwise specified by the applicable law, the applicant shall initiate such proceedings within two weeks of the date of the issue of the decision granting the remedy. The court can extend the period on the request of a party.

(2) If proceedings have not been initiated as required by Rule 188(1), the measure shall lapse, unless the court provides otherwise.

Rule 189. Review and appeal

(1) The court may, either on application of a party or on its own motion, modify, suspend, or terminate a provisional or protective measure if satisfied that a change in circumstances so requires.

(2) Decisions that grant, deny, modify, suspend or terminate provisional or protective measures are subject to appeal. Rule 179(3) applies accordingly.

Rule 190. Applicant liability

(1) If a provisional or protective measure is set aside, lapses, or if the proceedings are dismissed on procedural grounds or on their merits, the applicant must compensate the respondent for such loss or damage caused by the measure.

(2) The applicant is liable to compensate non-parties for any damages, and expenditure incurred as a consequence of complying with the measure.

Rule 191. Sanctions for non-compliance

Except in respect of interim payments, where there is non-compliance with a provisional or protective measure the court may impose a sanction under Rule 27, as appropriate.

Section 2 – Special Part

A Asset Preservation

Rule 192. Types of asset preservation measure

A court may grant, on application by a party, any of the following asset preservation orders for the purpose of protecting their claim:

(a) an attachment order, which is an order authorising provisional attachment of the respondent's assets,

(b) an asset restraining order, which is an interim order preventing the respondent from disposing of, or dealing with, their assets, or

(c) a custodial order, which is an order that the respondent's assets shall be placed in the custody of a neutral non-party (a custodian).

Rule 193. Criteria for awarding asset preservation orders

A party seeking an order under Rule 192 must show that:

(a) their claim for relief has a good chance of succeeding on its substantive merits, and

(b) it is likely that, without such an order, enforcement of a final judgment against the respondent will be impossible or exceedingly difficult.

Rule 194. Limitations on asset preservation orders

Asset Preservation Orders must ensure that a respondent is not prevented from receiving financial allowances, provided the amounts are reasonable, for

(a) ordinary living expenses, and/or

(b) legitimate business expenses, and/or

(c) to enable it to fund legal advice and representation in respect of the proceedings, including such as are necessary for it to respond to the order, including seeking its variation or discharge under Rules 186(4) or 189.

Rule 195. Notification of asset preservation orders and their effects to respondent

(1) At the earliest possible time after an order has been made under Rule 192, the respondent and any non-parties who are the addressees of an order must be given formal notice of it. Where necessary to enforce the order, non-parties may be given formal notice before the respondent.

(2) The applicant may, if it wishes, inform a non-party of an order before the respondent is given formal notice.

(3) The respondent or any non-parties who are the addressees of an order made under Rule 192 must comply with it as soon as they are notified of the order. In the event of breach, they will be subject (without limitation) to the sanctions listed in Rule 191.

B Regulatory Measures

Rule 196. Measures to perform or refrain from performing an action

The court may grant the applicant a measure to regulate the relationship between parties in relation to a non-pecuniary claim for relief on a provisional basis. Such a measure may require the respondent to act or to refrain from acting in a manner specified in the court's order.

Rule 197. Criteria for awarding a regulatory measure

A party seeking an order under Rule 196 must show:

(a) it has a good chance of succeeding in the proceedings; or

(b) where there is a significant risk that damages to the respondent will not be capable of providing adequate compensation for any interference with their rights if the proceedings are dismissed, that there is a very strong possibility that the applicant will succeed in the proceedings;

C Evidence Preservation

Rule 198. Evidence preservation orders

(1) The court has the power to secure evidence on the application of a party to proceedings through the following interim measures:

(a) hearing witness evidence or taking of witness evidence by a third party acting on its behalf;

(b) requiring the preservation or protection of evidence by the parties or by requiring it to be placed in the custody of a custodian;

(c) appointing an expert to provide expert opinion evidence.

(2) Evidence preservation orders may, where necessary, authorise access to the evidence. Access may be subject to such conditions as the court considers just.

Rule 199. Criteria for awarding an evidence preservation measure

A party seeking an evidence preservation order must show that:

(a) there is a real risk that unless the order is made the evidence will not be available for determining the substantive proceedings on their merits; and

(b) if the order requires access to a party's or non-party's property the applicant has a strong *prima facie* case in respect of the merits of the applicant's claim or proposed claim for relief.

D Interim Payment

Rule 200. Interim payment measures

A court may grant the claimant an interim payment order in relation to a monetary claim, either wholly or in part to satisfy the claim in the proceedings, in anticipation of the expected outcome.

Rule 201. Criteria for awarding an interim payment

(1) An applicant seeking an order under Rule 200 must show that:

(a) the defendant has admitted that they are liable to pay a monetary sum to the applicant, or the applicant has obtained a final judgment on liability, or it is highly likely that the applicant will obtain at least the amount sought in a final judgment; and

(b) they are in urgent need of payment by the defendant.

(2) In assessing whether to make an interim payment order the court should consider all the circumstances, including any potential or actual hardship to the applicant or the respondent as a result of refusing or granting the order.

(3) An interim payment order cannot be made on a without-notice basis.

(4) Where judgment in the proceedings is for a lesser amount than that paid, any over-payment must be repaid.

(5) An interim payment order will ordinarily be made subject to the applicant giving security. If the applicant's claim is absolutely well founded and the requirement to obtain security would frustrate the order's purpose of securing urgent relief for the applicant's economic distress, where that has been at least

partially caused by the defendant's delay, the court may grant an interim payment order without or upon reduced security.

Section 3 – Cross-Border Issues

Rule 202. International jurisdiction

(1) Within the scope of the European Union Regulations or international conventions, the international jurisdiction of the court in relation to provisional and protective measures is governed by those Regulations or conventions.

(2) In any event, the court having jurisdiction in respect of the proceedings will have jurisdiction to grant provisional and protective measures.

(3) Without prejudice to applicable European Union rules and international conventions, another court may grant such provisional and protective measures necessary to protect interests located within the jurisdiction or the subject-matter of which have a real connecting link with the territory of the court, or that are necessary to support proceedings brought in another country.

Rule 203. Recognition and enforcement

(1) Within the scope of European Union Regulations or international conventions, the recognition and enforcement of provisional and protective measures are governed by those Regulations or conventions.

(2) Where no European Union Regulation or international convention applies, provisional and protective measures will be recognised and enforced in accordance with domestic law.

(3) Courts should, at the request of the parties, take into account provisional and protective measures granted in another country and, where appropriate, and in accordance with these Rules, cooperate in order to secure the effectiveness of those measures.

Part XI – Collective Proceedings

Section 1 – Collective Interest Injunctions

Rule 204. Scope of application

(1) The Rules in Part XI, Section 1 apply to orders, known as collective interest injunction, made by a court, which direct any person to cease any conduct or behaviour that is infringing the law.

(2) A collective interest injunction cannot be made on an interim basis under Part X of these Rules.

Rule 205. Entitlement to apply for a collective interest injunction

(1) Any entity authorised under national law to bring actions in the collective interest may apply for a collective interest injunction that requires the cessation of any infringement of the law.

(2) Where appropriate the court may order additional measures such as the publication of its decision with a view to eliminating the continuing effects of the infringement.

Rule 206. Effect of collective interest injunctions
A collective interest injunction binds the defendant in all future proceedings.

Section 2 – Collective Proceedings

A General Part

Rule 207. Collective proceedings
Collective proceedings are proceedings brought by a qualified claimant on behalf of a group of persons who it is alleged are affected by an event giving rise to a mass harm, but where those persons, known as group members, are not parties to the action.

Rule 208. Claimants qualified to bring collective proceedings
A qualified claimant is:

(a) an organisation authorised, in accordance with national law, to bring collective proceedings and whose purpose has a direct relationship with the event giving rise to the mass harm,
(b) an entity which is established solely for the purpose of obtaining redress for group members and which satisfied the requirements of Rule 209; or
(c) a person who is a group member and who meets the requirements of Rules 209(a)–(c).

Rule 209. Requirements for qualified claimants
A person or entity shall not be a qualified claimant unless:

(a) they have no conflict of interest with any group member,
(b) they have sufficient capability to conduct the collective proceeding. In assessing this issue, the court shall take account of the financial, human and other resources available to the putative qualified claimant If appropriate, the court may require security for costs (see Rule 243),
(c) they are legally represented, and
(d) they are neither a lawyer nor exercising any legal profession.

Rule 210. Collective proceedings – Statement of claim

(1) A statement of claim in collective proceedings must include all relevant information available concerning

(a) the event giving rise to the mass harm,
(b) the group,
(c) the causal connection between the event of mass harm and the loss suffered by the group members,
(d) the similarity of the claims of the group members in law and fact,

(e) whether compensation or other collective remedies are sought,
(f) the financial and other resources available to the qualified claimant to pursue the collective proceeding,
(g) evidence of the qualified claimant's attempt to settle the group members' claims.

(2) Before commencing collective proceedings and upon the application of a qualified claimant, the court may issue an order preventing a potential defendant from bringing an action with respect to the event of mass harm.

Rule 211. Registration of collective proceedings

(1) Upon the qualified claimant submitting a collective proceedings statement of claim to the court, the court must enter the proceedings into a publicly accessible electronic register.

(2) After registration any other court must dismiss any collective proceedings against the same defendant(s) in respect of the same mass harm.

B Admissibility of Collective Proceedings

Rule 212. Conditions of admissibility

(1) The court may admit a collective proceeding if
(a) it will resolve the dispute more efficiently than joinder of the group members' individual claims,
(b) all of the claims for relief made in the proceeding arise from the same event or series of related events causing mass harm to the group members,
(c) the claims are similar in law and fact, and
(d) except in cases of urgency, the qualified claimant has allowed the defendant or defendants at least three months to respond to a settlement proposal.

(2) Upon application, the court may order any proceeding to continue as a collective proceeding.

Rule 213. Collective proceeding order

(1) An order made under Rule 212 must include the following information:
(a) the name and address, and other relevant contact details of the qualified claimant
(b) a concise description of the event of mass harm giving rise to the collective proceeding;
(c) the names or a description of all of the persons allegedly affected by the mass harm. The description must contain sufficient detail to enable any person allegedly affected by the event causing mass harm to know if they are within the group or not;
(d) the type of collective proceeding under Rule 215.

(2) Before making an order under this Rule the court shall advertise a draft of the order and set a deadline for any other potential qualified claimants to apply under Rule 207.
(3) The court shall determine which of several potential qualified claimants, if any, shall become the qualified claimant in the proceedings. It shall do so on the basis of the criteria set out in, among others, Rule 209. Where more than one qualified claimant is selected they must act jointly.
(4) The collective proceeding order shall be advertised in a manner which the court considers will best bring it to the attention of any person likely to be affected by the event causing mass harm on which the proceeding is based. The advertisement shall invite such persons to opt-in to the proceeding and shall give information on how to do so.
(5) The collective proceeding order or the refusal to grant such an order are subject to appeal by the qualified claimant and the defendant.

Rule 214. Obligation of qualified claimant
A qualified claimant must at all times act in the best interests of the whole group or sub-group, if a qualified claimant for a sub-group.

Rule 215. Types of collective proceeding
(1) Collective proceedings shall operate on an opt-in basis unless the court makes an order under Rule 215(2).
(2) The court may order that the proceedings will include all group members who have not opted-out of the proceedings under Rule 215(3) where it concludes that:
- (a) the group members' claims cannot be made in individual actions because of their small size; and
- (b) a significant number of group members would not opt-in to the collective proceeding.

(3) Where the court makes an order under Rule 215(2) it must set a deadline for group members to notify the court that they wish to opt-out. In exceptional circumstances the court may permit group members to opt-out after the deadline has expired.
(4) The court shall decide to whom and how notification under Rule 215(3) shall be given.

Rule 216. Opt-in proceedings
(1) Where collective proceedings operate on an opt-in basis, group members must notify the court if they wish to join the proceedings in the manner specified by the court.
(2) The court shall ensure that group member notifications are properly recorded in a public register, which may be established in accordance with Rule 220.

Rule 217. Individual actions

(1) Group members who have opted-in under Rule 216 or who have not opted-out under Rule 215(3) cannot bring an individual court action in respect of the same event of mass harm against a defendant to the collective proceeding.

(2) In cases under Rule 215(2) any group member who brings an individual action against a defendant to collective proceedings during the opt-out period shall be treated as having opted-out of the proceedings.

(3) Any time limit provided in national law for individual actions to be brought by a group member in respect of loss caused by the event of mass harm shall be suspended from the date of commencement of the collective proceeding. The period of suspension shall end when

- (a) the collective proceeding is withdrawn or dismissed; or
- (b) the group member opts-out under Rules 215(2)–(4).

(4) Where Rule 217(3)(a) or (b) applies the remaining limitation period for individual claims will start six months after the withdrawal, dismissal or the date on which the opt-out was effected.

C Case Management of Collective Proceedings

Rule 218. Case management powers

(1) In collective proceedings, the court has additional case management powers, including the power

- (a) to remove a qualified claimant of a group or any sub-group if they no longer satisfy the conditions in Rule 208 and Rule 209 or fails to act in the interests of all group members,
- (b) to authorise, with their consent, a new qualified claimant,
- (c) to modify the description of the group,
- (d) to divide a group into sub-groups and to authorise, with their consent, a qualified claimant for each sub-group,
- (e) to dismiss the collective proceeding or to order it to continue as individual proceedings if there is no longer a qualified claimant
- (f) to direct the correction of the group register (Rules 216(2) and 220).

(2) The court may hear any person it considers has an interest in the management of the case before making any case management order under this Rule.

Rule 219. Advertisements

(1) In collective proceedings the court shall advertise or shall require advertisement

- (a) when a qualified claimant is removed or authorised,
- (b) when the description of the group is modified or the group is divided into sub-groups,
- (c) when a collective settlement is offered,
- (d) when any order or judgment is made,
- (e) of information about the secure electronic platform under Rule 220; and

(f) if the collective proceeding is dismissed or withdrawn.

(2) The advertisement shall be made in a manner which the court considers will best attract the attention of any person likely to be affected by the event causing mass harm and in sufficient time to allow affected persons a reasonable opportunity to participate as they see fit in the proceedings.

Rule 220. Communication – Secure electronic platform

The court must create or authorise the creation of a secure electronic platform for the efficient management of the collective proceeding.

D Settlements in Commenced Collective Proceedings

Rule 221. Court approval

A group member will not be bound by any agreement settling a collective proceeding in whole or in part unless that agreement is approved by the court.

Rule 222. Application for the approval of a settlement agreement

(1) A party to a proposed settlement agreement may apply to the court for approval under Rule 221.

(2) The application for approval shall include:

(a) the description of the group whose members will be bound by the settlement;

(b) a copy of the proposed settlement agreement. In a collective proceeding for compensation, the proposed agreement shall include the total amount of compensation payable, and the criteria for distributing the compensation to each group member;

(c) the proposed administration of the compensation fund and method of distributing the compensation payment to group members; and

(d) a concise statement of reasons showing why the terms of the settlement agreement are fair and adequate.

Rule 223. Procedure for approving settlements

(1) Before approving a settlement the court may

(a) make any order necessary to obtain further information in order to assess the fairness and adequacy of the proposed settlement,

(b) appoint an expert to assist the court.

(2) The court must

(a) advertise the proposed settlement according to Rule 219, ensuring that it is clear that the court has not reached a conclusion on the fairness of the settlement,

(b) fix a period within which any comments may be made, and

(c) consider all comments made by the group members and the parties.

(3) The court may consider all other relevant comments received.

Rule 224. Settlement approval orders

The court shall not make an order approving a settlement agreement where

(a) the amount of compensation agreed for the group or any sub-group is manifestly unfair,

(b) the terms of any other undertaking by a defendant are manifestly unfair,

(c) the settlement is manifestly contrary to the public interest (*ordre public*) or

(d) the terms, whether contained in the proposed settlement agreement or not, as to the payment of legal and other associated costs of the action are manifestly unreasonable.

Rule 225. Approved settlements in opt-in actions

An approved settlement binds all group members who have opted-in at the time the order approving the settlement is made.

Rule 226. Approved settlements in opt-out proceedings

An approved settlement binds all group members unless they have opted-out of the collective proceedings at the time the order approving the settlement is made.

E Judgments in Collective Proceedings

Rule 227. Effect of final judgments

(1) A final judgment of the court in collective proceedings binds

(a) all of the parties, and all group members who have opted-in to the proceedings; or

(b) all of the parties, and all of the group members resident in the forum State who have not opted-out of the proceedings within the period set by the court in Rule 215(3).

(2) No other collective proceeding may be commenced in respect of any claims for relief determined in a final judgment.

(3) A final judgment may be enforced by the qualified claimant. If the qualified claimant does not enforce the final judgment within a reasonable time any group member, with the court's permission, may enforce the final judgment.

Rule 228. Amount of compensation

A final judgment that sets the amount of compensation in a collective proceeding shall include

(a) the total amount of compensation payable in respect of the group or any sub-group. If an exact calculation of this amount is impossible or excessively difficult, the court may estimate the amount,

(b) the criteria for distributing the compensation to each group member, and the method of administration of the compensation fund.

F Collective Settlements Outside Collective Proceedings

Rule 229. Standing to reach settlement

(1) Any entity fulfilling the requirements in Rules 208(a) and (b) to be a qualified claimant may reach a collective settlement agreement for a group even where a collective proceeding order has not been made.

(2) Any such collective settlement agreement shall be negotiated in good faith for the benefit of all group members.

Rule 230. Application for approval of collective settlement

(1) An application to the court for approval of a collective settlement agreement in accordance with Rule 229 must be made by all of the parties to it.

(2) The application shall include all of the information required under Rule 222(2). It shall also specify whether a binding settlement shall be reached on an opt-in or an opt-out basis.

Rule 231. Approval procedure

The procedure for approval of collective settlements in Rule 223 applies to any application to approve a collective settlement following an application under Rule 230.

Rule 232. Approval order and opt-in/opt-out procedure

The court must approve the proposed collective settlement on the basis of Rule 224.

(a) If the court does not approve the proposed collective settlement it must give its reasons for refusing to approve it, and must remit the agreement to the parties.

(b) The court must advertise the approved settlement in accordance with Rule 219(2), give information on whether the settlement shall become binding based on an opt-in or opt-out procedure, and fix a period of at least three months for the group members to opt-in or opt-out. The court shall decide to whom and how the notification to opt-in or to opt-out shall be given. If the terms of the settlement require a fixed number or percentage of group members to accept the settlement this must also be communicated clearly.

(c) After the period fixed for opt-in or opt-out notifications and, where applicable, if the necessary number or percentage of group members have opted-in or have not opted-out, the court shall declare the approved settlement binding. Otherwise the court shall declare that the approval proceedings have been terminated without a binding settlement.

(d) An approved settlement shall bind all of the persons who have opted-in to the settlement or who have not opted-out of the settlement.

Section 3 – Cross-Border Issues

Within the European Union

Rule 233. Recognition of qualified claimant

The recognition of a claimant as a qualified claimant by a court in an order made under Rule 213(1)(a) binds every other court in European Union Member States without the need for further application for recognition in relation to actions arising from the same event of mass harm.

Rule 234. Judicial co-ordination

(1) When a mass harm has cross-border effects, the registry entries for each collective proceeding shall be made available on the European e-justice platform or any similarly effective platform.

(2) European Union Member States' courts must use their best effort to co-ordinate collective proceedings in different Member States in order to avoid irreconcilable judgments or settlement approvals.

Rule 235. Group members outside the forum State

(1) The court shall ensure that group members outside the forum State are informed of the collective proceeding in accordance with Rule 219.

(2) No order made under Rule 215(2) binds group members outside the forum State.

(3) Group members outside the forum State must, if they choose, be allowed to opt-in.

(4) Rules 235(1)–(3) also apply to collective settlement proceedings under Rules 229–232.

Rule 236. Multiple substantive laws

(1) Group members shall not be prevented from participating in a single collective proceeding if they are subject to different substantive laws.

(2) In any case where group members are subject to different substantive law, the court may divide the group into sub-groups under Rule 218(1)(d).

Section 4 – Costs, Expenses and Funding

Rule 237. Third-party funding

(1) A qualified claimant may use third-party litigation funding.

(2) Rule 245 applies to any such third-party funding agreement. A court may, however, require a qualified claimant to disclose the details of any such funding agreement relevant for the instance at stake to the court and, in so far as appropriate, to the parties.

Rule 238. Costs and expenses of collective proceedings

(1) Only a qualified claimant is liable for the costs and expenses of a collective proceeding if it is unsuccessful.

(2) If the proceeding is successful, the total amount of compensation received by the qualified claimant shall form a common fund.

(3) The qualified claimant's costs and expenses incurred in bringing the proceeding must be paid from the common fund before any distribution of compensation to group members in accordance with Rule 228. Rule 245(4) applies accordingly.

Part XII – Costs

Rule 239. Decision on costs

(1) A court rendering a final judgment or terminating the proceedings in any other way shall determine which party is required to reimburse the other party or parties' costs of the proceedings, unless the parties have agreed otherwise. Any recovery of costs shall be limited to those that are reasonable and proportionate.
(2) If the parties enter into a settlement, each party shall bear its own costs unless they have agreed otherwise.

Rule 240. Scope and amount of costs

(1) Parties may seek to recover the costs of the proceedings, in particular
- (a) reasonable and proportionate costs of their legal representation in the proceedings,
- (b) court and other fees such as those of court-appointed experts, interpreters, court reporters etc.,
- (c) other reasonable financial outlays resulting from the conduct of the proceedings, such as costs of party-appointed experts, travel expenses, and fees for the service of documents.

(2) Costs under Rule 240(1) may also include costs reasonably incurred for the preparation of proceedings before they were commenced.
(3) Parties may only recover costs which they have reasonably and proportionately incurred for the conduct of the proceedings, taking into account the amount in dispute, the nature and complexity of the issues, the significance of the case for the parties.
(4) Where national law specify tariffs for the recovery of certain fees (such as, where relevant, court fees and fees for the parties' legal representation, for experts, and interpreters), any award of costs should nevertheless be consistent with the Rules of this Part.

Rule 241. General rule

(1) When determining upon which party the obligation to reimburse costs shall be placed under Rule 239, the court shall take into account the circumstances of the specific proceedings, in particular whether and to what extent the parties' claims were successful.

(2) The court may also take into account the parties' conduct, in particular, whether and to what extent they acted in good faith and contributed to the fair, efficient and speedy resolution of the dispute.

Rule 242. Review

(1) The court's decision on costs may be subject to an appeal.
(2) An appeal is limited to a review of whether the court exercised its discretion properly according to Rules 240 and 241.
(3) A decision on an appeal under Rule 242(2) is final and binding. It cannot be subject to a second appeal.

Rule 243. Security for costs

(1) A party may apply for the other party to provide reasonable security for costs.
(2) In deciding an application for security for costs, the court shall take into account
- (a) the likelihood that the applicant will be able to claim reimbursement of the costs of the proceedings,
- (b) the financial means of the parties and the prospect of enforcement of the costs decision against the other party,
- (c) whether such security for costs is compatible with the parties' right of access to justice and a fair trial.

Rule 244. Legal aid

(1) Parties are entitled to legal aid, as provided by national law, if their right of access to justice and to a fair trial so requires.
(2) Such legal aid should be sufficient to cover reasonable and proportionate legal representation where legal provisions, the complexity of the case, or the vulnerability of a party so require.

Rule 245. Third-party funding and success fees

(1) A party who receives funding for the proceedings from a professional third-party funder or from a crowd-funder shall disclose this fact and the identity of the funder to the court and the other party at the commencement of proceedings. The details of such a third-party funding arrangement are, however, not subject to this requirement.
(2) Such a third-party funding arrangement must be in accordance with applicable law and must not provide for inadequate compensation for the funder or enable the funder to exercise any undue influence on the conduct of the proceedings.
(3) Parties may enter into success fee arrangements with counsel or a third-party funder. Such arrangements must nevertheless be consistent with applicable law, the parties' access to fair legal representation and the integrity of the proceedings.

(4) A violation of the requirements of Rules 245(1), (2) and (3) does not constitute a defence against the claim of the party availing itself of third-party funding or a success fee arrangement. But, having made its decision on the claim, the court may ask for details of fee arrangements with a third party or counsel relevant for the instance at stake, and, upon consultation with the parties, it may take into account any disregard of applicable law or lacking fairness of the arrangement when it renders the final decision on costs determining the part of the claimant's costs to be reimbursed.
(5) As far as provided in Rules 237, 238(3), Rule 245 applies to collective proceedings.

Index

access to justice 72, 77, 93, 96–97, 107, 156–159, 161, 164, 170–171, 174, 221
affirmative defences 104
  in the context of *res judicata* 195–202
ALI-UNIDROIT Principles of Transnational Civil Procedure 5–6, 15, 28, 45–47, 51–52, 78, 99, 114, 136, 209–211, 257
  Principle 8 114
  Principle 9 28
  Principle 11 45–47, 51–52
  Principle 26 209
  Principle 27 210
antifragile, antifragility 257–258
appeal, means of review 3, 9, 11–13, 27, 36, 38, 59, 109, 129, 154, 180, 182, 185, 188, 193, 196, 208 ff., 242–244, 250, 253–254
  filtering standards, selective 217–218, 221, 253–254
  first appeal, second appeal 12–13, 213 ff., 242–243, 254
  jus litigatoris, jus constitutionis 215
  leapfrog appeal 220–221, 244
  right to 12, 211–213
  stare decisis 220
  time limits to 213–214, 222–224, 236
  uniform application of law 215, 217–220, 254
  value threshold 13, 216–218, 220–221
  waiver of, withdrawal of 27, 38, 212–215
applicable law 46–48, 64–66, 157, 162, 198, 233–234, 252
Aquinas, St. Thomas 30
Aristotle VII, 30, 50
artificial intelligence 8, 32–33
Augustinian interpretation 245
Austria 2–4, 18, 62, 199

Benjamin, Walter 237
best practices, best rule, better law approach 1, 5, 9–13, 19, 62, 99, 105, 256, 259
  as opposed to restatement 9, 99
  as opposed to *tronc commun* 9
Brazil 42, 110, 260
Bulgaria 93, 140

Calamandrei, Piero 44, 132
Canada 141, 244
Carnelutti, Francesco 43
case management 6–7, 14, 17, 22–31, 38–41, 47, 60, 63–66, 102, 106, 110, 240, 250–251
Césareo case 12
China 260
Chiovenda, Giuseppe 38, 53
civil code
  French 129, 232, 234
  Italian 175
  Spanish 122, 234
  Dutch 146–147
civil law 12, 31, 50, 129–132, 136, 140, 216, 230
code of civil procedure
  German 185
  Italian 101–102, 142
  Swiss 2, 4, 182, 185
  US Federal Rules of Civil Procedure 120–121, 128
Código Procesal Civil Modelo para Iberoamérica 7, 234
collective proceedings, collective redress 7, 109, 135 ff., 141–142, 165, 168, 170, 173, 254
  class actions 138, 143–147, 241
  ideological plaintiff 141
  individual, institutional claimant models 140–141, 144
  opt-in, opt-out 144, 151–154
  qualified entities 151, 154, 168, 173, 241
  ultra vires effect of *res judicata* 149–151
commercial courts 256–258
common law 12, 31, 65, 103, 121, 136, 140, 186, 190, 210, 216, 230–231
comparative law 1, 5, 9–10, 19, 69, 92, 98–99, 113, 122, 73, 149–150, 157, 184–185, 221, 228–232, 245–246, 250–253
competition 4, 21, 256–258

competition law 99, 113
compromise 9–12, 209, 216, 220, 229
Converium case 146–147
Court of Justice of the EU, ECJ 89–91, 148, 190–192, 202, 245, 260
Covid-19, corona, pandemic 32, 40, 53, 83, 93–95, 251
Croatia 85, 93, 96, 260
cross-border 6, 49, 80–81, 84, 86, 89, 100, 139, 148, 192, 236, 251–252, 255, 260
  collective actions 144–145

Denmark 88–89, 94, 140
dialogue, dialogical VII–VIII, 4–5, 27–30, 40, 58, 64, 260
discretion, discretionary 11, 119, 120, 148, 156, 159, 162–163, 179, 197, 217, 221–224
disposition, party disposition, *Dispositionsprinzip* 27, 37–44, 48–51, 156
  Befugnisdisposition 38
  Normdisposition 48
Draft Common Frame of Reference (DCFR) 110

ELI-UNIDROIT Model European Rules of Civil Procedure *passim*
  Rule 1 39
  Rule 2 19–20, 28, 39, 61, 161, 219
  Rule 3 19, 28, 39, 70, 161
  Rule 4 18–19, 20, 21, 46, 102, 110, 219, 240
  Rule 5 19, 119, 162
  Rule 6 19, 119, 161
  Rule 7 19, 161
  Rule 8 19, 161
  Rule 9 19
  Rule 10 19
  Rule 11 64, 239
  Rule 18 251
  Rule 21 27, 38
  Rule 22 47, 200–205, 233
  Rule 23 27, 38, 43, 197–199
  Rule 24 27, 37–38, 45–47, 65–66, 68, 70, 102
  Rule 25 10, 27, 37, 39, 65–66, 68, 101, 103, 105, 233
  Rule 26 27, 38, 46, 48, 66, 233–234
  Rule 27 68–69, 127, 210, 235
  Rule 33 244
  Rule 38 233
  Rule 40 188
  Rule 42 234
  Rule 43 234
  Rule 47 69
  Rule 49 23–24, 29, 39, 189, 219
  Rule 50 28, 40–41, 110, 244
  Rule 56 215
  Rule 57 48
  Rule 61 25, 29
  Rule 62 29
  Rule 63 25, 29, 244
  Rule 64 29
  Rule 65 121, 186, 189
  Rule 66 180–181, 189
  Rule 71 78
  Rule 73 79
  Rule 74 81, 84, 95
  Rule 75 81
  Rule 77 82
  Rule 78 82, 89, 90–91, 95
  Rule 79 80
  Rule 80 83–86, 91–94
  Rule 81 86–87
  Rule 82 81
  Rule 83 81
  Rule 84 81
  Rule 85 81
  Rule 86 81
  Rule 87 37
  Rule 88 103
  Rule 90 11
  Rule 92 28
  Rule 93 102, 237
  Rule 98 103–104
  Rule 99 127
  Rule 100 27, 105, 107
  Rule 102 105, 107
  Rule 103 103, 105
  Rule 104 105, 127
  Rule 105 105
  Rule 106 105–106
  Rule 107 105
  Rule 108 105
  Rule 109 105
  Rule 110 105

Rule 112 104
Rule 114 103
Rule 130 179, 181, 185
Rule 132 187, 236
Rule 133 187, 188, 189, 190, 244
Rule 138 126
Rule 139 182
Rule 140 236
Rule 147 190, 193
Rule 148 193, 244
Rule 149 12, 194–196, 198–205, 244
Rule 151 195
Rule 153 188, 211, 242
Rule 154 27, 38, 211, 214
Rule 155 220
Rule 156 214, 222–223
Rule 157 214, 222
Rule 158 214
Rule 162 210, 219
Rule 163 214
Rule 164 215
Rule 166 217, 221
Rule 167 38, 220
Rule 168 220
Rule 169 213
Rule 172 213, 217–220, 223, 254
Rule 174 213, 223
Rule 182 71
Rule 184 116–118, 124, 128
Rule 185 119, 124
Rule 186 70, 124, 244
Rule 187 119, 120, 124
Rule 188 118, 124
Rule 189 119, 124
Rule 190 120, 124
Rule 191 124, 127
Rule 192 121, 124
Rule 193 124, 126
Rule 194 124
Rule 195 124
Rule 196 124
Rule 197 124, 125–126
Rule 198 124
Rule 199 124–125, 127
Rule 200 123–124
Rule 201 123–126
Rule 204 138
Rule 206 151
Rule 207 151, 241
Rule 209 142
Rule 221 137
Rule 222 137
Rule 223 137
Rule 224 137
Rule 225 137, 152
Rule 226 137, 152
Rule 228 151
Rule 229 137
Rule 230 137
Rule 231 137
Rule 232 137, 153
Rule 237 172
Rule 239 159–160
Rule 240 159–160, 162
Rule 241 70, 159, 161
Rule 244 164
Rule 245 169, 172
Rule 285 139
Rule 286 139
steering committee 9, 59, 77–78, 209, 211
structure group 5–8, 98, 157, 211, 213, 215
working groups 3, 5–12, 8–11, 59–61, 77–78, 83, 88, 98, 104, 114, 136–137, 143, 157, 159, 163, 179, 181–183, 185, 204, 209, 211, 215–216, 224
enforcement of judgments 4, 8, 44, 51, 92–93, 117, 123, 138, 181, 204
provisional 209–210, 219
Estonia 93
EU legislation
acquis 1, 5, 80
Brussels I Regulation 49, 87, 115, 190, 192
Collective Redress Directive 137–139, 143–152, 165, 168, 172
Consumer ADR Directive 143
European Account Preservation Order Regulation 115
European Charter on Fundamental Rights 6
European Enforcement Order Regulation 87
Intellectual Property Directive 115, 158

Brussels I Regulation (*cont.*)
  Service Regulation 14, 80–81, 86, 89–90, 92, 255
  Evidence Regulation 14, 255

European Court of Human Rights 6, 92, 100, 260
evidence 7, 9–11, 14, 21–29, 37–40, 65, 67–69, 71, 73, 98 ff., 150, 152, 162, 185–186, 220–221, 237, 241, 250–251, 257–258
  access to information and 7, 9, 21, 68, 98, 101, 109, 257–258
  adverse inferences 69, 72–73
  burden of proof 37, 42, 67, 71, 99–100, 103–104, 111
  discovery 104–105, 240
  evaluation of 100, 103–104, 150
  fact-finding 39
  illegally obtained 11, 100, 260
  legal proof 103–104
  preservation of 117, 125, 127
  presumptions 104
  witness depositions 27, 29, 108

fictio juris 86, 201, 203
Finland 89–90
forum non conveniens 48, 148
forum shopping 49
France 1, 5, 12–13, 31, 42, 48, 62, 77, 79, 88, 90, 190, 210, 219–222, 234, 242, 244, 253–254
  French language 59, 78, 136, 227–232, 236–244
fundamental rights 208, 6, 11, 53
  human rights 260
funding 141–142, 144–145, 156, 159, 162–176

Germany 1, 5, 11–12, 26, 30–31, 68–69, 71, 77, 79, 85, 145, 163, 173, 182–185, 188, 191, 194, 199, 203, 205, 218, 221–222, 224, 236, 253, 256
Goldschmidt, James 41, 67
Gómez de la Serna, Pedro 129
Gothaer case 192
Gratian 7
Greece 77, 79
Grupo Mexicano de Desarrollo case 121
Gubisch case 191–192

harmonisation 1–4, 6, 9, 13, 99, 135, 149, 157, 211, 257–259
  approximation 2
  convergence 19, 257
  standardisation 4
  unification 2
Hegel, Georg Wilhelm Friedrich 36, 50–52
Henderson case 11, 89–90
Hippo, St. Augustine of 245
human action 4, 50
Hungary 90

IBA Rules on the Taking of Evidence 99, 109, 258
ICC Arbitration Rules 166–167
immediacy 23, 98
international arbitration 3, 26, 41–42, 51, 73–74, 99, 108–109, 115, 120, 157, 164, 166–167, 172, 180, 231–232, 256–259
international conventions
  Brussels Convention 49, 116
  Choice-of-Court Convention 49, 257
  European Convention on Human Rights 6
  Judgments Convention 49, 257
  New York Convention 256
  Service Convention 81, 240–241
Italy 1, 5, 13, 44, 48, 77, 79, 81, 90, 101–103, 105, 110, 138, 142, 149, 175, 182, 192, 236, 242–243, 252

joint application, *requête conjointe* 27, 48, 252
judgments 178 ff., *passim*
  default 181–185, 236
  early final 186–189
  final, partial 179–180, 184–187, 193
  provisional enforceability of 209–210, 219
  quantum 127, 180–181
  on preliminary procedural issues 179–181, 185, 193
  on specific legal issues on the merits 185, 193
  summary 185–186

judicial office, judicial organisation 31, 105, 157, 252–253, 259
jura novit curia / da mihi factum, dabo tibi jus 45–46, 65–66
jurisdiction 42, 48–49, 147–148, 180, 183, 192, 195, 213, 232
jus commune, solemnis ordo judiciorum, Romano-canonical procedure 32, 61, 122, 244, 260

Karesvaara case 92
Klein, Franz 19, 62

Latin (use of) 243–244
Latin America 15, 243, 260
legal aid 164, 174
legal costs 7, 70, 156–164, 170, 204
legal culture, heritage, tradition 1–5, 9–13, 19, 23, 29–31, 88, 103–104, 122, 131, 183, 216, 223, 231, 234, 242–244, 252–253, 256, 259
legal qualification of facts 45–48
legal reform 1, 236, 250, 260
  Italian 101, 252
legal standing 136, 171, 189, 212
  in collective proceedings 141–147, 166–168, 172–173
  legitimate interest 187–190, 211–212
legal transplant 253
lis pendens 7, 9, 11, 80, 178, 190–192, 201
  Kernpunkttheorie 191
Luxembourg 79, 90

modernity 53, 255
Montenegro 260

nemo contra se edere tenetur 65, 101, 105, 252
Netherlands 5, 7, 139–140, 146–148, 242
Norway 5, 19

obligations of parties, lawyers, and judges 58 ff.
  burdens 42, 58, 66–68, 71–73, 92, 99–100, 102–104, 106, 111, 150, 203–204
  duties 13, 18, 21, 26–27, 45, 47, 58–59, 66–67, 71–73, 85, 92–93, 101–102, 105, 108, 161–162, 167, 172, 240
  pre-commencement duties 13, 18–19, 62, 117–118
overriding objective 61, 254

parallel proceedings 49, 149, 190
parties to proceedings 109, 136, 143
party autonomy, private autonomy 19–20, 23, 26–28, 31, 36 ff., 135, 213, 250
  convençoes processuais 42
  contrats de procédure 42
  procedural contracts, *Prozessverträge* 28, 40–43, 110–111
  propter actionem, propter jurisdictionem, propter processum 42, 213
Portalis, Jean-Étienne 129, 229
Portugal 90
Prague Rules on the Taking of Evidence 109
predictability 3, 163
principles of civil procedure 6, 100, 257
  cooperation 6, 17–18, 20–21, 26–28, 30, 39, 41, 58, 61–65, 68, 71–72, 101–102, 108, 121, 161–162, 219, 254
  flexibility 28–29, 39–40, 100–101, 110
  proportionality 6, 11, 41, 62, 69, 101, 105, 107, 113–114, 119–120, 161–163, 254, 257
Principles of European Contract Law (PECL) 110
provisional measures, provisional and protective measures 7–8, 27, 38, 109, 113 ff., 162, 188, 193
  anticipatory 118, 123–126, 130–131
  asset preservation 121, 124–126
  evidence preservation 117, 125, 127
  fumus boni juris 107 124–125, 127–128
  Helsinki Principles 115
  instrumentality 118
  interim payments 118, 123–127
  periculum in mora 124–128, 188
  regulatory 118, 125–126, 130–131
  security 114, 119–120
  unnamed, atypical 128
  variability 119
purposes of civil justice 52

quæstio facti, quæstio juris 45, 48, 223

recognition 4
  exequatur 1, 257
relief sought, *causa petendi, petitum* 43–49, 118, 123, 139–140, 187–189, 194–201, 219, 233
  extra, ultra petita 198
res judicata 7, 9, 11–12, 149–153, 178, 184, 187, 190–205
  binding effect of 149–153, 193–195, 199–203
  claim preclusion, issue preclusion 204–205
  scope of 194–205
  ultra vires effect 149–151
right to be heard, right of defence 86, 46, 62, 77, 79, 91–93, 96
right to present one's case 86
Roman law 54, 130, 228, 244, 260
  actio 43, 45
  auctoritas, potestas 130
  legis actiones, manus injectio, pignoris capio 50
rule of law 3
Russia 231–232, 257

sanctions 58, 68–73, 100, 105–108, 121–122, 127, 161, 170
Satta, Salvatore 43
Serbia 260
service (electronic) 81–85, 88–89, 94–97, 251–252
  reasonable effort to discover address 85–86, 92–94
  right to disconnect 88
settlement 6, 13, 18, 21, 36, 42, 50, 52, 62–63, 105, 137, 163–164, 172, 175, 184
  collective 137, 143, 147–148, 151–152, 168
Shell case 146–147
Slovenia 148
soft law 3, 5, 108–110, 115, 250, 257
Spain 1, 12, 31, 87, 90, 92, 107, 117, 121–122, 123–124, 129, 130–131, 181, 189–190, 217, 234, 235–244
Stendhal 232
Storme commission, Project, report 5, 100, 115
structuralism 30, 228–230
structure of proceedings 26–30, 239
substantive law 23, 28, 42, 102–105, 135, 146, 161, 188–190, 198, 260
supreme courts 148, 216–217, 220, 224
  French 253
  Spanish 131, 217
  Swiss 192, 205
  US 121
Sweden 25, 88, 77, 140
Switzerland 2, 4, 182–183, 185, 188, 192, 199, 205, 244

teaching material (the Rules as) 260
technology, digitisation 8, 32–33, 83, 88, 251–252
  electronic service 81–85, 88–89, 94–97, 251–252
  social media 83, 93–96
translation 226 ff.
  and comparative law 228–231
  Augustinian, multilingual interpretation method 245
  faux amis 230–232
  functional equivalence 230, 242
  idiomaticity 232
  philology 226–227
  transcreation 230
travaux préparatories 229

UK, England and Wales 1, 5, 13, 18, 29, 31, 62, 77, 79, 93, 121, 140, 163, 190, 210, 215, 216, 242
Ukraine 257
Ulpian 54
UNCITRAL Model Law on International Commercial Arbitration 115, 258
UNIDROIT Principles of International Commercial Contracts 131, 246, 259
US, American 29, 31, 49, 93, 104, 108, 120–121, 128, 140–141, 143, 158, 161, 211

von Hayek, Friedrich 3–4

Woolf, Harry Kenneth 13, 29, 62

www.ingramcontent.com/pod-product-compliance
Lightning Source LLC
LaVergne TN
LVHW010556300926
849162LV00002B/342
9789004533240